OCR Anthology for Classical Greek GCSE

The following titles are available from Bloomsbury for the OCR specifications in Latin and Greek, first teaching September 2016

Cicero *Pro Milone*: A Selection, with introduction by Lynn Fotheringham and notes and vocabulary by Robert West

Ovid *Heroides*: A Selection, with introduction, notes and vocabulary by John Godwin

Propertius, Tibullus and Ovid: A Selection of Love Poetry, with introduction, notes and vocabulary by Anita Nikkanen

Seneca Letters: A Selection, with introduction, notes and vocabulary by Eliot Maunder

Tacitus *Annals* I: A Selection, with introduction by Roland Mayer and notes and vocabulary by Katharine Radice

Virgil *Aeneid* VIII: A Selection, with introduction, notes and vocabulary by Keith MacLennan

Virgil *Aeneid* X: A Selection, with introduction, notes and vocabulary by Christopher Tanfield

OCR Anthology for Classical Greek GCSE, covering the prescribed texts by Homer, Herodotus, Euripides, Lucian, Plato and Plutarch, edited by Judith Affleck and Clive Letchford

OCR Anthology for Classical Greek AS and A-level, covering the prescribed texts by Aristophanes, Homer, Plato, Sophocles, Thucydides and Xenophon, with introduction, notes and vocabulary by Malcolm Campbell, Rob Colborn, Frederica Daniele, Ben Gravell, Sarah Harden, Steven Kennedy, Matthew McCullagh, Charlie Paterson, John Taylor and Claire Webster

Supplementary resources for these volumes can be found at
www.bloomsbury.com/OCR-editions

Please type the URL into your web browser and follow the instructions to access the Companion Website. If you experience any problems, please contact Bloomsbury at contact@bloomsbury.com

OCR Anthology for Classical Greek GCSE

Edited by
Judith Affleck and
Clive Letchford

BLOOMSBURY ACADEMIC
LONDON • NEW YORK • OXFORD • NEW DELHI • SYDNEY

BLOOMSBURY ACADEMIC
Bloomsbury Publishing Plc
50 Bedford Square, London, WC1B 3DP, UK
1385 Broadway, New York, NY 10018, USA

BLOOMSBURY, BLOOMSBURY ACADEMIC and the Diana logo are trademarks of Bloomsbury
Publishing Plc

First published in Great Britain 2016
Reprinted 2017, 2018, 2019

A catalogue record for this book is available from the British Library.

Library of Congress Cataloging-in-Publication Data
Names: Affleck, Judith, editor. I Letchford, Clive, editor. I OCR (Organisation), editor.
Title: OCR anthology for classical Greek GCSE / edited by Judith Affleck &: Clive Letchford.
Description: London: Bloomsbury Academic, 2016.
Identifiers: LCCN 2016017990 (print) I LCCN 2016018843 (ebook) I ISBN 9781474265485 (pbk.) I
ISBN 9781474265508 (epdf) I ISBN 9781474265492 (epub)
Subjects: LCSH: Greek language–Readers.
Classification: LCC PA260 .O27 2016 (print) I LCC PA260 (ebook) I DDC 488.6/421–dc23
LC record available at https://lccn.loc.gov/2016017990

ISBN: PB: 978-1-47426-548-5
         ePDF: 978-1-47426-550-8
         eBook: 978-1-47426-549-2

Typeset by RefineCatch Limited, Bungay, Suffolk
Printed and bound in India

To find out more about our authors and books visit www.bloomsbury.com
and sign up for our newsletters.

CONTENTS

PREFACE

We are delighted that Bloomsbury has published this book to support GCSE Classical Greek. We hope it will prove useful not only as a GCSE textbook but as a flexible post-GCSE reader.

We are very aware of the challenges of reading a continuous Greek text for the first time, especially in unadapted prose or verse. We are also mindful of pressures on time, especially if Greek does not occupy a full place in the school curriculum. We hope that this book will give pupils enough help to be able to work independently on the text. We have tried to be aware of the vocabulary students are learning as they prepare for the GCSE language papers.

The texts are arranged in chronological order. As well as setting them briefly in context and encouraging students to think about the content, we have had two main aims in mind. First, we wanted to offer a commentary that encourages the application and consolidation of GCSE grammar. We have indicated nominatives (light blue) and verbs in the text (dark blue) to help the reader start off in a positive direction. Secondly, we wanted to encourage active engagement with the much more extensive vocabulary in these texts. The notes reinforce skills in word-recognition, a skill that is essential at any stage of learning to read Greek fluently, by suggesting derivations and drawing attention to related Greek words already met, especially those on the prescribed GCSE list.

We would like thank those who have seen earlier drafts and saved us from many errors: to students at the University of Warwick and King Edward VI, Stratford-upon-Avon, and especially to Stephen Anderson and Michael Atkinson.

Judith Affleck
Clive Letchford

INTRODUCTION

All dates referred to in this volume are BCE unless otherwise specified.

The texts in this volume range in time over about 1,000 years, from the dawn of Greek writing in the late eighth century to the height of Roman imperial rule in the second century CE, when Greek continued to be spoken in the eastern provinces. Geographically, they range widely too, with works by authors from Athens to Syria and subject matter from Africa to Elysium. What unites them is the language you have been learning to read and the sense of lively intellectual engagement typical of so many Greek texts.

The following historical outline is to help set your GCSE texts in their broad context.

Age of heroes

The Mediterranean landscape has plentiful traces of an ancient past typified by huge 'Cyclopean' walls, great hearths, colourful wall-paintings, and rooms full of storage jars, some with lists of their contents. The beginning of Greek culture goes back even earlier, as the figure of a minstrel from the islands around Greece carved in smooth white stone in the third millennium testifies, but it was to the Mycenaean period in particular (c. 1600–1200) that the Greek poets looked back. What they saw was an age of warriors in chariots, armed with bronze, valuing material possessions and honour in almost equal measure, living in palaces with great halls, where bards performed the latest songs and where, after death, men were buried or cremated with precious or highly crafted objects.

Colonization, Homer and the Greek alphabet

This Mycenaean palace culture collapsed at about the time that the legendary sack of Troy was believed to have taken place, traditionally in 1184. A technological shift from using bronze to iron followed, one of many discoveries of the 'Dark Age' (c. 1150–800), so-called because relatively little is known of it. This was the beginning of a period of exploration and colonization beginning with the settlement by Greeks of the eastern Aegean in the eleventh century, but extending all over the Mediterranean and Black Sea from the eighth century. Individual city-states became competitive, displaying their wealth through building projects, such as an early temple of Artemis at Ephesus, or sporting events, such as the Olympic games, traditionally inaugurated in 776. Establishing trade links and settlements led to contact with other cultures and new ideas: for example, law codes were created and Phoenician letters were adapted to create a versatile new Greek alphabet. **The Homeric poems** emerged during this period from the now well-established Greek settlements on the Aegean coast of Turkey. Contact with more sophisticated cultures in Egypt and the Middle East continued to produce new artistic discoveries, a wealth of stories about the gods and ideas about religion, astronomy and mathematics – ideas which permeated and shaped Greek art, literature and thought.

The rise of Persia

This contact also brought a threat to Greek independence, particularly along the western coast of Asia Minor. Cities like the highly cultured Miletus came under repeated attack and eventually became subject to the Persian king Cyrus the Great. The so-called 'Archaic Period' (*c.* 800–480) ends with the Persian Wars, when the huge forces of Persia and her subject allies crossed into Greece and destroyed Athens – but were then repelled. Our main source for this conflict was a Greek from Halicarnassus (40 km due south of Miletus), called **Herodotus**, later known as 'the father of history'. He explores the conflict between the Greek-speaking and 'barbarian' (non-Greek-speaking) worlds, which began with the 'Ionian revolt' in 499 against Persian rule and ended, unexpectedly, with Persian defeat twenty years later. In investigating this clash of cultures and power, he traces the rise of Persia in the sixth century under Cyrus the Great and his successors, Cambyses, Darius and Xerxes. His researches not only take him back in time, but also all over the known world from the fabulous wealth of Croesus, King of Lydia, to the ancient records of Egypt, the unique customs of India and, of course, to Greece. It is from Herodotus, writing in the mid-fifth century, that we get a vivid picture of the emerging characters of Greek city states and their different forms of government, from the prosperous tyrannies of wealthy states like Samos, the oligarchy of Sparta with its military discipline, and Athens, whose discovery of silver in Attica enabled her to establish democracy and develop a navy strong enough to defeat the Persians.

Athens and Sparta

The Athenian historian, Thucydides, writes of these two city states that there was nothing lasting in the physical remains of Sparta that would lead future generations to suspect her power, whereas the impression Athens produced was of a city twice as powerful as it really was. Athens had grown in power since the Persian wars: a successful defensive alliance against further threat from Persia to the Greeks in the Aegean, with its treasury on Delos, was transformed into an Athenian Empire. Under the leadership of the great Athenian statesman Pericles, a decision to preserve the 'ground-zero effect' of the Persian occupation of 479 was reversed, and Athens used her wealth (or, some argued, that of her subject-allies) to beautify the Acropolis with the marble temples that stand today. Relations between Athens, Sparta and other states like Corinth deteriorated and an uneasy cold war turned into a major conflict that lasted from 431–404. Even so, during the late fifth-century Athens attracted and nurtured not only great artists and architects, partly through the vision of men like Pericles, but also great thinkers and writers, many native to Athens, like the philosopher Socrates, the comic playwright Aristophanes, or the three great tragedians, Aeschylus, Sophocles and **Euripides**. Although these authors cover a range of genres, their works have common ground, centred on human nature and man's relationship with the world around him.

The power of myth

Herodotus is typical of these radical thinkers in trying to rationalize some of the myths of the remote past, stories like Jason and the Argonauts or the mythical Cadmus, a Phoenician exile who founded Thebes, to whom Herodotus ascribes the introduction of the worship of Dionysus and of the Greek alphabet. Regardless of their veracity or chronology, Greek myths continued to provide fertile ground for exploring contemporary themes. Euripides, for example, turns his Jason and Medea into a timeless example of a couple who have outlived their love for each other; he explores themes of love, revenge and fear of the unknown in sophisticated plays where gods and heroes rub shoulders with ordinary people. One function of the playwrights of ancient Athens, both tragic and comic, was seen to be as teachers of the male citizen body, stirring them out of complacency and making them clever and sophisticated.

Democratic Athens

Athenian theatrical performances reached audiences on an unprecedented scale; there was an appetite for debate and civic education. Athens was a city where engagement and debate were central to the political and legal processes. The Athenians would gather in huge numbers, the size of a football crowd, to make crucial decisions, like the fatal vote to help the Ionians in 499, where Herodotus comments drily on how it was easier to persuade 30,000 Athenians than one Spartan, or the foolish optimism with which they sent a full military expedition 1,368 km to Sicily while still at war with Sparta. For Athens, this decision contributed to her fall: the war ended in submission to Spartan terms.

Socrates and Plato

A vote by a large selection of the same citizen body five years later in 399 also led to the death sentence for their most celebrated thinker, Socrates. The reason, according to the elderly prisoner in the dock, was that he had provoked them by making them think too hard: they had decided, by swatting an irritating 'gadfly', to relieve themselves of his sting. **Plato** portrays him as a man given to engaging in philosophical argument with friends and rivals without demanding the payment usually expected. Although Socrates himself wrote nothing, Plato's depiction of him has given Socrates enormous influence.

The Hellenistic world

One 18-year-old who joined Plato's *Academy*, the philosophical school he established in Athens, was Aristotle, who in turn founded his own college, the *Lyceum*, before becoming tutor to the son of king Philip II of Macedon. The Athenians once again lost their independence, this time to Macedon, a military kingdom in the north of Greece, at the Battle of Chaeronea in 338. Two years later Philip was assassinated. Alexander the Great was his son and heir not only to the expanded kingdom of Macedon, but also to a greater ambition: the Greek conquest of the Persian empire. Alexander's extraordinary victories took him and his army near the edges of the known world, deep into the deserts of Egypt, through the vast kingdom that the Persian kings had united and further east, through the Hindu-Kush to India, where traces of Greek culture and language still survive. These conquests had a lasting impact despite Alexander's brief life (356–323): Greek was adopted as the language of Alexander's new Hellenistic world, texts were gathered together, catalogued and annotated by scholars in the great new library at Alexandria, and Greek was spoken, written and read throughout the Roman and Byzantine periods – until the conquest of Constantinople by the Ottoman Turks in 1453 CE.

Greeks in a Roman world: Plutarch's perspective

The ferocity of Athenian resistance to their Macedonian assailants is conveyed in the *Philippics*, a set of speeches by the fourth-century orator Demosthenes, whose style and passion was a model for the Roman orator and politician Cicero. Cicero's familiarity with these speeches resulted from travelling in Greece and learning Greek fluently, as educated Romans of the late republic and early empire did. The Roman poet Horace expresses the relationship graciously: *'captive Greece took her fierce conqueror captive'*. Others enjoyed drawing comparisons between the two great cultures, for example **Plutarch**, a Greek, used the structure of his *Parallel Lives* to contrast the legal and cultural foundations of Sparta, whose obsessive approach to military training was as fascinating to the Romans as it is today, with the legal foundation of the city whose military prowess would lead to the creation of the Roman empire.

The territorial struggle between Greeks and Romans was a long and bloody affair, beginning in Italy in the third century with the Greek Pyrrhus' bitter 'Pyrrhic victory', through a sequence of wars with Macedon and, after a decisive Roman victory at Pydna in 168, the sack of Corinth in 146. Greece continued to be despoiled by greedy governors even after it became a Roman province. The greatest depradations, which included seizing works of art and original texts as well as other treasures, came from Sulla in the early first century and Nero on his great tour of Greece in 66–67 CE. Nero's obsessive Greek fanaticism led him to neglect his responsibilities in Rome and, as later Greek rhetoricians would express it, by indulging his private passions for Greek sport, theatre, music, sex and art, to lose his empire. He was not the only emperor to indulge in Hellenistic fantasies or try to look like a Greek.

Lucian and the Second Sophistic

If you look at images of the Roman emperors you will notice that Hadrian ushers in the age of the Greek beard: he and his successors, Antoninus Pius and Marcus Aurelius, presided over a period of great stability and prosperity for the Roman empire. Each emperor reigned for about twenty years and died of natural causes. Marcus Aurelius even found time while on campaign to write a famous philosophical work, his *Meditations* – in Greek. Peace led to a flowering of art, literature and a revival of Greek known as the Second Sophistic. The wide range of authors it produced includes **Lucian**, the final author in our anthology. His witty answers to the earliest literary questions – Who was Homer? Was Helen to blame for the Trojan war? – are typical of his irreverent, post-modern playfulness.

Texts

The survival of these texts over the turbulent centuries is nothing short of miraculous. For a long period in European history some manuscripts were preserved in mediaeval monasteries, but almost no-one understood Greek: Petrarch, a fourteenth-century Italian poet, owned and treasured a Greek text of Homer but was unable to read it. In the early fifteenth century, Greek-speaking scholars, fleeing the spread of the Ottoman empire, arrived in Italy along with their learning and libraries of manuscripts. One of the first Greek texts to reach Italian humanists in 1423 CE was of Lucian. The invention of printing in the mid-fifteenth century and of a Greek typeface created by the Aldine Press in Venice meant that access to Herodotus, Euripides, Plato and Plutarch, as well as the Greek New Testament, became more widespread by the start of the sixteenth century among the wealthy elite. In England, for example, Edward VI learned enough Greek to enjoy writing it. Those who taught him and his sister Elizabeth helped introduce Greek into schools, some of which have taught it continuously since then. Today you can access almost any ancient Greek text electronically and there are more opportunities than ever to develop your knowledge of Greek, in summer schools, at university, through books or online.

Table of texts

	J292/02 Prose Lit A	J292/03 Prose Lit B	J292/04 Verse Lit A	J292/05 Verse Lit B
2018–2019	**Herodotus** Solon & Croesus How Alcmaeon was enriched by Croesus	**Plutarch** *Life of Lycurgus* 16–18 **Lucian** Anacharsis and Athletics	**Homer** *Odyssey* 6.48–159*	**Euripides** *Alcestis* 280–392*
2020–2021	**Herodotus** The Ethiopians The Power of Custom	**Lucian** The Isle of the Blest (Shangri La; The Homeric Question; The Face that Launched 1,000 Ships)	**Homer** *Iliad* 3.1–112	**Euripides** *Electra* 215–331*
2022–2023	**Herodotus** Psammetichus Crocodiles Mycerinus Pygmies	**Plato** *Phaedo* Section 59c10 to Section 118, line 19	**Homer** *Odyssey* 7.184–297*	**Euripides** *Bacchae* 434–508,* 800–838*

* In this volume lines are re-numbered starting at 1.

HOW TO USE THIS BOOK

Starting to read a literary text is always a challenging step. This book tries to guide you into doing this confidently in a number of ways:

1. There are three levels of introduction:

    i)   **Introduction**, p. 8 An overview of how your texts fit in to the wider picture of the history and culture of ancient Greece.

    ii) A more specific introduction to your author or genre (e.g. Homer, Greek Tragedy, Plato). In the case of Homer, this includes an introduction to his language.

    iii) **'The story so far . . .'** to help you set the extract you are reading in context, so that you know what's going on. At the end of your text there may also be a **'What happens next'** section, if the story continues.

Other reference pages you may find useful include a timeline, a map, some tips for translation, a glossary, and the GCSE word list at the back.

2. **Text pages** (on the left-hand side).

    i)   A brief heading in *italics* at the top of each page gives an overview.

    ii) At the bottom of each page there is a short list of words from the set GCSE vocabulary relevant to the page of text you are about to read. For reasons of space, this may be a selection rather than a complete list.

         •   If you have already learned the GCSE vocabulary, use this to revise from before you translate.

         •   If you are still working on the GCSE vocabulary list, look these words up before you begin.

    iii) **Colour coding in the text:** you will notice two colours are used in the text itself. This is to help you get started and to reinforce your grammatical understanding (see also Tips for Translation, p. 15).

         •   Words or phrases in light blue are in the nominative case. They should be a good starting point when translating.

         •   Words in dark blue are verbs (infinitives and participles not included). These are good anchor points in the sentence.

    iv) **Names and Places, Topics and Questions:** these are to help you understand and enjoy the text. Some of the questions on the text page are genuinely open; don't panic if you can't answer them all.

3. **Notes pages** (on the right hand side).

Vocabulary and translation help is arranged line by line. Try not to use this support until you have tried to work out what's going on for yourself.

i) Help with GCSE words may be given, especially if they have a slightly different meaning from the one you are used to or are in a less familiar form. GCSE words on the Notes page are in blue so that you can check them easily.

ii) New words that have appeared already may not be translated, but you may be directed back by a line reference to an earlier usage.

iii) Greek words taken directly from the text are in **bold**; English meanings or suggested translation are in *italics*. A larger font size is used for these words.

iv) English words in **bold**, if not explained in the context, will be found in the Glossary with a brief explanation.

v) The following symbols are used:

> This means the Greek word is derived from or related to a more familiar or simple Greek word. This is to help you understand its root meaning and perhaps remember it more easily.

< This means that an English word is derived from the Greek (a few Latin parallels have also been included). We have included some rather obscure examples, but hope to invite discussion or investigation; again, some may prove memorable.

= This is used where a less familiar word has the same meaning as (i.e. is synonymous with) one you may already know or recognize.

vi) Some standard abbreviations are used, like gen. = genitive, aor. = aorist, lit. = literally, i.e. = 'that is to say'.

Other useful books and resources

Morwood, J. (ed.) (2001) *Oxford Grammar of Classical Greek*, Oxford University Press

Morwood, J. and Taylor, J. (eds) (2002) *Pocket Oxford Classical Greek Dictionary*, Oxford University Press

Scott, R. and Liddell, H. G. (eds) (2010) *Intermediate Greek–English Lexicon*, Oxford University Press

Taylor, J. (2008) *Greek Beyond GCSE* (Bristol Classical Press)

Taylor, J. (2016) *Greek to GCSE I and II* (Bloomsbury)

There are also excellent online resources, such as:

Eton Greek Project (good for vocabulary and basic endings) http://www.etoncollege.com/GreekProject.aspx.

logeion.uchicago.edu for a dictionary linked to the ancient Greek texts.

Perseus and the app, *Attikos*, providing help with the major Greek texts.

TIPS·FOR TRANSLATION

1. Translating set texts (prose and verse texts)

- Use the colour-coding to help find your way into a sentence: identifying the subject and verb will help accurate translation.

- Read the sentence or passage through several times, letting the word order and particles guide you through until the sentence or phrase takes shape. After you have translated, continue this process of re-reading and be ready to develop or vary your translation to get closer to the Greek.

- Think about cases, registering what each is and questioning why.

- Check you understand the tense and form of verbs and look them up if you need to so that your grammatical understanding keeps developing. Start using a dictionary and grammar reference book. These are useful skills for A-level and beyond.

Intelligent deduction is an important skill to start developing. Unlike the GCSE unseen and comprehension passages, there will be lots of words you've never met before or aren't familiar with. In particular, word order or missing words may make things more confusing, especially in verse texts. Keep *trying* to work things out for yourself.

- Work from the known to the unknown. Keep re-reading until you can narrow down the problem(s). Use grammatical clues, in particular verb forms, case endings, and agreement.

- Try to work out the meaning of a word before seeking help on the opposite page. Break it down and think of derivations. Look out for synonyms – classical authors quite often pair words with similar meanings.

- Use the sense of the passage. Keep reading back over what has gone before and try to anticipate what might follow. If you are surprised, think about whether this might be part of a deliberate effect.

2. Translating from Greek to English (GCSE unseens and comprehensions)

Learning the set GCSE vocabulary thoroughly is best done as early as possible. The *Eton Greek Project* or electronic flashcards such as *Memrise* can help you to get started and refresh your memory. Make sure you don't learn only the meaning of a word, but also how its endings change. Sometimes this is a major challenge in Greek (especially with verbs) but it gets easier. Seeing different forms in context helps, so re-read old passsages as well as tackling new ones.

- **Identify the case** of each noun and question why it is in that case. The definite article is very helpful in Greek – use it. Finding the **nominative**, if there is one, and the **verb** is a good way into the sentence.

- Word order and phrasing in Greek is very important, so keep re-reading a phrase until the various elements fall into place. In particular, be sensitive to the 'sandwich construction', which keeps units together, to participles, which often act as 'staging posts' along the way, and to the unit a preposition forms with the noun that follows it.

- Be on the look-out for **genitive absolutes**, particularly near the start of a sentence.

- Pay special attention to words like δέ, γάϱ, οὖν, μέν ... δέ ... etc., since they are there to help direct your understanding; for example showing a change of subject (δέ), offering an explanation (γάϱ, often after a semi-colon), a causal connection (οὖν) or setting up a contrast (μέν ... δέ ...). You may not always translate them, but you should never ignore them. **Think of them as if they are attached to the word in front.**

- Take special care over τε, remembering that it often comes **after** the word it is connecting (like -*que* in Latin).

- Learn to check details: which case follows a preposition? Is this singular or plural? Have I thought about the tense, voice (active/middle/passive) and mood (subjunctive/optative, etc.) carefully enough?

3. Translating from English to Greek (GCSE short sentences)

This is the same process in reverse and the same things are important:

- Identify your subject and make sure it is in the nominative case. Change it into the plural if you need to. Have you included the definite article and does it agree?

- Identify your verb and take special care, if there is a stem change, to check your principal parts carefully before translating. Looking things up until you are completely confident is part of the learning process.

- No noun in your sentence other than the subject (or complement after the verb 'to be') should be nominative, so make sure you change the case of any other nouns in the sentence to fit the sense and rules, for example when dealing with prepositions.

- Adjectives must agree with the noun they describe in number, gender and case.

- Practise – and don't worry if you make lots of mistakes at first.

TIMELINE

Bronze Age	2500 2000–1200 1184	Great pyramids built at Giza in Egypt. Development of Greek island culture and Cycladic art. 1700 Minoan palace civilization flourished on Crete. 1450 Mycenaean palace civilization in Greece; Linear B. Traditional date of the Trojan War, calculated by Eratosthenes.
Iron Age	1150–700 700s	Migrations into Greece and across the Aegean. Period of colonization; growing contact with neighbouring powers. 776 1st Olympic Games. Alphabet adopted to write Greek. *Iliad* and *Odyssey* composed.
Archaic Greece c. 600–460	c. 594 546 525 546–527 510 499–494 490 480 479	Archonship of Solon. 1st Sacred War. Defeat of Croesus, king of Lydia, by Cyrus the Great. Conquest of Egypt by Cambyses, son of Cyrus the Great. Pisistratus, tyrant of Athens. Texts of *Iliad* and *Odyssey* copied. Hippias driven from Athens. The Ionian Revolt. Sack of Sardis by Ionians and Athenians. Darius invades Attica; Athenian victory at Marathon. **c. 484 birth of Herodotus; 480s birth of Euripides** Xerxes' invasion of Greece; Persian victory at Thermopylae; sack of Athens; Greek naval victory at Salamis; Xerxes' retreat. Final defeat of Persians at Plataea and Mycale.
Classical Greece c. 460–340	478 447 431–404 415–413 404 399	Formation of the Delian league; growing tensions between Athens, Sparta and their allies. Pericles' building programme on the Acropolis begins. The Peloponnesian War between Athens and Sparta. **431** *Alcestis* produced. **c. 428 Birth of Plato.** c. 416 *Electra*. Athen's unsuccessful expedition to Sicily. **c. 406 death of Euripides;** 405 *Bacchae* produced. Defeat of Athens by Sparta. **Execution of Socrates, aged 70.**
Hellenistic c. 340–31	338 336–323 264–146 146	Philip II of Macedon defeats Greeks at Chaeronea. Conquests of Alexander the Great. Rome at war with Pyrrhus, Philip V and Perseus of Macedon. Roman Provinces of Achaea and Macedonia established.
Roman Greece c. 146–CE 331	100–43 27 CE–68 CE 117 CE–180 CE	Dictatorship of Sulla; collapse of the Roman Republic. 44 assassination of Caesar; 43 murder of Cicero. The Julio-Claudian emperors ending with Nero 54–68 CE. **c. 50 CE birth of Plutarch.** Reigns of Hadrian d.138 CE, Antoninus Pius d.161 CE and Marcus Aurelius d.180. **c. 120 CE birth of Lucian.**
Byz	331 CE 1453 CE	Constantinople becomes the capital of the Roman empire. Ottoman conquest of Istanbul, capital of the Byzantine empire.

WHO'S WHO

Alcmaeon	6th C	Son of Megacles and member of the aristocratic Athenian family, the Alcmaeonids.
Alcestis	Pre-Trojan War	A wife who agrees to sacrifice her own life to save her husband; contemporary with Heracles.
Anacharsis	6th C	Legendary prince of Scythia renowned for his wisdom.
Bacchae		Followers of the god Bacchus, better known as Dionysus, god of wine, theatre and illusion.
Croesus	6th C	King of Lydia 560–546. His empire and its capital Sardis were captured by Cyrus the Great.
Electra	Post-Trojan War	She and Orestes avenge the murder of their father Agamemnon by their mother Clytaemnestra
Euripides	480s–406	One of the three great Athenian tragedians, along with Aeschylus and Sophocles.
Helen	Trojan War	Daughter of Leda and Zeus or Tyndareus, king of Sparta; blamed by many for the Trojan war.
Herodotus	480s–420s	Born in Halicarnassus, wrote the *Histories*, which includes an account of the Persian invasions of Greece.
Homer	Late 8th C	The name given to the author of the *Iliad* and *Odyssey*.
Lucian	*c.* 120 CE	Greek author and wit of the Second Sophistic. Born in Samosata, on the Turkish/Syrian border.
Lycurgus	7th C	Legendary founder of the Spartan code of laws and customs.
Mycerinus	*c.* 2500	King of Egypt, responsibile for the third great pyramid at Giza.
Pentheus	Pre-Trojan War	Legendary king of Thebes, grandson of Cadmus, who denies the divinity of Dionysus.
Phaedo	5th–4th C	A young follower and friend of Socrates.
Plato	*c.* 428–347	Athenian author of philosophical dialogues; our most important source for Socrates' teachings.
Plutarch	*c.* 50–120 CE	Greek author from Boeotia best known for his biographical work, *Parallel Lives*.
Psammetichus	7th C	King of Egypt 664–610; contemporary of Polycrates, tyrant of Samos.
Socrates	*c.* 469–399	Athenian philosopher; condemned to death for corrupting the young and atheism in 399.
Solon	6th C	Athenian statesman and poet whose political reforms contributed to the growth of democracy.

MAP OF THE ANCIENT

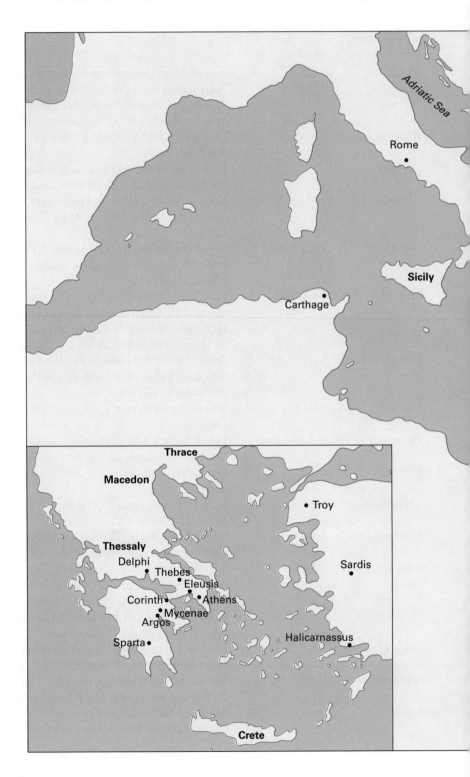

MEDITERRANEAN

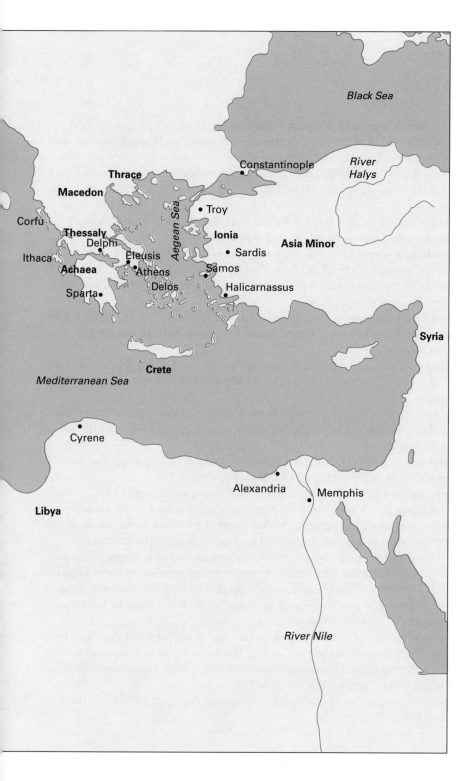

Black Sea

River Halys

Constantinople

Thrace

Macedon

Corfu

Thessaly
Delphi

Ithaca

Achaea

Sparta

Aegean Sea

Troy

Ionia

Sardis

Eleusis

Athens

Samos

Delos

Halicarnassus

Asia Minor

Syria

Crete

Mediterranean Sea

Cyrene

Alexandria

Memphis

Libya

River Nile

TECHNICAL TERMS

2-2 adjective – some compound adjectives that one might expect to go like σοφός –ή -όν (2-1-2) have no distinct first declension feminine endings. Feminine and masculine forms are both second declension.

accusative of respect – an idiomatic use of the accusative case used to show the part affected, e.g. I have a pain *with respect to the the head* – 'head' would be in the accusative case.

agent – where a verb is in the passive voice, there is often the preposition ὑπό + genitive to show the person by whom the action was done – the agent.

apposition – where a phrase uses one noun or phrase to elaborate on another, in the same case. An example in English '*Zeus, Father of gods and men, . . .*' where the phrase *Father of gods and men* is in apposition to the noun *Zeus*, and so *Father* would be in the same case as *Zeus*.

crasis – where Greek telescopes two words together, it shows this by using a sign similar to an apostrophe over a vowel where the words have merged, e.g. ταὐτά by crasis for τὰ αὐτά.

diaeresis – two dots over a letter show that two vowels which would normally be pronounced as a **diphthong** are pronounced separately. This is most commonly seen in Homer.

diphthong – two vowels that are pronounced together as one sound rather than separately. For example, in τιμαί the -αί is one sound but in ναυμαχία the -ία is two separate sounds.

dual – as well as the singular and plural, Greek has a set of endings for two of something – usually applying a pair of things, e.g. eyes.

elision – where one word ends in a vowel and the following word begins with a vowel, the first vowel gets cut ('elided') and the missing vowel is shown by an apostrophe.

genitive absolute – a participle agreeing with a noun or pronoun, both of which are in the genitive case and are not the subject or direct object of the sentence.

gnomic aorist – use of the aorist indicative not to show an action occurred in the past but to show a generalization. This should be translated as a present tense in English.

historic present – a verb in the present tense although referring to completed actions in the past. It should be translated as if an aorist tense, but the use of the present gives a sense of vividness to the story-telling.

-mi verb – a handful of verbs follow a different system of personal endings from παύω types. The present 'I' form ends in –μι. You have met some tenses of δίδωμι and φημί. Two others that are very common are ἵστημι (*stand*) and ἵημι (*send, let go*). You will be given appropriate help for person and tense.

partitive genitive – a genitive showing not possession but part of the whole, e.g. 'some of my friends'.

perfect tense – a tense, much less common than the aorist. It applies to a present state resulting from a past action. English uses the auxiliary verb 'have', so πέπαυκα = *I have stopped*. An English present tense may be a more idiomatic translation.

possessive dative – use of the dative case with the verb 'to be' in the structure 'X is to someone', which is a common way of saying 'someone has X'.

potential optative – use of the optative on its own to say something may/might/ would be the case rather than is/was.

stichomythia – a term used in verse, especially drama, where two characters speak alternate lines of verse.

DISCUSSING LITERARY STYLE

You have probably been used to commenting on the style of English writers, especially poets. Greek authors use similar techniques and you should be ready to comment on the style as well as the content of your set texts. If you can translate and understand the significance of the text, this should not present too much of a problem. A key difference between English and Greek is word order, which is much more flexible in Greek. Greek and Latin, unlike English, are inflected languages. This means that classical authors can arrange words in a variety of ways to alter the emphasis, while keeping the same basic meaning.

The following paragraphs set out some ways of analyzing style. The technical terms are a useful short-cut for describing what a writer is doing, but it is no substitute for properly understanding the content. Your first step when preparing for this type of discussion or exam question is to make sure you consider why the author is saying what he is saying as well as what he is saying. The questions set out on the left hand side and at the end of each section are designed to get you started on this.

There is often no right or wrong answer, and effects may be subtle, so be prepared to sharpen your wits and get into discussion with your fellow students and teacher.

Basics

1. Choice of words
An author makes many choices: for example, selecting from a number of words with the same basic meaning (synonyms), or including words, especially adjectives and adverbs, which may not be strictly necessary. This selection is sometimes termed **diction** (from the Latin *dico* – I say) or **lexis** (from λέγω).

2. Word order
When you start learning Greek, you get used to a fairly predictable word order, often involving a nominative at the start, and a verb at the end of the clause. Unusual word order is likely to be significant. For example, has an action been emphasized by placing the verb first? Has the subject been delayed, exciting the suspense of the reader? Try to take the Greek words as they come – how is the picture being built up, word-by-word?

Technical literary matters

Writers on literature have developed technical vocabulary to help describe some literary effects. Before setting out a few of these terms, it is worth emphasizing that as well as identifying an effect, it is important that you explain how it enhances the meaning.

Sound

alliteration – repeated consonantal sounds (e.g. 'π', 'κ', etc.) may draw a group of words together more tightly. In Greek this includes repeated sounds in any position in the word, not just at the start of a word. Listen out for the two sounds in the double letters ζ, ξ and ψ and remember that the aspirates θ, φ and χ are stronger versions of τ, π and κ.

assonance – similar to alliteration but refers to repeated vowel sounds rather than consonants.

onomatopoeia – where the sound of the word mirrors the meaning.

rhythm – verse authors (Homer and Euripides in this selection) wrote following a metrical framework; rhythm may be used flexibly to underline sense. If you want to understand more about rhythm, there is an introduction to the Homeric dactylic hexameter on the website.

Other terms

anaphora – a word is repeated at the start of successive clauses to give emphasis to an idea.

asyndeton – omission of conjunctions, often to speed up the narrative.

balance/contrast (antithesis) – Greek is fond of contrasting ideas, which it may signpost by using μέν and δέ.

chiasmus – elegant arrangement, reversing a word order, for example, nominative, accusative, accusative, nominative (A-B-B-A).

dramatic irony – a situation where what is being said or done has special significance because the audience or reader know more than the character(s) involved.

enjambement – a term used only in verse, where the sense runs over from one line to the next giving special emphasis to the word on the new line.

epithet – used particularly in Homer of adjectives or phrases attached to a particular character or noun.

juxtaposition – placing of two words next to each other to bring out clearly the contrast between them.

metaphor – one situation is described using language which is not literally the case, e.g. 'on fire with love'.

repetition – words are repeated to give additional emphasis to an important idea.

simile – where a situation or event is described as being like something else.

A good starting point for further consideration is Morwood, J. (ed.) (2001) *Oxford Grammar of Classical Greek*, which gives examples.

Homer

The *Iliad* and *Odyssey* emerged in their current form around the second half of the eighth century. Whether there was a person called Homer, and whether both works were by the same author or authors has been in dispute for well over 2,000 years. In many ways, it does not matter. The poems have been read and appreciated over the centuries for their deep understanding of human nature in what the characters say and how they act. However, we can develop a fuller appreciation of the texts if we understand some of their background.

The earliest evidence we have of written Greek is Linear B, a syllabic system found in the Mycenaean palaces several hundred years before Homer. The texts we have show that Linear B was used by scribes to record information about produce and animals. With the disappearance of the Mycenaean palaces in around 1200, writing vanished from the Greek world. In an age that could not keep written records, memory was the repository of knowledge and consequently became highly developed. Anthropologists have documented this in studies of pre-literate societies. Stories were performed from memory or through improvization by expert story-tellers and handed down across the generations. The *Iliad* and the *Odyssey* emerged towards the end of this long oral tradition.

We have evidence for this in the surviving texts of the *Iliad* and *Odyssey*. Within the poems, bards perform and can extemporize tales of gods and heroes, accompanying themselves on the lyre. There is evidence within the language itself of a long tradition with standard elements used repeatedly, as if the poet is drawing on a stock of expressions suited to the rhythm of the poem, for example, the sea is often '*wine-dark*', the Achaeans '*long-haired*'. We see standard phrases within common scenes – the dawn rising, performance of a sacrifice, launching a ship or a warrior arming. We also see alternative linguistic forms co-existing alongside each other, some of which suggest older forms have been retained from previous centuries. Tales could be told, retold and developed as they were handed down through the generations.

Writing was reintroduced into Greece in about 750, this time based on an alphabetical system used by one of their trading partners, the Phoenicians. It is probably no coincidence that these two poems date from the earliest period of writing. They come from the Ionian coast and, although they are closely related to the Greek of fifth-century Athens that you have been learning, you will see significant differences when starting to read Homeric Greek. While we know of other poems based on episodes from the Trojan war from the same period, none of them is anywhere near the length of the *Iliad* or *Odyssey*, nor do they show the same sophistication of overall structure or control of pace and shape. It seems likely that the introduction of an accessible system of writing enabled tales to develop on a grander scale, although we are unlikely to know definitively whether they were taken down from an oral story-teller or conceived and 'written' by their creators.

Note on the book divisions in Homer

The division of the texts of the *Odyssey* and *Iliad* each into 24 books was not the work of the original author and was determined in part by the practical mechanics of what could be conveniently contained on a papyrus scroll.

Some features of Homeric Greek

The language of the Homeric poems differs from the Greek you have been studying for three reasons: it is verse, not prose; the language evolved over the centuries; different regions had different dialects, for instance 'Attic Greek' is the Greek spoken by the Athenians and the Homeric poems are in an Ionic dialect.

1. Elision

Where a word ends in a short vowel (mainly ε or α), it may run into the next word, dropping the vowel. This is marked with an apostrophe to show where the missing letter was, in the same way as in English: e.g. do not = don't.

If the second word is aspirated (has a rough breathing) the 'h' sound may be reflected in the final consonant (e.g. τ becomes θ', π becomes φ', κ becomes χ').

e.g.	Od 6	δ' = δέ 1	δώμαθ' = δώματα 3
	Il 3	ἄμ' = ἄμα 1	καθ' = κατά 36
	Od 7	δ' = δέ 2	θ' = τε 1

2. Missing augments

In Attic Greek, all past tense indicative verbs have augments. This was not yet a fixed convention when the Homeric poems were written down.

e.g.	Od 6	βῆ = ἔβη 3	φέρεν = ἔφερεν 27
	Il 3	φύγον = ἔφυγον 4	φάτο = ἔφατο 28
	Od 7	φερόμην = ἐφερόμην 70	δῶκεν = ἔδωκεν 112

3. Uncontracted forms and other surprising vowels

i) Standard contractions are often left uncontracted.

e.g.	Od 6	κουράων = κουρῶν 75	χρυσέη = χρυσῇ 32
	Il 3	πεινάων = πεινῶν 25	ὄρεος = ὀροῦς 10
	Od 7	πετράων = πετρῶν 99	ξεῖνον = ξένον 7

ii) Additional short vowels are common.

e.g.	Od 6	ἐόντα = ὄντα 13	ἐνί = ἐν 15
	Il 3	προσέειπε = προσεῖπε 58	ἦεν = ἦν 41
	Od 7	ἔην = ἦν 108	ἔειπεν = εἶπεν 44

iii) η is often found where we would expect α, and vice versa.

e.g.	Od 6	τῇσι = ταῖς 54
	Il 3	βίη = βία 45
	Od 7	ἀμβροσίη = ἀμβροσία 100

iv) Long and short vowels may not be the familiar way round.

e.g.   **Od 6**   ἧος = ἕως 33
           Il 3   πόληι = πόλει 50
           Od 7   ἧος = ἕως 97

4. Tmesis > (τέμνω – *cut*)

In later Greek the preposition becomes attached as a prefix to the verb. This is often not the case in Homeric Greek, where you may find a prepositional prefix floating a word or two before the verb.

e.g.   **Od 6**   ἀπὸ … βαλοῦσαι = ἀποβαλοῦσαι (ἀποβάλλω) 53
           Il 3   ἐπὶ … ἥσιν = ἐφίησιν (ἐφίημι) 12
           Od 7   ἐκ … ἔπεσον = ἐξέπεσον 100 ἐπὶ … ἤλυθε = ἐπῆλθε 100–1

5. Epithets

Compound words are typical of Greek in general, but the epithet, usually a compound adjective, is a signature of Epic poetry.

e.g.   **Od 6**   λευκώλενος 54   γλαυκῶπις 65
           Il 3   θεοειδής 37, 58   καλλιγύναιξ 75   κορυθαίολος 83
           Od 7   λευκώλενος 50   πολύμητις 24

6. Alternative forms or words may exist side by side with more familiar ones

e.g.   **Od 6**   ἐς = εἰς 8 μιν = αὐτόν 8 πέλεται = ἐστί 61 τοί = σοί 15
           Il 3   ται = αὐταί 5   μιν = αὐτόν 35   ἠδέ = καί 67
           Od 7   μιν = αὐτόν 15 ἔπλετο = ἦν 34 οἱ = αὐτῷ 48 εἰς = εἶ 55

7. Alternative grammatical endings

Watch out especially for infinitives, genitive singular and dative plural endings.

e.g.   Infinitives (ending –αι –or –εμεν)
           Od 6   ἴμεναι = ἰέναι 3   τερσήμεναι = τέρσεσθαι 51
           Il 3   ἔμμεναι = εἶναι 44   ἀλέξεμεν = ἀλέξειν 9
           Od 7   ἐσθέμεναι = ἐσθίειν 37   πινέμεν = πίνειν 37

           Genitive singular (2nd Declension ending –οιο)
           Od 6   θαλάμοιο = θαλάμου 27   ποταμοῖο = ποταμοῦ 38
           Il 3   πεδίοιο = πεδίου 14   πολέμοιο = πολέμου 112
           Od 7   ἀνέμοιο = ἀνέμου 99

           Dative plurals: (ending –σι(ν))
           Od 6   ὄχθησιν = ὄχθαις 50   πρώτοισιν = πρώτοις 13
           Il 3   κορυφῇσι = κορυφαῖς 10   ὤμοισιν = ὤμοις 17
           Od 7   μεγάλῃσι = μεγάλαις 96   τοῖσι = τοῖς 2

ODYSSEY 6: 48–159 (here 1–112)

2018–2019 Prescription

See pages 24–6 for an introduction to Homer and his language.

The story so far . . .

The *Odyssey* tells the story of how Odysseus, one of the most famous Greek heroes to fight in the ten-year siege of Troy, made the journey home to his beloved island of Ithaca. The journey took him ten years, partly because, by blinding the Cyclops Polyphemus, he incurred the anger of the sea-god, Poseidon. When he finally reaches Ithaca, more troubles await him: his palace has been besieged by 108 suitors, keen to wed Penelope, Odysseus' loyal wife. In the first four books of the poem, we sense how much Odysseus is missed, in particular by his son Telemachus, who is standing on the threshold of manhood, uncertain if his father is alive or of how to keep hold of his inheritance. The goddess Athene sets in motion a two-fold plan, firstly instilling spirit in the son, then engineering the release of his father.

We first meet Odysseus in Book 5 of the *Odyssey*, where he has been kept prisoner for seven long years on a remote island by the beautiful nymph, Calypso, who has taken him as her lover. While Poseidon is temporarily absent from Mount Olympus, the gods, guided by Athene, agree that it is time for Odysseus to return home, since he is fated to return to his home and family in the twentieth year. Zeus sends Hermes to inform Calypso, who reluctantly comes to terms with the loss of her lover and helps him build a raft.

Odysseus sails for eighteen days until he is spotted by Poseidon on his return from Ethiopia. In a rage, the sea-god rouses a terrible storm which destroys the raft, leaving the hero to rely on his famous physical endurance and mental resources. With a little divine help, and after swimming for two days and nights, Odysseus reaches the coast of Scherie. Exhausted, he makes his way on to dry land and collapses into a deep sleep, after burying his naked body in a pile of leaves to protect himself from the cold and from wild animals.

Meanwhile Athene is thinking ahead. She realizes that Odysseus requires help to take his first steps back into civilized life. In particular he needs clothes, food and a way of getting back by ship to Ithaca.

At the start of Book 6, Athene herself goes to Scherie, where King Alcinous and Queen Arete rule over the sea-loving Phaeacians. In a dream, Athene appears to their beloved daughter, the princess Nausicaa, disguised as a friend, the daughter of Dymas. Athene plants the idea of going down to the sea for a day out washing clothes in the river, since marriage might soon be in the air and clean clothes are important in making a good impression.

Princess Nausicaa awakes and remembers a dream, sent by Athene on the previous
night, telling her to go to the sea to do some laundry.

Nominative *words or phrases are in* light blue, **verbs** *in* dark blue.

αὐτίκα δ' Ἠὼς ἦλθεν ἐΰθρονος, ἥ μιν ἔγειρε
Ναυσικάαν εὔπεπλον· ἄφαρ δ' ἀπεθαύμασ' ὄνειρον,
βῆ δ' ἴμεναι διὰ δώμαθ', ἵν' ἀγγείλειε τοκεῦσι,
πατρὶ φίλῳ καὶ μητρί· κιχήσατο δ' ἔνδον ἐόντας·
ἡ μὲν ἐπ' ἐσχάρῃ ἧστο σὺν ἀμφιπόλοισι γυναιξίν,   5
ἠλάκατα στρωφῶσ' ἁλιπόρφυρα· τῷ δὲ θύραζε
ἐρχομένῳ ξύμβλητο μετὰ κλειτοὺς βασιλῆας
ἐς βουλήν, ἵνα μιν κάλεον Φαίηκες ἀγαυοί.
ἡ δὲ μάλ' ἄγχι στᾶσα φίλον πατέρα προσέειπε·
'πάππα φίλ', οὐκ ἂν δή μοι ἐφοπλίσσειας ἀπήνην   10
ὑψηλὴν εὔκυκλον, ἵνα κλυτὰ εἵματ' ἄγωμαι
ἐς ποταμὸν πλυνέουσα, τά μοι ῥερυπωμένα κεῖται;'

Names and places
Ἠώς ἡ: *Dawn*

Ναυσικάα ἡ: *Nausicaa*
The daughter of Alcinous, king of Phaeacia.

Φαίηκες οἱ: *the Phaeacians*
A sea-faring nation who live on the island of Scherie (identified by some as modern Corfu), ruled over by
King Alcinous and Queen Arete.

Q.   What first impressions have you formed of Nausicaa and her relationship with
     her parents from lines 1–12?

Q.   Pick out two or three words that suggest the wealth and comfortable living
     style of the Phaeacian royal family.

GCSE vocabulary: *ἀγγέλλω, ἄγω, βαίνω, (aor: ἔβην), βασιλεύς, βουλή, γυνή, εἶπον*
(λέγω), ἦλθεν (ἔρχομαι), θαυμάζω, θύρα, ἵνα, καλέω, πατήρ, ποταμός, ὑψηλός, ὤν οὖσα
ὄν (εἰμί).

1   **αὐτίκα** – *straightaway, immediately;* δ′ = δέ (elision); **ἐΰθρονος -ον** (> εὖ + θρονος) – *lovely-throned;* **μιν** = αὐτόν/αὐτήν – *him/her;* **ἔγειρε** no augment, from ἐγείρω, aor: ἤγειρα – *awake, rouse.*

2   **εὔπεπλος -ον** (> εὖ + πέπλος) – *lovely-robed;* Nausicaa is in apposition to μιν; **ἄφαρ** – *at once, straightaway;* **ἀποθαυμάζω** – *be astonished;* **ὄνειρος ὁ** – *dream.*

3   **βῆ** = ἔβη (no augment), βῆ δ′ ἴμεναι – *she made her way* (lit. *she went to go* – ἴμεναι = ἰέναι) **διά** + acc. – *through* (often with this case rather than the genitive in Homer); **δώμαθ′** = δώματα – *house, palace;* **τοκεύς -έως ὁ** – *parent* (Nausicaa's parents are Arete and Alcinous, see p. 27); **ἵν′ ἀγγείλειε** purpose clause ἵνα + optative, after historic main verb (βῆ). In line 11 there is an example of ἵνα + subjunctive, ἄγωμαι.

4   **φίλος -η -ον** – *dear, beloved, own* (frequent in Homer); **κιχήσατο** (aorist of κιχάνομαι) – *find;* **ἔνδον** – *inside;* **ἐόντας** = ὄντας.

5   **ἡ μέν** (i.e. her mother, contrasting with τῷ δέ (6), her father); **ἐπί** + dat. – *on, at;* **ἐσχάρῃ ἡ** – *hearth, fire-side;* **ἧστο** (from ἧμαι) – *sat;* **σύν** + dat. – *with;* **ἀμφίπολος ἡ** – *maidservant, attendant.*

6   **ἠλάκατα τά** – *wool;* **στρωφάω** – *spin;* **ἁλιπόρφυρος -ον** – *sea-purple;* θύραζε – *out of the door* (lit. *out to the door*).

7   **ξύμβλητο** aorist of συμβάλλομαι + dat. – *meet;* **μετά** + acc. – *among;* **κλειτός -ή -όν** – *illustrious, famous;* **βασιλῆας** = βασιλέας – *lords,* since Alcinous is king.

8   **ἐς** = εἰς; **ἵνα** + indicative – *where;* **μιν** = αὐτόν; **κάλεον** = ἐκάλουν imperfect of καλέω – *call, invite;* **ἀγαυός -ή -όν** – *noble.*

9   **μάλα** – *very;* **ἄγχι** – *near, close;* **στᾶσα** aorist participle of ἵστημι – *standing;* **προσέειπε** (> πρός + λέγω) + acc. – *address.*

10   **πάππας -ου ὁ** – *daddy;* **φίλ′** = φίλε (*vocative*); **οὐκ ἄν** + optative (polite request) – *'would you mind . . .?';* **ἐφοπλίσσειας** aorist optative of ἐφοπλίζω (> ὅπλα = weapons, equipment) – *equip, get ready;* **ἀπήνη ἡ** – *waggon, cart.*

11   **εὔκυκλος -ον** (< cycle) – *well-wheeled, with fine wheels;* **κλυτός -ή -όν** – *glorious;* **εἵματα τά** – *clothes;* **ἄγομαι** (> ἄγω) – *take along.*

12   **πλυνέουσα** future participle – expressing purpose of πλύνω – *wash;* **τά** = ἅ (ὅς ἥ ὅ); **μοι** – *for me, my,* **ῥερυπωμένα** perfect passive participle of ῥυπόω – *dirty, left dirty;* **κεῖται** from κεῖμαι – *lie.*

Nausicaa persuades her father to let her travel down to the coast.

'καὶ δὲ σοὶ αὐτῷ ἔοικε μετὰ πρώτοισιν ἐόντα
βουλὰς βουλεύειν καθαρὰ χροῖ εἵματ' ἔχοντα.
πέντε δέ **τοι** φίλοι υἷες ἐνὶ μεγάροις γεγάασιν,   15
οἱ δύ' ὀπυίοντες, τρεῖς δ' ἠΐθεοι θαλέθοντες·
οἱ δ' **αἰεὶ ἐθέλουσι** νεόπλυτα εἵματ' ἔχοντες
ἐς χορὸν ἔρχεσθαι· τὰ δ' ἐμῇ φρενὶ πάντα μέμηλεν.'

ὣς ἔφατ'· αἴδετο γὰρ θαλερὸν γάμον ἐξονομῆναι
πατρὶ φίλῳ· ὁ δὲ **πάντα** νόει καὶ ἀμείβετο μύθῳ·   20

'οὔτε **τοι** ἡμιόνων φθονέω, **τέκος,** οὔτε τευ ἄλλου.
ἔρχευ· ἀτάρ **τοι** δμῶες ἐφοπλίσσουσιν ἀπήνην
ὑψηλὴν εὔκυκλον, ὑπερτερίῃ ἀραρυῖαν.'
ὣς εἰπὼν δμώεσσιν ἐκέκλετο, τοὶ δ' ἐπίθοντο.

Feminine beauty

λευκώλενος – '*white-armed*' (54) is an **epithet** often used of beautiful women. It was conventional for well-born women to keep their complexions fair: Nausicaa and her maids wear head-scarves (see 53) and Arete shows concern for her daughter's soft skin (32).

> Q.   What arguments does Nausicaa use to persuade her father?
>
> Q.   Which topic remains unspoken and why?
>
> Q.   What additional touch does Alcinous add when he grants Nausicaa her request?
>
> Q.   How is Alcinous characterized in lines 13–24?

GCSE vocabulary: *ἀεί, ἄλλος, αὐτός, γάρ, δύο, ἐθέλω, ἐμός, ἐν* + dat., *ἔχω, καλέω, μέγας, μῦθος, οὔτε . . . οὔτε . . ., πᾶς, πείθομαι, πέντε, πρῶτος, σοί (συ), τρεῖς, υἱός, φημί, ὡς.*

13 ἔοικε + dat. – *it is fit, it is right*; μετά + dat. – *among*; πρώτοισιν = πρώτοις; ἐόντα
    = ὄντα. Nausicaa refers to her father first in the dative (σοί αὐτῷ), then shifts to the accusative case
    (ἐόντα … ἔχοντα).

14 βουλήν βουλεύω – *'deliberate in council'*; καθαρός -ά -όν – *clean, fresh*; χροΐ
    (dat. of χρώς ὁ) – *skin*; εἵματα τά – *clothes* (11); ἔχοντα – often translated *'with'*.

15 τοι = σοί (also 21, 22); υἷες nom. pl. of υἱός; ἐνί = ἐν + dat.; μέγαρον τό
    (> μέγας) – *great hall*, pl. *palace*; γεγάασιν perfect of γίγνομαι – *are born*
    (*to you*) – i.e. *'you have'*.

16 οἵ δύ' – *'two of whom'*; ὀπυίω – *be married*; ἠίθεος ὁ – *unmarried youth,*
    bachelor; θαλέθω (< θάλλω) – *flourish, be full of life*.

17 αἰεί = ἀεί; νεόπλυτος -ον (> νέος + πλύνω 12) – *newly washed, freshly laundered*.

18 χορός ὁ – *dance, dancing*; φρήν φρένος ἡ – *mind, heart*; μέμηλεν perfect of μέλει
    + dat., with neuter plural subject – *are a concern to, concern*.

19 ὡς ἔφατο (φημί) – *'so he/she spoke'*, used formulaically to indicate the end of a speech;
    αἰδέομαι – *be embarrassed, feel shame*; θαλερός -ά -όν *youthful, blossoming*;
    γάμος ὁ (< polygamy) – *wedding, marriage*; ἐξονομῆναι aorist infinitive of ἐξονομαίνω
    (> ὄνομα) – *name, mention directly*.

20 νοέω – *notice, perceive*; ἀμείβομαι – *reply, answer in turn*; μῦθος ὁ – *story,*
    speech, word or words.

21 ἡμίονος ὁ, ἡ (< hemi-sphere) – *mule* (= half-donkey); φθονέω + gen. – *begrudge,*
    refuse; τέκος -εος τό – *child*; τευ = τινός (τις) – *'anything'*.

22 ἔρχευ = ἔρχου, imperative of ἔρχομαι; ἀτάρ – *but, yet*; δμῶες οἱ – *servants, domestic*
    slaves (also at 24); ἐφοπλίσσουσιν ἀπήνην (see 10–11).

23 ὑπερτερίη ἡ – *awning, shade*; ἀραρυῖαν + dat. perfect participle from
    ἀραρίσκω – *join, fit*, agreeing with ἀπήνην – *'fitted with'*.

24 ἐκέκλετο – Homeric aorist of κέλομαι – *call on, command*; τοὶ δ' = οἱ δε – *'and they'*
    marking a change of subject.

Preparations for a day at the beach.

οἱ μὲν ἄρ' ἐκτὸς ἄμαξαν ἐΰτροχον ἡμιονείην   25
ὅπλεον, ἡμιόνους θ' ὕπαγον ζεῦξάν θ' ὑπ' ἀπήνῃ·
κούρη δ' ἐκ θαλάμοιο φέρεν ἐσθῆτα φαεινήν.
καὶ τὴν μὲν κατέθηκεν ἐϋξέστῳ ἐπ' ἀπήνῃ,
μήτηρ δ' ἐν κίστῃ ἐτίθει μενοεικέ' ἐδωδὴν
παντοίην, ἐν δ' ὄψα τίθει, ἐν δ' οἶνον ἔχευεν   30
ἀσκῷ ἐν αἰγείῳ· κούρη δ' ἐπεβήσετ' ἀπήνης.
δῶκεν δὲ χρυσέῃ ἐν ληκύθῳ ὑγρὸν ἔλαιον,
ἧος χυτλώσαιτο σὺν ἀμφιπόλοισι γυναιξίν.
ἡ δ' ἔλαβεν μάστιγα καὶ ἡνία σιγαλόεντα,
μάστιξεν δ' ἐλάαν· καναχὴ δ' ἦν ἡμιόνοιϊν·   35
αἱ δ' ἄμοτον τανύοντο, φέρον δ' ἐσθῆτα καὶ αὐτήν,
οὐκ οἴην, ἅμα τῇ γε καὶ ἀμφίπολοι κίον ἄλλαι.

Q.   How is Arete characterized in lines 29–33?

Q.   What sort of atmosphere is created by the detailed description of preparations
     in this passage? Pick out details that make the scene vivid.

GCSE vocabulary: αὐτός, βαίνω, βήσομαι (*future of* βαίνω), γε, δή, ἔδωκα, ἐκ + gen., ἕως,
ἦν (*imperfect of* εἰμί), λαμβάνω, ἔλαβον, μήτηρ, οἶνος, φέρω, χρυσός.

25   οἱ μέν – *they* (the servants, contrasted with κούρη, 27); ἄρ' = ἄρα – *then*; ἐκτός (adv.) –
outside; ἅμαξα ἡ (= ἀπήνη) – *cart, waggon*; ἐΰτροχος -ον (> τρέχω) = *smooth-running*; ἡμιονείος -η -ον – *mule* (adj.).

26   ὁπλέω – *make ready*; θ' = τε (elision before a rough breathing); ὑπάγω
(> ἄγω) – *lead under*; ζεῦξαν aorist of ζεύγνυμι – *yoke*; ὑπό + dat./gen. – *under*.

27   κούρη ἡ – *girl, maiden*; θαλάμοιο 2nd declension genitive ending, from θάλαμος ὁ –
chamber, bedroom; φέρεν = ἔφερεν; the imperfect tense suggests more than one trip;
ἐσθής -ῆτος ἡ – *clothing, clothes*; φαεινός -ή -όν – *shining, splendid*.

28   τὴν μέν (i.e. the clothes); κατέθηκεν aorist of κατατίθημι – *set down, put*; ἐΰξεστος
-ον – *well-polished*; ἐπί + dat. – *on*.

29   κίστη ἡ – *basket, hamper*; ἐτίθει imperfect of τίθημι – *put, place* (30); μενοεικής -ες
– *nourishing*; ἐδωδή ἡ – *provisions, food*.

30   παντοῖος -α -ον – *of every kind*; ἐν δ' (i.e. ἐν τῇ κίστῃ); ὄψα τά – *delicacies,
savouries*; ἔχευεν (aorist of χέω) – *pour*.

31   ἀσκός ὁ – *wine-skin, flagon*; αἴγειος -η -ον – *of goat-skin*; ἐπεβήσετ' aorist of
ἐπιβαίνομαι – *get up onto* + gen.

32   δῶκεν = ἔδωκεν (the subject is Arete); χρύσεος -α/η -ον (> χρυσός) – *of gold*; λήκυθος
ἡ – *oil-flask, bottle*; ὑγρός -ά -όν – *fluid, liquid*; ἔλαιον τό – *olive oil*.

33   ἧος = ἕως + opt.– *until, for when, so that*; χυτλόομαι – *anoint oneself after
bathing*; σὺν ἀμφιπόλοισι (5).

34   μάστιξ -ιγος ἡ – *whip*; ἡνία τά – *reins*; σιγαλόεις -εσσα -εν – *shining, splendid*.

35   μαστιγόω – *whip*; ἐλάαν infinitive of ἐλαύνω – '*to drive them on*'; καναχή ἡ – *clatter,
ring*; ἡμιόνοιϊν – a dual genitive form – *of the two mules* (21).

36   αἱ δέ – i.e. the mules; ἄμοτον – *vigorously*; τανύομαι – *strain, pull ahead*; ἐσθής
-ῆτος ἡ (27).

37   οἶος -η -ον – *alone, on one's own*; ἅμα (adv.) – *along with, together*; καί – *also,
as well*; κίον imperfect of κίω – *went*; ἄλλαι – '*as well*' (lit. 'as others').

Nausicaa and her maids wash the clothes.

αἱ δ' ὅτε δὴ ποταμοῖο ῥόον περικαλλέ' ἵκοντο,
ἔνθ' ἦ τοι πλυνοὶ ἦσαν ἐπηετανοί, πολὺ δ' ὕδωρ
καλὸν ὑπεκπρορέει μάλα περ ῥυπόωντα καθῆραι,   40
ἔνθ' αἵ γ' ἡμιόνους μὲν ὑπεκπροέλυσαν ἀπήνης
καὶ τὰς μὲν σεῦαν ποταμὸν πάρα δινήεντα
τρώγειν ἄγρωστιν μελιηδέα· ταὶ δ' ἀπ' ἀπήνης
εἵματα χερσὶν ἕλοντο καὶ ἐσφόρεον μέλαν ὕδωρ,
στεῖβον δ' ἐν βόθροισι θοῶς ἔριδα προφέρουσαι.   45
αὐτὰρ ἐπεὶ πλῦνάν τε κάθηράν τε ῥύπα πάντα,
ἑξείης πέτασαν παρὰ θῖν' ἁλός, ἧχι μάλιστα
λάϊγγας ποτὶ χέρσον ἀποπλύνεσκε θάλασσα.
αἱ δὲ λοεσσάμεναι καὶ χρισάμεναι λίπ' ἐλαίῳ
δεῖπνον ἔπειθ' εἵλοντο παρ' ὄχθησιν ποταμοῖο,   50
εἵματα δ' ἠελίοιο μένον τερσήμεναι αὐγῇ.

Q.   What makes this long description of washing clothes engaging? Which details
      stand out most vividly and why?

GCSE vocabulary: *ἀπό* + gen., *δεῖπνον*, *εἷλον* (*αἱρέω*), *ἐπεί*, *ἔπειτα*, *ἦσαν*
(*imperfect of εἰμί*), *θάλασσα*, *καλός*, *μάλιστα*, *μέν . . . δε*, *μένω*, *πολύς πολλή πολύ*, *πρός* +
acc., *ὕδωρ*, *χερσίν* (*dat. pl. of χείρ*).

38   ὅτε – *when*; ποταμοῖο (gen. sg.); ῥόος ὁ – *stream, current*; περικαλλής -ές (> καλός) – *very lovely, idyllic*; ἵκοντο aorist of ἱκνέομαι = ἀφικνέομαι – *they reached*.

39   ἔνθα – *where*; ἤ τοι – *indeed, in truth*; πλυνός ὁ – *washing place*; ἐπηετανός -όν – *never-failing, brimming*.

40   ὑπεκπροϱέει (> ῥέω – *flow* + three prepositional prefixes: προ- ἐκ- ὑπο-) – *flow out*; μάλα – *very*; περ = καίπερ + participle (ῥυπόωντα, 12) – '*although being very dirty*', i.e. '*even the dirtiest things*'; καθῆραι aorist infinitive, expressing result, of καθαίρω (< catharsis) – *cleanse, purify, 'so as to cleanse . . .'*.

41   ἔνθα – *there*; αἵ γε – *the girls*; ὑπεκπροέλυσαν (> λύω – *release, loose* + προ- ἐκ- ὑπο- – *forth out from under* + gen. (40)); ἀπήνη ἡ (10).

42   τὰς μέν – *the mules*; σεύω aorist ἔσευα – *chase off, let go*; παρά + acc. (< parallel) – *alongside, along*; δινήεις -εσσα -εν – *swirling, eddying*.

43   τρώγειν infinitive expressing purpose, of τρώγω – *nibble, graze*; ἄγρωστις -ιδος ἡ – *long grass*; μελιηδής -ές – *honey-sweet, delicious*; ταὶ δ' – '*Then they . . .'*.

44   εἵματα (11); ἕλοντο = εἷλον; ἐσφόρεον = εἰσέφερον + acc.; μέλας μέλαινα μέλαν (< melancholy) – *black, dark*.

45   στείβω – *trample, tread* (to get the dirt out); βόθρος ὁ – *channel*; θοῶς – *swiftly*; ἔρις -ιδος ἡ – *rivalry, competitiveness*; προφέρω (> φέρω) – *display, show off*.

46   αὐτάρ – *but, moreover*; πλῦνάν (πλύνω 12); κάθηραν (καθαίρω, ἐκάθηρα 40); ῥύπα τά (> ῥυπόω 12) – *dirt*.

47   ἑξείης (adv.) – *in order, in a row*; πέτασαν from πετάννυμι – *spread out*; παρά (42); θίς θινός ὁ – *shore, beach*; ἅλς ἁλός ὁ – *sea*; ἧχι – *where*.

48   λᾶϊγξ λάϊγγας ἡ – *pebble*; ποτί = πρός + acc. *to, towards*; χέρσος ἡ – *land, shore*; ἀποπλύνεσκε (ἀποπλύνω) – *wash up* -σκ- gives a frequentative sense: '*would wash up*'.

49   λοεσσάμεναι aorist participle of λούομαι – *wash oneself*; χρισάμεναι from χρίομαι – *anoint oneself*; λίπα (< lipids) – *richly*; ἐλαίον τό (32).

50   ἔπειθ' = ἔπειτα; παρά + dat. – *beside, by*; ὄχθησιν (ὄχθη ἡ) – *bank, dune*.

51   εἵματα τά (14); ἠελίοιο gen. of ἥλιος (< helium) – *sun*; τερσήμεναι infinitive of τέρσομαι – *dry, get dry*; αὐγή ἡ – *ray, light, beam*.

Nausicaa looks like Artemis as she plays on the beach with her maids.

αὐτὰρ ἐπεὶ σίτου τάρφθεν δμῳαί τε καὶ αὐτή,
σφαίρῃ ταί γ' ἄρα παῖζον, ἀπὸ κρήδεμνα βαλοῦσαι·
τῇσι δὲ Ναυσικάα λευκώλενος ἄρχετο μολπῆς.
οἵη δ' Ἄρτεμις εἶσι κατ' οὔρεα ἰοχέαιρα.   55
ἢ κατὰ Τηΰγετον περιμήκετον ἢ Ἐρύμανθον,
τερπομένη κάπροισι καὶ ὠκείης ἐλάφοισι·
τῇ δέ θ' ἅμα νύμφαι, κοῦραι Διὸς αἰγιόχοιο,
ἀγρονόμοι παίζουσι· γέγηθε δέ τε φρένα Λητώ·
πασάων δ' ὑπὲρ ἥ γε κάρη ἔχει ἠδὲ μέτωπα,   60
ῥεῖά τ' ἀριγνώτη πέλεται, καλαὶ δέ τε πᾶσαι·
ὣς ἥ γ' ἀμφιπόλοισι μετέπρεπε παρθένος ἀδμής.
ἀλλ' ὅτε δὴ ἄρ' ἔμελλε πάλιν οἶκόνδε νέεσθαι
ζεύξασ' ἡμιόνους πτύξασά τε εἵματα καλά,

Names and places

Ἄρτεμις ἡ: *Artemis;* **Λητώ ἡ:** *Leto*
Leto was the mother of Artemis, virgin goddess of hunting, and her twin brother Apollo; their father was Zeus. They were born on the island of Delos.

Τηΰγετος ... Ἐρύμανθος: *Taygetus ... Erymanthus*
Two mountain ranges in the Peloponnese.

Διὸς αἰγιόχοιο (gen. case): *aegis-bearing Zeus*
The aegis was a goatskin cloak, fringed with snakes and often emblazoned with the head of the Gorgon, Medusa; it offered protection and filled any opponent with dread. Athene used the aegis in battle in the great hall to terrify Odysseus' enemies out of their wits in *Odyssey* 22.295ff.

Similes

Similes play an important part in epic poetry. As well as having a primary point of comparison, Homeric similes often bring surprising insights or subtle shading to the narrative, adding touches of humour, irony or pathos, for example. There are two similes in this section of *Odyssey* 6 (lines 55–61 and 83–7).

Q.   What is the primary point of correspondence in the simile in lines 55–62?

Q.   What additional details are introduced and what effect do these have? Why in
       particular is Leto mentioned?

GCSE vocabulary: *ἀλλά, ἀποβάλλω, ἄρχομαι* + gen., *Διός, εἶσι (from εἶμι), ἤ ... ἤ ...,
καλός, κατά* + acc., *οἶκος, ὄρος, σῖτος.*

52 αὐτάρ (46); τάρφθεν aorist of τέρπομαι – *they had delighted in, enjoyed their fill of* + gen.; δμωαί αἱ (= ἀμφίπολοι, feminine form of δμῶες οἱ (22)) – *maids.*

53 σφαίρη ἡ (< sphere) – *ball;* ἄρα – *then* (25); παῖζον (> παῖς) – *play;* ἀπὸ. . .βάλλω (tmesis); κρήδεμνον τό – *veil, head-scarf.*

54 τῇσι = ταῖς – *for them;* λευκώλενος -ον – *white-armed* (a common epithet for beautiful women); μολπή ἡ – *song, singing.*

55 οἵη – *like* from οἷος – *of the sort which,* agreeing with Nausicaa and introducing a simile – *like . . . Artemis, when she ranges over . . .;* εἶσι from εἶμι – *I go;* οὖρος -εος τό = ὄρος; ἰοχέαιρα ἡ – *archer, shooter of arrows.*

56 περιμήκετος -ον – *lofty, high.*

57 τέρπομαι + dat. (52) – *delight in;* κάπρος ὁ – *wild boar;* ὠκείης = ὠκείαις (f. dat. pl of ὠκύς, -εῖα -ύ) – *swift;* ἔλαφος ἡ – *deer.*

58 θ΄= τε (τε can be used when a generalization is being made; it is used four times in the simile in this way); ἅμα + dat.– *along with, together with* (τῇ – *her*); νύμφη ἡ – *nymph;* κούρη ἡ *maid* (27), '*daughter*'; αἰγίοχος -ον – *aegis-bearing.*

59 ἀγρονόμος -ον – *wild, roaming the countryside;* παίζουσι (see 53 – the verb within the simile of Artemis and her attendant nymphs picks up the verb used of Nausicaa and her maids); γέγηθε (perfect of γηθέω) – *feels joy;* φρήν φρενός ἡ – *mind, heart* (accusative of respect) '*in her heart*'.

60 ὑπέρ + gen. (πασάων = πασῶν) – *above, over;* κάρη τό – *head;* ἠδέ – *and;* μέτωπον τό – *brow.*

61 ῥεῖά – *easily;* ἀρίγνωτος -η -ον – *distinct, recognizable;* πέλεται – *is* (πέλομαι, a common verb in the Homeric poems, means simply '*be*'); καλαὶ δέ τε πᾶσαι – '*but all are beautiful*'.

62 ὥς (= οὕτως) – used to close the simile *so, just so . . .;* ἥ γ΄ – i.e. Nausicaa; μετέπρεπε (from μεταπρέπω + dat.) – *be distinguished amongst;* παρθένος ἡ – *maiden, virgin;* ἀδμής -ῆτος – *unmarried, untamed.*

63 ὅτε (38); ἄρ΄ (25); πάλιν – *back, back again;* οἴκόνδε – *(to) home, homewards;* νέεσθαι infinitive of νέομαι – *to go, come.*

64 ζεύξασα . . . πτύξασα aorist participles of ζεύγνυμι – *yoke* and πτύσσω – *fold.*

Athene contrives a way of waking Odysseus.

ἔνθ' αὖτ' ἄλλ' ἐνόησε θεὰ γλαυκῶπις Ἀθήνη,   65
ὡς Ὀδυσεὺς ἔγροιτο, ἴδοι τ' εὐώπιδα κούρην,
ἥ οἱ Φαιήκων ἀνδρῶν πόλιν ἡγήσαιτο.

σφαῖραν ἔπειτ' ἔρριψε μετ' ἀμφίπολον βασίλεια·
ἀμφιπόλου μὲν ἅμαρτε, βαθείῃ δ' ἔμβαλε δίνῃ,
αἱ δ' ἐπὶ μακρὸν ἄϋσαν. ὁ δ' ἔγρετο δῖος Ὀδυσσεύς,   70
ἑζόμενος δ' ὅρμαινε κατὰ φρένα καὶ κατὰ θυμόν·

'ὤ μοι ἐγώ, τέων αὖτε βροτῶν ἐς γαῖαν ἱκάνω;
ἦ ῥ' οἵ γ' ὑβρισταί τε καὶ ἄγριοι οὐδὲ δίκαιοι,
ἦε φιλόξεινοι, καί σφιν νόος ἐστὶ θεουδής;
ὥς τέ με κουράων ἀμφήλυθε θῆλυς ἀϋτή,   75
νυμφάων, αἳ ἔχουσ' ὀρέων αἰπεινὰ κάρηνα
καὶ πηγὰς ποταμῶν καὶ πίσεα ποιήεντα.
ἦ νύ που ἀνθρώπων εἰμὶ σχεδὸν αὐδηέντων;
ἀλλ' ἄγ', ἐγὼν αὐτὸς πειρήσομαι ἠδὲ ἴδωμαι.'

Names and places

Ἀθήνη ἡ: *Athene*

Athene is the daughter of Zeus and warrior goddess of wisdom. She supports Odysseus and his family throughout the *Odyssey*, driving the plot forward to help her favourite hero get home and avenge the wrongs to his household.

Ὀδυσεύς or **Ὀδυσσεύς** (70, 88) **ὁ:** *Odysseus*

Odysseus' travels

Whenever the hero arrives in a strange land in the *Odyssey*, he is alert to the danger of savages. In this case, unlike Odysseus, we know the true situation and his initial anxiety is amusing. Odysseus has just spent seven years on Calypso's remote island with no-one but the goddess to talk to and there could be excitement as well as weariness or caution in his words.

Q.   How well devised have the details of Athene's plans been so far?
      What details make this scene dramatic?
Q.   What sort of hero does Odysseus seem to be from his opening words?

GCSE vocabulary: ἀνήρ ἀνδρός, ἄνθρωπος, δίκαιος, ἐγώ, ἐμβάλλω, θεά, ἴδοι (ὁράω), μέλλω, ξένος, πειράομαι, φιλός.

65   ἔνθα – *then, there* (41), *where* (39); αὖτε – *in turn, again*; ἄλλο (ἄλλος -η -ο);
ἐνόησε (from νοέω) *think, realize, notice* (20) *turn one's thoughts to*; γλαυκῶπις
– *bright-eyed* (Athene's epithet).

66   ὡς + opt. – *so that*; ἔγροιτο – aorist middle optative of ἐγείρω – *awake, rouse* (1);
εὐῶπις -ιδος – *lovely-eyed, fair-faced.*

67   ἤ + optative ἡγήσαιτο aorist optative of ἡγέομαι + dat. – *lead*: here *who might lead, to
lead* (expression of purpose); οἱ = αὐτῷ.

68   σφαῖρα (53); ῥίπτω – *throw*; μετά + acc. – '*to*'; βασίλεια ἡ – *princess.*

69   ἁμαρτάνω, ἥμαρτον + gen. – *miss*; βαθύς -εῖα -ύ – *deep*; ἐμβάλλω = ἐν + βάλλω;
δίνη ἡ – *eddy, whirlpool, swirling water.*

70   ἐπὶ . . . αὔω – *cry out, shriek*; μακρόν – '*loudly*' (literally 'long'); ἔγρετο – poetic
aorist of ἐγείρω (66); δῖος -α -ον – *noble, god-like.*

71   ἕζομαι = καθίζω – *sit, sit up*; ὁρμαίνω – *ponder*; κατά + acc. – *throughout, 'in*';
φρήν (18) *mind, heart*; θυμός ὁ – *heart, spirit.*

72   ὦ μοι ἐγώ – *Alas for me!*; τέων = τίνων – *whose?*; αὖτε (65) – *in turn, 'this time*';
βροτός ὁ (< ambrosia) – *mortal*; γαῖα = γῆ; ἱκάνω – *reach, come to.*

73   ἦ ῥ' οἵ γ' . . . ἦε – '*are they. . .or. . .?*'; ὑβριστής -οῦ ὁ (< hubris) – *insolent, violent
person*; ἄγριος -α -ον (< ἀγρός) – *wild, uncivilized*; οὐδέ – *and not.*

74   φιλόξεινος -ον (< φίλος + ξένος) – *friendly to strangers*; σφιν = αὐτοῖς; νόος = νοῦς
– *mind*; θεουδής -ές – *godly, god-fearing.*

75   ὥς τέ – *as of* + gen. (58); κουράων = κουρῶν; ἀμφήλυθε = ἀμφ + ἤλυθε = ἦλθε –
surround; θῆλυς – *female, feminine*; ἀϋτή ἡ – *war-cry, shout, shriek* (from αὔω
70).

76   νυμφάων – in apposition to κουράων; αἵ (ὅς ἥ ὅ); ἔχω – *have, inhabit*; ὀρέων (ὄρος τό);
αἰπεινός -ή -όν – *high, lofty*; κάρηνον τό – *peak, head.*

77   πηγή ἡ – *spring, source*; πίσεα τά – *meadows*; ποιήεις -εσσα -εν – *grassy.*

78   ἤ νύ που ἤ introduces a question, νύ and που suggest inference – *perhaps, then?*, σχεδόν
+ gen. – *near*; αὐδήεις -εσσα -εν (> αὐδάω – speak) – *with human speech.*

79   ἀλλ' ἄγε – *but come* – the hero rouses himself to action; ἐγών = ἐγώ; πειρήσομαι
subjunctive of πειράομαι; ἠδέ – *and*; ἴδωμαι (< ὁράω) – '*let me try for myself and
see . . .*'.

Odysseus emerges from the undergrowth like a hungry lion.

ὣς εἰπὼν θάμνων ὑπεδύσετο δῖος Ὀδυσσεύς,   80
ἐκ πυκινῆς δ' ὕλης πτόρθον κλάσε χειρὶ παχείῃ
φύλλων, ὡς ῥύσαιτο περὶ χροῒ μήδεα φωτός.
βῆ δ' ἴμεν ὥς τε λέων ὀρεσίτροφος, ἀλκὶ πεποιθώς,
ὅς τ' εἶσ' ὑόμενος καὶ ἀήμενος, ἐν δέ οἱ ὄσσε
δαίεται· αὐτὰρ ὁ βουσὶ μετέρχεται ἢ ὀΐεσσιν   85
ἠὲ μετ' ἀγροτέρας ἐλάφους· κέλεται δέ ἑ γαστὴρ
μήλων πειρήσοντα καὶ ἐς πυκινὸν δόμον ἐλθεῖν·
ὣς Ὀδυσεὺς κούρῃσιν ἐϋπλοκάμοισιν ἔμελλε
μίξεσθαι, γυμνός περ ἐών· χρειὼ γὰρ ἵκανε.
σμερδαλέος δ' αὐτῇσι φάνη κεκακωμένος ἅλμῃ,   90
τρέσσαν δ' ἄλλυδις ἄλλη ἐπ' ἠϊόνας προὐχούσας·
οἴη δ' Ἀλκινόου θυγάτηρ μένε· τῇ γὰρ Ἀθήνη
θάρσος ἐνὶ φρεσὶ θῆκε καὶ ἐκ δέος εἵλετο γυίων.

Q.   How far does the vase painting below capture or differ from the situation
     described in lines 80–93?

Q.   What is the primary point of correspondence in this simile (lines 83–7)? What
     additional details are introduced and what effect do these have?

Q.   Pick out two or three words where their sound may contribute to the overall
     effect of the passage.

Q.   Could there be an element of humour in this passage?

GCSE vocabulary: *εἶσι (εἶμι), θυγάτηρ, ὕλη, φαίνομαι.*

Figure 1 *Sixth-century
red-figure vase depicting
Odysseus, Athena and Nausicaa.*
Photo: DEA Picture Library/De
Agostini/Getty Images.

80 θάμνος ὁ – *bush*; ὑπεδύσετο ὑποδύομαι + gen. – *slink out, creep out from.*

81 πυκινός -ή -όν – *dense, thick, crowded*; πτόρθος ὁ – *branch*; κλάω – *break off*; παχύς -εῖα -ύ – *sturdy.*

82 φύλλον τό – *leaf* (πτόρθος φύλλων – '*leafy branch*'); ὡς = ἵνα + opt.; ῥύομαι – *shield, offer protection* (the subject is πτόρθος, μήδεα is the object); περί + dat. – *for, round*; χρώς ὁ – *skin, flesh, body* (14); μήδεα τά – *genitals*; φώς φωτός ὁ (= ἀνήρ) – *man, male.* It might help to translate ῥύσαιτο twice: . . . *offer his body protection, shielding his male parts.*

83 βῆ δ᾽ ἴμεν – (3); ὥς τε (opens the simile, see 58); λέων -οντος ὁ – *lion*; ὀρεσίτροφος -ον (> ὄρος τό) – *mountain-reared*; ἀλκί (dat.) – *strength*; πεποιθώς + dat. (from πείθομαι) – *trusting in.*

84 τ᾽ – see 58; εἶσι (εἶμι – go); ὕω – *rain, rain on*; ἄημι – *blow, blow on*; ἐν οἱ = ἐν αὐτῷ; ὄσσε τώ – (*two*) *eyes*; (neuter dual with a singular verb).

85 δαίομαι – *blaze*; βοῦς ὁ (< Latin: bovis < bovine) – *ox, cow*; μετέρχομαι + dat. – *go among*; ὄϊεσσιν (dat. pl. of ὄϊς < Latin: ovis < ovine) – *sheep.*

86 ἠέ = ἤ; μετά + acc. – *after*; ἀγρότερος -α -ον – *wild*; ἔλαφος ἡ – *deer* (57); κέλομαι (= κελεύει) – *bid*; ἑ = αὐτόν; γαστήρ -τρός ὁ – *stomach, belly.*

87 μῆλα τά – *sheep, flocks*; πειρήσοντα from πειράω – *make an attempt on* future participle indicates purpose; πυκινός -ή -όν (81); δόμος ὁ – *house.*

88 κούρῃσιν = κούραις; ἐϋπλόκαμος -ον – *lovely-haired.*

89 μίξεσθαι future infinitive of μίγνυμι after μέλλω – *mix, mingle, have intercourse with*; γυμνός -ή -όν (< gymnasium) – *naked*; περ ἐών = καίπερ ὤν; χρείω ἡ – *want, need, necessity*; ἱκάνω (72) – *come over, reach.*

90 σμερδαλέος -η -ον – *terrible, terrifying*; αὐτῇσι = αὐταῖς; φάνη from ἐφάνην = aorist of φαίνομαι – *appear, seem*; κεκακωμένος perfect passive participle of κακόω (> κακός) – *fouled with, caked in*; ἅλμη ἡ – *brine, sea-salt.*

91 τρέσσαν (from τρέω) – *flee in panic*; ἄλλυδις ἄλλη (lit: a different girl in a different direction) – *all in different directions*; ἐπί + acc. – *along*; ἠϊών -όνος ἡ – *shore*; προὐχούσας (from προ+ ἔχων-ουσα-ον) – *jutting.*

92 οἶος -η -ον – *alone, only*; τῇ = αὐτῇ.

93 θάρσος τό – *courage*; ἐνί + θῆκε (tmesis) = ἐντίθημι + dat. – *put in*; ἐκ + εἵλετο (tmesis) = ἐξαιρέομαι – *take out, remove*; φρεσί dat. of φρήν (18); δέος τό – *fear*; γυῖα τά – *limbs.*

Supplication.

στῆ δ' ἄντα σχομένη· ὁ δὲ μερμήριξεν Ὀδυσσεύς,
ἢ γούνων λίσσοιτο λαβὼν εὐώπιδα κούρην,   95
ἦ αὔτως ἐπέεσσιν ἀποσταδὰ μειλιχίοισι,
λίσσοιτ', εἰ δείξειε πόλιν καὶ εἵματα δοίη.
ὣς ἄρα οἱ φρονέοντι δοάσσατο κέρδιον εἶναι,
λίσσεσθαι ἐπέεσσιν ἀποσταδὰ μειλιχίοισι,
μή οἱ γοῦνα λαβόντι χολώσαιτο φρένα κούρη.   100
αὐτίκα μειλίχιον καὶ κερδαλέον φάτο μῦθον·
'γουνοῦμαί σε, ἄνασσα· θεός νύ τις ἦ βροτός ἐσσι;
εἰ μέν τις θεός ἐσσι, τοὶ οὐρανὸν εὐρὺν ἔχουσιν,
Ἀρτέμιδί σε ἐγώ γε, Διὸς κούρη μεγάλοιο,
εἶδός τε μέγεθός τε φυήν τ' ἄγχιστα ἐΐσκω·   105
εἰ δέ τίς ἐσσι βροτῶν, τοὶ ἐπὶ χθονὶ ναιετάουσι,
τρισμάκαρες μὲν σοί γε πατὴρ καὶ πότνια μήτηρ,
τρισμάκαρες δὲ κασίγνητοι· μάλα πού σφισι θυμὸς
αἰὲν ἐϋφροσύνῃσιν ἰαίνεται εἵνεκα σεῖο,
λευσσόντων τοιόνδε θάλος χορὸν εἰσοιχνεῦσαν.   110
κεῖνος δ' αὖ περὶ κῆρι μακάρτατος ἔξοχον ἄλλων,
ὅς κέ σ' ἐέδνοισι βρίσας οἶκόνδ' ἀγάγηται.

Decisions

Making the right decisions at critical moments is key to Odysseus' character in the *Odyssey*: he is defined by and survives because of his mental agility (see Book 5.465ff. and in Book 16.225ff.). As at lines 71–4, the hero ponders the situation (ὅρμαινε 71, μερμήριξεν 94) before deciding on a course of action. Line 98, with minor variations, recurs seven times in the Odyssey.

Supplication

Odysseus deliberates about how to approach Nausicaa. He decides against grasping her knees (γούνων λαβών), the traditional way to seek help from a position of weakness. This act, known as supplication, placed the stronger party under an obligation. Helping might entail risk, but refusing went against a moral code sanctioned by Zeus.

Q.   What does Odysseus want to achieve by his supplication?

Q.   Why does Odysseus decide to speak '**ἀποσταδά**'? How do the the words **καὶ κερδαλέον** (101) affect the way we listen to the speech that follows?

Q.   How insightful is Odysseus? Analyse his persuasive powers in this speech.

GCSE vocabulary: *εὐρύς, μήτηρ.*

94 στῆ = ἔστη – strong aorist of ἵστημι – *stood*; ἄντα – *face to face*; σχομένη (ἔχω) *'holding her ground'*; μερμηρίζω – *ponder*.

95 ἤ . . . ἤ . . . + opt. – *whether . . . . or . . .* (indirect question); γούνων (gen. pl. of γόνυ τό – *knee*); λαμβάνω + gen. – *take hold of*; λίσσομαι – *entreat, beg, beseech*; εὐῶπις -ιδος (66).

96 αὔτως – *just so, as he was*; ἐπέεσσιν dat. pl. of ἔπος τό – *word*; ἀποσταδά – *standing apart, from afar*; μειλίχιος -α -ον – *gentle, soothing* (also 99).

97 εἰ + opt. – *'in case she might'*, *'to see if she would . . .'*; δείξειε (δείκνυμι) – *show*; εἵματα τά (11); δοίη (< δίδωμι) – *give*.

98 ὡς ἄρα points to line 99 – *'This, then, is how'*; οἱ = αὐτῷ (see 100); φρονέω – *think, reflect*; δοάσσατο – *it seemed*; κέρδιον – *better*.

100 μή + optative – *lest*; χολόομαι – *grow angry with* + dat.

101 αὐτίκα – *straightaway, directly*; μειλίχιος -α -ον (96); κερδαλέος -α -ον (> κέρδος τό – *profit*) *crafty, winning*; φάτο = ἔφατο (< φημί); μῦθος (20).

102 γουνέομαι (> γόνυ τό – knee) – *supplicate, grasp the knees*; ἄνασσα ἡ – *queen, lady*; νύ – *perhaps, then* (78); ἦ = ἤ; βροτός (72); ἐσσι = εἶ (εἰμί).

103 εἰ μέν . . . (εἰ δέ – 106), introducing two conditional clauses: *'if you are . . .'* (ἐσσι), *then I liken you* (ἔϊσκω, 105), (*but if . . .*); τοί = οἵ; ἔχουσιν (76).

105 εἶδός τό – *looks*; μέγεθος τό – *height*; φυή ἡ – *nature*; ἄγχιστα – *most closely*; ἔϊσκω – *liken x* (acc. – σε) *to y* (dat.) *in respect of z* (acc.).

106 τίς = τις; τοί = οἵ; ἐπί + dat. – *on*; χθών -ονός ἡ – *earth*; ναιετάω – *live, dwell*.

107 τρισμάκαρες – *thrice-blessed* (εἰσί is understood); πότνια – *revered, lady*.

108 κασίγνητος ὁ – *brother*; μάλα πού – *I'm sure*; σφισι = αὐτοῖς – *'their'*.

109 αἰέν = ἀεί; ἐϋφροσύνη ἡ – *joy, delight, happiness*; ἰαίνω – *warm, cheer*; εἵνεκα + gen. *for the sake of*; σεῖο = σοῦ.

110 λεύσσω – *see, look at*, *'of them seeing'*, *'when they saw'*; τοιόνδε – (τοιόσδε) *such as this*; θάλος τό – *shoot, sapling*; χορός ὁ – *dance, dancing* (18); εἰσοιχνεῦσαν (pres. participle of εἰσοιχνέω) – *enter into, join*.

111 κεῖνος = ἐκεῖνος; αὖ – *in turn*; περί – *most*; κῆρ -ρος τό *heart*; μακάρτατος -η -ον (superl. of μάκαρ, see 107); ἔξοχον + gen. – *beyond*.

112 ὅς κέ – *whoever it is that* (κέ + subj. gives an indefinite sense); σ' = σε; ἐέδνα τά – *bridal gifts*; βρίθω – *outweigh, win*; οἰκόνδε (63); ἀγάγηται (> ἄγω).

What happens next?

Odysseus' supplication is successful and Nausicaa treats the stranger with courtesy, showing courage and good judgement. When Odysseus has bathed and put on some of the clean clothes – and the goddess Athene has enhanced his appearance – Nausicaa gazes in admiration at his transformation. She lets Odysseus follow along with her maids part way back to the city and then gives him directions so that he can make his own way to the palace without involving her in any scandal.

Odysseus wins the respect of the Phaeacians, eventually revealing his identity, and he stays with them for long enough to tell the story of his adventures after Troy (Books 9–12). They in return provide him with generous guest-gifts and a safe passage home to Ithaca.

Odysseus and Nausicaa meet once more in the palace in Book 8, a scene famously imagined in a painting by Lord Frederic Leighton, where Odysseus says farewell and thanks her graciously (8.460ff.).

Final questions

- To what extent do you think the poet hints at a romantic attachment between Odysseus and Nausicaa?
- How 'normal' does Phaeacian society seem to you?
- Does Odysseus act in a way you would expect of a hero?
- What, if anything, can you learn about the status of women in Homeric poems from this extract?
- What do you find most memorable in this story?
- What are Homer's strengths as a story-teller?

ILIAD 3: 1–112

2020–2021 Prescription

See pages 24–6 for an introduction to Homer and his language.

The story so far . . .

Many suppose that the *Iliad* tells the story of the Trojan war, the ten-year struggle between the Greeks and Trojans following the abduction of Helen from Sparta. In fact, the whole poem, which amounts to over 12,000 lines of Greek verse and which takes around 15 hours to recite, focuses on a period of a few weeks near the end of the war. Of the 24 books, Books 2 to 22 cover only four days of fighting and a two-day truce. As the opening line states, the *Iliad* focuses on the wrath of Achilles. His anger at being denied his due honour – τιμή – by Agamemnon, leader of the Greek forces, leads him to withdraw from the battlefield and the Greeks suffer in his absence. It is only on his return to battle that the tide turns and he kills Hector, the best fighter on the Trojan side (Book 22). From this point, it is clear that Troy is doomed. Although the episode of the Trojan horse is beyond the scope of the poem, the familiar story of the ultimate destruction of Troy is foreshadowed in the closing books.

We are also given a sense of the first nine years of fighting in the opening books. In Book 3, for example, Helen identifies the main Greek heroes for king Priam as if he were seeing them for the first time, and the first clash of armies feels like an initial encounter between Greek and Trojan forces. The centrepiece of the book is a duel between Menelaus, Helen's rightful husband, and Paris (also called Alexander), the man who abducted Helen and took her back home to Troy. Their agreement, that Helen will belong to the winner to avoid a full-scale war, would make more logical sense when the Greeks first arrived in Troy. Thus, although the *Iliad* deals with only a few weeks of fighting in the final year, the concentrated focus on a brief episode conveys the emotional intensity of the whole ten-year campaign.

In the opening of Book 3 we see each side advancing into battle and they are characterized very differently: the Greeks, led by king Agamemnon, who fights alongside his brother Menelaus to avenge the abduction of Helen, are formidable in their silence and discipline. This picture contrasts with impressions so far in the *Iliad* of the Greek forces (also known as *Achaean*, *Argive* or *Danaan*), where the argument between Agamemnon and Achilles has escalated quickly in Book 1 and Agamemnon has come close to losing control of his forces when he decides to test their morale in Book 2.

Our first glimpse of the Trojans in the *Iliad* comes at the end of Book 2, after the huge massed forces of the Greeks have been listed. The Trojans are ruled over by king Priam and queen Hecuba, but their eldest son, Hector, commands the fighting forces and bears on his shoulders the weight of responsibility for protecting the besieged Trojan women, children and old men. He also has his own wife, Andromache, and baby son to protect. Hector's fighting forces consist of the Trojans and their allies. Hector's many brothers fight alongside him, of whom Paris, the man responsible for bringing war to Troy, is one.

The armies of the Greeks and the Trojans advance on each other.

Nominative *words or phrases are in* light blue, **verbs** *in dark blue.*

αὐτὰρ ἐπεὶ κόσμηθεν ἅμ' ἡγεμόνεσσιν ἕκαστοι,
Τρῶες μὲν κλαγγῇ τ' ἐνοπῇ τ' ἴσαν ὄρνιθες ὥς,
ἠΰτε περ κλαγγὴ γεράνων πέλει οὐρανόθι πρό,
αἵ τ' ἐπεὶ οὖν χειμῶνα φύγον καὶ ἀθέσφατον ὄμβρον
κλαγγῇ ταί γε πέτονται ἐπ' Ὠκεανοῖο ῥοάων   5
ἀνδράσι Πυγμαίοισι φόνον καὶ κῆρα φέρουσαι·
ἠέριαι δ' ἄρα ταί γε κακὴν ἔριδα προφέρονται·
οἳ δ' ἄρ' ἴσαν σιγῇ μένεα πνείοντες Ἀχαιοί,
ἐν θυμῷ μεμαῶτες ἀλεξέμεν ἀλλήλοισιν.

Names and places

Τρῶες οἱ: *Trojans;* **Ἀχαιοί οἱ:** *Achaeans, Greeks*
The Trojans lived in Troy in what is now modern Turkey. Several different names are used in the *Iliad* for
the Greeks. Achaea is in the northern Peloponnese in Greece.

Ὠκεανός -οῖο ὁ: *Ocean*
The river that was conceived of as flowing around the edge of the world.

Πυγμαῖοι οἱ: *Pygmies* (*πυγμή* = fist, suggesting either their size or character).
The battle of cranes and Pygmies was a popular story in Greek mythology.

Similes (1)

Similes are a notable feature of Homeric style. They take us away from the immediate action, often to a
more familiar world or natural setting. Homeric similes tend to have one primary point of contact and
further details may add atmosphere or shading. There are five similes in the lines you are about to read,
an unusually high density.

> Q.   What is the main point of comparison made in the simile (lines 2–7)?
>
> Q.   How does the vivid picture of the cranes affect our view of the Trojans?
>
> Q.   What key elements in the way the Greeks advance are brought out?
>
> Q.   How do the two sides differ as they enter battle? Does either side seem
>   stronger?

GCSE vocabulary: *ἀνήρ, ἐν* + dat., *ἐπεί, ἡγεμών, κακός, οὖν, σιγή, φεύγω, χειμών.*

1   αὐτάρ – *but, however*; κόσμηθεν = ἐκοσμήθησαν, from κοσμέω – *set in order* (the
     augment is often omitted in Homeric Greek); ἅμ' = ἅμα + dat. (elision) – *together with*;
     ἡγεμόνεσσιν – dat. pl. of ἡγεμών ὁ; ἕκαστοι – the plural refers to '*each side*'.

2   Τρῶες μέν ... contrasts with οἵ δ' ... Ἀχαιοί (8); κλαγγή ἡ (< clang) – *harsh noise,
     cry*; ἐνοπή ἡ – *shout, scream*; τε ... τε = τε ... καί; ἴσαν = ἦσαν (imperfect of εἶμι –
     go); ὄρνις -ιθος ὁ/ἡ (< ornithologist) – *bird*; ὄρνιθες ὥς – '*like birds*' (the accent on
     ὥς shows that it belongs with the previous word).

3   ἠΰτε πέρ – *just as when* (πέρ gives emphasis; the diaeresis (¨) shows that the two vowels are
     pronounced separately); γέρανος ὁ (< geranium, also called cranesbill) – *crane*; πέλω –
     rise; πρό – *ahead*; οὐρανόθι (> οὐρανός) '*in the sky*'.

4   αἵ τ' ἐπεὶ οὖν ... φύγον – '*when they flee ...*'; τ' = τε – indicates a generalization, as
     does the aorist φύγον (= ἔφυγον), known as a **gnomic aorist**; οὖν is best untranslated here, but
     means '*then, in that case*'; ἀθέσφατος – *inexpressibly great, endless*; ὄμβρος ὁ –
     rain.

5   κλαγγή ἡ (2); ταί γε (= αὐταί) – *they*, reinforced by γε; πέτομαι – *fly*; ἐπ' = ἐπί (elision)
     + gen. - *towards*; ῥοή ἡ – *stream* (ῥοάων = ῥοῶν).

6   φόνος ὁ (> φονεύω) – *slaughter*; κήρ -ός ἡ – *death*.

7   ἠέριος -η -ον – *early in the morning, high in the air*; ἄρα – *then* (different accent
     from ἆρα;); ταί = αὐταί; ἔρις -ιδος ἡ – *strife, battle*; προφέρομαι (> πρό + φέρω) –
     bring on, 'start'.

8   οἵ δε (see 2, the two sides are contrasted); ἴσαν (> εἶμι – go); μένος τό (μένεα = μένη τά) –
     strength, courage; πνείω (< pneumatic) – *breath*.

9   θυμός ὁ – *heart, mind, spirit* (can refer either to the seat of the emotions or the seat of
     reason); μεμαῶτες perfect participle of μάω – '*eager*'; ἀλεξέμεν (Homeric infinitive form
     of ἀλέξω + dat. (= βοηθέω) – *come to help, assist*; ἀλλήλους
     (> ἄλλος) – *each other*.

A cloud of dust arises as they advance. Paris readies his weapons for the fight.

εὖτ' ὄρεος κορυφῇσι Νότος κατέχευεν ὀμίχλην   10
ποιμέσιν οὔ τι φίλην, κλέπτῃ δέ τε νυκτὸς ἀμείνω,
τόσσον τίς τ' ἐπιλεύσσει ὅσον τ' ἐπὶ λᾶαν ἵησιν·
ὣς ἄρα τῶν ὑπὸ ποσσὶ κονίσαλος ὄρνυτ' ἀελλὴς
ἐρχομένων· μάλα δ' ὦκα διέπρησσον πεδίοιο.
οἳ δ' ὅτε δὴ σχεδὸν ἦσαν ἐπ' ἀλλήλοισιν ἰόντες,   15
Τρωσὶν μὲν προμάχιζεν Ἀλέξανδρος θεοειδής,
παρδαλέην ὤμοισιν ἔχων καὶ καμπύλα τόξα
καὶ ξίφος· αὐτὰρ δοῦρε δύω κεκορυθμένα χαλκῷ
πάλλων Ἀργείων προκαλίζετο πάντας ἀρίστους
ἀντίβιον μαχέσασθαι ἐν αἰνῇ δηϊοτῆτι.   20

Names and places

Νότος ὁ: *South Wind*

Ἀλέξανδρος ὁ: *Alexander or Paris*
Paris, son of Priam, caused the Trojan war by abducting Menelaus' wife, Helen. The Trojan hero is also named Alexander in the *Iliad*. In Book 3 he is called Alexander twenty-one times and Paris on only three occasions.

Ἀργεῖοι οἱ: *Argives, Greeks*
Properly, Greeks from the kindom of Argos, the area surrounding Agamemnon's city of Mycenae, but usually used to refer to all the Greeks.

Similes (2)

This second simile builds up an atmosphere of confusion as the two sides come together, raising so much dust on the plain that they can barely see ahead. The starts and ends of similes in the Homeric poems are clearly indicated, with words like εὖτε/ ἠΰτε, ὥσπερ and ὥς (13).

> Q.   How does the mention of a κλέπτης (11) affect the mood of the simile?
>
> Q.   How is Paris dressed and armed? What sort of a fighter does he seem to be, judging from lines 16–20?

GCSE vocabulary: ἄριστος (ἀγαθός), ἔρχομαι, ἦσαν, ἰών ἰοῦσα ἰόν, κλέπτω, μάχομαι, νύξ, ξίφος, ὄρος, πᾶς, πούς.

10   εὖτε (= ἠῦτε, 3) – *as when* (introducing a second simile); **κορυφή ἡ** – *peak*; **καταχέω** – *pour down on*; **ὀμίχλη ἡ** – *mist*.

11   **ποιμήν -ένος ὁ** – *shepherd*; **οὔ τι** – *not at all*; **φίλος** – *dear (to), loved by*; **κλέπτης ὁ** (> κλέπτω) – *thief*; **τε** – indicates a generalization, commonly in a simile (4); **ἀμείνω** (> ἀγαθός) = acc. sg. – *better* (comparative, followed by genitive).

12   **τόσσον τε ... ὅσον τε** – *as far ... as*; **τίς** (= τις) – *someone, 'a person'*; **ἐπιλεύσσω** – *see ahead*; **λᾶας -ος ὁ** – *stone*; **ἐπὶ ... ἵησιν** (3rd sg. present of ἵημι) – *throw, hurl*; tmesis in later Greek ἐπί would become attached to the verb as a prepositional prefix, = ἐφίημι – *throw*.

13   **ὥς** – *thus, just so* (ὡς is used to open and **ὥς** (= οὕτως) to close a simile); **ἄρα** – *then* (7); **τῶν** = αὐτῶν; **ὑπό** + dat. – *under*; **κονίσαλος ὁ** – *dust cloud*; **ὄρνυτο** imperfect of ὄρνυμι – *rise*; **ἀελλής -ές** – *thick, swirling*.

14   **ἐρχομένων** agrees with τῶν (13) *'of them as they were going'* (enjambment); **μάλα** (> μάλιστα) – *very*; **ὦκα** – *swiftly*; **διαπρήσσω** + gen. – *traverse, cross*; **πέδιον -οιο τό** – *plain*.

15   **ὅτε** – *when*; **σχεδόν** – *near*; **ἐπί** + dat. – *against* (often it has the sense of hostile intent, as is the case here); **ἀλλήλους** (> ἄλλος) – *each other*.

16   **προμαχίζω** (> πρό + μάχομαι) – *fight in front, come forward as a champion*; **θεοειδής -ές** (> θεός + εἶδος τό ('*looks*') – *looking like a god*; Paris' epithet emphasises his beauty (see also 39, 45)

17   **παρδαλέη ἡ** – *leopard-skin*; **ὦμος ὁ** – *shoulders*; **καμπύλος -ον** – *curved*; **τόξον τό** (plural for singular) – *bow*.

18   **αὐτάρ** – *but* (a stronger form of δέ); **δόρυ τό** – *spear* (δοῦρε is acc. dual – i.e. there were two spears); **κεκορυθμένος** (perfect passive participle of κορύσσω) – *tipped with*; **χαλκός ὁ** – *bronze*.

19   **πάλλω** – *shake, brandish*; **προκαλίζομαι** (> πρό + καλέω) – *call forward, challenge*; **ἄριστος** (> ἀγαθός) – *best, 'nobles'*.

20   **ἀντίβιον** (adv.) (> ἀντί + βία) – *force opposing force, 'full on'*; **αἰνός -ή -όν** – *terrible, grim*; **δηϊοτής -τῆτος ἡ** – *battle, combat*.

Menelaus is ready to oppose Paris.

τὸν δ᾽ ὡς οὖν ἐνόησεν ἀρηΐφιλος Μενέλαος
ἐρχόμενον προπάροιθεν ὁμίλου μακρὰ βιβάντα,
ὥς τε λέων ἐχάρη μεγάλῳ ἐπὶ σώματι κύρσας
εὑρὼν ἢ ἔλαφον κεραὸν ἢ ἄγριον αἶγα
πεινάων· μάλα γάρ τε κατεσθίει, εἴ περ ἂν αὐτὸν   25
σεύωνται ταχέες τε κύνες θαλεροί τ᾽ αἰζηοί·
ὣς ἐχάρη Μενέλαος Ἀλέξανδρον θεοειδέα
ὀφθαλμοῖσιν ἰδών· φάτο γὰρ τείσεσθαι ἀλείτην·
αὐτίκα δ᾽ ἐξ ὀχέων σὺν τεύχεσιν ἆλτο χαμᾶζε.
τὸν δ᾽ ὡς οὖν ἐνόησεν Ἀλέξανδρος θεοειδὴς   30
ἐν προμάχοισι φανέντα, κατεπλήγη φίλον ἦτορ,
ἂψ δ᾽ ἑτάρων εἰς ἔθνος ἐχάζετο κῆρ᾽ ἀλεείνων.

Names and places

Μενέλαος ὁ: *Menelaus* ('strength of the people')
Agamemnon's brother and husband of Helen, until Paris/Alexander stole her away to Troy. Menelaus
wants to get his wife back and to avenge the dishonour done to him.

Combat in the *Iliad*

In this world of heroes, attention is focused on one-on-one combat, very different from the emphasis on
hoplite warfare of Greece in the fifth century. Combatants would generally drive into battle on a chariot
and dismount to fight hand-to-hand with a notable opponent they had picked out. Each would have a full
set of armour comprizing crested helmet, breast-plate, shield, greaves (shin protectors), sword and spear.
Paris is unusual in carrying a bow (17).

Q.   As in the first simile, there is repetition of the key point of comparison
      (κλαγγή in lines 2–5): here it is ἐχάρη (23–7). How and why does Menelaus
      rejoice on seeing the man who abducted his wife? What do we learn from this
      passage about Menelaus?

Q.   What do the actions of Paris in this passage suggest about his character (lines
      22 and 30–2)?

GCSE vocabulary: αὐτός, γάρ, εἰς + acc., εὑρίσκω, μέγας, σῶμα, ἐφάνην (φαίνομαι).

21 τόν = αὐτόν; **νοέω** – *I notice* (+ participle); **ἀρηϊφιλος** – *loved by Ares or loving Ares* (= *loving war*, an example of metonymy).

22 **προπάροιθεν** + gen. – *out in front of*; **ὅμιλος ὁ** – *throng, crowd*; **μακρός -ά -όν** – *long* (here n.pl. = adverb); **βιβάω** – *stride*; '*taking long strides*'.

23 **ώς τε** – *just as, as* (see 13); **λέων -οντος ὁ** – *lion*; **ἐχάρη** (χαίρομαι) – *rejoice*, another gnomic aorist, see 4; **ἐπί ... κύρω** + dat. – *chance upon, encounter* (tmesis).

24 **ἔλαφος ὁ** – *fawn*; **κεραός -ά -όν** – *with antlers, horned*; **ἄγριος -α -ον** – *wild*; **αἰξ αἰγός ὁ** – *goat*.

25 **πεινάω** – *be hungry*; **μάλα** (> μάλιστα) – *very, 'eagerly'*; **κατεσθίω** (> ἐσθίω) – *devour*; **εἰ πέρ** (+ subjunctive) – *even if*.

26 **σεύομαι** – *I harry, chase, pursue*; **τε ... τε** = τε ... καί; **κύων κυνός ὁ** – *dog*; **θαλερός -ά -όν** – *strong, vigorous*; **αἰζηός ὁ** (= νεανίας) – *young man*.

27 **θεοειδής -ές** (16) (-εα is acc. sg. in an uncontracted form).

28 **ὄφθαλμός ὁ** – *eye*; **ἰδών** (> ὁράω); **φάτο** (= ἔφατο > φημί) – *think, say*; **τείσομαι** future of τίνομαι – *be avenged on*; **ἀλείτης ὁ** – *offender, culprit, scoundrel* (i.e. Paris, who had stolen Helen).

29 **αὐτίκα** – *immediately*; **ὅχεα τά** – *chariot*; **σύν** + dat. – *with*; **τεύχεα τά** – *armour*; **ἄλλομαι** aorist ἄλτο – *leap*; **χαμᾶζε** – *to the ground* (-ζε = σδε, the suffix -δε indicates motion towards).

30 See 21. Only the name and epithet at the end have changed, indicating the influence of oral composition on the poem.

31 **πρόμαχος ὁ** (> μάχη, 16) – *champion*; **φανέντα** (aorist participle of φαίνομαι) – *appear*; **κατεπλήγη** (aorist passive of καταπλήσσω) – *shake*; **φίλος -η -ον** – *dear, one's own, his/her* (a common meaning in Homer); **ἦτορ τό** – *heart* (accusative of respect, literally '*shaken as to his heart*').

32 **ἄψ** – *back, back again*; **ἔταρος ὁ** – *companion*; **ἔθνος -εος τό** (< ethnic) – *people, host*; **χάζομαι** – *shrink back*; **κῆρ -ός ή** – *death* (6); **ἀλείνω** – *avoid*.

Paris' courage fails; Hector criticizes him to his face.

ὡς δ' ὅτε τίς τε δράκοντα ἰδὼν παλίνορσος ἀπέστη
οὔρεος ἐν βήσσῃς, ὑπό τε τρόμος ἔλλαβε γυῖα,
ἂψ δ' ἀνεχώρησεν, ὠχρός τέ μιν εἷλε παρειάς,   35
ὣς αὖτις καθ' ὅμιλον ἔδυ Τρώων ἀγερώχων
δείσας Ἀτρέος υἱὸν Ἀλέξανδρος θεοειδής.
τὸν δ' Ἕκτωρ νείκεσσεν ἰδὼν αἰσχροῖς ἐπέεσσιν·

'Δύσπαρι εἶδος ἄριστε, γυναιμανές, ἠπεροπευτά,
αἴθ' ὄφελες ἄγονός τ' ἔμεναι ἄγαμός τ' ἀπολέσθαι·   40
καί κε τὸ βουλοίμην, καί κεν πολὺ κέρδιον ἦεν
ἢ οὕτω λώβην τ' ἔμεναι καὶ ὑπόψιον ἄλλων.
ἦ που καγχαλόωσι κάρη κομόωντες Ἀχαιοί,
φάντες ἀριστῆα πρόμον ἔμμεναι, οὕνεκα καλὸν
εἶδος ἔπ', ἀλλ' οὐκ ἔστι βίη φρεσὶν οὐδέ τις ἀλκή.   45

Names and places

Ἀτρεύς -έος ὁ: *Atreus*

Agamemnon and Menelaus are both frequently referred to as the sons of Atreus or Atreidae.

Ἕκτωρ -ορος ὁ: *Hector*

Hector, the eldest son of King Priam, was the great champion of Troy. The *Iliad* ends with laments over Hector's corpse, which his father retrieves by venturing into the Greek camp to beg Achilles, who had killed Hector and mutilated his corpse, to let him have his son's body back.

Character of Paris

Paris is characterized in this passage partly through a fourth simile, and partly through the reproachful words of Hector, his older brother. Although Paris has stolen Helen from Sparta because, according to Hector, he is woman-mad (γυναιμανής), he does not have the skills or courage to fight Menelaus and assert his rights over her.

Q.   How effective is the simile in helping the audience or reader to visualize Paris' reaction to Menelaus?

Q.   How fair are Hector's criticisms of Paris?

Q.   How does Hector convey the shame Paris is bringing upon himself and others? Consider his choice of words (**diction**) and how they sound.

GCSE vocabulary: *ἄλλος, ἀναχωρέω, βία, βούλομαι, εἷλον (αἱρέω), καλός, λαμβάνω, οὕτω, πολύς, τις, υἱός.*

33   ὡς δ' ὅτε – *as when* (introducing a simile, see 13); τίς τε – *someone*; δράκων -οντος
     ὁ (< dragon) – *snake*; παλίνορσος -ον – *back*; ἀπέστη (gnomic aorist; ἀφίσταμαι) –
     stand away from.

34   οὔρεος (gen. of ὄρος τό); βήσση ἡ – *glen*; τρόμος ὁ – *trembling*; γυῖα τά – *limbs*;
     ὑπό ... ἔλλαβε (tmesis) – *'takes his knees from underneath'.*

35   ἄψ – *back, back again*; ὠχρος ὁ – *paleness, pallor* (< ochre); μιν = αὐτόν; παρειά
     ἡ – *cheek* (accusative of respect). In the simile, note the generalizing τε and the four **gnomic
     aorists** which should be translated in the present tense.

36   ὡς – *just so* (13); αὖτις = αὖθις; ὅμιλος ὁ – *crowd*; καθ' = κατά ... δύω (tmesis)
     – *sink into*; ἀγερώχος -ον – *noble, lordly.*

37   δείδω – *fear.*

38   νεικέω – *I rebuke*; αἰσχρός -ά -όν – *'causing shame', 'insulting'*; ἔπος -εος τό
     (< epic) – *word.*

39   Δύσπαρις – *evil Paris, ill-starred Paris*; εἶδος τό (< θεοειδής) – *appearance* (accusative
     of respect); γυναιμανής -ές (> γυνή, + < maniac) – *mad about women*; ἠπεροπευτής
     ὁ – *cheat.* There are four vocatives in this line.

40   αἴθ' ὄφελες + infinitive expresses a wish for the past – *if only you had . . .*, ('*how it would
     have been better for you to*'); ἄγονος -ον – *unborn*; ἔμεναι = εἶναι; ἄγαμος -ον –
     unmarried; ἀπολέσθαι aorist infinitive of ἀπόλλυμαι – *perish, die.*

41   καί ... καί – *both . . . and*; κε = ἄν + potential optative – '*would*'; τό = τοῦτο; κέρδιον
     – *better*; ἦεν = ἦν (κε + indic. for what should have happened – '*would have been . . .*').

42   ἤ – *than, rather than*; λώβη ἡ – *cause of outrage, disgrace*; ἔμεναι = εἶναι (40);
     ὑπόψιος -ον – *cause of suspicion* (lit. looking (ὀψ-) from under (ὑπό)); ἄλλων (gen. after
     ὑπόψιος) – '*amongst others'.*

43   ἦ – *indeed*; που – *I suppose*; καγχαλάω – *laugh at*; κάρη κομόωντες – '*long-
     haired'* (lit. '*long-haired as to their heads*') a frequent Homeric epithet.

44   φάντες (participle from φημί) – *thinking* (introduces an indirect statement with infinitive);
     ἀριστεύς ὁ (< aristocrat) – *prince*; πρόμος ὁ – *champion*; ἔμμεναι = ἔμεναι; οὕνεκα
     – *because.*

45   ἔπ' = ἔπεστι – *be upon, be available, 'he has/you have'*; βίη = βία; φρένες αἱ –
     heart, mind; ἀλκή ἡ – *courage, strength.*

Hector continues to criticize Paris, detailing his responsibility for the Trojan war.

ἦ τοιόσδε ἐὼν ἐν ποντοπόροισι νέεσσι
πόντον ἐπιπλώσας, ἑτάρους ἐρίηρας ἀγείρας,
μιχθεὶς ἀλλοδαποῖσι γυναῖκ' εὐειδέ' ἀνῆγες
ἐξ ἀπίης γαίης, νυὸν ἀνδρῶν αἰχμητάων,
πατρί τε σῷ μέγα πῆμα πόληΐ τε παντί τε δήμῳ,   50
δυσμενέσιν μὲν χάρμα, κατηφείην δὲ σοὶ αὐτῷ;
οὐκ ἂν δὴ μείνειας ἀρηΐφιλον Μενέλαον;
γνοίης χ' οἵου φωτὸς ἔχεις θαλερὴν παράκοιτιν·
οὐκ ἄν τοι χραίσμη κίθαρις τά τε δῶρ' Ἀφροδίτης,
ἥ τε κόμη τό τε εἶδος ὅτ' ἐν κονίῃσι μιγείης.   55
ἀλλὰ μάλα Τρῶες δειδήμονες· ἦ τέ κεν ἤδη
λάϊνον ἔσσο χιτῶνα κακῶν ἕνεχ' ὅσσα ἔοργας.'

Names and places
Ἀφροδίτη ἡ: *Aphrodite*
Goddess of love. Paris was a particular favourite of hers among the heroes of the Trojan war because he chose her when asked to judge which goddess was most beautiful.

Q.   The English word 'hectoring' means acting like a bully and is derived from the Trojan hero's name. What gives this passage a hectoring tone (think about sounds – for example in line 50 – as well as **diction** and word order)?

Q.   Do you feel more sympathetic towards Hector or Paris as you listen to this speech? Is Hector too harsh on his brother or does Paris deserve it?

Q.   What part did Aphrodite play in starting the Trojan war? (You may have to research this.) What defence could Paris offer against these accusations?

GCSE vocabulary: *ἀνήρ, γιγνώσκω, γυνή, δῆμος, δῶρον, μέγας, μένω, ναῦς, πατήρ, πόλις.*

46　ἤ introduces a question; **τοιόσδε** – *of such a kind, like this*; **ἐών** = ὤν (participle of εἰμί); **ἤ τοιόσδε ἐών** – '*Is this the sort of man you were when …?*'; **ποντοπόρος -ον** – *sea-going*; **νέεσσι** = ναυσί(ν). There is a series of participles leading up to the main verb ἀνῆγες at the end of line 48; the question ends at line 51.

47　**πόντος ὁ** – *sea*; **ἐπιπλέω** (> ἐπί + πλέω) – *I sail on*; **ἔταρος ὁ** – *companion*; **ἐρίηρος -η -ον** – *trusty*; **ἀγείρω** – *collect, gather.*

48　**μιχθείς** + dat. (aorist participle of μίγνυμαι) – *mix, mingle, have intercourse with*; **ἀλλοδαπός -ον** (> ἄλλος) – *foreign*; **γυναῖκ'** = γυναῖκα; **εὐειδής -ές** (> εὖ + εἶδος) – *well-shaped, good-looking*; **ἀνάγω** (> ἀνά + ἄγω) – *bring back.*

49　**ἄπιος -η -ον** (> ἀπό) – *far-away*; **γαῖα ἡ** (< Gaia) = γῆ; **νυός ἡ** – *daughter-in-law (of), kinswoman,* the first of four words in apposition to γυναῖκα (also πῆμα (50), χάρμα, κατηφείην (51)); **αἰχμητής ὁ** – *spearman.*

50　**πῆμα -ατος τό** – *pain, cause of suffering.*

51　**δυσμενής -ές** (> δυσ + μένος) – *hostile*; **χάρμα τό** – *joy*; **κατήφεια ἡ** – *cause of shame.*

52　**οὐκ ἄν μείνειας** (potential optative) – '*could you not wait for?*'; **ἀρηΐφιλος -ον** (21).

53　**γνοίης** aor. opt. from γιγνώσκω; **χ'** = κε = ἄν + potential optative – '*you would know*'; **οἷος -α -ον** – *what kind of?*; **φώς -τός ὁ** – *man*; **θαλερός -ά -όν** – *flourishing, blossoming*; **παράκοιτις ἡ** – *wife.*

54　**τοι** = σοί; **χραισμέω** + dat. – *defend, protect, help*; **κίθαρις ἡ** – *lyre.*

55　**κόμη ἡ** – *hair*; **κονίαι αἱ** – *dust*; **μιγείης** – '*you mix*' (48); 'mix with the dust', means lie dead on the ground, but there is also an erotic charge to this word, appropriate to Hector's view of Paris.

56　**δειδήμων -ον** (> δείδω 37) – *cowardly, scared* (understand 'εἰσί'); **ἦ τέ** – *indeed,* (ἦ has an emphatic, often sarcastic, force; τέ reinforces it).

57　**λάϊνος -η -ον** – *made of stone*; **ἔσσο** (pluperfect of ἕννυμι) – *wear,* '*you would* (κεν) *have been wearing*'; **χιτών -ῶνος ὁ** – *tunic*; **ἔνεχ** = ἕνεκα – *because of*; **ὅσσα** (> ὅσος) – *as many as,* '*the many*' (with κακῶν being a partitive genitive); **ἔργω** perf. ἔοργα – *do,* '*because of the many evils you have done*'. 'Tunic of stones' is a grim metaphor for stoning a person to death, in this case, perhaps, as a punishment for adultery.

Paris defends his record and proposes how to settle the war – winner takes all, including Helen.

τὸν δ' αὖτε προσέειπεν Ἀλέξανδρος θεοειδής·
Ἕκτορ, ἐπεί με κατ' αἶσαν ἐνείκεσας οὐδ' ὑπὲρ αἶσαν
αἰεί τοι κραδίη πέλεκυς ὥς ἐστιν ἀτειρής,   60
ὅς τ' εἶσιν διὰ δουρὸς ὑπ' ἀνέρος, ὅς ῥά τε τέχνη
νήϊον ἐκτάμνησιν, ὀφέλλει δ' ἀνδρὸς ἐρωήν·
ὣς σοὶ ἐνὶ στήθεσσιν ἀτάρβητος νόος ἐστί·
μή μοι δῶρ' ἐρατὰ πρόφερε χρυσέης Ἀφροδίτης·
οὔ τοι ἀπόβλητ' ἐστὶ θεῶν ἐρικυδέα δῶρα,   65
ὅσσα κεν αὐτοὶ δῶσιν, ἑκὼν δ' οὐκ ἄν τις ἕλοιτο·
νῦν αὖτ' εἴ μ' ἐθέλεις πολεμίζειν ἠδὲ μάχεσθαι,
ἄλλους μὲν κάθισον Τρῶας καὶ πάντας Ἀχαιούς,
αὐτὰρ ἔμ' ἐν μέσσῳ καὶ ἀρηΐφιλον Μενέλαον
συμβάλετ' ἀμφ' Ἑλένῃ καὶ κτήμασι πᾶσι μάχεσθαι·   70
ὁππότερος δέ κε νικήσῃ κρείσσων τε γένηται,
κτήμαθ' ἑλὼν εὖ πάντα γυναῖκά τε οἴκαδ' ἀγέσθω·

Similes (3)

This simile, rather than being within the narrative, is part of a speech. Paris accuses Hector of being too hard on him.

Q. How well-chosen do you think Paris' choice of simile for describing Hector is? What is the primary point of comparison?

Q. How reasonable does Paris seem in deflecting the criticism of Hector in lines 64–6?

Q. Does Paris' proposal that he and Menelaus fight a dual seem in keeping with his character?

Q. Have your views of either brother altered by line 72 (or by line 75, when the speech finishes)?

GCSE vocabulary: ἀεί, ἄλλος, γίγνομαι, διά + gen., εἶσι (εἶμι), ἔδωκα (δίδωμι), ἐθέλω, εἶλον (αἱρέω), μάχομαι, νικάω, ὅς.

58   τόν = αὐτόν; αὖτε – *in turn*; προσέειπε + acc. (> πρός + εἶπον) – *address*.

59   κατά + acc. – *in accordance with*; αἶσα ἡ – *destiny, share*; κατ' αἶσαν – *'fairly'*
     νεικέω – *criticize*; ὑπέρ – *beyond*; ὑπὲρ αἶσαν – *'unfairly'*.

60   αἰεί = ἀεί; τοι = σοί; κραδίη ἡ – *heart*; πέλεκυς ὁ – *axe*; πέλεκυς ὥς (= ὡς
     πέλεκυς, opening a simile); ἀτειρής -ές – *unyielding*.

61   τ' = τε – generalizing τε (4); εἰσιν (> εἶμι – go); δουρός (gen. sg. from δόρυ τό) – *wood,*
     plank, shaft, spear; ὑπ' = ὑπό + gen. – *by, 'driven by'*; ἀνέρος = ἀνδρός; ὅς ῥά τε –
     'who'; τέχνη ἡ (< technique) – *skill*.

62   νήϊον τό – *ship's timber*; ἐκτάμνησιν present subjunctive of ἐκτάμνω – *cut down,*
     hew into shape; ὀφέλλω – *increase, strengthen* (the subject changes back to the axe,
     indicated by the δ'); ἐρωή ἡ – *power*.

63   σοί – possessive dative; ἐνί = ἐν + dat.; στῆθος ὁ (< stethoscope) – *chest*; ἀτάρβητος
     -ον – *fearless*; νόος ὁ – *mind, purpose*.

64   μή + imperative – *do not*; ἐρατός – *lovely*; προφέρω (προ + φέρω) – *bring up*
     against, reproach x (dat.) *with y* (acc.); χρύσεος -η -ον (> χρυσός) – *golden*.

65   τοι (emphatic) – *indeed, let me tell you*; ἀπόβλητος (> ἀπό + βάλλω) – *to be rejected,*
     despised; ἐρικυδής (< kudos) – *very famous, glorious*.

66   ὅσσα – *whatever (things)*; δῶσιν (> δίδωμι) aorist subjunctive with an indefinite sense –
     'they (may) give'; ἑκών – *willingly, wanting, 'even if he wanted'* (concessive use);
     οὐκ ἄν τις ἕλοιτο (αἱρέομαι) – aorist optative used potentially – *'a man could not take*
     them for himself'.

67   αὖτε – (58) μ' = με; πολεμίζω (> πόλεμος) – *fight, do battle*; ἠδέ – *and*.

68   καθίσον (aorist imperative of καθίζω) – *seat, make sit down*.

69   αὐτάρ – *but*; ἔμ' = ἔμε; μέσσος ὁ (= μέσος, < mesolithic) – *middle, middle of*.

70   συμβάλλω (> σύν + βάλλω) – *throw together, match, pit* (plural imperative addressing
     both sides); ἀμφί + dat. (< amphitheatre) – *around, 'for'*; κτήματα τά (> κτάομαι) –
     possessions.

71   ὁππότερος -α -ον – *whichever one*; κε + subj. for indefinite meaning; κρείσσων -ον
     – *stronger*; γένηται (aor. subj. of γίγνομαι) – *becomes stronger, i.e. 'gains the upper*
     hand'.

72   ἑλών – (αἱρέω); εὖ – reinforces the idea of taking absolutely everything; οἴκαδε (> οἰκία + -δε
     suffix indicating motion towards); ἀγέσθω (> ἄγω) 3rd person imperative – *'let him lead,*
     take'.

Hector settles the Trojans; Agamemnon, the Greeks.

οἱ δ' ἄλλοι φιλότητα καὶ ὅρκια πιστὰ ταμόντες
ναίοιτε Τροίην ἐριβώλακα, τοὶ δὲ νεέσθων
Ἄργος ἐς ἱππόβοτον καὶ Ἀχαΐδα καλλιγύναικα.'   75

ὣς ἔφαθ', Ἕκτωρ δ' αὖτε χάρη μέγα μῦθον ἀκούσας,
καί ῥ' ἐς μέσσον ἰὼν Τρώων ἀνέεργε φάλαγγας,
μέσσου δουρὸς ἑλών· τοὶ δ' ἱδρύνθησαν ἅπαντες.
τῷ δ' ἐπετοξάζοντο κάρη κομόωντες Ἀχαιοὶ
ἰοῖσίν τε τιτυσκόμενοι λάεσσί τ' ἔβαλλον·   80
αὐτὰρ ὁ μακρὸν ἄϋσεν ἄναξ ἀνδρῶν Ἀγαμέμνων·

'ἴσχεσθ', Ἀργεῖοι, μὴ βάλλετε κοῦροι Ἀχαιῶν·
στεῦται γάρ τι ἔπος ἐρέειν κορυθαίολος Ἕκτωρ.'

ὣς ἔφαθ', οἳ δ' ἔσχοντο μάχης ἄνεῴ τ' ἐγένοντο
ἐσσυμένως· Ἕκτωρ δὲ μετ' ἀμφοτέροισιν ἔειπε·   85

Names and places
Ἄργος -εος τό: *Argos*
A city in the Peloponnese near Mycenae, home of Agamemnon.

Ἀχαΐς -ίδος ἡ: *the land of Achaea (Greece)*

Q.   Do his closing words suggest that Paris anticipates the outcome of the duel? What is the impact of his final word (καλλιγύναικα, 75)?

Q.   How realistic do you find the description of settling the two armies (77–85)?

Q.   Are Agamemnon and Hector shown to be equally strong leaders?

Q.   What is the effect of placing ἐσσυμένως on line 85 (**enjambement**)?

GCSE vocabulary: *ἀκούω, βάλλω, εἶπον (λέγω), ἐρέω (λέγω), ἰών ἰοῦσα ἰόν, μάχη, μή, μῦθος, φημί.*

73   οἱ δ' ἄλλοι . . . τοὶ δέ (74) – '*the rest (of you) . . . while they*', Paris sketches a peaceful
outcome for both sides; φιλότης -ητος ἡ (> φίλος) – *friendship*; ὅρκιον τό – *oath*;
πιστός – *trustworthy, reliable*; τάμνω, ἔταμον – *cut*, '*seal*'. 'Cutting an oath' involves
animal sacrifice to solemnize the oath. The phrase occurs six times in the Iliad. φιλότητα καὶ ὅρκια
πιστά literally translated '*friendship and reliable oaths*' means '*reliable oaths of friendship*', an
example of **hendiadys**.

74   ναίοιτε (ναίω – *dwell*, the optative is used to express a wish for the future) – '*may you
dwell in*'; ἐριβῶλαξ (> ἐρι- 'very', see 65) – *very fertile*; τοί = οἱ (i.e. the Greeks); νέομαι
(3rd person imperative) – *return*, '*may they return*'.

75   ἐς = εἰς + acc.; ἱππόβοτος – *horse-nourishing*; καλλιγύναιξ (καλός + γυνή) – *with
beautiful women*.

76   ὡς ἔφατο (φημί) – '*so he spoke*', a common expression to mark the end of a speech (84, 95,
111); ἐχάρη aorist of χαίρομαι (23, 27); μέγα – *greatly* (neuter sg. used as an adverb).

77   ῥ' = ῥά = ἄρα (61); μέσσος ὁ (69); ἰών participle of εἰμι; ἀνέργω – *keep back*; φάλαγξ
-αγγος ἡ (< phalanx) – *battle-line*.

78   δουρός gen. sg. – *spear* (61); αἱρέω + gen. (verbs of touching, holding usually have their
object in the genitive case); τοί = οἱ (i.e. the Trojans); ἱδρύομαι – *sit down*; ἅπαντες =
πάντες.

79   τῷ = αὐτῷ (i.e. Hector); ἐπιτοξάζομαι – *shoot arrows at*, '*they began to shoot
arrows*' reflects the use of imperfect to show that an action was started; κάρη κομόωντες
– see 43 for this **epithet**.

80   ἰός ὁ – *arrow*; τιτύσκομαι – *I aim*; λᾶας ὁ – *stone*.

81   ὁ – '*he*' (Agamemnon); μακρόν – '*loudly*' literally 'far' (see 22); αὖω – *shout*; ἄναξ
-ακτος ὁ – *lord*; ἄναξ ἀνδρῶν – Agamemnon's stock **epithet**.

82   ἴσχομαι – *stop*; μή – (64) κοῦρος ὁ – *son*.

83   στεῦται (from στεῦμαι) + future infin. – *be about to*; ἔπος τό – *word, speech*; ἐρέειν
= ἐρεῖν (> λέγω); κορυθαίολος -η -ον – *of the gleaming helmet* – Hector's stock
epithet.

84   ὡς ἔφαθ' (76); ἔχομαι + gen. – *keep from*; ἄνεῳ (nom. pl. of ἄνεως) – *silent*.

85   ἐσσυμένως – *eagerly*; μετά + dat. – *among*, '*to*'; ἀμφότερος -α -ον – *both*,
pl. '*both sides*'.

The proclamation to both sides.

'κέκλυτέ μευ, Τρῶες καὶ ἐϋκνήμιδες Ἀχαιοί,
μῦθον Ἀλεξάνδροιο, τοῦ εἵνεκα νεῖκος ὄρωρεν.
ἄλλους μὲν κέλεται Τρῶας καὶ πάντας Ἀχαιοὺς
τεύχεα κάλ' ἀποθέσθαι ἐπὶ χθονὶ πουλυβοτείρῃ,
αὐτὸν δ' ἐν μέσσῳ καὶ ἀρηΐφιλον Μενέλαον   90
οἴους ἀμφ' Ἑλένῃ καὶ κτήμασι πᾶσι μάχεσθαι.
ὁππότερος δέ κε νικήσῃ κρείσσων τε γένηται
κτήμαθ' ἑλὼν εὖ πάντα γυναῖκά τε οἴκαδ' ἀγέσθω·
οἱ δ' ἄλλοι φιλότητα καὶ ὅρκια πιστὰ τάμωμεν.'

ὣς ἔφαθ', οἱ δ' ἄρα πάντες ἀκὴν ἐγένοντο σιωπῇ·   95
τοῖσι δὲ καὶ μετέειπε βοὴν ἀγαθὸς Μενέλαος·

'κέκλυτε νῦν καὶ ἐμεῖο· μάλιστα γὰρ ἄλγος ἱκάνει
θυμὸν ἐμόν, φρονέω δὲ διακρινθήμεναι ἤδη
Ἀργείους καὶ Τρῶας, ἐπεὶ κακὰ πολλὰ πέπασθε
εἵνεκ' ἐμῆς ἔριδος καὶ Ἀλεξάνδρου ἕνεκ' ἀρχῆς·   100
ἡμέων δ' ὁπποτέρῳ θάνατος καὶ μοῖρα τέτυκται
τεθναίη· ἄλλοι δὲ διακρινθεῖτε τάχιστα.

Repetition

Repetition is a feature of the *Iliad* and *Odyssey*, not only at the level of individual words or phrases, like epithets (adjectives) or the formulaic phrase ὣς ἔφατο – *so he spoke* – (lines 76, 84, 95), but also of episodes, like performing a sacrifice or putting on armour. A frequent use is to report a message that has already been delivered, often repeating the original words, perhaps with minor changes, some of them revealing. These various kinds of repetition are familiar elements in oral composition and, as well as varying the pace, help the audience follow and feel involved in the story-telling.

Q. Why do you think Hector speaks to the armies rather than Paris? How accurately does he deliver Paris's offer to fight (compare lines 69–75 with 90–4)?

Q. How important has the reaction of the armies been in making this scene dramatic?

Q. What impression of Menelaus do you get from this opening to his speech (97–102)?

GCSE vocabulary: ἀγαθός, ἄγω, ἀρχή, βοή, ἐπεί, ἤδη, θάνατος, κακός, μάλιστα, πολύς, τάχιστα (*superlative adverb of* ταχύς).

86   κλύω + acc. + gen. – *hear something from someone*; μευ = μου; ἐϋκνήμις -ιδος – *well-greaved, with fine greaves* (greaves protected the lower leg).

87   εἵνεκα + gen. – *because of*; τοῦ = οὗ – *of whom* (i.e. Paris); νεῖκος τό – *quarrel, dispute*; ὄρωρεν (perfect of ὄρνυμι) – *has arisen*.

88   ἄλλους μέν (73); κέλομαι = κελεύω (subject is Paris).

89   τεύχεα τά – *armour*; ἀποθέσθαι (from ἀποτίθεμαι) – '*to put aside*'; χθών -ονός ἡ – *ground*; πουλυβότειρα (= πολυβότειρα) – *much-nourishing*.

90   μέσσος -η -ον (77).

91   οἶος -α -ον – *alone*.

94   A variation on line 73, but with the participle ταμόντες changed to a jussive subjunctive τάμωμεν – '*let us cut/seal*.' The two words are metrically equivalent.

95   ἀκήν – *silent, hushed*; σιωπῇ – *in silence*.

96   μετέειπε = εἶπε; βοὴν ἀγαθός – another of Menelaus' stock epithets, '*master of the war cry*', lit. '*good in respect of shouting*' (accusative of respect). The war cry was an important element in keeping the ranks together and motivated.

97   καί – *too*; ἐμεῖο = ἐμοῦ; ἄλγος τό (< analgesic) – *pain, suffering*; ἱκάνω – *come, reach*. Menelaus begins with almost the same form of words as Hector at 86.

98   θυμός ὁ – *heart, mind, spirit* (9); φρονέω (> φρένες) – *think, 'think it right'* introducing an indirect statement with infinitive; διακρινθήμεναι (aorist passive infinitive of διακρίνω) – *to be separated*. Menelaus uses the same verb when giving his command in 102.

99   πέπασθε – perfect active πάσχω.

100   εἵνεκα or ἕνεκα + gen. – *because of, on account of* (87); ἔρις -ιδος ἡ – *quarrel*; ἀρχή ἡ – *beginning*, i.e. Menelaus is indicating that Paris began the quarrel.

101   ὁππότερος -α -ον – *whichever one* (71); ἡμέων = ἡμῶν; μοῖρα ἡ – *fate*; τέτυκται perfect passive of τεύχω *make ready* – '*is prepared*'.

102   τεθναίη – optative showing a wish for the future '*may he die*'; διακρινθεῖτε – also optative, but effectively a command (98).

Menelaus proposes a solemn oath to seal the agreement.

οἴσετε ἄρν', ἕτερον λευκόν, ἑτέρην δὲ μέλαιναν,
Γῆ τε καὶ Ἡελίῳ· Διὶ δ' ἡμεῖς οἴσομεν ἄλλον·
ἄξετε δὲ Πριάμοιο βίην, ὄφρ' ὅρκια τάμνῃ   105
αὐτός, ἐπεί οἱ παῖδες ὑπερφίαλοι καὶ ἄπιστοι,
μή τις ὑπερβασίῃ Διὸς ὅρκια δηλήσηται.
αἰεὶ δ' ὁπλοτέρων ἀνδρῶν φρένες ἠερέθονται·
οἷς δ' ὁ γέρων μετέῃσιν, ἅμα πρόσσω καὶ ὀπίσσω
λεύσσει, ὅπως ὄχ' ἄριστα μετ' ἀμφοτέροισι γένηται.'   110

ὣς ἔφαθ', οἱ δ' ἐχάρησαν Ἀχαιοί τε Τρῶές τε
ἐλπόμενοι παύσασθαι ὀϊζυροῦ πολέμοιο.

Names and places
Γῆ ἡ: *Earth*

Ἡελίος (= Ἥλιος) ὁ: *Sun*
Earth and Sun, older gods than the Olympians, were often invoked at the taking of an oath. Perhaps this is a more sacred oath than could be sworn by the Olympian gods, who are not independent but take sides in the conflict. Alternatively, this could be a calculated snub from Menelaus, if these older gods are good enough for the Trojans but not the Greeks.

Performing sacrifices
For the Greeks, a sacrifice was a contract between a human and a god. A mortal offers a sacrifice before making a request. If the sacrifice pleases the god, then he or she may grant the request, but is under no obligation to do so. The gods generally favoured animal sacrifice: the smell of roasting meat rose to the heavens and the thigh-bones covered in fat were reserved for them. The rest of the animal was shared out amongst mortals in a feast. The preparation of meat by cutting it up and putting it onto spits before roasting it on a fire is perhaps the earliest description of a barbecue.

Q.   Why does Menelaus want to involve Priam in the agreement and what qualities does he think the old king will bring?

Q.   Do you think he has anyone particular in mind when he refers to Priam's sons as ὑπερφίαλοι καὶ ἄπιστοι (106)?

GCSE vocabulary: *ἄριστα (superlative adverb of ἀγαθός), βία, γέρων, γῆ, γίγνομαι, ἐλπίζω, ἡμεῖς, οἴσω (future of φέρω), παῖς, παύω, πόλεμος.*

103 οἴσετε (> φέρω) imperative; ἄρνε (**dual** form of ἀρήν, ἄρνος τό – *lamb*) – '*pair of lambs*'; ἕτερος (< heterosexual) *one* (masc.), . . . *the other* . . . (fem.); λευκός -ή -όν – *white*; μέλας -αινα -αν (< melancholy) – *black*.

105 ἄξετε – imperative (103); βίη = βία – *force* (*of Priam*), an idiomatic phrase meaning '*mighty Priam*'; ὄφρα = ἵνα; ὅρκια τάμνη (73, 94).

106 οἱ – *to him*, '*his*' (possessive dative); ὑπερφίαλος -ον – *arrogant*; ἄπιστος -ον – *untrustworthy*.

107 μή τις – *lest anyone, so that no-one*; ὑπερβασίη ἡ (> ὑπερ beyond + βαίνω) – *transgression, violence*; δηλέομαι – *hurt, spoil, break*.

108 ὁπλοτέρος -η -ον – *younger*; φρένες αἱ – *heart, mind*; ἠερέθομαι (< air) – *float, be unstable*.

109 οἷς – '*in matters which*'; ὁ γέρων – '*an old man*' (generalized with the subjunctive verb); μέτειμι – *be involved with*, a subjunctive is used here because it is indefinite; πρόσσω (> πρός) – *forwards*; ὀπίσσω – *backwards*.

110 λεύσσω – *look, see* (the subject is ὁ γέρων); ὅπως – *so that*, '*at how*'; ὄχ' ἄριστα – '*by far the best*'; μετά + dat. – *amongst*, '*for*'; ἀμφοτέρος -α -ον – *both* (85).

111 ἐχάρησαν – (23, 76).

112 ἔλπομαι (= ἐλπίζω); παύομαι + gen. – *cease from*; ὀϊζυρός -ά -όν – *miserable, wretched*.

What happens next?

The duel does not proceed as in the 2004 film *Troy*. The two warriors clash and Menelaus quickly proves his superiority as a fighter. He grabs Paris by the helmet and whirls him around the battle-field. Paris is rescued by Aphrodite, who snaps the helmet strap and whisks the prince away to Helen's bedroom (who is not enthusiastic about giving in to his charms this time), leaving Menelaus roaming furiously in search of his victim. Needless to say, the truce is broken and battle recommences.

Final questions

- How vivid a picture of the conflict and of the two sides involved in it do we get from this extract?
- Which character do you find most sympathetic, Hector, Paris or Menelaus? Who is the most commanding?
- Which of the similes in this selection do you find most effective and why?
- What are Homer's strengths as a story-teller?

ODYSSEY 7: 184–297 (here 1–114)

2022–2023 Prescription

See pages 24–7 for an introduction to Homer and his language and for what happens in Book 6.

The story so far . . .

In *Odyssey* 7, Odysseus is a guest on the island of Scherie, home of the sea-loving Phaeacians. He has arrived there with nothing – no companions, no clothes and nothing to eat – after being targeted at sea by the hostile god Poseidon. Odysseus is fortunate, however, in having the support of the goddess Athene who, working behind the scenes for fear of offending Poseidon, has arranged things in such a way that the first person Odysseus meets after landing on Scherie is the daughter of the king and queen. Princess Nausicaa has come down to the beach, with her maids and a generous picnic, to wash her clothes and those of her brothers and father. She is thus well-equipped to help Odysseus with his most urgent needs of food, drink, a bath and something to wear. She also helps him with directions to the city and to her father's palace, where she advises him to make sure he wins the support of queen Arete, if he wants to secure an escort back home to his island of Ithaca.

The composition of the Odyssey is sophisticated in that it is not a linear narrative, beginning with Odysseus leaving Troy and tracing the story of his travels in order. Instead, it starts midway through the action ('*in medias res*'), so that the beginning of the story has to be explained later, by the hero himself. The first books of the poem begin on Ithaca and follow the adventures of Telemachus, Odysseus' son; we don't actually meet Odysseus until the fifth book of the poem, where he is languishing on Calypso's remote island, unable to escape but filled with longing for his wife, Penelope, and the life he left behind when he went to fight at Troy.

In this section, Odysseus tells part of his story – the full version follows in Books 9–12 of the *Odyssey*. Specifically, he accounts for how he comes to be wearing clothes that Arete recognizes. In particular, we hear how he first came to arrive on Calypso's island after losing his companions, then how Calypso looked after for him for seven years until releasing him and helping him on his way. Finally we hear how, after further adventures at sea, he arrived on the shores of Scherie and met Nausicaa.

King Alcinous addresses the Phaeacian leaders about hospitality for their guest.

Nominative *words or phrases are in* light blue, **verbs** *in* dark blue.

αὐτὰρ ἐπεὶ σπεῖσάν τ' ἔπιόν θ' ὅσον ἤθελε θυμός,
τοῖσιν δ' Ἀλκίνοος ἀγορήσατο καὶ μετέειπε·
'κέκλυτε, Φαιήκων ἡγήτορες ἠδὲ μέδοντες,
ὄφρ' εἴπω τά με θυμὸς ἐνὶ στήθεσσι κελεύει.
νῦν μὲν δαισάμενοι κατακείετε οἴκαδ' ἰόντες·   5
ἠῶθεν δὲ γέροντας ἐπὶ πλέονας καλέσαντες
ξεῖνον ἐνὶ μεγάροις ξεινίσσομεν ἠδὲ θεοῖσιν
ῥέξομεν ἱερὰ καλά, ἔπειτα δὲ καὶ περὶ πομπῆς
μνησόμεθ', ὥς χ' ὁ ξεῖνος ἄνευθε πόνου καὶ ἀνίης
πομπῇ ὑφ' ἡμετέρῃ ἣν πατρίδα γαῖαν ἵκηται   10
χαίρων καρπαλίμως, εἰ καὶ μάλα τηλόθεν ἐστί,
μηδέ τι μεσσηγύς γε κακὸν καὶ πῆμα πάθῃσι
πρίν γε τὸν ἧς γαίης ἐπιβήμεναι· ἔνθα δ' ἔπειτα
πείσεται ἄσσα οἱ αἶσα κατὰ Κλῶθές τε βαρεῖαι
γιγνομένῳ νήσαντο λίνῳ, ὅτε μιν τέκε μήτηρ.   15

Names and places
Ἀλκίνοος ὁ: *Alcinous*; Φαίηκες οἱ: *the Phaeacians*
Alcinous was King of the Phaeacians. His epithet is θεοειδής – *looking like a god* (48); the Phaeacians were a nation of sea-farers who live on the island of Scherie. Odysseus is destined to make the final journey home to Ithaca with their help (5.31ff.).

Κλῶθες αἱ: *The Fates*
In Greek thought, the metaphor of a thread is used to represent a man's life: his destiny is spun, measured and cut by three old women who are almost blind, called the Fates.

Xenia
ξενία (> ξένος) is a key element in Greek culture. If a stranger appears at your door, you have responsibilities towards him (or her), in particular caring for his immediate physical needs of food, drink, clothes and a bed, before asking about his identity and helping him on his way. Depending on the status of the guest and the success of the visit, the host might also offer gifts.

Q.   What plan does Alcinous set before the Phaeacian leaders?

Q.   Identify the elements of xenia offered by Alcinous. Which details suggest that he is a god?

GCSE vocabulary: γέρων, γίγνομαι, ἐθέλω, εἶπον (λέγω), ἐπεί, ἔπειτα, ἡμέτερος, ἱερός, ἰών ἰοῦσα ἰόν, κακός, καλέω, κελεύω, μήτηρ, νῦν, ξένος, πάσχω, πείθομαι, περί + gen., πλέονες (πολύς), πίνω, ὡς.

1   αὐτάρ – *but, moreover*; σπεῖσαν = ἔσπεισα, aorist of σπένδω – *pour a libation* (drink
    offering to the gods); τ′ = τε (elision); θ′ = τε (elision, before a rough breathing); ὅσον – *as
    much as*; θυμός ὁ – *heart, spirit.*

2   τοῖσιν = αὐτοῖς; δ′ = δέ; ἀγορήσατο = ἠγορήσατο, aorist of ἀγοράομαι – *speak to,
    address*; μετέειπε (> μετά + λέγω) – *address, speak among.*

3   κέκλυτε pl. imperative of κλύω – *hear, listen*; ἡγήτωρ -ορος ὁ – *leader, commander*;
    ἠδέ = καί; μέδων -οντος ὁ – *guardian, advisor.*

4   ὄφρα + subj. – *so that*; τά = ἅ – *the things which*; με = ἐμέ; ἐνί + dat. = ἐν;
    στήθεσσι dative plural of στῆθος -εος τό (< stethoscope) – *chest, breast.*

5   νῦν μέν – *for now* (contrasts with ἠῶθεν δέ, 6); δαισάμενοι – aorist participle of δαίνυμαι
    – *join a feast, banquet*; κατακείετε imperative of κατάκειμαι – *lie down*; οἴκαδ′ - the
    suffix -δε indicates *homewards, (to) home*; ἰόντες participle of εἶμι.

6   ἠῶθεν – *at dawn*; ἐπί + καλέω (tmesis) – *call upon, invite*; πλέονας (πλέων -ον is
    the comparative of πολύς πολλή πολύ) – *more.*

7   ξεῖνος = ξένος; μέγαρον τό – *great hall, hall*, pl. *palace*; ξεινίσσομεν a subjunctive
    of ξεινίζω – '*let us entertain*', the first of three subjunctives; ἠδέ (3); θεοῖσιν = θεοῖς.

8   ῥέξομεν subj. of ῥέζω – *perform*; ἱερά τά – *holy sacrifices*; πομπή ἡ – *escort.*

9   μνησόμεθα subj. of μνάομαι – *be mindful of, think about*; ὥς χ′ + subj. – *so that
    then* (somehow); χ′ = κε (elision). Like ἄν, κε has an indefinite or potential sense. ἄνευθε +
    gen. = ἄνευ; πόνος ὁ – *toil*; ἀνίη ἡ – *distress.*

10 ὑφ′ = ὑπό + dat. – *under*; ἥν = ἑήν, from ἑός-ή-όν – *his own*; πατρίς -ίδος ἡ –
    fatherland, country; γαῖα = γῆ ἡ; ἵκηται (ἱκνέομαι = ἀφικνέομαι) – *reach.*

11 χαίρω – *rejoice*; καρπαλίμως – *swiftly*; εἰ καί – *even if*; μάλα – *very*; τηλόθεν
    (< telecommunications) – *from afar, far off.*

12 μή + subj. '*let him not . . .*'; μεσσηγύς – *in the meantime*; πῆμα -ατος τό – *pain,
    trouble*; πάθῃσι = πάθῃ (πάσχω).

13 πρίν – *before* x (acc.) *does* y (infinitive); τόν = αὐτόν; ἧς = ἑῆς (10); ἐπιβήμεναι =
    ἐπιβῆναι (βαίνω has the irregular aorist infinitive βῆναι); ἔνθα – *there.*

14 πείσεται future of πάσχω; ἅσσα (= ἅτινα from ὅστις) – *whatever*; οἱ = αὐτῷ; αἶσα ἡ –
    fate; κατά (15); βαρύς -εῖα -ύ – *heavy, oppressive.*

15 νήσαντο (from νέομαι) – *spin*; with κατά (adv.) – '*(spin) out*'; λίνον τό – *thread*; ὅτε
    – *when*; μιν = αὐτόν; τέκε = ἔτεκε (aorist of τίκτω) – *give birth.*

Alcinous entertains the idea that their guest might be a god.

εἰ δέ τις ἀθανάτων γε κατ' οὐρανοῦ εἰλήλουθεν,
ἄλλο τι δὴ τόδ' ἔπειτα θεοὶ περιμηχανόωνται.
αἰεὶ γὰρ τὸ πάρος γε θεοὶ φαίνονται ἐναργεῖς
ἡμῖν, εὖτ' ἔρδωμεν ἀγακλειτὰς ἑκατόμβας,
δαίνυνταί τε παρ' ἄμμι καθήμενοι ἔνθα περ ἡμεῖς.　　　　20
εἰ δ' ἄρα τις καὶ μοῦνος ἰὼν ξύμβληται ὁδίτης,
οὔ τι κατακρύπτουσιν, ἐπεί σφισιν ἐγγύθεν εἰμέν,
ὥς περ Κύκλωπές τε καὶ ἄγρια φῦλα Γιγάντων.'

τὸν δ' ἀπαμειβόμενος προσέφη πολύμητις Ὀδυσσεύς·
'Ἀλκίνο', ἄλλο τί τοι μελέτω φρεσίν· οὐ γὰρ ἐγώ γε　　　　25
ἀθανάτοισιν ἔοικα, τοὶ οὐρανὸν εὐρὺν ἔχουσιν,
οὐ δέμας οὐδὲ φυήν, ἀλλὰ θνητοῖσι βροτοῖσιν.
οὕς τινας ὑμεῖς ἴστε μάλιστ' ὀχέοντας ὀϊζὺν
ἀνθρώπων, τοῖσίν κεν ἐν ἄλγεσιν ἰσωσαίμην.

Names and places

Κύκλωπες οἱ: *the Cyclopes;* **Γιγάντες οἱ:** *the Giants*

The Giants and the Cyclopes were the 'Earth-born' children of Ge and Ouranos. The Phaeacians were once neighbours of the Cyclopes, a race of one-eyed giants, but moved away because the Cyclopes kept ravaging their land (*Odyssey* 6.4–6). The most famous Cyclops, Polyphemus, was blinded by Odysseus (*Odyssey* 9).

Gods and men

There are many stories in Greek mythology where gods come down to earth to test how strangers are treated. Wrongdoers risked punishment from Zeus. Lycaon, for example, was turned into a wolf for his cruel treatment of strangers. Alcinous knows it is wise to be cautious.

Q.　Explain what makes the Phaeacians' relationship with the gods so special.

Q.　How does Odysseus deal with the compliment from Alcinous?

GCSE vocabulary: *ἀεί, ἀλλά, ἄλλος, ἄνθρωπος, γάρ, δή, ἐγώ, εἰ, ἐν + dat., εὐρύς, ἔχω, ἡμεῖς, θεός, μάλιστα, μόνος, ὅδε, ὅς, οὐρανός, τις, ὑμεῖς.*

16   ἀθάνατος ὁ – *immortal*; εἰλήλουθα (perfect of ἔρχομαι) – *have come*.

17   περιμηχανάομαι – *devise, contrive*; ἄλλο τι – '*something new*' = τόδ' δὴ (ἐστίν) ἄλλο τι; ἔπειτα – *then, in that case*.

18   αἰεί = ἀεί; τὸ πάρος – *in the past*; ἐναργής -ές – *visible, manifest*.

19   εὖτε + subj. – *whenever*; ἔρδω – *do, make, offer*; ἀγακλειτός -όν – *glorious*; ἑκατόμβη ἡ – *hecatomb, major public sacrifice* (literally of 100 oxen).

20   δαίνυμαι – *join a feast, banquet* (5); τε (links the verbs φαίνονται and δαίνυνταί); παρά + dat. – *beside, alongside*; ἄμμι = ἡμῖν; κάθημαι – *sit*; ἔνθα περ – *there where*.

21   εἰ τις – *if someone*; ἄρα – *then*; καί – *even*; μοῦνος = μόνος; ἰών (participle of εἶμι); ξύμβληται aor. subj. of συμβάλλομαι – *meet*; ὁδίτης -ου ὁ (> ὁδός ἡ) – *traveller*.

22   τι – *at all*; κατακρύπτω – *hide away*; σφισιν = αὐτοῖς; ἐγγύθεν – *close*; εἰμέν = ἐσμέν.

23   ὥς περ – *like, as*; ἄγριος -α -ον – *savage, wild*; φῦλον τό – *tribe*.

24   τὸν δ' is the object of προσέφη (from προς + φημί) – *addressed*; ἀπαμειβόμενος from ἀπαμείβομαι – *in reply, in turn*; πολύμητις – *of many wiles, crafty*. Variants of this line appear many times in the poem.

25   τοι = σοί – '*your*'; μελέτω + dat. 3rd person imperative of μέλει – '*let it concern*'; φρεσίν dat. pl. of φρήν φρενός ἡ – *mind, heart*.

26   ἀθανάτοισιν (16); ἔοικα – *be like* (+ dat.) in respect of (+ acc.); τοί = οἵ (ὅς ἡ ὁ); ἔχω – *have, live in*.

27   δέμας τό – *body, build*; οὐ . . οὐδέ – *neither . . . nor*; φυή ἡ – *nature*; θνητός -ή -όν (> ἀποθνῄσκω) – *mortal*; βροτός ὁ – *man, mortal* (dat. after ἔοικα 26).

28   ἴστε (from οἶδα) – *you know*; ὀχέω – *bear, endure*; ὀϊζύς ἡ – *misery, suffering*. οὕς τινας . . . ἀνθρώπων – '*of all the men whom . . .*'.

29   τοῖσιν = αὐτοῖς; κέν + opt. – '*would*', '*could*', '*might*'; ἄλγος -εος τό (< analgesic) – *pain*; ἰσωσαίμην (< isosceles) from ἰσόω – *consider as equal*.

Odysseus shows how eager he is first to eat and then to get home.

καὶ δ' ἔτι κεν καὶ μᾶλλον ἐγὼ κακὰ μυθησαίμην,   30
ὅσσα γε δὴ ξύμπαντα θεῶν ἰότητι μόγησα.
ἀλλ' ἐμὲ μὲν δορπῆσαι ἐάσατε κηδόμενόν περ·
οὐ γάρ τι στυγερῇ ἐπὶ γαστέρι κύντερον ἄλλο
ἔπλετο, ἥ τ' ἐκέλευσεν ἕο μνήσασθαι ἀνάγκη
καὶ μάλα τειρόμενον καὶ ἐνὶ φρεσὶ πένθος ἔχοντα,   35
ὡς καὶ ἐγὼ πένθος μὲν ἔχω φρεσίν, ἣ δὲ μάλ' αἰεὶ
ἐσθέμεναι κέλεται καὶ πινέμεν, ἐκ δέ με πάντων
ληθάνει ὅσσ' ἔπαθον, καὶ ἐνιπλήσασθαι ἀνώγει.
ὑμεῖς δ' ὀτρύνεσθε ἅμ' ἠοῖ φαινομένηφιν,
ὡς κ' ἐμὲ τὸν δύστηνον ἐμῆς ἐπιβήσετε πάτρης   40
καί περ πολλὰ παθόντα· ἰδόντα με καὶ λίποι αἰὼν
κτῆσιν ἐμήν, δμῶάς τε καὶ ὑψερεφὲς μέγα δῶμα.'

Persuasive speaking

Of the heroes who fought at Troy, Odysseus was the greatest exponent of skilful speaking. The ability to use words well was a quality widely admired as heroic: in the *Iliad* King Priam recalls Odysseus' unrivalled power of speech, his words *'like snowflakes in winter'* (*Iliad* 3.222). When Odysseus eventually tells the Phaeacians the story of his sufferings, his gripping account lasts for hours (*Odyssey* 9–12).

Q.   After this speech we are told that the Phaeacians approve Odysseus' speech as
     spoken κατὰ μοῖραν (44). How well-suited to the occasion do you think
     Odysseus' words are and why?

Q.   Odysseus expresses his readiness to die once he has seen three things: what are
     they?

GCSE vocabulary: *γε, ἐάω, ἕκαστος, ἐμός, ἐσθίω, ἔτι, κακός, κελεύω, μᾶλλον, μέγας, μέν . . . δέ . . ., καίπερ, λείπω, μέγας, εἶδον (ὁράω), πάσχω, πᾶς, πέμπω, πίνω.*

30   **κακά τά** = *troubles, ills*; **κεν . . . μυθησαίμην** (from μυθέω > μῦθος) – '*I could tell of*'.

31   **ὅσσα** – *as many as*; **ξύμπαντα** (= πάντα); **ὅσσα γε δὴ ξύμπαντα** – '*yes* (γε) *indeed, all the many things . .*'; **ἰότης -ητος ἡ** – *will, desire*; **μογέω** – *suffer*.

32   **δορπῆσαι** aorist infinitive of δορπέω – *eat*; **ἐάσατε** aorist imperative of ἐάω – *allow, let*; **κήδομαι** – *be care-worn, troubled*; **πέρ** = καίπερ + participle.

33   **στυγερός -ά -όν** – *wretched, hateful*; **ἐπί** + dat. – *after*, i.e. '*than*'; **γαστήρ -έρος ἡ** – *stomach*; **κύντερος -α -ον** (comparative > κύων – dog) – *more base, more dog-like*.

34   **ἔπλετο** = ἐστί; **ἥ τ'** – *which*; **ἕο** = ἑαυτῆς; **μιμνήσκομαι** + gen. – *remember*; **ἀνάγκη κή** (> ἀναγκάζω) – *necessity*. The aorist verbs are **gnomic**, expressing what tends to happen.

35   **καί . . . . καί . . .** (+ participles) – *although being, even when one is x and y*; **μάλα** – *very*; **τείρω** – *wear out*; **ἐνὶ φρεσί** (25); **πένθος -εος τό** – *grief, sorrow, pain*.

36   **ἡ δε** – changes the subject back to the insistent γαστήρ of Odysseus.

37   **κέλομαι** = κελεύω; **ἐσθέμεναι . . . πινέμεν** = ἐσθίειν . . . πίνειν; **ἐκ** (tmesis, see 38).

38   **ἐκ .. ληθάνω** (< lethargic) – *make someone* (acc.) *forget something* (gen.) *completely*; **ὅσσα** – *as many as*, '*all the*' (31); **ἐνιπλήσασθαι** aorist middle infinitive of ἐμπίπλημι – *eat one's fill*; **ἀνώγω** – *urge, command*.

39   **ὀτρύνεσθε** imperative of ὀτρύνομαι – *stir oneself, get going*; **ἅμα** + dat. *along with*; **ἠοῖ** (dat. of ἠώς ἡ) – *dawn*; **φαινομένηφιν** = φαινομένη – '*when dawn appears*'.

40   **ὥς** = ἵνα; **δύστηνος -ον** – *miserable, wretched*; **ἐπιβήσετε** (> βαίνω) + gen. – *set down on*; **πάτρη ἡ** (= πατρίς -ίδος ἡ) – *fatherland, homeland* (10).

41   **καί περ** (= καίπερ); **λίποι** (λείπω, optative expressing a wish); **αἰών ὁ** (< aeon) – *life*.

42   **κτῆσις ἡ** (> κτάομαι) – *possessions*; **δμῶη ἡ** – *housemaid, serving woman*; **ὑψερεφής -ές** – *high-roofed*; **δῶμα -ατος τό** – *house*.

Odysseus wins the Phaeacians over with his words, but left alone with the King and Queen, Odysseus is questioned further by Arete.

ὣς ἔφαθ', οἱ δ' ἄρα πάντες ἐπήνεον ἠδ' ἐκέλευον
πεμπέμεναι τὸν ξεῖνον, ἐπεὶ κατὰ μοῖραν ἔειπεν.
αὐτὰρ ἐπεὶ σπεῖσάν τ' ἔπιον θ' ὅσον ἤθελε θυμός,   45
οἱ μὲν κακκείοντες ἔβαν οἰκόνδε ἕκαστος,
αὐτὰρ ὁ ἐν μεγάρῳ ὑπελείπετο δῖος Ὀδυσσεύς,
πὰρ δέ οἱ Ἀρήτη τε καὶ Ἀλκίνοος θεοειδὴς
ἥσθην· ἀμφίπολοι δ' ἀπεκόσμεον ἔντεα δαιτός.
τοῖσιν δ' Ἀρήτη λευκώλενος ἄρχετο μύθων·   50
ἔγνω γὰρ φᾶρός τε χιτῶνά τε εἵματ' ἰδοῦσα
καλά, τά ῥ' αὐτὴ τεῦξε σὺν ἀμφιπόλοισι γυναιξί·
καί μιν φωνήσασ' ἔπεα πτερόεντα προσηύδα·
'ξεῖνε, τὸ μέν σε πρῶτον ἐγὼν εἰρήσομαι αὐτή·
τίς πόθεν εἰς ἀνδρῶν; τίς τοι τάδε εἵματ' ἔδωκεν;   55
οὐ δὴ φῆς ἐπὶ πόντον ἀλώμενος ἐνθάδ' ἱκέσθαι;'
τὴν δ' ἀπαμειβόμενος προσέφη πολύμητις Ὀδυσσεύς·

Names and places
Ἀρήτη ἡ: *Arete*
Queen of the Phaeacians. Nausicaa has told Odysseus that it is more important to win over her mother Arete than her father the king, if he wants to secure an escort home (*Odyssey* 6.297–315).

What is Odysseus wearing?
The picture on p. 40 shows Odysseus' first appearance on Phaeacia as a wild, naked man. In *Odyssey* 6, Homer tells how Athene arranged things so that at the moment when Odysseus was in desperate need of food, drink and clothes, the beautiful Phaeacian princess Nausicaa was washing clothes for her brothers on the beach with a picnic, near where Odysseus had collapsed.

Q.   What impressions of the Phaeacians have you formed so far?

Q.   How can we tell from lines 50–6 that Arete is a shrewd and intelligent queen?

GCSE vocabulary: *ἄρχομαι, αὐτός, γιγνώσκω, ἔδωκα (δίδωμι), ἐθέλω, ἐπεί, καλός, κελεύω, μῦθος, πρῶτον, τίς;, φημί.*

43   ὣς ἔφατο from φημί – 'so he spoke,' a formulaic phrase indicating the end of a speech; ἄρα
     – then (21); ἐπαινέω – praise; ἠδέ (3).

44   πεμπέμεναι infinitive of πέμπω – 'escort'; κατὰ μοῖραν – fittingly; ἔειπεν = εἶπεν.

45   αὐτὰρ ἐπεὶ σπεῖσάν τ' ἔπιον θ' ὅσον ἤθελε θυμός = line 1.

46   οἱ μέν – this opens a contrast between the Phaeacian leaders, who depart home, and the king and
     queen (δέ 48); κακκείοντες (= κατακείοντες from κατακείω) – go to lie down; ἔβαν =
     ἔβησαν; οἰκόνδε (5).

47   μέγαρον (7); ὑπολείπω – leave behind; δῖος – noble, godlike, a common epithet.

48   πάρ + dat. – beside; οἱ = αὐτῷ; θεοειδής -ές – looking like a god.

49   ἥσθην imperfect of ἥμαι, a dual form – (the two of them) sat; ἀμφίπολος ἡ – maid;
     ἀποκοσμέω (< cosmetic) – arrange, tidy away; ἔντεα τά – equipment, 'the dishes';
     δαίς δαιτός ἡ – feast, banquet.

50   τοῖσιν = αὐτοῖς (Odysseus and Alcinous); λευκώλενος -ον (< leukaemia) – white-armed,
     a frequent epithet for well-born women; ἄρχομαι + gen. – begin, opened; μῦθος ὁ –
     word, talk.

51   ἔγνω root aorist of γιγνώσκω; φᾶρος τό – cloak; χιτών -ῶνος ὁ – tunic; εἵματα τά
     – clothes.

52   τά ῥ' = ἅ ἄρα; τεῦξε aorist of τεύχω – make; σύν + dat. – with; ἀμφίπολος ἡ (49).

53   μιν = αὐτόν; φωνέω – speak, utter; ἔπος -εος τό – word (< epic); πτερόεις -εσσα
     -εν (< pterodactyl) – winged (words fly from the speaker to the listener); προσηύδα + acc.
     imperfect of προσαυδάω – address.

54   τὸ μέν . . . πρῶτον – 'this first' – we expect a δέ, but further questions prove unnecessary;
     ἐγών = ἐγώ; αὐτή – Arete makes it clear that she will lead the conversation now; εἰρήσομαι
     future of εἴρομαι – ask.

55   πόθεν; – from where?; εἰς = εἶ (εἰμί); τοι = σοί; τάδε (ὅδε ἥδε τόδε); εἵματα (51). τάδε
     suggests that Arete gestures towards Odysseus's clothes.

56   φῆς = ἔφης (φημί); πόντος ὁ – sea; ἀλάομαι – wander, roam; ἱκνέομαι – reach
     (10).

57   τὴν δ' Odysseus addresses the queen (compare with 24).

Odysseus does not immediately answer Arete's question about his clothes, but begins the story of his troubles.

'ἀργαλέον, βασίλεια, διηνεκέως ἀγορεῦσαι
κήδε', ἐπεί μοι πολλὰ δόσαν θεοὶ οὐρανίωνες·
τοῦτο δέ τοι ἐρέω ὅ μ' ἀνείρεαι ἠδὲ μεταλλᾷς.   60
Ὠγυγίη τις νῆσος ἀπόπροθεν εἰν ἁλὶ κεῖται,
ἔνθα μὲν Ἄτλαντος θυγάτηρ, δολόεσσα Καλυψώ
ναίει ἐϋπλόκαμος, δεινὴ θεός· οὐδέ τις αὐτῇ
μίσγεται οὔτε θεῶν οὔτε θνητῶν ἀνθρώπων.
ἀλλ' ἐμὲ τὸν δύστηνον ἐφέστιον ἤγαγε δαίμων   65
οἶον, ἐπεί μοι νῆα θοὴν ἀργῆτι κεραυνῷ
Ζεὺς ἔλσας ἐκέασσε μέσῳ ἐνὶ οἴνοπι πόντῳ.
ἔνθ' ἄλλοι μὲν πάντες ἀπέφθιθεν ἐσθλοὶ ἑταῖροι,
αὐτὰρ ἐγὼ τρόπιν ἀγκὰς ἑλὼν νεὸς ἀμφιελίσσης
ἐννῆμαρ φερόμην· δεκάτῃ δέ με νυκτὶ μελαίνῃ   70
νῆσον ἐς Ὠγυγίην πέλασαν θεοί, ἔνθα Καλυψώ
ναίει ἐϋπλόκαμος, δεινὴ θεός, ἥ με λαβοῦσα
ἐνδυκέως ἐφίλει τε καὶ ἔτρεφεν ἠδὲ ἔφασκε
θήσειν ἀθάνατον καὶ ἀγήραον ἤματα πάντα·
ἀλλ' ἐμὸν οὔ ποτε θυμὸν ἐνὶ στήθεσσιν ἔπειθεν.   75

Names and places
Καλυψώ ἡ: *Calypso;* **Ὠγυγίη ἡ;** *Ogygia;* **Ἄτλας -αντος ὁ:** *Atlas*
Odysseus was rescued by the nymph Calypso, daughter of Atlas, when he was washed up, shipwrecked, on her beautiful but remote island of Ogygia.

Odysseus' shipwreck
Zeus punished Odysseus' crew, who had been repeatedly warned that they must not eat the cattle of the Sun (*Odyssey* 12.260ff.), by sending a terrible storm which destroyed Odysseus' last remaining ship. Odysseus survived the sea by clinging to the wreckage and outwitting the great whirlpool Charybdis.

Q.   How does Odysseus try to get the sympathy of Arete at the start of his tale in lines 58–67?

Q.   How far does Odysseus answer Arete's questions (55–6) in lines 68–75?

GCSE vocabulary: *αἱρέω, δεινός, δέκα, ἐρέω (λέγω), θυγάτηρ, λαμβάνω, ναῦς, νῆσος, νύξ, οὔτε . . . οὔτε . . ., ὅς, πολύς, πείθω, φέρω.*

58   ἀργαλέος -α -ον – *difficult, painful*; βασίλεια ἡ – *queen*; διηνεκέως – *right through, from start to finish*; ἀγορεῦσαι (aor. inf. of ἀγορεύω) – *speak of*.

59   κῆδος -εος τό – *care, trouble, suffering*; δόσαν = ἔδοσαν (δίδωμι); οὐρανίωνες (> οὐρανός) – *heaven-dwelling, heavenly*.

60   τοι = σοί; ἐρέω future of λέγω; ὅ (ὅς ἥ ὅ); ἀνείρεαι from ἀνέρομαι – '*you enquire*', '*you ask*'; μεταλλάω – *ask about, investigate*.

61   ἀπόπροθεν – *far off*; εἰν = ἐν; ἅλς ἁλός ἡ – *sea*; κεῖμαι – *lie*.

62   ἔνθα – *there* (13); δολόεις -εσσα -εν – *crafty, devious*.

63   ναίω – *live, dwell*; ἐϋπλόκαμος -ον – *lovely-haired*; οὐδέ τις – *and no-one*.

64   μίσγεται present of μίγνυμαι – *mix with, have dealings with, sleep with*; οὔτε . . . οὔτε (reinforces οὐδέ); θνητός -ή -όν – *mortal* (27).

65   δύστηνος -ον (40); ἐφέστιον (< Hestia) – *to the hearth*; δαίμων ὁ (< demon) – *god*.

66   οἶος -α -ον – *alone*; μοι dat. –'*my*'; νῆα acc.sg. of ναῦς; θοός -ή -όν – *swift*; ἀργής -ῆτος – *shining, bright*; κεραυνός ὁ – *lightning-bolt*.

67   ἔλσας aorist participle of εἴλω – *smite, strike*; ἐκέασσε aorist from κεάζω – *shatter, smash*; μέσος -η -ον (< mesolithic) – *middle of*; οἶνοψ -οπος (> οἶνος) – *wine-dark*; πόντος ὁ (56).

68   ἔνθα – *there* (62); ἀπέφθιθεν aorist passive of ἀποφθίνω – *perish*; ἐσθλός -ή -όν – *excellent, fine*; ἑταῖρος ὁ – *companion*.

69   τρόπις ἡ – *keel*; ἀγκάς (adv.) – *in my arms*; ἑλών (αἱρέω); νεός = νεώς (gen. of ναῦς); ἀμφιέλισσα (< helix) – *curved at both ends*.

70   ἐννῆμαρ – *for nine days*; φερόμην imperfect of φέρομαι – *be carried, borne along, swept away*; μέλας -αίνα -αν (< melancholy) – *black*.

71   πελάζω – *bring near, draw near*. For line 72 see line 63.

73   ἐνδυκέως – *considerately*; τρέφω – *nurture, tend*; φάσκω – *keep saying*.

74   θήσειν future infinitive of τίθημι in an indirect statement – '*would make me*'; ἀθάνατος -ον (16); ἀγήραος -ον – *ageless, not subject to ageing*; ἦμαρ -ατος τό (= ἡμέρα) – *day*.

75   οὔ ποτε – *never*; θυμὸν ἐνὶ στήθεσσιν (4)

Odysseus explains how he left Calypso's island and how his raft was wrecked.

ἔνθα μὲν ἑπτάετες μένον ἔμπεδον, εἴματα δ' αἰεὶ
δάκρυσι δεύεσκον, τά μοι ἄμβροτα δῶκε Καλυψώ·
ἀλλ' ὅτε δὴ ὀγδοόν μοι ἐπιπλόμενον ἔτος ἦλθε,
καὶ τότε δή μ' ἐκέλευσεν ἐποτρύνουσα νέεσθαι
Ζηνὸς ὑπ' ἀγγελίης, ἢ καὶ νόος ἐτράπετ' αὐτῆς.   80
πέμπε δ' ἐπὶ σχεδίης πολυδέσμου, πολλὰ δ' ἔδωκε,
σῖτον καὶ μέθυ ἡδύ, καὶ ἄμβροτα εἵματα ἕσσεν,
οὖρον δὲ προέηκεν ἀπήμονά τε λιαρόν τε.
ἑπτὰ δὲ καὶ δέκα μὲν πλέον ἤματα ποντοπορεύων,
ὀκτωκαιδεκάτῃ δ' ἐφάνη ὄρεα σκιόεντα   85
γαίης ὑμετέρης, γήθησε δέ μοι φίλον ἦτορ
δυσμόρῳ· ἦ γὰρ μέλλον ἔτι ξυνέσεσθαι ὀϊζυῖ
πολλῇ, τήν μοι ἐπῶρσε Ποσειδάων ἐνοσίχθων,
ὅς μοι ἐφορμήσας ἀνέμους κατέδησε κελεύθου,
ὤρινεν δὲ θάλασσαν ἀθέσφατον, οὐδέ τι κῦμα   90
εἴα ἐπὶ σχεδίης ἀδινὰ στενάχοντα φέρεσθαι.

Names and places

Ποσειδάων -άωνος ὁ: *Poseidon*
Brother of Zeus and lord of the sea. He persecuted Odysseus after Odysseus blinded his son, Polyphemus the Cyclops.

Ζηνός (alternative genitive to Διός): *Zeus*

Enjambement

There have been several moments in this text when a significant word has been delayed in the sentence to hang at the start of a new line. We find this effect, called **enjambement**, used in lines 87 and 88. Enjambement can produce a number of effects by throwing emphasis onto the word on the new line, for example, suspense, irony, paradox, pathos and humour.

Q.   What picture of Calypso does Odysseus give? Is he sympathetic to her?

Q.   Summarize Odysseus' experiences after he left Calypso. How clear a view do we get of his emotions along the way?

Q.   Consider the specific impact of the examples of **enjambement** mentioned above, and any others you've noticed earlier in the text (e.g. lines 49, 66).

GCSE vocabulary *ἀλλά, ἄνεμος, δέκα, ἑπτά, ἔτι, ἔτος, ἡδύς, ἦλθον (ἔρχομαι), κελεύω, μέλλω, μένω, ὅς, πέμπω, σῖτος, τότε, ὑμέτερος, φαίνομαι.*

76   ἑπτάετες (= ἑπτά + ἔτος); μένον= ἔμενον; ἔμπεδον – *constantly, without a break*;
     εἵματα (51); αἰεί = ἀεί.

77   δάκρυ τό – *tear*; δεύεσκον imperfect of δεύω – *'would soak, drench'*, -σκ- has a
     frequentative sense (see 73); τά = ἅ; ἄμβροτος -ον – *immortal* (also 82).

78   ὅτε – *when*; ὄγδοος -η -ον (< octopus) – *eighth*; ἐπιπλόμενον aorist participle of
     ἐπιπέλομαι – *come round, be upon.*

79   καὶ τότε δή – *then, that was when*; ἐποτρύνω – *urge, command* (39); νέομαι –
     return, go back.

80   ὑπό + gen. – *because of* (usually only used of agent); ἀγγελίη ἡ – *message*; ἢ καί – *or
     even*; νόος ὁ – *mind, 'feelings'*; ἐτράπετο aorist of τρέπομαι – *turn, change*. Zeus sent
     Hermes to tell Calypso to release the hero (*Odyssey 5*).

81   πέμπε = ἔπεμπε; ἐπί + gen. – *on*; σχεδίη ἡ – *raft*; πολύδεσμος -ον – *bound-fast.*

82   μέθυ τό (< methylated) – *wine*; ἕσσεν aorist of ἕννυμι – *clothe.*

83   οὖρος ὁ – *fair wind, breeze*; προέηκεν aorist of προίημι – *send forth*; ἀπήμων
     -ονος – *trouble-free, gentle*; λιαρός -ά -όν – *warm, balmy.*

84   πλέον = ἔπλεον; ἤματα (74); ποντοπορεύω – *journey by sea, be at sea.*

85   ὀκτὼ -και -δεκάτη (ἡμέρᾳ) – *time 'when'*; ἐφάνη aorist of φαίνομαι – *appeared*;
     ὄρεα τά (ὄρος τό) – *mountain*; σκιόεις -εσσα -εν – *shadowy.*

86   γαῖα (< Gaia) = γῆ; γήθησε aorist of γηθέω – *rejoice*; μοι = ἐμοί – *'my'*; φίλος -η -ον
     – *dear, own*; ἦτορ τό– *heart.*

87   δύσμορος -ον – *ill fated*: agrees with μοι – *'ill fated though I was'*; ἦ – *indeed, in
     truth*; μέλλον = ἔμελλον (+ future infinitive); ἔτι – *still, yet, in the future, 'to come'*;
     ξυνέσεσθαι from σύνειμι – *meet with*; ὀϊζύς ἡ – *misery, suffering.*

88   τήν = ἥν (ὅς ἥ ὅ); ἐπῶρσε aorist of ἐπόρνυμι – *stir up, rouse*; ἐνοσίχθων
     (> χθών < chthonic) – *earth-shaker.*

89   ἐφορμάω + dat. (< hormone) – *stir up, let loose at*; καταδέω + gen. – *check, stop,
     block from*; κέλευθος ἡ – *journey, path, course.*

90   ὀρίνω – *rouse, stir up*; ἀθέσφατος -ον – *unspeakable, inexpressibly awful*;
     οὐδέ τι – *not at all*; κῦμα -ατος τό – *wave.*

91   εἴα imperfect of ἐάω – *allow* (με is understood) + infinitive; ἐπὶ σχεδίης (81); ἀδινά –
     loudly, heavily; στενάχω – *groan*; φέρομαι (70).

Saved from the sea, Odysseus sleeps soundly, not waking until the next afternoon.

τὴν μὲν ἔπειτα θύελλα διεσκέδασ'· αὐτὰρ ἐγώ γε
νηχόμενος τόδε λαῖτμα διέτμαγον, ὄφρα με γαίη
ὑμετέρῃ ἐπέλασσε φέρων ἄνεμός τε καὶ ὕδωρ.
ἔνθα κέ μ' ἐκβαίνοντα βιήσατο κῦμ' ἐπὶ χέρσου,   95
πέτρῃς πρὸς μεγάλῃσι βαλὸν καὶ ἀτερπέϊ χώρῳ·
ἀλλ' ἀναχασσάμενος νῆχον πάλιν, ἧος ἐπῆλθον
ἐς ποταμόν, τῇ δή μοι ἐείσατο χῶρος ἄριστος,
λεῖος πετράων, καὶ ἐπὶ σκέπας ἦν ἀνέμοιο.
ἐκ δ' ἔπεσον θυμηγερέων, ἐπὶ δ' ἀμβροσίη νὺξ   100
ἤλυθ'. ἐγὼ δ' ἀπάνευθε διιπετέος ποταμοῖο
ἐκβὰς ἐν θάμνοισι κατέδραθον, ἀμφὶ δὲ φύλλα
ἠφυσάμην· ὕπνον δὲ θεὸς κατ' ἀπείρονα χεῦεν.
ἔνθα μὲν ἐν φύλλοισι, φίλον τετιημένος ἦτορ
εὗδον παννύχιος καὶ ἐπ' ἠῶ καὶ μέσον ἦμαρ·   105
δείλετό τ' ἠέλιος καί με γλυκὺς ὕπνος ἀνῆκεν.

Dramatic irony

Odysseus tells many stories about himself in the Odyssey, many of them complete lies. This story is different because it is a brief version of adventures the audience or reader has already heard described at greater length in Books 5–6 as a third person narrative. This speech re-caps the story so far and gives an insight into Odysseus' character and perspective on those experiences. The audience in some cases knows more than the hero, particularly about the role played by Athene.

Q.   How is the impression of Odysseus' long sleep conveyed?

Q.   Odysseus' **stock epithets** are '*much-enduring*' (πολύτλας) and '*resourceful*' (πολύμητις 57, > μῆτις = *wisdom, cunning*). What evidence is there of these qualities in his speech?

GCSE vocabulary: *βάλλω, ἐκβαίνω, ἔπειτα, ἔπεσον (πίπτω), καθεύδω, μέγας, νύξ, ὅδε, πίπτω, ποταμός, ὕδωρ, ὕπνος.*

92   τὴν μέν (i.e. the raft, contrasted with αὐτὰρ ἐγώ γε); θύελλα ἡ – *storm*; διεσκέδασε from
      διασκεδάννυμι – *scatter, split apart.*

93   νήχομαι – *swim*; λαῖτμα -ατος τό – *gulf, bay, expanse*; διέτμαγον (aorist of
      διατμήγω) – *cut through*; ὄφρα – *until*; γαῖα (86).

94   ἐπέλασσε + dat. aorist of πελάζω (71) – *bring near to*; ἄνεμός τε καὶ ὕδωρ are each the
      subject.

95   κε + aorist indicative – '*would have*'; βιήσατο aorist of βιάομαι (> βία) – *force, power,
      drive*; κῦμα -ατος τό (90); ἐπί + gen. – *onto, upon*; χέρσος ἡ – *shore.*

96   πέτρης = πέτραις (< petrification) – *rock*; πρός + dat. *against*; μεγάλῃσι = μεγάλαις;
      βαλόν neuter aorist participle of βάλλω; ἀτερπής -ές – *joyless, miserable*; χῶρος ὁ (>
      χώρα) – *place.*

97   ἀναχάζομαι – *draw back*; νῆχον imperfect of νήχω = νήχομαι (93); πάλιν – *back
      again*; ἦος = ἕως; ἐπῆλθον (ἐπέρχομαι) – *come to.*

98   ἐς = εἰς; τῇ – *where*; ἐείσατο aorist of εἴδομαι + dat. – *seem*; χῶρος ὁ (96); ἄριστος
      -η -ον (superlative of ἀγαθός).

99   λεῖος -α -ον – *smooth, free from* + gen.; πετράων (96); ἐπὶ . . . ἦν (tmesis) ἔπεστι –
      be at hand; σκέπας τό – *shelter*; ἀνέμοιο gen. sg. – '*from the wind*'.

100   ἐκ . . . ἔπεσον (tmesis) – *fell out, tumbled out*; θυμηγερέω – *gather one's spirits*;
      ἐπί (see 101); ἀμβρόσιος -ον (< ambrosia) – *immortal, divine.*

101   ἐπί . . . ἤλυθ' aorist of ἐπέρχομαι – *come on*; ἀπάνευθε + gen. – *away from*; διιπετής
      -ές (> Διός + πίπτω) – *heaven-sent*; ποταμοῖο for case, see 99.

102   ἐκβάς aorist participle of ἐκβαίνω; θάμνος ὁ – *bush*; κατέδραθον aorist of καταδαρθάνω
      – *fall asleep*; ἀμφί (adv.) – *around*; φύλλον τό – *leaf.*

103   ἠφυσάμην aorist middle of ἀφύσσω – *heaped up for myself*; κατ' . . . χεῦεν aorist of
      καταχέω – *pour down*; ἀπείρων -ον – *unlimited, endless.*

104   φύλλοισι (102); τετίημαι – *be sorrowful, grieve*; φίλον ἦτορ (86) – acc. of respect.

105   εὗδον imperfect of εὕδω = καθεύδω – *sleep*; παννύχιος (> πᾶν + νύξ) – *all night long*;
      ἐπί + acc. – *up to*; ἠῶ (acc. of ἠώς ἡ) – *dawn* (39); μέσος -η -ον (67); ἦμαρ τό (74).

106   δείλομαι – *head into the afternoon*; ἠέλιος = ἥλιος ὁ (< helium) – *sun*; γλυκύς -εῖα
      -ύ (< glucose) – *sweet*; καί – translate idiomatically as '*when*'; ἀνῆκεν aorist of ἀνίημι –
      let go, release.

Odysseus describes how he sees the princess Nausicaa and her maids on the beach and asks them for help.

ἀμφιπόλους δ' ἐπὶ θινὶ τεῆς ἐνόησα θυγατρὸς
παιζούσας, ἐν δ' αὐτὴ ἔην ἐϊκυῖα θεῆσι.
τὴν ἱκέτευσ'· ἡ δ' οὔ τι νοήματος ἤμβροτεν ἐσθλοῦ,
ὡς οὐκ ἂν ἔλποιο νεώτερον ἀντιάσαντα   110
ἐρξέμεν· αἰεὶ γάρ τε νεώτεροι ἀφραδέουσιν.
ἥ μοι σῖτον δῶκεν ἅλις ἠδ' αἴθοπα οἶνον
καὶ λοῦσ' ἐν ποταμῷ καί μοι τάδε εἵματ' ἔδωκε.
ταῦτά τοι ἀχνύμενός περ ἀληθείην κατέλεξα.'

Supplication

The verb **ἱκετεύω** in line 109 means supplicate: when someone in need asks another more powerful person for help, he grasps their knees and touches their chin. He becomes their suppliant and the person supplicated has a responsibility to help. Odysseus had supplicated Nausicaa from afar, concerned that she might be alarmed by his nakedness. She responds with courage and generosity and Odysseus praises these qualities in one so young. Nausicaa is probably in her mid-teens, since she is beginning to think of marriage.

> Q.   If you were Arete, would you feel that your questions had been satisfactorily answered?
>
> Q.   Would you describe Odysseus as a persuasive speaker?

GCSE vocabulary: *ἀληθής, ἐλπίζω, θεά, θυγάτηρ, νέος, οἶνος, ταῦτα (οὗτος).*

107 ἀμφίπολος ἡ (49); ἐπί + dat. – *on*; θίς θινός ὁ/ἡ – *shore*; τεῆς = σῆς (σός-ἡ-όν);
νοέω – *notice*.

108 παίζω (> παῖς) – *play*; ἐν ... ἔην (ἔνειμι) – *be among*; ἐϊκώς -υῖα -ός +
dat. – *like, resembling*; θεῆσι = θεαῖς – '*a goddess*'. When this meeting is described in
Book 6 Odysseus asks Nausicaa if she is a goddess, likening her specifically to Artemis.

109 τήν = αὐτήν; ἱκετεύω – *supplicate, beseech*; ἡ δ' (change of subject); οὔ τι – *in no
way, not at all* (90); νόημα -ατος τό – *sense*; ἤμβροτον aorist of ἁμαρτάνω + gen. –
miss, be missing, lack; ἐσθλός -ή -όν – *excellent, fine* (68).

110 ὡς οὐκ ἂν ἔλποιο (+ acc. + future infinitive) – '*not as you might expect that*';
νεώτερος -α -ον (> νέος) – *younger, 'a younger person*'; ἀντιάω – *meet, 'on
meeting (someone)*'.

111 ἐρξέμεν future infinitive of ἔρδω – *do, manage, act*; αἰεὶ γάρ τε (one of the uses of τε (also
at 34) is to express a generalization) – '*always tend to*'; νεώτεροι – '*the young*';
ἀφραδέω – *lack sense, be thoughtless*.

112 ἅλις – *enough* (suggesting a snack rather than a banquet); ἠδέ (3); αἴθοψ -οπος –
gleaming.

113 λοῦσ' = ἔλουσε from λούω – *wash*. In fact, Nausicaa ordered her maids to wash Odysseus and
he refused, expressing embarrassment and preferring to wash himself (*Odyssey* 6. 209–37); τάδε
– see 55.

114 ταῦτα (< οὗτος); τοι = σοί; ἀχνύμενος – *grieving*; πέρ = καίπερ (+ participle); ἀληθείη
ἡ (> ἀληθής) – *truth*; καταλέγω (< catalogue) – *relate, recount, tell*.

What happens next?

Arete and Alcinous show extreme hospitality towards their guest, whom they value more and more over the course of his visit. As well as offering him fine food, wine and a bed, they entertain him with athletic contests, dancing and music: the bard Demodocus sings stories, some of which reduce Odysseus to tears as he relives memories of the part he played in the Trojan war. Eventually the hero reveals his identity and holds the Phaeacians spell-bound with stories of his adventures after he left Troy. Alcinous' appreciation of the value of his guest is clear from the way he eagerly increases the value of the guest-gifts they load him with on his departure. They also provide a ship and fifty rowers to convey him and his gifts home to Ithaca. The crew leave him asleep on the shore of his beloved island, surrounded by riches (*Odyssey* 8–13).

There is a sad epilogue to the way this generosity is rewarded (*Odyssey* 13.125–87). The god Poseidon is resentful of the Phaeacians' mastery of the seas and offer of safe passage to all wayfarers – especially Odysseus. He teaches them a lesson by turning their ship and fifty young rowers to stone as they return to harbour. This punishment had been prophesied to the Phaeacians, but they had continued to help visitors get home. The rock stands as a reminder to the Phaeacians of the power of the sea-god.

Final questions

- How well do you think the three main characters are developed? Pick out key words for each character (Odysseus, Alcinous and Arete).
- What impressions have you formed of Phaeacian society?
- Do you find Odysseus a sympathetic hero? Do you admire him?
- Do you think the values of Homeric society, like **xenia** and **supplication**, are recognized at all in today's society?
- What makes Homer a good story-teller?

Herodotus

Herodotus is in many ways a natural successor to Homer. He was born in Halicarnassus (*c.* 484), not far from the various Ionian states that claimed Homer as their own. The original Greek text has elements of the Ionic dialect in common with the Homeric poems, like the use of an η where you would expect an α, but the prose text in this edition has been simplified to reinforce the Greek you have been studying so far. These extracts come mainly from the first three books of the *Histories*, a work in nine books.

Like Homer, Herodotus wrote an epic work about a great conflict between East and West, an account of the Persian Wars of 490–479. His brief mention of the Trojan War, the subject of Homer's *Iliad*, gives an insight into Herodotus' aims and methods. Herodotus claims that Homer was aware of, but chose not to use, a tradition that Helen never reached Troy and instead was detained in Egypt after leaving Sparta. To learn whether this version contained more truth than Homer's, Herodotus questioned Egyptian priests during his travels in Egypt and recorded his 'research' or 'ἱστορίη'; this Greek word gives us both the title of his work, *The Histories*, and our word, history.

In the Persian Wars, the Persians attempted to gain a foothold in Europe. This ended in a spectacular and unexpected victory for the Greeks. Herodotus' work is not simply the patriotic celebration such a Greek victory might justify. He, like Homer, shows a balanced interest in both sides, and shapes his work with the skill of a story-teller. To understand the conflict, he traced the expansion of the Persian empire over a vast area and explored the geography and customs of the lands and peoples that paid tribute to Persia as carefully and fully as he was able, given the great obstacles of time, distance and language. This is a world of gods as well as men and Herodotus' stories have a strong moral aspect to them, but the spirit of enquiry which drives his work forward is marked by a curiosity and scepticism typical of fifth-century Greek thought.

The scope of Herodotus' work is vast, but the audience is entertained along the way with travellers' tales of ants bigger than foxes that dig for gold (3.102) or headless men with eyes in their chests (*'well, that's what the Libyans say'*) (4.191). The reader's understanding of their own contemporary world is simultaneously challenged and strengthened. Simple observations – like the ideas that 'great powers were once small', that 'no man can truly be called happy until he is dead', that *hubris* (arrogant pride) is susceptible to *nemesis* (retribution), or that you can make no absolute assumptions about what is right or wrong – often result in profound lessons, learned not only by the memorable characters in his work, but also by the generations that have read them since they were first circulated in the 420s.

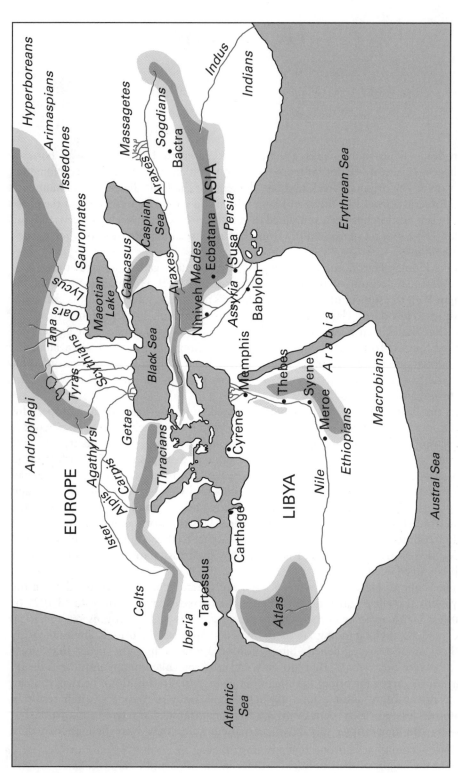

This map attempts to reconstruct Herodotus' view of the world c. 450.

HISTORIES, 1.30–4, 86–7, 6.125

Solon and Croesus; How Alcmaeon was enriched by Croesus

2018–2019 Prescription

*This selection corresponds as follows to **Tales from Herodotus**, ed. Farnell and Goff:*

Pages 86 to 99: Section IX: **Solon and Croesus** (*Histories 1.30–4 and 1.86–7*)
Pages 98 to 102: Section XIVa: **How Alcmaeon was enriched by Croesus** (*Histories 6.125*)

The story so far . . .

The tales that follow describe two separate visits to the court of **Croesus**, king of Lydia, at the height of his prosperity by the Athenians, **Solon** and **Alcmaeon**.

Solon won a reputation for wisdom that made him one of the 'Seven Sages' of Greece. He was an Athenian statesman and poet whose political and social reforms in the 590s laid the foundations for the development in Athens, over the next hundred years, of the world's first democracy. His reputation for wisdom was based partly on the fact that, after making radical reforms, he persuaded the Athenians to live with his laws for ten years before changing anything. During this time Solon left Athens and travelled widely.

Croesus ruled Lydia *c.* 560–546. The Lydians had risen to wealth and power under King Gyges (*c.* 680–645). Sardis, the capital of their empire, was situated on the river Pactolus, where, according to Greek myth, Midas, King of Phrygia, washed off his Golden Touch, and the Lydians are credited with minting the first coinage using gold and silver from this river. Croesus' kingdom extended east to the river Halys and west to the Greek cities on the coast of the Aegean, places like Miletus, Ephesus and Halicarnassus, where Herodotus was born. Some of Croesus' wealth found its way to Greece, specifically to the sanctuary of Apollo at Delphi. Croesus, after testing a number of oracles, believed Delphi was reliable in its prophecies. He chose this oracle when he wanted to ask if he should attack the Persian empire rising under King Cyrus east of his border. The oracle's words reassured Croesus: he was told that if he went to war, a great empire would fall. Blinded by his own assumptions, Croesus failed to see the ambiguity in this prophecy. The story of Solon and Croesus introduces how human complacency can have catastrophic results.

Alcmaeon was an Athenian who, along with Solon, had fought to open Delphi up to the outside world during the First Sacred War (*c.* 590) by preventing control of visitors by the local port, Crisa. Herodotus seems to suggest that Alcmaeon gave a personal welcome to Croesus' legates from Sardis and for that reason Croesus summoned him to Sardis and rewarded him for his services.

Both accounts are chronologically improbable, given that Solon and Alcmaeon were at the height of their political activity in the 590s and Croesus reigned *c.* 560–546. Some scholars think Herodotus may have confused Croesus with his father, Alyattes and/or Alcmaeon with his son, Megacles.

Solon and Croesus

Solon, the Athenian statesmen and philosopher, is asked a question while on his travels by Croesus, the fabulously rich king of Lydia, and gives a surprising reply. Herodotus *Histories 1.30*

Nominative words or phrases are in light blue, **verbs** in dark blue.

ἐκδημήσας ὁ Σόλων εἰς Σάρδεις ἀφίκετο παρὰ Κροῖσον.
ἀφικόμενος δὲ ἐξενίζετο ἐν τοῖς βασιλείοις ὑπὸ τοῦ Κροίσου·
μετὰ δέ, ἡμέρᾳ τρίτῃ ἢ τετάρτῃ, κελεύσαντος Κροίσου, τὸν
Σόλωνα θεράποντες περιῆγον κατὰ τοὺς θησαυρούς, καὶ
ἐπεδείκνυσαν πάντα ὄντα μεγάλα τε καὶ ὄλβια.   5
θεασάμενον δὲ αὐτὸν πάντα ἤρετο ὁ Κροῖσος τάδε, 'ξένε
Ἀθηναῖε, παρ' ἡμᾶς περὶ σοῦ λόγος ἀφῖκται πολύς, καὶ
σοφίας ἕνεκα τῆς σῆς καὶ πλάνης· νῦν οὖν ἵμερος ἐπῆλθέ με
ἐπερωτᾶν εἴ τινα ἤδη πάντων εἶδες ὀλβιώτατον.'

ὁ μὲν ἐλπίζων εἶναι ἀνθρώπων ὀλβιώτατος ταῦτα ἐπηρώτα·   10
Σόλων δέ, οὐδὲν ὑποθωπεύσας ἀλλὰ τῷ ὄντι χρησάμενος,
λέγει 'ὦ βασιλεῦ, Τέλλον Ἀθηναῖον.' ἀποθαυμάσας δὲ
Κροῖσος τὸ λεχθὲν ἤρετο ἐπιστρεφῶς, 'πῶς δὴ κρίνεις
Τέλλον εἶναι ὀλβιώτατον;'

Names and places

Σόλων ὁ: *Solon*
An Athenian statesman famous for his wisdom.

Κροῖσος ὁ: *Croesus*
King of Lydia, the central figure in the opening section of Herodotus' *Histories*.

Σάρδεις αἱ: *Sardis*
The wealthy capital city of the Lydian empire in Asia Minor (modern Turkey).

Q.   Give two reasons why Croesus thinks Solon will be able to give a good answer to his question.

GCSE vocabulary: *ἄγω, Ἀθηναῖος, ἄνθρωπος, αὐτός, ἀφικνέομαι, βασιλεύς, δέ, δή, εἰ, εἶδον (ὁράω), εἶναι (εἰμί), εἰς + acc., ἤ, ἤδη, ἦλθον (ἔρχομαι), ἡμεῖς, ἡμέρα, ἠρόμην (ἐρωτάω), καί, κελεύω, λέγω, λόγος, με (ἐγώ), μέγας, νῦν, ξένος, ὅδε, οὖν, πᾶς, περί + gen., πολύς, πῶς, . . . τε . . . καί, σός, σύ, τέταρτος, τις, τρίτος, ὑπό + gen., ὤν οὖσα ὄν (εἰμί).*

1   ἐκδημέω – *go abroad, leave home* (> δῆμος); **παρά** + acc. – *into the presence of, before* (7). Herodotus often postpones the subject until after the verb or participle.

2   ξενίζω (> ξένος) *entertain, welcome as a guest;* **βασίλεια τά** (> βασιλεύς) *royal palace;* **ὑπό** + gen. indicates 'agent', a good clue that there is a passive verb.

3   **μετὰ δέ** – not the preposition (μετά+ acc. = *after*), but an adverb, *afterwards;* ἡμέρᾳ τρίτῃ ἢ τετάρτῃ, the dative indicates 'time when'; κελεύσαντος Κροίσου, genitive absolute.

4   **θεράπων -οντος ὁ** (< therapy) – *attendant, helper;* **περιῆγον** – *led around* (> περὶ and ἄγω); **κατά** + acc. – *throughout, all around;* **θησαυρός ὁ** – *treasure chamber.*

5   **ἐπιδείκνυμι** – *point out, show;* **ὄλβιος -α -ον** – *blessed, fortunate, happy, rich,* it may refer to wealth/riches and/or to a person's prosperity, blessings or happiness in a wider sense: πάντα ὄντα μεγάλα τε καὶ ὄλβια – '*all the great wealth that there was*' or '*all the great blessings that were there*'.

6   **θεάομαι** (< theatre) – *look at, gaze at;* **τάδε** (ὅδε ἥδε τόδε) introducing direct speech: '*these (words)*', '*the following*', '*this*'.

7   **παρ'** = παρά (1), the missing final vowel (-α) is an example of **elision;** ἀφῖκται, perfect tense (ἀφικνέομαι) – '*has arrived*'.

8   **ἕνεκα** + gen. – *on account of, because of;* **πλάνη ἡ** – *wanderings, travel;* **ἵμερος ὁ** – *longing, desire;* **ἐπέρχομαι** (> ἔρχομαι) – *come over.*

9   **ἐπερωτάω** (> ἐρωτάω) – *ask a question;* **ὀλβιώτατος -α -ον** (5).

10   **ἐπηρώτα** – imperfect tense of an alpha-contracted verb; **ἐλπίζων** – '*supposing*' here not with the usual future infinitive.

11   **ὑποθωπεύω** – *use flattery;* **τῷ ὄντι** –'*the truth*', '*reality*'; **χράομαι** + dat. – *use, employ.* Instead of fawning like a courtier, Solon speaks the truth.

12   **λέγει** – present tense, can be translated either as a past or as a vivid present; **ἀποθαυμάζω** – the ἀπο-prefix suggests open astonishment.

13   **τὸ λεχθέν** (> λέγω) – '*what had been said*'; **ἐπιστρεφῶς** – *eagerly, sharply;* **κρίνω** (< critical) – *judge.*

Solon explains why he considers Tellus the Athenian to be so fortunate.
Croesus asks him whom he considers to be the next happiest. 1.30

ὁ δὲ εἶπε, 'Τέλλῳ τοῦτο μὲν παῖδες ἦσαν καλοί τε κἀγαθοί,   15
καὶ εἶδεν ἅπασιν αὐτοῖς τέκνα ἐκγενόμενα, καὶ πάντα
παραμείναντα· τοῦτο δὲ τελευτὴ τοῦ βίου λαμπροτάτη
ἐπεγένετο· γενομένης γὰρ Ἀθηναίοις μάχης πρὸς τοὺς
ἀστυγείτονας ἐν Ἐλευσῖνι, βοηθήσας καὶ τροπὴν ποιήσας
τῶν πολεμίων, ἀπέθανε κάλλιστα. καὶ Ἀθηναῖοι δημοσίᾳ τε   20
ἔθαψαν αὐτὸν ᾗπερ ἔπεσε, καὶ ἐτίμησαν μεγάλως.'

ὡς δὲ τὰ κατὰ τὸν Τέλλον διηγήσατο ὁ Σόλων, ἐπηρώτα
ὁ Κροῖσος τίνα δεύτερον μετ' ἐκεῖνον ἴδοι, δοκῶν πάνυ
δευτερεῖα γοῦν οἴσεσθαι. ὁ δὲ εἶπε, 'Κλέοβίν τε καὶ Βίτωνα·
τούτοις γὰρ, οὖσι γένος Ἀργείοις, βίος τε ἀρκῶν ὑπῆν, καὶ   25
πρὸς τούτῳ, ῥώμη σώματος τοιάδε· ἀθλοφόροι τε ἀμφότεροι
ὁμοίως ἦσαν, καὶ δὴ καὶ λέγεται ὅδε ὁ λόγος.

Names and places
Τέλλος ὁ: *Tellus*
An unknown Athenian whose name may be a pun on τέλος – *end/fulfilment*.

Ἐλευσῖνι (dat.): *Eleusis*
This battle at Eleusis, 20km west of Athens, may be the one that took place against Megara over control of the island of Salamis *c.* 570. If so, the Athenian victory is better known for the leadership of Peisistratus, who later became tyrant of Athens, by building on his success in this battle (*Histories* 1.59).

Κλέοβις ὁ: *Cleobis;* Βίτων ὁ: *Biton;* Ἀργεῖοι οἱ: *Argives, citizens of Argos*
The two young Argives are known only from this story (but see fig. 2).

Prizes
The Greeks were highly competitive and winning prizes brought increased status and material rewards; Olympic victors in Athens, for example, were awarded free meals for life.

Q.   Explain Solon's two reasons for making Tellus his choice.

Q.   What do we learn about Cleobis and Biton from Solon's introduction?

Q.   Do you think Croesus is being ironic, witty, genuinely competitive or bitter when he asks about the second prize? How intelligent does he seem?

GCSE vocabulary: ἀγαθός, οἱ Ἀθηναῖοι, ἀποθνήσκω, βίος, βοηθέω, γίγνομαι, δεύτερος, εἶδον (ὁράω), ἐκεῖνος, θάπτω, θαυμάζω, καλός, εἶπον (λέγω), λόγος, μάχη, μένω, μετά + acc., οὐδείς, παῖς, ἔπεσον (πίπτω), ποιέω, οἱ πολέμιοι, πρός + acc., σῶμα, τιμάω, τοῦτο, ταῦτα (οὗτος), . . . τε . . . καί, χράομαι + dat., ὤν οὖσα ὄν, ὡς.

15   Τέλλῳ – *'In Tellus' case . . .'.* The dative sets Tellus up clearly at the start of Solon's
     explanation. τοῦτο μέν . . . τοῦτο δέ . . . (17) – *for one thing, . . . and for another,
     . . .*; ἦσαν + dat. – *'there were (to Tellus)'*, i.e. *'he had . . .'*; καλοὶ τε κἀγαθοί –
     'gentlemen' (lit., *fine/noble and good*), a standard Greek phrase where καὶ ἀγαθοί, is
     routinely written as one word (**crasis**).

16   ἅπας (= πᾶς); ἅπασιν αὐτοῖς – *'to all of them . . .'*, i.e. *'they all had'* (15); τέκνα
     τά – *children*; ἐκγίγνομαι (> γίγνομαι) – *be born.*

17   παραμένω (> μένω) – *survive;* τελευτή ἡ (> τέλος) – *end;* λαμπρός -ά -όν
     (< lamp) – *bright, brilliant, glorious.* Low survival rates for children are common in pre-
     industrial societies; Tellus was unusually fortunate in seeing all his grandchildren survive.

18   ἐπιγίγνομαι (> γίγνομαι) – *occur, come upon, be.*

19   ἀστυγείτονες οἱ – *people from the nearby town, neighbours;* τροπή ἡ – *turn,
     rout;* τροπὴν ποιέω + gen.– *rout, put to flight.*

20   κάλλιστα (> καλός) adverb – *most nobly;* δημοσίᾳ (> δῆμος) – *at public expense;*

21   ἥπερ – *where, in the place where.*

22   τὰ κατὰ τὸν Τέλλον – *'Tellus' situation';* διηγέομαι – *explain, describe;*
     ἐπηρώτα (10).

23   τίνα; – *whom?* introducing an indirect question, which may be followed either by an indicative
     (εἶδες 9), or by an optative (ἴδοι); δοκέω (> δοκεῖ) – *seem, think, expect;* πάνυ (> πᾶς) –
     definitely, certainly.

24   δευτεραῖα τά – *second prize;* γοῦν (> γε + οὖν) – *at least, at any rate;* φέρομαι
     (future: οἴσομαι) – *carry off for oneself, win.*

25   τούτοις – possessive dative: *'they had'* (15); οὖσι (participle from εἰμί) agrees with τούτοις;
     γένος τό (< genocide) – *race,* accusative of respect (*Argive in respect of their race*); βίος ὁ
     – *life, livelihood;* ἀρκῶν – *sufficient;* ὕπειμι + dat. – *be, be available.*

26   πρός + dat. – *in addition to;* ῥώμη ἡ (< Rome) – *strength;* τοιόσδε τοιάδε τοιόνδε
     – *of this sort, of the following kind;* ἀθλοφόρος -α -ον (ἆθλον + φέρω) – *prize-
     winning, successful in competition;* ἀμφότεροι – *both.*

27   ὁμοίως (< homogeneous) – *equally;* καὶ δὴ καί – *moreover.*

The story of Cleobis and Biton. 1.31

οὔσης ἑορτῆς τῇ Ἥρᾳ ἔδει πάντως τὴν μητέρα αὐτῶν ζεύγει
κομισθῆναι εἰς τὸ ἱερόν· οἱ δὲ βόες ἐκ τοῦ ἀγροῦ οὐ
παρεγίγνοντο ἐν ὥρᾳ. οἱ δὲ νεανίαι, ὑποδύντες αὐτοὶ   30
ὑπὸ τὴν ζεύγλην, εἷλκον τὴν ἄμαξαν, ἐπὶ δὲ τῆς ἀμάξης
ᾠχεῖτο ἡ μήτηρ. σταδίους δὲ πέντε καὶ τετταράκοντα
διακομίσαντες ἀφίκοντο εἰς τὸ ἱερόν· ταῦτα δὲ ποιήσασιν
αὐτοῖς καὶ ὀφθεῖσι ὑπὸ τῆς πανηγύρεως τελευτὴ τοῦ βίου
ἀρίστη ἐπεγένετο· διέδειξέ τε ἐν τούτοις ὁ θεὸς ὡς ἄμεινον εἴη   35
ἀνθρώπῳ τεθνάναι μᾶλλον ἢ ζῆν. Ἀργεῖοι μὲν γὰρ περιστάντες
ἐμακάριζον τῶν νεανιῶν τὴν ῥώμην, αἱ δὲ Ἀργεῖαι τὴν μητέρα
αὐτῶν οἵων τέκνων ἐκύρησε· ἡ δὲ μήτηρ περιχαρὴς οὖσα
τῷ τε ἔργῳ καὶ τῇ φήμῃ, στᾶσα ἀντίον τοῦ ἀγάλματος ηὔχετο
τὴν θεὸν δοῦναι Κλεόβει τε καὶ Βίτωνι ὃ ἀνθρώπῳ τυχεῖν   40
ἄριστόν ἐστι.

Names and places

Ἥρα ή: Hera
Queen of the gods, whose famous sanctuary or Heraion, is situated about 5km south of Mycenae and 8km north of the city of Argos.

God or gods?

It may seem surprising that Herodotus speaks of a single god in line 35, perhaps meaning Apollo or Hera (40). Herodotus was a polytheist, but absorbed a wide range of views on the nature of the gods: he explains to his readers, for example, that the Persian concept of god was not anthropomorphic (1.131). On the Ionian coast, where Herodotus was born, Greek philosophers like Xenophanes of Colophon had long been debating the nature of the gods; the word scepticism comes from a Greek word, σκέψις, meaning *investigation*.

Q. What are the different reactions of the Argive men and women to Cleobis and Biton when they arrive at the temple?

Q. What two things delight their mother?

Q. What prayer does the mother make to the goddess Hera?

Q. How does Herodotus suggest in this passage that the reaction of the crowd is as important as the deed itself?

GCSE vocabulary: ἀγρός, ἄμεινων, ἄριστος (ἀγαθός), γάρ, δεῖ, ἐκ + gen., ἔργον, θεός, ἱερόν, μᾶλλον, μέν . . . δε . . ., μήτηρ, νεανίας, οὐ, πέντε, ὤφθην (ὁράω).

28 ἑορτή ἡ – *festival*; παντῶς (> πᾶς) – *entirely, absolutely*; ζεῦγος τό – *cart, wagon* (pulled by a pair of animals yoked together).

29 κομισθῆναι (aorist passive infinitive of κομίζω) – *to be conveyed*; βοῦς ὁ (< bovis (Latin), bovine) – *ox*.

30 παραγίγνομαι – *appear*; ὥρα ἡ – *hour, suitable time*; ὑποδύντες (participle of ὑποδύνω) – *slipping under*.

31 ζεύγλη ἡ – *yoke-strap*; ἕλκω (imperfect εἷλκον) – *drag, pull*; ἅμαξα ἡ – *cart, waggon*; ἐπί + gen. – *on*.

32 ὀχέομαι – *be conveyed, ride*; μήτηρ ἡ – later named Cydippe by Cicero and Plutarch; στάδιοι (< stadium) – *distance of a stade, stade* (approx. 185 m; 45 stades is just over 8 km); τετταράκοντα (> τέσσαρες) – *forty*.

33 διακομίζω – *convey, carry*; ποιήσασιν dative plural aorist participle.

34 ὀφθεῖσι (ὁράω) aorist passive participle; πανήγυρις -εως ἡ (> πᾶς + ἀγορά) – *festive gathering*; τελευτή ἡ – *end, ending*.

35 ἐπιγίγνομαι (> γίγνομαι) – *occur, happen, be* (18); διέδειξε (aorist of διαδείκνυμι) – *show, demonstrate*; ὡς = ὅτι + opt. (εἴη) – indirect statement.

36 τεθνάναι (perfect infinitive of ἀποθνήσκω) – *to die*; ζῆν (infinitive of ζάω < zoo) – *to live*; περιστάντες (< static) – *standing around*.

37 μακαρίζω – *count as blessed, congratulate*; ῥώμη ἡ (26); Ἀργεῖα αἱ – *women of Argos*, contrasted in the μέν ... δέ ... clauses with the Argive men.

38 οἷος – *the sort of*; τέκνον τό – *child*; κυρέω + gen. – *come upon, have*, (ἐμακάριζον) οἵων τέκνων ἐκύρησε – (*considered her blest*) *for the sort of children she had*; περιχαρής -ές – *overjoyed*.

39 φήμη ἡ (> φημί) – *talk, reputation*; στᾶσα (36) – *standing*; ἀντίον + gen. (< anti) – *opposite, facing, before*; ἄγαλμα -ατος τό – *image, statue*; εὔχομαι + acc. (< eucharist) – *pray to*.

40 δοῦναι (infinitive of δίδωμι) – *to give*; ὅ (ὅς ἥ ὅ) – '*that which*', '*what*'; τυχεῖν aorist infinitive of τυγχάνω (> τύχη) to *chance upon, meet with*. ὃ ἀνθρώπῳ τυχεῖν ἄριστόν ἐστί – lit. *that which it is best for a man to chance upon*, i.e. '*the best fortune a man can meet with*'.

The Argives set up statues of Cleobis and Biton in Delphi. Solon tries to explain his choices to Croesus. 1.31

μετὰ δὲ ταύτην δὲ τὴν εὐχήν, ὡς ἔθυσάν τε καὶ εὐωχήθησαν,
κατακοιμηθέντες ἐν αὐτῷ τῷ ἱερῷ οἱ νεανίαι οὐκέτι ἀνέστησαν,
ἀλλ' ἐν τέλει τούτῳ ἔσχοντο. Ἀργεῖοι δὲ εἰκόνας αὐτῶν ποιησάμενοι
ἀνέθεσαν εἰς Δελφούς, ὡς ἀνδρῶν ἀρίστων γενομένων.'   45

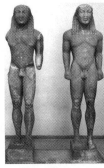

Figure 2 *This pair of statues of youths from c. 570 in the museum at Delphi is generally identified as Cleobis and Biton. A damaged inscription shows the sculptor was from Argos and possibly names Biton. The stylistic representation of the youths' hair and body is characteristic of early sixth-century Archaic Greek art. By setting the funerary monuments up in Delphi, a pan-Hellenic sanctuary, the Argives were displaying their values to the wider Greek world and beyond.*
Photo by PHAS/UIG via Getty Images.

Σόλων μὲν δὴ εὐδαιμονίας δευτερεῖα ἔνεμε τούτοις·
Κροῖσος δὲ σπερχθεὶς εἶπεν, 'ὦ ξένε Ἀθηναῖε, ἡ δὲ ἡμετέρα
εὐδαιμονία οὕτω τοι ἀπέρριπται εἰς τὸ μηδέν, ὥστε οὐδὲ
ἰδιωτῶν ἀνδρῶν ἀξίους ἡμᾶς ἐποίησας;' ὁ δὲ εἶπεν, 'ὦ Κροῖσε,
ἐπιστάμενόν με τὸ θεῖον πᾶν φθονερόν τε καὶ ταραχῶδες ὂν   50
ἐπερωτᾷς ἀνθρωπείων πραγμάτων πέρι. ἐμοὶ δὲ σὺ καὶ πλουτεῖν
μὲν μέγα φαίνει, καὶ βασιλεὺς πολλῶν εἶναι ἀνθρώπων·
εὐδαίμονα δὲ οὔπω σε ἐγὼ λέγω, πρὶν ἂν τελευτήσαντά σε
καλῶς τὸν αἰῶνα πύθωμαι. σκοπεῖν δὲ χρὴ παντὸς χρήματος
τὴν τελευτήν πῇ ἀποβήσεται· πολλοῖς γὰρ δὴ ὑποδείξας ὄλβον   55
ὁ θεὸς προρρίζους ἀνέτρεψε.'

Names and places
Δελφοί οἱ: *Delphi*
Believed to be at the centre of the world; site of the famous oracle of Apollo.

Solon's wisdom
Solon calculates that an average life span of 70 years consists of 26,250 days; on any of these days misfortune can fall.

Q.   Why did the Argives set up statues of these two youths in Delphi?

Q.   What can these statues tell us about Greek values?

GCSE vocabulary: *ἀλλά, ἀνήρ, ἄξιος, ἡμέτερος, θύω, μετά* + acc., *μηδείς, οὕτω, πυνθάνομαι, φαίνομαι (φαίνει = 2nd sg.), χρή* + inf, *ὥστε.*

42   εὐχή ἡ – *prayer* (39); εὐωχήθησαν (aor. pass. of εὐωχέω) – *entertain with a banquet.*

43   κατακοιμηθέντες (aor. participle of κατακοιμάομαι) – *go to sleep* (κοιμάω < cemetery); οὐκέτι – *no longer, not anymore*; ἀνέστησαν (strong aor. of ἀνίστημι) – *rise, get up.*

44   τέλος τό – *the end*; ἔχω - have, hold ἐν τέλει τούτῳ ἔσχοντο – lit. *'they were held in this end',* i.e. *'this was the end they had'*; εἰκών -όνος ὁ (< icon) – *statue, likeness.*

45   ἀνέθεσαν (aorist of ἀνατίθημι) – *set up, dedicated*; εἰς – *'at'*; ὡς – *on the grounds that* (+ genitive absolute).

46   εὐδαιμονία ἡ – *happiness, good fortune*; νέμω – *distribute, award.*

47   σπερχθείς – *hastily, quickly* (from σπέρχω, drive on, urge); ἡμέτερος -α -ον – Croesus refers to himself in the plural.

48   τοι – *indeed*; ἀπέρριπται (perfect pass. of ἀπορρίπτω) – *discarded, flung away*; εἰς τὸ μηδέν – *'as nothing'*; οὕτω ... ὥστε (result); οὐδέ – *not even.*

49   ἰδιώτης ὁ (< idiot) – *private individual, common person*; ἄξιος + gen. *worthy of, of as much value as*; ποιέω – *do, make, consider* i.e. *'that you have not even considered us worth as much as'.*

50   ἐπίσταμαι – *know*; θεῖον τό (> θεός) – *divine power, god*; φθονερός -ά -όν – *envious, spiteful*; ταραχῶδης -ες – *troublesome, unruly*; the main verb is ἐπερωτᾷς (51) – *you ask me ... but I know that ...* (ἐπιστάμενόν με) + indirect statement with the participle ὄν.

51   ἀνθρώπειος -α -ον – *mortal, of man* (contrasting with θεῖον, 50); πρᾶγμα -ατα τό – *matter, affair*; περί + gen. – the noun precedes it here; πλουτέω – *be wealthy.*

52   μέγα – acc. neuter sg. used as an adverb.

53   εὐδαίμων -ον – *happy, fortunate* (46); οὔπω – *not yet*; λέγω – *say, speak of*; οὔπω ... πρὶν ἄν + subjunctive – *not until such time as ...*; τελευτάω – *end, finish, die.*

54   αἰών -ῶνος ὁ – *life*; πύθωμαι aor. subj. of πυνθάνομαι; σκοπέω (< microscope) – *examine, look at*; χρῆμα -ατος τό – *thing, matter, affair.*

55   πῆ – *how*; ἀποβήσομαι (fut. of ἀποβαίνω) – *turn out*; ὑποδείκνυμι – *show, offer a glimpse of*; ὄλβος ὁ – *wealth, blessings, happiness.*

56   προρρίζος -ον (ῥίζα = root) – *'utterly', 'root and branch'*, supply αὐτούς; ἀνατρέπω – *overturn, upturn, upset.* This **gnomic aorist** should be translated as a present tense.

As Solon departs, Croesus considers him to be a fool. Only after Croesus' defeat by Cyrus the Great does he understand Solon's wisdom. 1.33–4 and 1.86

ταῦτα λέγων τῷ Κροίσῳ οὔ πως ἐχαρίζετο ὁ Σόλων· λόγου δὲ
αὐτὸν ποιησάμενος οὐδενὸς ἀποπέμπεται ὁ Κροῖσος, κάρτα
δόξας ἀμαθῆ εἶναι, ὃς τὰ παρόντα ἀγαθὰ μεθεὶς τὴν τελευτὴν
παντὸς χρήματος ὁρᾶν ἐκέλευε.   60

μετὰ δὲ Σόλωνα οἰχόμενον ἔλαβεν ἐκ θεοῦ νέμεσις μεγάλη
Κροῖσον, ὡς εἰκάσαι, ὅτι ἐνόμισεν ἑαυτὸν εἶναι ἀνθρώπων
ἁπάντων ὀλβιώτατον. οἱ γὰρ Πέρσαι τάς τε Σάρδεις εἷλον,
καὶ αὐτὸν Κροῖσον ἐζώγρησαν, ἄρξαντα ἔτη τεσσαρεσκαίδεκα·
λαβόντες δὲ αὐτὸν ἤγαγον παρὰ Κῦρον. ὁ δὲ συννήσας πυρὰν   65
μεγάλην ἀνεβίβασεν ἐπ᾽ αὐτὴν τὸν Κροῖσόν τε ἐν πέδαις
δεδεμένον καὶ δὶς ἑπτὰ Λυδῶν παρ᾽ αὐτὸν παῖδας. τῷ δὲ Κροίσῳ,
ἑστῶτι ἐπὶ τῆς πυρᾶς, εἰσῆλθε, καίπερ ἐν κακῷ ὄντι τοσούτῳ,
τὸ τοῦ Σόλωνος, ὡς εἴη σὺν θεῷ εἰρημένον, τὸ 'μηδένα εἶναι τῶν
ζώντων ὄλβιον.' ἀνενεγκάμενος δὲ καὶ ἀναστενάξας ἐκ πολλῆς   70
ἡσυχίας εἰς τρὶς ὠνόμασε Σόλωνα·

Names and places

Σάρδεις αἱ: *Sardis*

Croesus experienced a sequence of misfortunes after Solon's departure, all foretold by the oracles to which he had sent such lavish gifts. His son was killed by a stranger he had welcomed (1.34–45), and his carefully considered decision to attack Cyrus resulted in the siege and capture of his capital city, Sardis (1.46–55 and 69–85). Croesus himself was taken prisoner by Cyrus.

Κῦρος ὁ: *Cyrus*; **Πέρσαι οἱ:** *the Persians*

Cyrus the Great, king of the Persians. His father was a Persian and his mother a Mede. He overthrew Astyages, king of the Medes, in 550 before going on to defeat the Lydians in 546 and Babylonians in 439. He died *c.* 530 and was buried near Pasargadae, a city he built on the site of his victory over the Medes.

Hubris

Herodotus' guess (62) about why Croesus met with great retribution from the gods implies that Croesus had committed *hubris*, by showing excessive pride. Greek mythology is full of examples of *hubris* followed by divine *nemesis*, like Arachne, who is turned into a spider for boasting that she was the best weaver. In the *Histories*, the Persian king Xerxes, who led the second invasion of Greece in 480, is depicted as *hubristic*: he whips the sea for breaking his bridge of boats over the Hellespont. *Nemesis* follows when he is defeated by the Greeks.

> Q.   Do you think that Croesus is guilty of *hubris*?

GCSE vocabulary: *ἄρχω, ἑαυτόν, εἷλον (αἱρέω), ἔτος, ἤγαγον (ἄγω), καίπερ + partic., κακός, λαμβάνω, τρίς.*

57 οὐ πως – *in no way*; χαρίζομαι + dat. – *please, be agreeable to*; λόγος ὁ – *'account'*

58 ποιέομαι + acc. + gen. – *consider someone worthy of*; ἀποπέμπεται – (middle form) – *'has him sent away'*; κάρτα – *very much*.

59 δοκέω – *think, form an opinion*; ἀμαθής -ές (> μανθάνω) – *ignorant*; τὰ παρόντα ἀγαθά – *'present good fortune'*; μεθείς (aorist participle of μεθίημι) – *having let go, disregarded*; τελευτή ἡ (> τέλος) – *end, conclusion* (17).

60 χρῆμα -ατος τό (54).

61 οἴχομαι – *depart, be gone*; νέμεσις -εως ἡ – *indignation, retribution, nemesis*.

62 ὡς εἰκάσαι (aorist infinitive of εἰκάζω – *guess*) – *'presumably'*; ὅτι – *because*. Herodotus suggests that Croesus pays for being too confident.

63 ἅπας = πᾶς; ὀλβιώτατος -η -ον (5).

64 ζωγρέω – *take prisoner, capture alive*; ἔτη τεττωρεσκαίδεκα (> τέσσαρες + δέκα) – acc. of time: how long.

65 παρά + acc. – *into the presence of* (1); συννήσας (aorist participle of συννέω) – *heap up, build up*; πυρά ἡ – *a pyre, funeral-pyre*.

66 ἀναβιβάζω – *force up onto, make ascend*; πέδη ἡ (> πούς) – *fetter, chain*.

67 δεδεμένος (perfect passive participle of δέω) – *'bound', 'tied'*; δίς – *twice*.

68 ἑστῶτι (dat. sg. perfect participle of ἵστημι) – *'standing'*. The subject is τὸ τοῦ Σόλωνος (69).

69 τὸ τοῦ Σόλωνος – *'advice', 'wisdom' of Solon*; ὡς εἴη – *that it was . . .* (35); σύν + dat. – *with*; σὺν θεῷ – *'with divine inspiration'*; εἰρημένον (perfect passive participle of λέγω) – *spoken*, τό – *'the words'*.

70 ζώντων (present participle of ζάω – *live, be alive*; ἀνενεγκάμενος (aorist participle of ἀναφέρομαι) – *collect oneself*; ἀναστενάξας (from ἀναστενάζω) – *groan, sigh aloud*.

71 ἡσυχία ἡ – *calm, silence* ἐκ πολλῆς ἡσυχίας – *'after a long silence'*; εἰς τρίς – *'three times'*; ὠνόμασε (from ὀνομάζω) – *'call on by name'*.

Cyrus is intrigued by Croesus' words and asks his interpreters to explain. Cyrus, too, begins to understand the wisdom of Solon. 1.86

καὶ ὁ Κῦρος ἀκούσας ἐκέλευσε τοὺς ἑρμηνέας ἐπέρεσθαι
τὸν Κροῖσον τίνα ἐπικαλοῖτο· καὶ οἱ δὲ προσελθόντες ἐπηρώτων.
Κροῖσος δὲ τέως μὲν σιγὴν εἶχεν ἐρωτώμενος· μετὰ δὲ ἔλεγεν
ὡς ἔλθοι ποτὲ ὁ Σόλων, ὢν Ἀθηναῖος, καὶ θεασάμενος πάντα   75
τὸν ἑαυτοῦ ὄλβον ἀποφλαυρίσειε· καὶ πάντα ἑαυτῷ ἀποβεβήκοι
ᾗπερ ἐκεῖνος εἶπεν, οὐδέν τι μᾶλλον εἰς ἑαυτὸν λέγων ἢ
εἰς ἅπαν τὸ ἀνθρώπινον καὶ μάλιστα τοὺς παρ' ἑαυτοῖς ὀλβίους
δοκοῦντας εἶναι. ὁ μὲν Κροῖσος ταῦτα ἀφηγεῖτο, τῆς δὲ πυρᾶς
ἤδη ἡμμένης ἐκαίετο τὰ περιέσχατα. καὶ ὁ Κῦρος, ἀκούσας παρὰ   80
τῶν ἑρμηνέων ἃ Κροῖσος εἶπε, μεταγνούς τε καὶ ἐννοήσας ὅτι
καὶ αὐτὸς ἄνθρωπος ὢν ἄλλον ἄνθρωπον, γενόμενον ἑαυτοῦ
εὐδαιμονίᾳ οὐκ ἐλάττω, ζῶντα πυρὶ διδοίη, ἐκέλευε σβεννύναι
τὴν ταχίστην τὸ καιόμενον πῦρ, καὶ καταβιβάζειν Κροῖσόν τε
καὶ τοὺς μετὰ Κροίσου. καὶ οἱ δὲ πειρώμενοι οὐκ ἐδύναντο ἔτι   85
τοῦ πυρὸς ἐπικρατῆσαι.

Figure 3 *Croesus is shown sitting alone on the pyre as it is lit. This detail is from a red-figure amphora in the Louvre that dates from about 490, long before Herodotus wrote his* Histories. *It is unusual in depicting a historical scene rather than a mythological one. A poet called Bacchylides, commemorating a victory in 468 (Ode 3), also tells the story of Croesus on the pyre. In his version, Croesus builds the pyre for himself, his wife and daughters, but Zeus puts the fire out and Apollo whisks the family away to the Hyperboreans ('beyond the north wind') as a reward for Croesus' piety.*
Photo by Hulton Archive/Getty Images.

Q.   Why did Cyrus order the pyre to be extinguished as quickly as possible?

Q.   How does the image above differ from Herodotus' account?

Q.   How does Herodotus bring out the drama in this passage (see also 87–91)?

GCSE vocabulary: *ἀκούω, ἄλλος, εἶπον (λέγω), εἶχον (imperfect of ἔχω), ἔτι, ἦλθον (ἔρχομαι), ἤνεγκα (aorist of φέρω), ἠρόμην (aorist of ἐρωτάω), καίω, καλέω, κελεύω, μᾶλλον, μάλιστα, πειράομαι, πῦρ, σιγή, τάχιστος, τίς.*

72   ἑρμηνεύς ὁ – *interpreter*; ἐπερέσθαι (ἐπερωτάω, ἐπηρόμην) – *ask, question* (9).

73   ἐπικαλοῖτο from ἐπικαλέω (> καλέω) – *call upon, invoke*, present middle optative in an indirect question; ἐπηρώτων (72).

74   τέως – *for a time*; σιγὴν ἔχω – *keep silent*; μετὰ δέ - *afterwards* (3).

75   ὡς + optative – '*that he had come*', indirect statement with ὡς instead of ὅτι (35); ποτε – *once*; θεασάμενος from θεάομαι (6).

76   ὄλβος ὁ – *wealth, riches*; ἀποφλαυρίσειε optative, still in indirect speech, of ἀποφλαυρίζω – *belittle, dismiss as trivial*; ἀποβεβήκοι perfect optative of ἀποβαίνω – *turn out*.

77   ἤπερ – *as, in the way that*; ἐκεῖνος – *that man*, i.e. Solon; οὐδέν τι μᾶλλον εἰς ἑαυτὸν λέγων – '*speaking no more of himself* (i.e. Croesus) *than any mortal*' (i.e. a universal truth, applicable not just to Croesus).

78   εἰς ἅπαν – '*to each person*' (63); ἀνθρώπινος -η -ον (> ἄνθρωπος) – *mortal, human*; παρ' ἑαυτοῖς – *to themselves, 'in their own eyes'*; ὄλβιος (5).

79   δοκοῦντας (δοκέω) – *thinking, seeming* (23); ἀφηγέομαι – *explain, relate*.

80   ἡμμένης perfect middle participle of ἅπτω – *set alight*; τὰ περιέσχατα (> περί + ἔχω) – *the outer edges*; παρά + gen. – *from*.

81   ἑρμηνεύς (72); μεταγνούς aorist participle of μεταγιγνώσκω – *have a change of heart, mind*; ἐννοέω – *realise* introducing the indirect statement ὅτι... διδοίη (83).

82   γενόμενον (> γίγνομαι) – '*was*'.

83   εὐδαιμονία ἡ – *happiness*; οὐκ ἐλάττω acc. sg. masc. – *no less*, i.e. '*his equal*'; ζῶντα from ζάω – *be alive*; διδοίη optative from δίδωμι – *give, offer up*; σβεννύναι present active infinitive of σβέννυμι (< asbestos) – *quench, extinguish*.

84   τὴν ταχίστην – *as quickly as possible*; καταβιβάζειν opposite of ἀναβιβάζω (66) – *make descend, get down*.

85   τοὺς μετὰ Κροίσου – *those with Croesus* (fourteen Lydian youths); ἐδύναντο imperf. of δύναμαι (< dynamic) – *be able*; οὐκ ... ἔτι – *no longer, not ... any longer*.

86   ἐπικρατῆσαι aorist infinitive of ἐπικρατέω + gen. – *master, control*.

Apollo intervenes, ending the story of Croesus and Solon. 1.87

ἐνταῦθα Κροῖσος, μαθὼν τὴν Κύρου μετάγνωσιν, ἐπεβοήσατο
τὸν Ἀπόλλωνα ἐπικαλούμενος παραστῆναι καὶ ῥύσασθαι
αὐτὸν ἐκ τοῦ παρόντος κακοῦ. ὁ μὲν δακρύων ἐπεκαλεῖτο
τὸν θεόν· ἐκ δὲ αἰθρίας τε καὶ νηνεμίας συνέδραμεν ἐξαίφνης   90
νέφη, καὶ χειμών τε κατερράγη καὶ ὗσεν ὕδατι λαβροτάτῳ,
κατεσβέσθη τε ἡ πυρά.

Q.   How was the pyre eventually extinguished (lines 87–92)?

Q.   In the unadapted version Herodotus writes, '*The Lydians say that* . . .', before
      he describes Apollo's intervention. What difference does this make?

How Alcmaeon was enriched by Croesus

The story of how Alcmaeon was enriched by Croesus. 6.125

οἱ Ἀλκμαιωνίδαι ἦσαν μὲν καὶ πάλαι λαμπροὶ ἐν ταῖς Ἀθήναις,
ἀπὸ δὲ Ἀλκμαίωνος καὶ αὖθις Μεγακλέους ἐγένοντο καὶ κάρτα
λαμπροί. ὁ γὰρ Ἀλκμαίων συμπράκτωρ ἐγίγνετο τοῖς ἐκ Σάρδεων   95
Λυδοῖς παρὰ Κροίσου ἀφικνουμένοις καὶ συνελάμβανε προθύμως·
καὶ Κροῖσος πυθόμενος ταῦτα μεταπέμπεται αὐτὸν εἰς Σάρδεις.
ἀφικόμενον δὲ δωρεῖται χρυσῷ τοσούτῳ ὅσον ἂν δύνηται
τῷ ἑαυτοῦ σώματι ἐξενεγκέσθαι εἰσάπαξ.

Names and places
Ἀπόλλων ὁ: *Apollo,* the god of prophecy.

Ἀλκμαιωνίδαι οἱ: *the Alcmaeonids*
This powerful Athenian family fell under the 'Curse of Cylon' when Alcmaeon's father, opposing Cylon's attempt to become tyrant of Athens, caused the deaths of some of Cylon's men who had sought protection at an altar. The Alcmaeonids offer another example of how easily human fortune can change.

Ἀλκμαίων ὁ: *Alcmaeon;* **Μεγακλῆς ὁ:** *Megacles*
Megacles was Alcmaeon's son. He married Agariste, daughter of the tyrant of Sicyon, Cleisthenes. Like his grandfather (also called Megacles), he opposed an attempt at tyranny by Peisistratus and eventually fell victim to his political enemies.

Λυδοί οἱ: *the Lydians*

GCSE vocabulary: *αὖθις, βοάω, δακρύω, ἔδραμον (τρέχω), ἐξήνεγκα (ἐκφέρω), μανθάνω, πέμπω, πυνθάνομαι, σιγή, ὕδωρ, χειμών, χρυσός.*

87 ἐνταῦθα – *then*; μετάγνωσις -εως ἡ – *change of heart, mind* (81) μετα- as a prefix can mean 'change' – e.g. metamorphosis; ἐπεβοήσατο aorist of ἐπιβοάομαι (> βοή) – *shout out to*.

88 ἐπικαλέω – *call upon* (73); παραστῆναι aorist infinitive from παρίστημι – *stand beside*; ῥύσασθαι from ῥύομαι – *rescue, deliver*.

89 πάρειμι – *be present*.

90 αἰθρία ἡ (< aether) – *clear sky*; νηνεμία ἡ – *calm*; συντρέχω (> τρέχω) – *run together, gather*; ἐξαίφνης – *suddenly*.

91 νέφος τό – *cloud*; κατερράγη aorist passive of καταρρήγνυμι – '*broke out*'; ὗσεν from ὕω – *rain*; λάβρος -α -ον – *furious, violent*.

92 κατεσβέσθη aorist passive of κατασβέννυμι – *put out, extinguish* (83).

93 λαμπρός -ά -όν (< lamp) – *bright, illustrious, famous* (17); καὶ πάλαι – *also in the past*.

94 ἀπό + gen. – *from the time of*; καὶ αὖθις Μεγακλέους – '*and later from the time of Megacles*'; καὶ κάρτα – *especially*.

95 συμπράκτωρ (> πράσσω) – *helper, supporter*.

96 παρά + gen. – *from*; συλλαμβάνω – *receive*; προθύμως – *willingly, enthusiastically*.

97 μεταπέμπομαι (> πέμπω) – *send for, summon*.

98 δωρέομαι (+ dat.) (> δῶρον) – *make a gift of, present with*; τοσούτῳ ... ὅσον ἂν δύνηται subjunctive of δύναμαι + inf. (85) – *be able to* – '*as much as he could ...*'.

99 τῷ ἑαυτοῦ σώματι – '*on his own body*'; ἐξενεγκέσθαι (> φέρω) – *to carry off*; εἰσάπαξ – *in one go, at one time*.

Alcmaeon's quick response. 6.125

ὁ δὲ Ἀλκμαίων ἐνδὺς χιτῶνα μέγαν καὶ κόλπον βαθὺν 　　100
καταλιπόμενος τοῦ χιτῶνος, καὶ κοθόρνους οὓς ηὕρισκεν
εὐρυτάτους ὄντας ὑποδησάμενος, ἤει εἰς τὸν θησαυρόν.

εἰσπεσὼν δὲ εἰς σωρὸν ψήγματος πρῶτον μὲν παρέσαξε
παρὰ τὰς κνήμας ὅσον τοῦ χρυσοῦ ἐχώρουν οἱ κόθορνοι,
μετὰ δὲ, τὸν κόλπον πάντα πλησάμενος τοῦ χρυσοῦ καὶ εἰς 　　105
τὰς τρίχας τῆς κεφαλῆς διαπάσας τοῦ ψήγματος, καὶ ἄλλο
λαβὼν εἰς τὸ στόμα, ἐξήει ἐκ τοῦ θησαυροῦ ἕλκων μὲν μόγις
τοὺς κοθόρνους, παντὶ δέ τινι εἰκὼς μᾶλλον ἢ ἀνθρώπῳ· τό
τε γὰρ στόμα ἐβέβυστο καὶ πάντα ἐξώγκωτο. ἰδόντα δὲ
τὸν Κροῖσον γέλως εἰσῆλθε, καὶ αὐτῷ πάντα τε ἐκεῖνα 　　110
δίδωσι, καὶ προσέτι ἕτερα οὐκ ἐλάττω ἐκείνων.

An Olympic victory

The story of Alcmaeon ends with the following words from Herodotus: '*In this way his house became extremely rich and Alcamaeon kept a four-horse chariot team and won an Olympic victory*' (*Histories* 6.125).

A record of Olympic victors with their dates was preserved. Alcmaeon's Olympic victory is generally dated to 592 and cited as evidence that the encounter with Croesus was chronologically impossible.

Q. Draw two sketches of Alcmaeon, before and after he went into the treasure store, labelling it in Greek.

Q. How much does it matter that the earlier sections of Herodotus' *Histories* are chronologically vague?

GCSE vocabulary: γελάω, ἔπεσον (πίπτω), ἐκ + gen. ἐκεῖνος, εὑρίσκω, εὐρύς, ἤει (εἶμι), ἰδών (*aor. partic.* ὁράω), κεφαλή, οἰκία, οὕς (ὅς ἥ ὅ), πρῶτον.

100 ἐνδύς aor. participle from ἐνδύω – *put on*; χιτών -ῶνος ὁ – *tunic*; κόλπος ὁ – *fold*;
βαθύς – *deep, large*.

101 καταλείπω – *leave*; τοῦ χιτῶνος – '*in the tunic*'; κοθόρνος ὁ – *boot, buskin*
(calf or knee length boots).

102 ὑποδέομαι – *put on* (a shoe); ᾔει imperf. of εἶμι – *went*; θησαυρός ὁ (4); κοθόρνους
οὓς ηὕρισκεν εὐρυτάτους ὄντας – '*the widest boots he could find*'.

103 σωρός ὁ – *heap, pile*; ψῆγμα -ατος τό – *dust, gold-dust*; παρέσαξε aorist of
παρασάττω – *stuffed in.*

104 παρά + acc. *alongside, 'down'*; κνήμη ἡ – *shin, lower leg*; ὅσον – *as much as*
(98); χωρέω – *go, 'hold'*; τοῦ χρυσοῦ and ψήγματος (103) are partitive genitives: '*as much
(of) gold...; (some) of the gold-dust*'.

105 μετὰ δέ – adverbial (3, 74), pointing towards the main verb in ἐξήει (107); κόλπος ὁ (100);
πλησάμενος aorist middle participle of πίμπλημι + acc. + gen. – *fill x with y.*

106 τριχαί αἱ – *hair*; διαπάσας aorist participle of διαπάττω + gen. – *having sprinkled . . .
with*; ἄλλο (ἄλλος -η -ο) – '*more*'.

107 στόμα -ατος τό – *mouth*; ἐξήει (102); ἕλκω – *pull, drag*; μόγις – *with difficulty.*

108 κοθόρνος ὁ (101); εἰκώς -υῖα -ός (+ dat.) – *like, resembling*; παντὶ δέ τινι . . .
μᾶλλον ἤ – '*anything rather than', 'anything other than*'.

109 στόμα -ατος τό (107); ἐβέβυστο pluperfect passive of βύω – '*had been stuffed*',
'*crammed*'; ἐξώγκωτο pluperfect passive of ἐξογκόω – '*had become swollen*'.

110 γέλως -ωτος ὁ (> γελάω) – *laughter.*

111 δίδωσι the verb is suddenly a vivid present tense, lit: '*and he gives*'; προσέτι – *in
addition*; ἕτερος -α -ον – *other 'more'* (106); ἐλάττω = ἐλάττονα (n. pl.)
(> ὀλίγος) – *less.* ἕτερα οὐκ ἐλάττω ἐκείνων – *other things no less than those* i.e. '*the same
amount again*'.

What happens next?

After Croesus was spared, he won the trust and admiration of Cyrus by offering him wise advice: while Cyrus' troops were sacking and plundering Sardis, for example, Croesus pointed out to the king that it was now Cyrus' own property that was being pillaged. Croesus outlived Cyrus, who died in war. In Herodotus' account, Cyrus, shortly before his death, entrusted Croesus to his son, Cambyses, the next Persian king. Croesus won Cambyses' affections with a piece of well-timed flattery: when asked whether Cyrus or Cambyses was the greater king Croesus risked Cambyses' wrath by replying that Cyrus was – because Cambyses had not yet produced a son like that of Cyrus (*Histories* 3.34).

As for Alcmaeon, his family (the 'Alcmaeonids') became one of the most powerful in Athens. Herodotus says of them at one point, '*there were no men better thought of and more honoured in Athens*' (*Histories* 6.124). Alcmaeon's grandson, Cleisthenes, introduced important democratic reforms in 508/507, two years after the expulsion of the tyrant Hippias, son of Peisistratus. The wealth of the Alcmaeonids, supported by contributions from Croesus and Amasis of Egypt, was also used to rebuild the temple at Delphi after it was burned down in 548 at a cost of 300 talents. It was completed in 505 and withstood the Persian invasion (*Histories* 8.36–9). The name of the Alcmaeonids continued to suggest wealth and influence but the family lost power after the Persian wars, when they were accused of colluding with the Persians in 490. These allegations are hotly disputed by Herodotus (*Histories* 6.121). Both Pericles and Alcibiades were descendants of Alcmaeon's family.

Final questions

- Which scenes from this selection stand out most vividly in your mind and why?
- How well characterized are the figures of Croesus, Solon, Cyrus and Alcmaeon in these tales?
- What general principles do the stories of Croesus and Alcmaeon illustrate?
- What do you think Herodotus' use of direct speech adds or detracts from the effectiveness of his writing?
- Do you think these accounts are better described as 'tales' or as 'history'? Can they be both?

HISTORIES, 3.17–25, 38

The Ethiopians; The power of custom

2020–2021 Prescription

See pages 83–4 for an introduction to Herodotus.

*This selection corresponds as follows to **Tales from Herodotus**, ed. Farnell and Goff:*

Pages 104 to 117: Section XVb: **The Ethiopians**   (*Histories 3.17–25*)
Pages 118 to 119: Section XX: **The power of custom**   (*Histories 3.38*)

The story so far . . .

The stories in this selection are set in the reigns of two Persian kings, **Cambyses** (530–521) and **Darius** (522–486), who is best known for the attack on Greece in 490 that led to the battle of Marathon and an unexpected victory for Athens. Both kings extended the Persian empire and, in the course of their campaigns, came into contact with unfamiliar cultures on the edges of the known world. Herodotus shows as much interest in these cultures as he does in the military campaigns themselves, often implying that the boundaries between 'civilization' and 'barbarism' are less clear than one might think.

Cambyses became king of Persia on the death of his father Cyrus the Great in 530. He conducted a successful military campaign against Egypt, making it part of the Persian empire, but his military ambitions extended further into Africa. Herodotus writes that after conquering Egypt, Cambyses started to plan three new campaigns against the Carthaginians, the Ammonians and the Ethiopians. The account you will read describes his first contact with the **Ethiopians**. The ancient name refers to people living south of Egypt, a wider area than modern Ethiopia. In Homer's *Iliad* and *Odyssey*, the Olympian gods travel a long distance to feast with the Ethiopians, and in Herodotus' work, too, they retain a semi-mythical quality.

Darius succeeded Cambyses, but it was not a dynastic succession. It seems likely that Darius was keen to establish his authority by blackening the reputation of his predecessor. The picture we have of Cambyses is of a madman who tramples on the customs of other people. For example, Herodotus expresses his outrage at Cambyses' treatment of the dead Egyptian king Amasis, whose body he removed from its tomb and had whipped, plucked and burned; Herodotus explains that cremation of a corpse, the usual practice in Greece, was a sacrilegious offence against both Persian and Egyptian customs.

The picture of Darius's reign is very different, partly because he promoted a powerful and positive image of himself through strong administration, building works and inscriptions. The best known of these is the Behistun inscription in Iran, a record of his accession and achievements written in three languages. Darius' campaigns reached east and west, and he encountered different peoples whose customs were completely opposed. In the last anecdote, we learn how Darius compared the customs of the people he encountered in his campaigns, the Indian tribes to the east and the Greeks to the west.

The Ethiopians

Cambyses, king of Persia, sends men to spy on the Ethiopians and, in particular, to find out about the mysterious Table of the Sun. Herodotus *Histories* 3.17–18

Nominative *words or phrases are in* light blue, **verbs** *in* dark blue.

ἐβουλεύσατό ποτε ὁ Καμβύσης στρατείαν ἐπὶ τοὺς
μακροβίους Αἰθίοπας οἰκουμένους Λιβύης ἐπὶ τῇ νοτίᾳ
θαλάττῃ. ἔδοξε δὲ αὐτῷ πρῶτον κατόπτας ἀποστέλλειν,
ὀψομένους τε τὴν ἐν τούτοις τοῖς Αἰθίοψι λεγομένην εἶναι
ἡλίου τράπεζαν εἰ ἔστιν ἀληθῶς, καὶ πρὸς ταύτῃ τὰ ἄλλα   5
κατοψομένους, δῶρα δὲ τῷ λόγῳ φέροντας τῷ βασιλεῖ
αὐτῶν.

ἡ δὲ τράπεζα τοῦ ἡλίου τοιάδε τις λέγεται εἶναι. λειμών ἐστιν
ἐν τῷ προαστείῳ ἐπίπλεως κρεῶν ἑφθῶν πάντων τῶν
τετραπόδων, εἰς ὅν τὰς μὲν νύκτας τιθέασι τὰ κρέα οἱ ἐν   10
τέλει ὄντες, τὰς δὲ ἡμέρας δαίνυται προσιὼν ὁ βουλόμενος.
οἱ δὲ ἐπιχώριοί φασι ταῦτα τὴν γῆν αὐτὴν ἀναδιδόναι
ἑκάστοτε. ἡ μὲν δὴ τράπεζα τοῦ ἡλίου καλουμένη λέγεται
εἶναι τοιάδε.

Names and places
Καμβύσης ὁ: *Cambyses*
King of Persia from 530 – 521.

Αἰθίοπες οἱ (sg. Αἰθίοψ ὁ): *Ethiopians*; **Λιβύη ἡ:** *Libya, Africa*
The people living south of Egypt, a wider area than modern Ethiopia.
The Greek name for the continent of Africa is Libya.

Spies
Since Cambyses was thinking of embarking on an extended campaign into unknown territory, scouting out the land ahead was sensible; these spies seem as interested as Herodotus in learning about curious local customs.

Q.   How is an impression of deception established in paragraph 1?

Q.   What do you think the truth behind the Table of the Sun is and why do you think Cambyses was so curious about it?

GCSE vocabulary: αὐτός, βασιλεύς, βούλομαι, δοκεῖ (μοι), δῶρον, ἡμέρα, θάλασσα, καλέω, λόγος, λέγω, νύξ, ὄψομαι (ὁράω), οὗτος, πρῶτον, στρατιά.

1   βουλεύομαι (> βουλή) – *plan*; ποτε – *once, at one time*; στρατεία ἡ (> στρατιά) –
    expedition; ἐπί + acc. – *against*.

2   μακρόβιος -ον (> βίος) – *long-lived*; οἰκημένος -η -ον (> οἰκία, perfect participle of
    οἰκέομαι) – *settled, dwelling*; ἐπί + dat. – *on, at*; νότιος -α -ον – *southern*, i.e. the
    African coast of the Indian ocean, modern Somalia.

3   θάλαττα ἡ (= θάλασσα) – the Arabian Sea and Indian Ocean; ἔδοξε δὲ αὐτῷ – *'he
    decided'*; κατόπτης -ου ὁ – *spy*; ἀποστέλλω – *dispatch, send off*.

4   ὀψόμενος – future participle of ὁράω expressing purpose – *'to see if'* (εἰ, 5); τε – *both* . . .
    (καί follows in line 5), key to the structure of the sentence: the spies are sent with **two** sets of
    instructions; τὴν ... λεγομένην – keep this phrase together: *'what, amongst these
    Ethiopians, is said . . .'*.

5   ἥλιος ὁ (> helium) – *sun*; τράπεζα ἡ – *table*; ἀληθῶς (> ἀληθής) (adv.), i.e. *if it truly
    exists* (ἐστιν); πρὸς ταύτη – *in addition to this* (i.e. table).

6   κατοψόμενος (> κατόπτης), future participle of καθοράω – *spy*; τῷ λόγῳ – *'as a pretext'*,
    'in theory'.

8   τοιόσδε τοιάδε τοιόνδε – *of this sort* (the – δε suffix indicates something you can point
    to, or point ahead to); τοιάδε τις – *'something like this'*; λειμών -ῶνος ὁ – *meadow*.

9   προάστειον τό – *suburbs, outskirts*; ἐπίπλεως -ων + gen. – *full of*; κρέα τά –
    meat; ἐφθός -ή -όν – *boiled*.

10 τετράπουν -ποδος τό – *four-footed animal*; ὅν (ὅς ἥ ὁ); τὰς νύκτας – *'at night'*;
    τιθέασι 3rd pl. present of τίθημι – *put, place*; οἱ goes with ὄντες, bracketing the words in
    between.

11 οἱ ἐν τέλει ὄντες – *those in authority* (τέλος τό – end, ultimate power); δαίνυμαι –
    feast, dine; προσιών participle of πρόσειμι – *go forward*; ὁ βουλόμενος (from
    βούλομαι) – *the one wanting*, i.e. *'anyone who wants'*.

12 ἐπιχώριοι οἱ (> χώρα) – *locals*; φασί (φημί), expect an indirect statement with an infinitive
    (and accusative); ταῦτα – accusative after ἀναδιδόναι; ἀναδιδόναι the present infinitive of
    ἀναδίδωμι – *give up, offer up*.

13 ἑκάστοτε (> ἕκαστος + τότε) – *on each occasion, each time*; καλούμενος -η -ον
    from καλέω, see λεγομένην (4) – *'so-called'*.

14 The virtual repetition of the phrase from line 8, bringing this section of the work to a clear
    conclusion, is known as 'ring-composition'; the Table of the Sun is mentioned again in lines 84–5.

*As well as the spies, Cambyses sends for interpreters whom he dispatches to the
Ethiopian king with gifts and instructions of what to say. 3.19–20*

Καμβύσῃ δὲ ὡς ἔδοξε πέμπειν τοὺς κατασκόπους, αὐτίκα   15
μετεπέμπετο ἐξ Ἐλεφαντίνης πόλεως τῶν Ἰχθυοφάγων
ἀνδρῶν τινας ἐπισταμένους τὴν Αἰθιοπίδα γλῶτταν.
ἐπεὶ δὲ ἀφίκοντο, ἔπεμπεν αὐτοὺς εἰς τοὺς Αἰθίοπας,
ἐντειλάμενος ἃ λέγειν χρῆν, δῶρα φέροντας πορφυροῦν τε
εἷμα καὶ χρυσοῦν στρεπτὸν περιαυχένιον καὶ ψέλια καὶ   20
μύρου ἀλάβαστρον καὶ φοινικείου οἴνου κάδον.

The Ethiopians have a special way of selecting their king.

οἱ δὲ Αἰθίοπες οὗτοι λέγονται εἶναι μέγιστοι καὶ κάλλιστοι
ἀνθρώπων πάντων. νόμοις δὲ καὶ ἄλλοις χρῶνται
κεχωρισμένοις τῶν ἄλλων ἀνθρώπων καὶ δὴ καὶ κατὰ τὴν
βασιλείαν τοιῷδε· ὃν ἂν τῶν ἀστῶν κρίνωσι μέγιστόν τε εἶναι   25
καὶ κατὰ τὸ μέγεθος ἔχειν τὴν ἰσχύν, τοῦτον ἀξιοῦσι
βασιλεύειν.

Names and places
Ἐλεφαντίνη ἡ: *Elephantine*
This city is about 1,200 km up the river Nile at the First Cataract (now Aswan). Herodotus tells us that
this is as far south as he got in his travels (*Histories* 2.29).

Ἰχθυοφάγοι οἱ: *Fish-eaters* (> ἰχθύς – fish + ἔφαγον), *Ichthyophagi*
These coastal inhabitants of the Red Sea might have traded with their southern neighbours.

Gifts
Giving and receiving gifts play an important part in the Homeric poems and in Greek culture. In particular
it is a way of establishing and demonstrating friendship – either φιλία or ξενία. Gifts were also important
in Persian culture, often as rewards for loyalty from the king.

Q.   How well thought-through are Cambyses' preparations?

Q.   Why does Cambyses send gifts?

Q.   Discuss the advantages and disadvantages of the Ethiopians' method of
     selecting a king?

GCSE vocabulary: ἀνήρ, ἄνθρωπος, γλῶσσα, ἔχω, εἶναι (εἰμί), κάλλιστος, λέγω, μέγιστος,
νόμος, οἶνος, οὗτος, πᾶς, πέμπω, πόλις, τις, χράομαι + dat.

15   δέ . . . this answers the μέν of line 13 and takes us back to the structure established in the first
      paragraph (3); ὡς + indicative – *when*; κατάσκοπος ὁ (> σκοπεω – *see, investigate*
      < periscope) – *spy, scout* (3); αὐτίκα – *straightaway, immediately*.

16   μεταπέμπομαι + acc. – *send for*.

17   ἐπίσταμαι (< epistemology) – *know*; γλῶττα ἡ = γλῶσσα (< glossary, polyglot).

18   ἔπεμπεν – '*sent*', Herodotus uses the imperfect tense rather than an aorist as the action is not
      yet complete (see also 29, 75, 96).

19   ἐντειλάμενος -η -ον aorist participle of ἐντέλλομαι – *give instructions, command*; ἅ
      (ὅς ἥ ὅ); χρῆν = ἐχρῆν from χρή + inf.; δῶρα – '*as gifts*' in apposition to the list that follows;
      πορφυροῦς -ᾶ -οῦν (= -έος) – *purple*; τε – *both* (4).

20   εἷμα -ατος τό – *robe, clothing*; χρυσοῦς -ῆ -οῦν (> χρυσός) – *golden, of gold*;
      στρεπτός -ή -όν – *twisted*; περιαυχένιον τό (> περί + αὐχήν – *neck*) – *necklace,
      torque*; ψέλιον τό – *bracelet*.

21   μύρον τό (< myrrh) – *perfume*; ἀλάβαστρος ὁ (< alabaster) – *perfume bottle, flask*;
      φοινίκειος -α -ον (< Phoenician) – *from a palm-tree, palm*; κάδος ὁ – *casket*.

22   λέγονται + inf. – '*are said to*', Herodotus often reports stories or opinions without
      commenting on their reliability himself, leaving his readers to judge; μέγιστος -η -ον (μέγας)
      – '*the tallest*'.

23   καὶ ἄλλοις . . . καὶ δὴ καί – Greek says, '*other things and especially x*' whereas in English
      we write '*x and other things*': '*they employ other customs . . . including this one,*' or
      '*amongst other customs, they also use . . .*'.

24   κεχωρισμένος -η -ον perfect passive participle of χωρίζω + gen. – '*different from*'; καὶ
      δὴ καί – *moreover, 'including'* (23); κατά + acc. – *concerning, in respect of*.

25   βασιλεία ἡ – *royal power*; τοιόσδε – *of this kind*, dative after χρῶνται (23); ὃν ἄν
      – *whomever, whichever man*; ἀστός ὁ – *citizen*; κρίνω – *judge*, subjunctive in an
      indefinite clause after ἄν); τε (19).

26   κατά + acc. – '*to match*'; μέγεθος -ους τό (> μεγας) – *size*; ἰσχύς -υος ἡ (> ἰσχυρός)
      – *strength*; τοῦτον (picks up ὃν ἄν, 25); ἀξιόω – *think worthy*.

27   βασιλεύω (> βασιλεύς) – *be king, rule*.

Cambyses' interpreters deliver his message and receive the Ethiopian king's reply.
3.21

εἰς τούτους δὴ οὖν τοὺς ἄνδρας ὡς ἀφίκοντο οἱ Ἰχθυοφάγοι,
διδόντες τὰ δῶρα τῷ βασιλεῖ αὐτῶν ἔλεγον τάδε, 'βασιλεὺς
ὁ Περσῶν Καμβύσης βουλόμενος φίλος καὶ ξένος   30
σοι γενέσθαι ἡμᾶς τε ἀπέπεμψεν, εἰς λόγους ἐλθεῖν
κελεύων, καὶ δῶρα ταῦτά σοι δίδωσι, οἷς καὶ αὐτὸς μάλιστα
ἥδεται χρώμενος.'

ὁ δὲ Αἰθίοψ μαθὼν ὅτι κατόπται ἥκοιεν λέγει πρὸς αὐτοὺς
τοιάδε, 'οὔτε ὁ Περσῶν βασιλεὺς δῶρα ὑμᾶς ἔπεμψε   35
φέροντας βουλόμενος ἐμοὶ ξένος γενέσθαι, οὔτε ὑμεῖς
λέγετε ἀληθῆ (ἥκετε γὰρ κατόπται τῆς ἐμῆς ἀρχῆς),
οὔτε ἐκεῖνος ἀνήρ ἐστι δίκαιος· εἰ γὰρ ἦν δίκαιος, οὔτ' ἂν
ἐπεθύμησε χώρας ἄλλης ἢ τῆς ἑαυτοῦ, οὔτ' ἂν εἰς
δουλοσύνην ἀνθρώπους ἦγεν ὑφ' ὧν οὐδὲν ἠδίκηται.   40

νῦν δὲ αὐτῷ τόξον τόδε διδόντες τάδε ἔπη λέγετε,
'βασιλεὺς ὁ Αἰθιόπων συμβουλεύει τῷ Περσῶν βασιλεῖ τότε
ἐπ' Αἰθίοπας τοὺς μακροβίους στρατεύεσθαι ἐπὴν οὕτως
εὐπετῶς Πέρσαι ἕλκωσι τὰ τόξα ὄντα μεγέθει τοσαῦτα·
μέχρι δὲ τούτου θεοῖς εἰδέναι χάριν, οἳ οὐκ ἐπὶ νοῦν   45
τρέπουσιν Αἰθίοψι γῆν ἄλλην προσκτᾶσθαι τῇ ἑαυτῶν.'
ταῦτα δὲ εἰπὼν καὶ ἀνεὶς τὸ τόξον παρέδωκε τοῖς ἥκουσι.

Names and places
Πέρσαι οἱ (sg. Πέρσης -ου ὁ): *the Persians*
The Persians rose quickly to power under Cyrus the Great and his successors.

Ethiopian warriors
Ethiopians joined Xerxes' invasion of Greece in 480. Herodotus describes their equipment: they wore the
skins of leopards or lions and were armed with clubs, spears tipped with antelope horn, and bows six foot
long which shot small, stone-tipped arrows. Before battle they would paint their bodies white and red
with chalk and vermillion. *Histories* 7.69

> **GCSE vocabulary:** *ἄγω, ἀδικέω, ἀληθής, ἄλλος, ἀρχή, ἀφικνέομαι, γίγνομαι, δή, δίδωμι,*
> *δίκαιος, ἑαυτόν, ἐκεῖνος, ἐλθεῖν (ἔρχομαι), ἐπί + acc., ἡμεῖς, κελεύω, μάλιστα, μανθάνω,*
> *ξένος, ὅδε, οὖν, οὔτε . . . οὔτε, πέμπω, ὑμεῖς, φέρω, φίλος.*

28   τούτους τοὺς ἄνδρας (i.e. the Ethiopians).

29   διδόντες present participle of δίδωμι; ἔλεγον (18); τάδε from ὅδε ἥδε τόδε; speeches are usually introduced with this or the vaguer τοιάδε (35).

31   ἀποπέμπω – send off, send; εἰς λόγους ἐλθεῖν – 'enter into talks'.

32   δίδωσι (3rd sg. present of δίδωμι); οἷς (ὅς ἥ ὅ, dat. after χράομαι).

33   ἥδομαι (> ἡδύς -εῖα -ύ < hedonist) + participle – enjoy, take pleasure in.

34   ὅτι + optative (indirect statement); κατόπται – 'as spies' (3); ἥκω – have come; λέγω πρός – speak to, address (λέγω is usually with the dative).

37   κατόπται (34); ἀρχή ἡ – empire, kingdom, realm.

38   εἰ γὰρ ἦν δίκαιος, ἦν may be translated either 'if he were' or 'if he had been', depending on the other half of the unfulfilled conditional clause, οὔτ' ἄν ... οὔτ' ἄν – 'neither would he have . . . nor would he be . . .'.

39   ἐπιθυμέω + gen. – desire, οὔτ' ἄν ἐπεθύμησε – 'would not have . . .'.

40   δουλοσύνη ἡ (> δοῦλος) – slavery; οὔτ' ἄν . . . ἦγεν (ἄγω) – 'would not be leading' (imperfect); ὑφ' (elision) = ὑπό + gen. – by (expressing agent); ἠδίκηται, perfect passive of ἀδικέω – 'has been wronged'.

41   τόξον τό – bow; ἔπος -εος τό (< epic) – word; λέγετε (imperative).

42   συμβουλεύω + dat. – advise; τότε – then, at that time pointing towards a 'when' at some point in the future; τότε may be left untranslated.

43   μακροβίος -ον (2); στρατεύομαι (> στρατιά) – march against, campaign; ἐπήν = ἐπεί + ἄν – when, 'only when' (42), ἄν + subjunctive gives an indefinite sense; οὕτως – thus, so, 'as . . . as this'.

44   εὐπετῶς – easily; ἕλκω – pull, 'draw'; τὰ τόξα – 'a bow'; μεγέθει dat. sg. (26).

45   μέχρι + gen. – until, μέχρι δὲ τούτου – until then, referring back to τότε (42); εἰδέναι infin. of οἶδα parallel with στρατεύεσθαι after συμβουλεύει; εἰδέναι χάριν – to thank, be grateful infinitive following on from συμβουλεύει (42); οἵ (ὅς ἥ ὅ) refers back to οἱ θεοί.

46   ἐπὶ νοῦν τρέπω – turn someone's (dat.) thoughts to; Αἰθίοψι, dat. pl.; προσκτάομαι – acquire x (acc.) in addition to y (dat.); τῇ (γῇ) ἑαυτῶν.

47   ἀνείς aorist participle of ἀνίημι – loosen, let go, 'unstring'; παραδίδωμι – hand over; τοῖς ἥκουσι dat. pl. participle – 'to those who . . .'.

The Ethiopian king's opinion of the Persian king's gifts. 3.22

Before translating, list in Greek the five gifts of the Persian king (lines 19–21).

λαβὼν δὲ τὸ εἶμα τὸ πορφυροῦν ἤρετο ὅ τι εἴη καὶ ὅπως
πεποιημένον· εἰπόντων δὲ τῶν Ἰχθυοφάγων τὴν ἀλήθειαν
περὶ τῆς πορφύρας καὶ τῆς βαφῆς, δολεροὺς μὲν τοὺς   50
ἀνθρώπους ἔφη εἶναι, δολερὰ δὲ αὐτῶν τὰ εἵματα.

δεύτερον δὲ περὶ τοῦ χρυσοῦ περιαυχενίου ἤρετο καὶ
περὶ τῶν ψελίων· ἐξηγουμένων δὲ τῶν Ἰχθυοφάγων,
γελάσας ὁ βασιλεὺς καὶ νομίσας αὐτὰ εἶναι πέδας
εἶπεν ὡς παρ' ἑαυτοῖς εἰσι ῥωμαλεώτεραι τούτων πέδαι.   55

τρίτον δὲ ἤρετο περὶ τοῦ μύρου· εἰπόντων δὲ αὐτῶν περὶ τῆς
ποιήσεως καὶ ἀλείψεως, τὸν αὐτὸν λόγον ὃν καὶ περὶ τοῦ
εἵματος εἶπεν. ὡς δὲ εἰς τὸν οἶνον ἀφίκετο καὶ ἐπύθετο αὐτοῦ
τὴν ποίησιν, ὑπερησθεὶς τῷ πώματι ἐπήρετο ὁ βασιλεὺς ὅ τι
σιτοῦνται οἱ Πέρσαι καὶ ὁπόσον χρόνον μακρότατον ἀνὴρ   60
Πέρσης ζῇ. οἱ δὲ σιτεῖσθαι μὲν τὸν ἄρτον ἔφασαν,
ἐξηγησάμενοι τῶν πυρῶν τὴν φύσιν, ὀγδοήκοντα δὲ ἔτη ζωῆς
πλήρωμα μακρότατον ἀνδρὶ προκεῖσθαι.

Anthropology

One of Herodotus' interests was in exploring how different peoples had different values – both material
and moral. This story makes the point clearly and entertainingly: the Ethiopian, who lives at the furthest
reaches of the known world and might therefore be expected to be less sophisticated than the wealthy
king of a vast empire, eloquently mocks these false gifts, undermining their value and ridiculing the giver.

Q. What criticisms does the Ethiopian king make of the first four gifts? What does
    he think of the last gift?

Q. How valuable are these gifts?

Q. What do Persians eat? How long could a Persian live?

GCSE vocabulary: *γελάω, δεύτερος, εἶπον (λέγω), ἔτος, ἔφη (φημί), ἠρόμην (ἐρωτάω),
λαμβάνω, νομίζω, περί* + gen., *ποιέω, πυνθάνομαι, σῖτος, τρίτος, χρόνος, χρύσος.*

See lines 19–21 for some of the key words in this passage.

48   ἤρετο (ἐρωτάω, ἠρόμην); ὅ τι – *what* (indirect question form of τί;); εἴη optative of εἰμί;
      ὅπως – *how* (indirect question form of πῶς;).

49   πεποιημένον ('εἴη' is understood – perfect passive optative) – '*had been made*'; εἰπόντων
      δὲ τῶν Ἰχθυοφάγων (the first of three genitive absolutes on this page); ἀλήθεια ἡ (>
      ἀληθής) – *truth*.

50   πορφύρα ἡ – *purple*; βαφή ἡ (< baptism) – *dipping, dyeing process*; δολερός -ά
      -όν – *deceitful, crafty*.

51   ἔφη (φημί).

52   δεύτερον (adv.) – *secondly*; περιαυχένιον τό (20).

53   ἐξηγέομαι (> ἡγεμών) – *relate, explain*.

54   πέδη ἡ – *chain, fetter*.

55   εἶπεν ὡς (= ὅτι); παρά + dat. – *with, amongst*; ῥωμαλεώτερος -α -ον (comparative
      of ῥωμαλέος-α-ον) – *strong, mighty*.

56   τρίτον (adv.) follows on from δεύτερον (52).

57   ποίησις -εως ἡ (> ποιέω) – *making, manufacture*; ἄλειψις -εως ἡ – '*use*' (as
      ointment); τὸν αὐτὸν λόγον ὅν καί – '*the same remark which ... also*'; λόγον
      λέγω – *make a remark*.

59   ὑπερησθείς + aorist participle of ὑπερήδομαι (> ἥδομαι 33) – *overjoyed, delighted*;
      πῶμα -ατος τό – *drink*; ἐπερωτάω (= ἐρωτάω); ὅ τι (48).

60   σιτέομαι (> σῖτος) – *eat food*; ὁπόσος -η -ον indirect question form of πόσος – *how
      great, 'what'*; μακρός -ά -όν – *long*.

61   ζῇ present indicative of ζάω (< zoo) – *live*; οἱ δέ (the Fish-eaters speak for the Persians);
      ἄρτος ὁ – *bread*; ἔφασαν (imperfect of φημί).

62   ἐξηγησάμενοι (53); πυρός ὁ – *wheat, grain*; φύσις -εως ἡ (< physical) – *nature*;
      ὀγδοήκοντα (> ὀκτώ) *eighty*; ζωή ἡ (< zoology) – *life*.

63   πλήρωμα -ατος τό – *full extent, span*; πρόκειμαι – *lie before, extend*.

Why the Ethiopians are called long-lived. 3.22–3

πρὸς ταῦτα ὁ Αἰθίοψ ἔφη οὐδὲν θαυμάζειν εἰ σιτούμενοι
κόπρον ἔτη ὀλίγα ζῶσιν· οὐδὲ γὰρ ἂν τοσαῦτα ἔφη δύνασθαι　　　65
ζῆν αὐτούς, εἰ μὴ τῷ πώματι ἀνέφερον (φράζων τὸν οἶνον)·
τούτῳ γὰρ ἑαυτοὺς ὑπὸ Περσῶν ἡττᾶσθαι.

ἀντερομένων δὲ τὸν βασιλέα τῶν Ἰχθυοφάγων περὶ τῆς ζωῆς
καὶ διαίτης, ἔφη ἔτη μὲν εἰς εἴκοσι καὶ ἑκατὸν τοὺς πολλοὺς
αὐτῶν ἀφικνεῖσθαι, ὑπερβάλλειν δέ τινας καὶ ταῦτα, σίτησιν　　　70
δὲ εἶναι κρέα ἑφθὰ καὶ πῶμα γάλα. θαῦμα δὲ ποιουμένων
τῶν κατασκόπων περὶ τῶν ἐτῶν, ἐπὶ κρήνην αὐτοῖς ἡγήσατο
ἀφ' ἧς λουόμενοι λιπαρώτεροι ἐγίγνοντο, καθάπερ εἰ ἐλαίου
ἡ κρήνη εἴη, ὦζε δ' ἀπ' αὐτῆς ὡς εἰ ἴων. ἀσθενὲς δὲ τὸ ὕδωρ
τῆς κρήνης ταύτης οὕτω δή τι ἔλεγον εἶναι οἱ κατάσκοποι　　　75
ὥστε μηδὲν οἷόν τ' εἶναι ἐπ' αὐτοῦ ἐπιπλεῖν, μήτε ξύλον μήτε
ὅσα ξύλου ἐστιν ἐλαφρότερα, ἀλλὰ πάντα χωρεῖν εἰς βυθόν.
καὶ διὰ τὸ ὕδωρ τοῦτο, εἰ ἔστιν ἀληθῶς οἷόν τι λέγεται,
μακρόβιοι ἂν εἶεν, εἰς πάντα χρώμενοι.

Different lifestyles

Other differences between cultures are explored here. Why do some races live longer than others? What is the secret of a long life? Does diet make a difference? The king draws his own conclusions, and the spies communicate an alternative view to the Persian king. Herodotus, meanwhile, conveys the mysteries of an exotic and magical world to his readers, not so remote from travellers' tales in the *Odyssey* like the hero's visit to the fantastic Lotus-eaters, whose diet keeps them in a state of lethargy, or the Cyclops' reaction to delicious Greek wine (*Odyssey* 9).

Q.　What elements in the speech of the Ethiopian king suggest that he is deliberately provoking Cambyses (lines 64–7)?

Q.　Does the Ethiopian king's enthusiasm for the wine suggest sophistication or naivety?

Q.　What, according to the scouts, is the real reason for the Ethiopians' living so long?

GCSE vocabulary: ἀληθής, ἀπό + gen., ἀσθενής, ἀφικνέομαι, βασιλεύς, γίγνομαι, δή, εἰ, ἔτος, θαυμάζω, μηδείς, μήτε . . . μήτε . . ., οἷός τ'εἰμί, οὐδείς, ὀλίγος, οὕτω, πολύς, ὕδωρ, χράομαι, ὡς, ὥστε.

64   πρὸς ταῦτα – *in response to this*; οὐδέν – *not at all*; θαυμάζειν (the Ethiopian king is the subject of the infinitive).

65   κόπρος ἡ – *dung, excrement*; ἔτη (ἔτος-ους) acc. n. pl. time 'how long'; ζῶσιν, 3rd pl. present of ζάω (61); οὐδέ – *not even*; τοσαῦτα (τοσοῦτος) – *so many, 'that many'* (*years*); ἔφη – οὔ φημί = *say . . . not* + acc. (αὐτούς 66) + inf. (δύνασθαι, ἄν gives a potential sense); δύναμαι (< dynamic) – *be able.*

66   ζῆν infinitive of ζάω (61); εἰ μή – *if not, unless*; πώματι (59), instrumental dat. ἀναφέρω – *recover, refresh themselves*; φράζω – *refer to.*

67   τούτῳ – i.e. τὸ πῶμα; ἑαυτούς (the Ethiopians); ἡττάομαι (> ἥττων – comparative of κακός) – *be inferior to, be bettered by* infinitive, continuing the indirect speech.

68   ἀντέρομαι – *ask in return*; ζωή ἡ – *life-span* (62).

69   δίαιτα ἡ (< diet) – *life-style, diet*; εἴκοσι – *twenty*; ἑκατόν – *one hundred*; οἱ πολλοί – *most, the majority.*

70   ἀφικνέομαι εἰς – *'reach'*; ὑπερβάλλω – *exceed, go beyond*; καὶ ταῦτα – *even this*; σίτησις -εως ἡ (> σῖτος) – *food, sustenance.*

71   κρέα ἑφθά (9); γάλα -ακτος τό (< galaxy) – *milk*; θαῦμα -ατος τό – *wonder*; θαῦμα ποιέομαι – *consider amazing, express amazement.*

72   κατάσκοπος ὁ (15); κρήνη ἡ – *spring, fountain*; ἡγέομαι + dat. – *lead.*

73   ἀφ' = ἀπό + gen.; ἧς from ὅς ἥ ὅ; λούω – *wash*; λιπαρός -ά -όν – *sleek, shiny, glossy*; καθάπερ εἰ – *(just) as if*; ἔλαιον τό – *olive oil.*

74   εἴη (optative of εἰμί); ὄζει (impersonal) – *there is a fragrance, smell*; ὡς εἰ – *as if*; ἴον τό – *violet*; ἀσθενής -ές – *weak, soft, 'light'*, i.e. lacking density.

75   οὕτω . . . ὥστε (76), result clause + infinitive (expected result, negative μή); τι λέγω – *make a point, mention.*

76   ἐπί + gen. – *on*; ἐπιπλέω (> πλέω) – *sail on, float*; ξύλον τό (< xylophone) – *wood*; μήτε . . . μήτε . . . (reinforcing μηδέν).

77   ὅσα – *as many as*; ἐστίν (n. pl. with sg. verb), *'anything' (which is)'*; ξύλου (gen. of comparison); ἐλαφρός -ά -όν – *light*; χωρέω – *go*; βυθός ὁ – *bottom, depths.*

78   εἰ ἐστὶν ἀληθῶς (5); οἷος -α -ον – *of the sort which*; οἷόν τι – *'anything like'*; λέγεται – *is said, 'they say'.*

79   μακρόβιος -ον (2); ἂν εἶεν – *they are (be likely to be)* potential optative; εἰς πάντα – *for everything*; χρώμενοι – causal participle – *'since . . .'.*

A final guided tour of the prison and one other famous sight. 3.23–5

ἀπὸ τῆς κρήνης δὲ ἀπαλλαχθέντων αὐτῶν, ἤγαγεν ὁ   80
βασιλεὺς εἰς τὸ δεσμωτήριον, ἔνθα οἱ πάντες ἐν πέδαις
χρυσαῖς ἐδέδεντο. ἔστι δὲ ἐν τούτοις τοῖς Αἰθίοψι ὁ χαλκὸς
πάντων σπανιώτατον καὶ τιμιώτατον. θεασάμενοι δὲ τὸ
δεσμωτήριον ἐθεάσαντο καὶ τὴν τοῦ ἡλίου λεγομένην
τράπεζαν. θεασάμενοι δὲ πάντα ἀπαλλάττονται ὀπίσω.   85

The Fish-eaters report back to Cambyses.

ἀπαγγειλάντων δὲ τῶν κατασκόπων ταῦτα, αὐτίκα ὁ
Καμβύσης ὀργὴν ποιησάμενος ἐστρατεύετο ἐπὶ τοὺς
Αἰθίοπας, οὔτε παρασκευὴν σίτου οὐδεμίαν παραγγείλας
οὔτε λόγον ἑαυτῷ δοὺς ὅτι εἰς τὰ ἔσχατα γῆς ἤμελλε
στρατεύσεσθαι· οἷα δὲ ἐμμανής τε ὢν καὶ οὐ φρενήρης, ὡς   90
ἤκουσε τῶν Ἰχθυοφάγων, ἐστρατεύετο πάντα τὸν πεζὸν ἅμα
ἀγόμενος. πρὶν δὲ τῆς ὁδοῦ τὸ πέμπτον μέρος διεληλυθέναι
τὴν στρατιάν, αὐτίκα τὰ σιτία ἐπελελοίπειν αὐτούς, μετὰ δὲ
τὰ σιτία καὶ τὰ ὑποζύγια ἐπέλιπε κατεσθιόμενα.

ἡ τιμή – *price, worth, value, honour*
A land where gold is commonplace is irresistibly enticing to a culture that places a high value on this rare metal, as both the Greeks and Persians did; for example, tales of gold in Central and South America led to many adventures and misadventures, real and fictional, in search of El Dorado. The inversion of this is where something relatively common, such as bronze was for the Greeks, is highly prized by others. Herodotus implies that there is no such thing as a gold-standard.

Q.   What was strange about the prison?

Q.   What was the last visit on the Fish-eaters' itinerary?

Q.   Explain why Cambyses was so incensed by the Fish-eaters' report.

Q.   How is it clear that he was very angry? Refer both to the content and style of
lines 86–94.

GCSE vocabulary: *ἀκούω, ἤγαγον (ἄγω), δίδωμι, ἐσθίω, λείπω, λόγος, μέλλω, μετά +
acc., ὁδός, οὐδείς, πέμπτος.*

80 ἀπαλλαχθέντων aorist participle of ἀπαλλάττομαι – *depart, leave*.

81 δεσμωτήριον τό – *prison*; ἔνθα – *where*; οἱ πάντες – *everybody*; πέδη ἡ – *chain, fetter* (54).

82 ἐδέδεντο – pluperfect passive of δέω – '*had been bound*'; ἐν + dat. pl. – *amongst*; Αἰθίοψι dat. pl. of Αἰθίοψ ὁ; χαλκός ὁ – *bronze*.

83 σπάνιος -α -ον – *rare, scarce*; τίμιος -α -ον (> τιμή) – *valuable, highly-prized*; add 'thing' for these neuter adjectives; θεάομαι (< theatre) – *watch, look at*.

84 τράπεζαν this brings us full-circle to the start of the story.

85 ἀπαλλάττομαι (80); ὀπίσω – *back again*.

86 ἀπαγγέλλω (> ἀγγέλλω) – *report back*; αὐτίκα – *immediately, straightaway* (15).

87 ὀργή ἡ – *anger*; ὀργὴν ποιέομαι = ὀργίζομαι; στρατεύομαι (43).

88 παρασκευή ἡ (> παρασκευάζω) – *preparation*; οὐδεμίαν (οὐδείς -μία -έν) – *not any*; παραγγέλλω (> ἀγγέλλω) – *give orders*.

89 λόγον … δούς (aorist participle of δίδωμι) – '*taking into account*'; ἔσχατα τά – *ends, 'edge'*; ἤμελλε = ἔμελλε, imperfect of μέλλω.

90 οἷα + participle – *since, as*; ἐμμανής -ές (< maniac) – *mad*; φρενήρης -ες – *in one's right mind*; ὡς + indicative – *when*.

91 πεζός ὁ – *infantry, foot-soldiers*; ἅμα (adv.) – *along with*.

92 ἀγόμαι – *take along*; πρίν + accusative (τὴν στρατιάν) + infinitive – *before*; μέρος τό (< polymer) – *part*; διεληλυθέναι perfect infinitive of διέρχομαι – *get through, go through*.

93 σιτία τά (> σῖτος) – *provisions*; ἐπελελοίπειν 3rd person sg. pluperfect of ἐπιλείπω (> λείπω) + acc. – *had run out on*. The perfect tense represents a present state resulting from a past action: *I have eaten*; the pluperfect represents that state in the past: *I had eaten*.

94 καί – *also, as well*; ὑποζύγιον τό – *baggage animal*; ἐπιλείπω (93); κατεσθίω – *eat, devour* κατεσθιόμενα causal participle (79).

Cambyses' expedition ends in disaster. 3.25

εἰ μέν νυν μαθών ταῦτα ὁ Καμβύσης ἐγνωσιμάχει καὶ 95
ἀπῆγεν ὀπίσω τὸν στρατόν, ἐπὶ τῇ ἀρχῆθεν γενομένῃ
ἁμαρτάδι ἦν ἂν ἀνὴρ σοφός· νῦν δὲ οὐδένα λόγον
ποιούμενος ἤει ἀεὶ εἰς τὸ πρόσω. οἱ δὲ στρατιῶται, ἕως μέν τι
εἶχον ἐκ τῆς γῆς λαμβάνειν, ποιηφαγοῦντες διέζων·
ἐπεὶ δὲ εἰς τὴν ψάμμον ἀφίκοντο, δεινὸν ἔργον αὐτῶν τινες 100
εἰργάσαντο· ἐκ δεκάδος γὰρ ἕνα ἑαυτῶν ἀποκληρώσαντες
κατέφαγον.

πυθόμενος δὲ ταῦτα ὁ Καμβύσης, δείσας τὴν ἀλληλοφαγίαν,
ἀφεὶς τὸν ἐπ' Αἰθίοπας στόλον ὀπίσω ἐπορεύετο, καὶ
ἀφικνεῖται εἰς Θήβας πολλοὺς ἀπολέσας τοῦ στρατοῦ. 105

Names and places
Θῆβαι αἱ: *Thebes* (= *Luxor*)
A city in Egypt about 225 km north of Elephantine on the river Nile. (There is also a city of Thebes in Greece.)

Cambyses' military record
Cambyses was forced to cut short his military campaigns in 522 because of news of a revolt by his brother; his death and that of his brother followed one year later, and so ended the dynasty of Cyrus the Great. During his brief reign Cambyses defeated the Egyptians, Libyans, Cyreneans and Phoenicians. He had further designs on the Ethiopians, Carthaginians and Ammonians.

Q. What picture of Cambyses emerges from this passage? Do you find Herodotus' impression of him consistent?

Q. Which translation of ἀπολέσας (105) do you prefer and why?

Q. How coherent do you find the whole account of Cambyses' campaign against the Ethiopians?

Q. How successful is Herodotus in maintaining the interest of his audience? (Refer to this passage only, or to the campaign against the Ethiopians as a whole).

GCSE vocabulary: ἀεί, ἀπάγω, γῆ, δεινός, εἰς μία ἕν, εἶχον (ἔχω), ἔργον, ἤει (εἶμι), μανθάνω, νῦν, οὐδείς, πορεύομαι, πυνθάνομαι, σοφός, στρατιώτης, ταῦτα (οὗτος).

95   εἰ μέν the conditional clause leads to ἦν ἄν (97) – '*if he had . . . he would have been . . .*';
γνωσιμαχέω (> μάχη) – '*fought his feelings*', (the imperfect suggests an ongoing state of
mind).

96   ἀπῆγεν (ἀπάγω) for this use of the imperfect see 18; ὀπίσω – *back* (85); στρατός ὁ
(= στρατιά); ἐπί + dat. – *after, following upon*; ἀρχῆθεν (> ἀρχή) – '*at the start*'.

97   ἁμαρτάς -άδος ἡ – *mistake*; ἦν ἄν – '*would have been*'; νῦν δέ – '*but as it was*';
οὐδένα (οὐδείς) – *no, not any*.

98   λόγον ποιέομαι – *take into account, consider important*; ἤει (3rd person imperfect
of εἶμι); ἀεί – *always, ever*; εἰς τὸ πρόσω – *forwards, onwards*; ἕως – *while, until,
for as long as*.

99   εἶχον imperfect of ἔχω + infinitive – *be able*; ποιηφαγέω (> ἔφαγον) – *eat grass*; διέζων
imperfect of διαζάω – *live through, stay alive*.

100   ψάμμος ἡ – *sand, desert*.

101   ἐργάζομαι (> ἔργον) – *do, commit*; δεκάς -άδος (> δέκα) – *group of ten*; ἕνα (εἷς μία
ἕν); ἀποκληρόω – *select by lot*.

102   κατέφαγον (> ἐσθίω) – *eat, devour* (94).

103   δείσας aorist participle of δείδω, *fear* – '*alarmed by*'; ἀλληλοφαγία ἡ (> ἀλλήλων – one
another + ἔφαγον) – *cannibalism*.

104   ἀφείς aorist participle of ἀφίημι – *dismiss, let go* (47); στόλος ὁ – *expedition*; ὀπίσω
(96).

105   ἀπολέσας aorist participle of ἀπόλλυμι – *having lost, having destroyed*; στρατός ὁ
(96).

The power of custom

The power of custom: King Darius conducts an experiment. 3.38

ἕκαστοι νομίζουσι πολύ τι καλλίστους τοὺς ἑαυτῶν νόμους.
τοῦτο δὲ πολλοῖς τε ἄλλοις τεκμηρίοις πάρεστι σταθμώσασθαι
καὶ δὴ καὶ τῷδε. Δαρεῖος ἐπὶ τῆς ἑαυτοῦ ἀρχῆς καλέσας Ἕλληνάς
τινας ἤρετο ἐφ' ὁπόσῳ ἂν χρήματι βούλοιντο τοὺς πατέρας
ἀποθνήσκοντας κατασιτεῖσθαι· οἱ δὲ ἐπ' οὐδενὶ ἔφασαν ἔρδειν   110
ἂν τοῦτο. Δαρεῖος δὲ μετὰ ταῦτα καλέσας Ἰνδῶν τοὺς
καλουμένους Καλλατίας, οἳ τοὺς γονέας κατεσθίουσιν, ἤρετο
(παρόντων τῶν Ἑλλήνων καὶ δι' ἑρμηνέως μανθανόντων τὰ
λεγόμενα) ἐπὶ τίνι χρήματι δέξαιντ' ἂν τελευτῶντας τοὺς
πατέρας κατακάειν πυρί· οἱ δέ, ἀναβοήσαντες μέγα,   115
εὐφημεῖν αὐτὸν ἐκέλευον.

Names and places

Δαρεῖος ὁ: *Darius*
Darius was Cambyses' successor. He sent the first expedition against Greece, which resulted in a Persian defeat at Marathon in 490.

Ἕλληνες οἱ (sg. Ἕλλην): *the Greeks*
The term was not restricted to those living in Greece, but included all who spoke Greek as their first language. This included Greeks living on the Ionian coast, part of the Persian empire.

Ἰνδοί οἱ: *the Indians*
In a list of the provinces which paid tribute to the Persians Herodotus says that the Indians contributed most (3.95). Like the Ethiopians, they took part in Xerxes' invasion of Greece.

Καλλατίαι οἱ: *the Callatiae*
A remote Indian tribe.

Cannibalism

Cambyses is horrified when his men resort to cannibalism, an event which finally leads him to abort his expedition against the Ethiopians (103–5). In this passage, however, Herodotus shows that even the greatest taboos may be challenged: moral values, while they might stem from common sense factors like hygiene, are relative and not based on any absolute truth.

Q.   Why would a Persian king be running this experiment?

Q.   Does the experiment seem to you clever or contrived?

GCSE vocabulary: ἀποθνήσκω, βοάω, βούλομαι, δέχομαι, διά + gen., ἑαυτόν, ἕκαστος, ἠρόμην (ἐρωτάω), καίω, καλέω, κελεύω, πατήρ, πῦρ, χρήματα.

106 ἕκαστοι (the plural means each set of people) – *each group, 'each nation'*; πολύ τι (adv.) – *by far, by quite some way.*

107 τοῦτο δέ (i.e. this view); πολλοῖς τε ἄλλοις (23–4); τεκμήριον τό – *piece of evidence, proof*; πάρεστι – *it is possible*; σταθμόομαι – *weigh up, assess.*

108 καὶ δὴ καὶ τῷδε – *'including/especially this one'*, (23–4); ἐπὶ τῆς ἑαυτοῦ ἀρχῆς – *in the time of his own rule, 'during his reign'.*

109 ἠρόμην (ἐρωτάω) followed by an indirect question (see 48ff.); ἐπί + dat. – *'for'*; ὁπόσος -η -ον indirect question form of πόσος – *how great, how much* (60); ἂν βούλοιντο – *'would be willing'*, ἄν gives a potential sense, matched in the reply, (111).

110 κατασιτέομαι (> σῖτος) – *eat* (60); ἀποθνήσκοντας – *'dead'* (lit. *'as they died'*); ἐπ' οὐδενί – *not for anything, 'at no price'*; ἔρδω – *do*; ἄν (109).

111 καλούμενος -η -ον – *'known as'* (13).

112 οἵ (ὅς ἥ ὅ); γονεύς -έως ὁ – *parent*; κατεσθίουσιν (94).

113 παρόντων present participle of πάρειμι – *be present*; ἑρμηνεύς -έως ὁ – *interpreter.*

114 ἐπὶ τίνι χρήματι (109); δέχομαι + infinitive – *'be prepared to'* (the optative + ἄν has a potential sense here); τελευτάω – *come to an end, die.*

115 κατακαίω (= καίω); ἀναβοάω (> βοάω) – *shout, cry out*; μέγα (adv.) – *'loudly'.*

116 εὐφημέω (< euphemism) – *be quiet*, literally *'speak well'*, but commonly used in religious rituals to establish respectful silence.

What happens next . . .

Cambyses' reputation as a tyrant

Herodotus writes at one point, '*It is absolutely clear to me that Cambyses was utterly mad*' (3.38) His evidence includes a number of tyrannical acts of impiety. When Cambyses entered the city of Memphis after suffering a major set-back (an entire army sent against the Ammonians was lost in the desert), he was furious to find the city celebrating a festival and stabbed the object of their veneration, the sacred Apis bull, in the thigh. It later died from its wounds. Cambyses' early death is presented as punishment for this sacrilegious behaviour: he dies from a minor wound in exactly the same part of the body as the bull. Herodotus' picture of Cambyses' reign has been challenged by modern scholars using inscriptional evidence from Egypt. It seems likely that Cambyses was at least in part a victim of the propaganda of his successor, the usurper Darius.

If you want to read more about this, the section of Herodotus that deals with Darius' accession is *Histories* 3.61–88. The story of how the Athenians came to provoke Darius to attack Greece comes in *Histories* 5.97–103.

Final questions

- Have you found Herodotus' style of writing engaging? Which moments in the text you have read do you remember most vividly and why?

- How good a historian do you consider Herodotus to be? What makes a good historian?

- Is it clear that this account was written from the perspective of a Greek?

- From your reading do you think that Herodotus was more interested in characters, events or themes? Are there other areas of his interest not included in these categories?

HISTORIES, 2.2, 69–70, 129–33, 31–2

Psammeticus; Crocodiles; Mycerinus; Pygmies

2022–2023 Prescription

See pages 83–4 for an introduction to Herodotus.

*This selections correspond as follows to **Tales from Herodotus**, ed. Farnell and Goff:*

Pages 122 to 125: Section II: **Psammetichus**   (*Histories* 2.2)
Pages 126 to 127: Section III: **Crocodiles**   (*Histories* 2.69–70)
Pages 128 to 131: Section IV: **Mycerinus**   (*Histories* 2.129–33)
Pages 132 to 137 Section XVa: **Pygmies**   (*Histories* 2.31–2)

The story so far. . . .

The selection that follows includes some of the highlights of Herodotus' travels and research in Egypt, extracts from a long digression in the second of his nine books of *Histories*. In theory, Herodotus is tracing the growth of Persian power and specifically the conquest of Egypt by Cambyses in 525; in practice, he ranges over the whole continent of Africa, known to Herodotus as Libya, and over the well-documented history of the Egyptians, exploring some of the questions that still fascinate the world: who built the pyramids, what is the source of the Nile and why did the Egyptians mummify crocodiles? You will be introduced to two kings of Egypt, the legendary figure of **Mycerinus** (Menkaure, *c.* 2532–2503), who built the third great pyramid at Giza, and **Psammetichus** (Psamtik I, 664–610), who first introduced Greeks to Egypt.

Greeks in Egypt

Herodotus describes how **Psammetichus** became king of Egypt (*Histories* 2.151–7). Originally one of twelve joint rulers he was driven into exile when the other eleven suspected his ambition. A prophecy from the oracle at Buto told him that '*bronze men from the sea*' would help him seek revenge. These turned out to be Greeks from Ionia and Caria wearing bronze armour, as yet unknown in Egypt. These Greek mercenaries, possibly sent by Gyges of Lydia, helped Psammetichus to establish the 26th Dynasty and in return were given land in Egypt and Egyptian boys to train as Greek interpreters; '*they were the first foreigners to settle in Egypt*', writes Herodotus. Psammetichus faced a further challenge in ending the Assyrian occupation of Egypt (656–639), driving out Ashurbanipal to reunite the kingdom of Egypt. Greeks continued to fight as mercenaries in Egypt. Some left their graffiti in 593 on the great statues at Abu Simbel, over 1,000km from the coast. The Greeks were later helped by Amasis I (570–526) who gave them the trading port of Naucratis.

Psammetichus

The Egyptian king Psammetichus decides to find out which is the oldest nation. 2.2

Nominative *words or phrases are in* light blue, **verbs** *in* dark blue.

οἱ Αἰγύπτιοι, πρὶν μὲν ἢ Ψαμμήτιχον σφῶν βασιλεῦσαι,
ἐνόμιζον ἑαυτοὺς πρώτους γενέσθαι πάντων ἀνθρώπων·
ἐπειδὴ δὲ Ψαμμήτιχος βασιλεύσας ἠθέλησεν εἰδέναι οἵτινες
γένοιντο πρῶτοι, ἀπὸ τούτου χρόνου νομίζουσι Φρύγας
προτέρους γενέσθαι ἑαυτῶν, τῶν δὲ ἄλλων ἑαυτούς.   5

Ψαμμήτιχος δὲ ὡς οὐκ ἐδύνατο πυνθανόμενος πόρον οὐδένα
τούτου ἀνευρεῖν, οἳ γένοιντο πρῶτοι ἀνθρώπων, ἐπιτεχνᾶται
τοιόνδε. παιδία δύο νεογνὰ ἀνθρώπων τῶν ἐπιτυχόντων
δίδωσι ποιμένι τρέφειν, ἐντειλάμενος μηδένα ἀντίον αὐτῶν
μηδεμίαν φωνὴν ἱέναι, ἐν στέγῃ δὲ ἐρήμῃ ἐφ' ἑαυτῶν   10
κεῖσθαι αὐτά, καὶ ἐν ὥρᾳ τὸν ποιμένα ἐπάγειν αὐτοῖς αἶγας,
πλήσαντα δὲ τοῦ γάλακτος τἆλλα διαπράττεσθαι.

Names and places

Αἰγύπτιοι οἱ: *Egyptians*
Egypt extends along the river Nile. Upper and Lower Egypt were united under the First Dynasty in the fourth millennium.

Ψαμμήτιχος ὁ: *Psammetichus (Psamtich I)*
Psammetichus established the 26th Dynasty and ruled Egypt 664–610

Φρύγες οἱ (sg. Φρύξ Φρυγός): *Phrygians*
The Phrygians were believed to have migrated south in the second millennium into the north-west of modern Turkey.

Goats' milk

Greek myths and legends are full of babies being suckled by a range of animals, wild and domesticated. Zeus himself was tended by a she-goat, Amalthea, while hidden from his father Cronus on Crete.

Q.   Why would an Egyptian king be interested in the question of which was the oldest race?

Q.   How plausible do you find this tale? What elements make you suspicious?

Q.   How good an understanding of child-care does Herodotus appear to have?

GCSE vocabulary: *ἄλλος, ἄνθρωπος, γίγνομαι, δίδωμι, ἑαυτόν, ἐθέλω, εἰδέναι (οἶδα), ἐπεί, εὑρίσκω, μηδείς, νομίζω, οὐδείς, τοῦτο (οὗτος), πᾶς, πρῶτος, πυνθάνομαι, φωνή.*

1   πρὶν ... ἤ + accusative and infinitive – *before*; **σφῶν** = αὐτῶν; **βασιλεῦσαι** aorist infinitive of βασιλεύω (> βασιλεύς) – *rule, be king, become king.*

2   **ἐνόμιζον** instead of αὐτοί (nominative and infinitive) this indirect statement uses **ἑαυτούς** (i.e. *'that they themselves were ...'*).

3   **ἐπειδή** (= ἐπεί); **εἰδέναι** an indirect question follows this verb; **οἵτινες** – the indirect question form of τίνες.

4   **γένοιντο** aorist optative of γίγνομαι in an indirect question; **ἀπὸ τούτου χρόνου** – *from this time on.*

5   **πρότερος -α -ον** – *earlier, previous, 'older'*; **ἑαυτῶν** gen. of comparison: *'earlier than ...'*; **τῶν δὲ ἄλλων ἑαυτούς** – δέ indicates a contrast, i.e. the Phrygians may be older than the Egyptians, but the Egyptians are older than the rest (οἱ ἄλλοι) of the world.

6   **ὡς** + indicative – *as, when*; **ἐδύνατο** aorist of δύναμαι (< dynamic) – *be able, can*; **πόρος ὁ** – *way, means, path, solution*; **οὐδένα** (οὐδείς -μία -έν) – *no, not any*; **οὐκ ... οὐδένα** the second negative reinforces the first.

7   **τούτου** (οὗτος) i.e. this question; **ἀνευρεῖν** aorist infinitive of ἀνευρίσκω (> εὑρίσκω) – *discover*; **οἵ** (= οἵτινες, 3); **ἐπιτεχνάομαι** (< technique) – *devise.*

8   **τοιόνδε** pointing forward to what comes next – *such a thing, 'the following'*; **παιδίον τό** (> παῖς) – *small child, baby*; **νεογνός -ή -όν** (> νέος) – *new-born*; **ἐπιτυχών ὁ** – *person met by chance, random person.*

9   **δίδωσι** (3rd sg. present of δίδωμι); **ποιμήν -ένος ὁ** – *shepherd*; **τρέφω** – *rear, look after*; **ἐντειλάμενος** aorist participle of ἐντέλλομαι – *give instructions, command*; a list of instructions for the shepherd follows using the accusative and infinitive (negative μή, not οὐ): introduce with *'that'*; **μηδένα** (μηδείς -μία -έν); **ἀντίον** + gen. – *in the presence of.*

10   **μηδεμίαν** as in line 6, the second negative reinforces the first; **φωνή ἡ** (< telephone) – *utterance, word*; **ἰέναι** present infinitive of ἵημι – *let out*; **στέγη ἡ** – *roof, room*; **ἐρῆμος -η -ον** – *empty, deserted*; **ἐφ' ἑαυτῶν** – *on their own, by themselves.*

11   **κεῖμαι** – *lie, lie down*; **αὐτά** – i.e. τὰ παιδία, (8); **ὥρα ἡ** (< Latin hora) – *hour, time*; **ἐν ὥρᾳ** – *'from time to time'*; **ποιμένα** (9); **ἐπάγω** (> ἄγω) – *lead to, bring to*; **αἴξ αἰγός ἡ** – *goat, she-goat.*

12   **πλήσαντα** acc. sg. aorist participle of πίμπλημι + gen. – *fill with*; **γάλα -ακτος τό** (< galaxy) – *milk*; **τἄλλα** = τὰ ἄλλα (crasis – when two words run together) – *the rest, the other things*; **διαπράττομαι** – *do, sort out.*

What Psammetichus discovers. 2.2

ταῦτα δ' ἐποίει τε καὶ ἐνετέλλετο ὁ Ψαμμήτιχος, ἐθέλων
ἀκοῦσαι ἥντινα φωνὴν ῥήξουσι πρώτην οἱ παῖδες,
ἀπαλλαχθέντων τῶν ἀσήμων κνυζημάτων. ἅπερ οὖν καὶ   15
ἐγένετο· ὡς γὰρ διετὴς χρόνος ἐγεγόνει, τῷ ποιμένι
ἀνοίγοντι τὴν θύρην καὶ εἰσιόντι τὰ παιδία ἀμφότερα
προσπίπτοντα 'βεκὸς' ἐφώνουν, ὀρέγοντα τὰς χεῖρας.

τὰ μὲν δὴ πρῶτα ἀκούσας ἥσυχος ἦν ὁ ποιμήν· ὡς δὲ
πολλάκις φοιτῶντι αὐτῷ καὶ ἐπιμελομένῳ πολὺ ἦν τοῦτο τὸ   20
ἔπος, οὕτω δὴ σημήνας τῷ δεσπότῃ ἤγαγε τὰ παιδία εἰς ὄψιν
τὴν ἐκείνου. ἀκούσας δὲ καὶ αὐτὸς ὁ Ψαμμήτιχος,
ἐπυνθάνετο οἵτινες ἀνθρώπων 'βεκός' τι καλοῦσι·
πυνθανόμενος δὲ ηὕρισκε Φρύγας καλοῦντας τὸν ἄρτον.
οὕτω συνεχώρησαν Αἰγύπτιοι, τοιούτῳ σταθμησάμενοι   25
πράγματι, τοὺς Φρύγας πρεσβυτέρους εἶναι ἑαυτῶν.

Herodotus' research

Herodotus discusses his research into this story about Psammetichus, saying that he learned it at first hand from the priests at Memphis (20 km south of modern Cairo). He says there are other versions circulated by Greeks, including one where the babies are attended by women whose tongues have been cut out. He says that he travelled down first to Thebes and then up to Heliopolis in the Delta to corroborate the Memphis version (*Histories* 2.3).

Q.   Is this the outcome to the story you (or Psammetichus) expected?

Q.   Is the argument that early human development can be understood from the behaviour of two babies flawed? Can you think of any other reason for their first word being or sounding like 'βεκός'?

Q.   Why do you think Herodotus took so much trouble over this story?

GCSE vocabulary: ἀκούω, δεσπότης, εἶναι (εἰμί), ἐκεῖνος, ἤγαγον (ἄγω), ἦν (εἰμί), θύρα, καλέω, οὕτω, παῖς, πίπτω, πολλάκις, πυνθάνομαι, τοιοῦτος, χείρ.

13   ταῦτα (> οὗτος αὕτη τοῦτο); ἐντέλλομαι – *instruct, give instructions* (9).

14   ἀκοῦσαι aorist infinitive; ἥντινα (> ὅστις ἥτις ὅ τι) indirect question form of τίς (3) – *what*;
      ῥήξουσι future of ῥήγνυμι – *break out*, '*utter*', the future indicative preserves the tense of
      the original question.

15   ἀπαλλαχθέντων aorist participle of ἀπαλλάττομαι – *leave off, depart*; ἄσημος -ον
      (> σῆμα – sign) – *insignificant, meaningless*; κνύζημα -ατος τό – *burbling, babble*
      the genitive absolute is temporal '*after the* . . .', '*once the* . . .'; ἅπερ ὅς ἥ ὅ, strengthened by –περ
      – *which*, '*which is what*'; καί – '*actually*'.

16   ὡς + indicative – *when*; διετής -ές (> ἔτος) – *of two years, two-year*; ἐγεγόνει –
      pluperfect of γίγνομαι – '*had happened*', '*had passed*'.

17   ἀνοίγοντι present participle of ἀνοίγω – *open*; θύρη ἡ (= θύρα); εἰσιόντι (= εἰς +
      ἰών ἰοῦσα ἰόν from εἶμι); παιδίον τό (8); ἀμφότεροι -αι -α – *both*.

18   προσπίπτω – *run up to*; βεκός – '*bekos*'; φωνέω – *utter, say*; ὀρέγω – *stretch
      out*.

19   τὰ πρῶτα – '*for the first time*'; ἥσυχος -η -ον – *calm, quiet*; ἦν (εἶμί) – *was*,
      '*kept*', '*stayed*'.

20   φοιτάω – *come and go*; ἐπιμέλομαι – *look after, take care of*; πολύ – *much*,
      '*much-spoken*'.

21   ἔπος -ους τό – *word*; σημήνας aorist participle of σημαίνω (> σῆμα < semaphore) –
      signal, indicate; ὄψις -εως ἡ (< optician) – *sight*.

22   καὶ αὐτός – '*for himself*'.

23   ἐπυνθάνετο, ηὕρισκε (24), the imperfect suggests persistent enquiry; οἵτινες (3);
      ἀνθρώπων partitive genitive; τι – *something, anything*.

24   ηὕρισκε + accusative and participle; καλέω – *call*, '*use the word to mean*'; ἄρτος ὁ
      – *bread*.

25   συγχωρέω + accusative + infinitive – *go along with, agree that*; σταθμάομαι
      (> σταθμός – a weight) – *assess, weigh up*.

26   πρᾶγμα -ατος τό – *matter*, '*procedure*'; τοιούτῳ (25); πρεσβύτερος -α -ον –
      older, senior; ἑαυτῶν – gen. of comparison (5).

Crocodiles

A difference of opinion on how crocodiles should be treated. 2.69–70

τοῖς μὲν δὴ τῶν Αἰγυπτίων ἱεροί εἰσιν οἱ κροκόδειλοι, τοῖς δ'
οὔ, ἀλλ' ἅτε πολεμίους περιέπουσι. οἱ δὲ περί τε Θήβας καὶ
τὴν Μοίρεως λίμνην οἰκοῦντες καὶ κάρτα ἡγοῦνται αὐτοὺς
εἶναι ἱερούς. ἕνα δὲ ἑκάτεροι τρέφουσι κροκόδειλον,   30
δεδιδαγμένον εἶναι χειροήθη· ἀρτήματα δὲ εἰς τὰ ὦτα
ἐνθέντες καὶ ἀμφιδέας περὶ τοὺς προσθίους πόδας, καὶ σιτία
ἀποτακτὰ διδόντες καὶ ἱερεῖα, περιέπουσιν ὡς κάλλιστα
ζῶντας· ἀποθανόντας δὲ ταριχεύοντες θάπτουσιν ἐν ἱεραῖς
θήκαις.   35

οἱ δὲ περὶ Ἐλεφαντίνην πόλιν οἰκοῦντες καὶ ἐσθίουσιν
αὐτούς, οὐχ ἡγούμενοι ἱεροὺς εἶναι. ἄγραι δὲ αὐτῶν πολλαὶ
καθεστήκασι καὶ παντοῖαι· ἡ δ' ἔμοιγε δοκεῖ ἀξιωτάτη
ἀφηγήσεως εἶναι ταύτην γράφω. ἐπειδὰν νῶτον ὑὸς δελεάσῃ
τις περὶ ἄγκιστρον, μεθίησι εἰς μέσον τὸν ποταμόν· αὐτὸς δὲ 40
ἐπὶ τοῦ χείλους τοῦ ποταμοῦ ἔχων δέλφακα ζωήν, ταύτην
τύπτει. ἐπακούσας δὲ τῆς φωνῆς ὁ κροκόδειλος ἵεται κατὰ
τὴν φωνήν· ἐντυχὼν δὲ τῷ νώτῳ καταπίνει, οἱ δὲ ἕλκουσι.
ἐπειδὰν δὲ ἐξελκυσθῇ εἰς γῆν, πρῶτον ἁπάντων ὁ θηρευτὴς
πηλῷ κατέπλασεν αὐτοῦ τοὺς ὀφθαλμούς· τοῦτο δὲ ποιήσας   45
κάρτα εὐπετῶς τὰ λοιπὰ χειροῦται· μὴ ποιήσας δὲ σὺν πόνῳ.

Names and places

Θῆβαι αἱ: *Thebes (= Luxor)*
A city nearly 1,000 km from the Mediterranean on the east bank of the Nile.

Μοίρεως λίμνη ἡ: *Lake Moeris*
A large lake west of the Nile south of Memphis, *c.* 600 km north of Thebes.

Ἐλεφαντίνη ἡ: *Elephantine*
A city *c.* 225 km south of Thebes, where the Aswan dam is now. Herodotus tells us that this is as far south as he got in his travels (*Histories* 2.29).

Crocodiles

Herodotus describes the crocodile in detail: its eggs are the size of a goose's; the inside of its mouth fills up with leeches; it is the only animal without a tongue. Crocodiles have excellent hearing; their ears are directly behind their eyes.

Q.   How does Herodotus hint that he has been selective in chosing what to record in this passage?

GCSE vocabulary: *ἀλλά, ἄξιος, ἀποθνήσκω, γῆ, γράφω, δοκεῖ (μοι), ἔχω, θάπτω, ἱερός, ποιέω, πολέμιοι, πόλις, πολύς, ποταμός, πούς, πρῶτον, φωνή.*

27 τοῖς μέν . . . τοῖς δέ . . . – *for some* . . . – *for others*; Herodotus shows how customs in the north of Egypt differ from those of the south; **κροκόδειλος ὁ** – *crocodile*.

28–9 **ἀλλά** – '*rather*'; **ἅτε** + participle – *since, as*; **περιέπω** (here, dat. pl. participle) – *treat, handle*; **οἱ δὲ . . . οἰκοῦντες** (29) – '*those living*', '*those dwelling*'; **καὶ κάρτα** – *very definitely, most certainly*; **ἡγέομαι** – *think, consider* + acc. + inf. indirect statement.

30–1 **ἕνα** (εἰς μία ἕν); **ἑκάτεροι** – *the people from both places*; **τρέφω** – *rear, look after*; **δεδιδαγμένος -η -ον** perfect passive participle of διδάσκω – *taught, trained*; **χειροήθης -ες** (> χείρ) – *tame, used to being handled*; **ἄρτημα -ατος τό** – *earring*; **οὖς ὠτός τό** – *ear*.

32 **ἐνθέντες** aorist participle of ἐντίθημι – *put in*; **ἀμφιδέα ἡ** (> δέω – *tie*) – *bracelet, anklet*; **πρόσθιος -α -ον** – *front*; **σιτία τά** (= σῖτος) – *food*.

33 **ἀποτακτός -όν** – *special*; **διδόντες** pres. participle δίδωμι; **ἱερεῖον τό** (> ἱερός) – *sacrifice, holy offering*; **περιέπω** (28).

34–5 **ζῶντας** pres. participle of ζάω – *live, be alive*; **ταριχεύω** – *embalm, mummify*; **θήκη ἡ** (35) – *box, coffin, case*.

36–7 **καί** (36) – '*actually*'; **ἡγέομαι** (29); **ἄγρα ἡ** – *method of hunting*.

38 **καθέστηκα** perfect tense – *be established, exist*; **παντοῖος -α -ον** – *of all kinds, of every sort*; **ἥ** (ὅς ἥ ὅ) – '*the one which*' (refers back to ἄγρα); **ἔμοιγε** = ἐμοί strengthened by γε.

39 **ἀφήγησις -εως** – *explanation*; **ταύτην** refers to ἥ (38); **ἐπειδάν** + subj. – *when(ever)*; **νῶτον τό** – *back*; **ὗς ὑός ὁ/ἡ** – *pig, pork*; **δελεάσῃ** aor. subj. of δελεάζω – *use as bait*, τις (40) is the subject.

40 **ἄγκιστρον τό** – *hook*; **μεθίησι** 3rd sg. present of μεθίημι – *drop*; **μέσος -η -ον** – *middle of*.

41 **ἐπί** + acc. – *on*; **χεῖλος -ους τό** – *edge, bank*; **δέλφαξ -ακος ἡ** – *piglet*; **ζωός -ή -όν** – *alive, living*.

42 **τύπτω** – *hit, beat*; **ἐπακούσας** + gen. (= ἀκούω); **φωνή ἡ** – *voice, 'squeal'*; **ἵεμαι** – *rush off*; **κατά** + acc. – *in the direction of*.

43 **ἐντυχών** aorist participle of ἐντυγχάνω + dat. – *come upon, 'find'*; **νῶτον τό** (39); **καταπίνω** (> πίνω) – *gulp down*; **ἕλκω** – *drag, pull*.

44 **ἐπειδάν** + subj. (39); **ἐξελκυσθῇ**, aorist passive of ἐξ + ἕλκω (43); **ἁπάντων** (= πάντων); **θηρευτής ὁ** – *hunter*.

45 **πηλός ὁ** – *mud*; **καταπλάττω** – *plaster* the aorist here suggests what traditionally happens (gnomic use); **ὀφθαλμός ὁ** – *eye*.

46 **κάρτα** – *very*; **εὐπετῶς** – *easily*; **τὰ λοιπά** – *the rest*; **χειρόομαι** (χείρ) – *handle*; **μὴ ποιήσας** μή shows there is a conditional sense – '*if he doesn't do this. . .*'; **σύν** + dat. – *with*; **πόνος ὁ** – *work, effort, labour*.

Mycerinus

Mycerinus, King of Egypt, was a more liberal ruler than his father and uncle, but was beset by misfortune. 2.129, 133

Μυκερίνῳ τὰ μὲν τοῦ πατρὸς ἔργα ἀφήνδανε· ὁ δὲ τά τε ἱερὰ
ἀνέῳξε, καὶ τὸν λεών, τετρυμένον εἰς τὸ ἔσχατον κακοῦ,
ἀνῆκε πρὸς ἔργα τε καὶ θυσίας· δίκας δέ αὐτοῖς πάντων
βασιλέων δικαιοτάτας ἔκρινεν. ὄντι δὲ ἠπίῳ τῷ Μυκερίνῳ   50
κατὰ τοὺς πολίτας καὶ ταῦτα ἐπιτηδεύοντι πρῶτον κακῶν
ἦρξεν ἡ θυγάτηρ ἀποθανοῦσα, ἣ μόνον αὐτῷ ἦν ἐν τοῖς
οἰκίοις τέκνον. μετὰ δὲ τὸ τῆς θυγατρὸς πάθος, δεύτερα
τούτῳ τῷ βασιλεῖ τάδε ἐγένετο. ἦλθεν αὐτῷ μαντεῖον ἐκ
Βουτοῦς πόλεως, ὡς μέλλοι ἓξ ἔτη μόνον βιοὺς τῷ ἑβδόμῳ   55
τελευτήσειν. ὁ δὲ δεινὸν ποιησάμενος ἔπεμψεν εἰς
τὸ μαντεῖον τῷ θεῷ ὀνείδισμα, ἀντιμεμφόμενος τάδε,
'ὁ μὲν πατήρ ἐμοῦ καὶ πάτρως, ἀποκλείσαντες τὰ ἱερά,
καὶ θεῶν οὐ μεμνημένοι ἀλλὰ καὶ τοὺς ἀνθρώπους φθείροντες,
ἐβίωσαν ἐπὶ πολὺν χρόνον· ἐγὼ δ' εὐσεβὴς ὢν μέλλω ταχέως οὕτω   60
τελευτήσειν.'

Names and places
Μυκερῖνος ὁ: *Mycerinus* (Menkaure, King of Egypt, 2532–2503)

Βουτώ -οῦς ἡ: *Buto*
A city in the Nile delta, near the Mediterranean coast, famous for its oracle.

The great pyramids of Giza
Mycerinus built the third pyramid at Giza (modern Cairo). The two more impressive pyramids were built by his father Cheops and his uncle Chephren. Herodotus describes in detail the construction of the Great Pyramid by Cheops, which took thirty years to build, and measured both it and Chephren's pyramid for himself (2.124–5). Cheops and Chephren are presented by Herodotus as tyrannical rulers who forced the people to labour like slaves for their building projects. They also closed the temples, forbidding traditional religious practices. Cheops is alleged to have prostituted his daughter, who built her own pyramid by charging customers in blocks of stone.

Q.   How admirable does Mycerinus seem (pick out details from lines 47–73)?

Q.   Does your impression seem consistent with his statue on p. 130? What makes people consider a king good or bad?

GCSE vocabulary: *ἀλλά, ἄνθρωπος, ἀποθνήσκω, ἄρχω, βασιλεύς, βίος, γίγνομαι, δεινός, δεύτερος, δίκαιος, ἐγώ, εἰς + acc., ἐκ + gen., ἕξ, ἔργον, ἔτος, θεός, θυγάτηρ, ἦλθον (ἔρχομαι), ἱερόν, κακός, μέλλω, μόνον, ὅδε, οὕτω, πᾶς, πατήρ, πέμπω, ποιέω, πολίτης, πολύς, πρῶτον, ταχύς, χρόνος.*

47   ἀφανδάνω + dat. – *displease, be displeasing to* with a singular verb after n. pl. subject;
     ὁ δέ – *he* = Mycerinus, whose acts are contrasted with those of his father and uncle.

48   ἀνέῳξε aorist of ἀνοίγω – *open*; λεώς ὁ (= δῆμος) – *people*; τετρυμένος -η -ον perfect
     passive participle of τρύω – *wear down, grind down*; ἔσχατον τό – *edge, limit*;
     κακόν τό – *trouble, misery, suffering*.

49   ἀνῆκε aorist of ἀνίημι – *let go, release*; ἔργα (i.e. their usual employment and tasks);
     θυσία ἡ (> θύω) – *sacrifice*; δίκη ἡ – *justice, law-suit* (50).

50   βασιλεύς ὁ – *King* (Egyptians rulers were not called Pharoahs until *c.* 1500 during the New
     Kingdom); δίκην κρίνω – *make a legal judgement*; ὄντι (ὢν οὖσα ὄν) used
     concessively, 'although . . .'; ἤπιος -α -ον – *gentle, kind*.

51   κατά + acc. – *towards*; ἐπιτηδεύω – *attend to* the object, ταῦτα, refers to his acts
     described above; πρῶτον κακῶν – 'the first of his troubles' in apposition to the subject
     ἡ θυγάτηρ ἀποθανοῦσα.

52   ἦρξεν (ἄρχω, but = ἄρχομαι) – 'started', 'began'; ἥ (ὅς ἥ ὅ); μόνος -η -ον agrees with
     τέκνον.

53   οἰκία τά – *household*; τέκνον τό – *child*; πάθος τό – *suffering*, 'affliction';
     δεύτερος -α -ον n. pl. agrees with τάδε – *second*, 'next'.

54   τάδε (ὅδε ἥδε τόδε) points to what comes next – *this*, 'the following'; μαντεῖον τό –
     prophecy, oracle.

55   πόλεως gen. of πόλις; ὡς (= ὅτι) – *that*; ἔτη acc. 'time how long'; βιούς nom. sg. aorist
     participle of βιόω) – *having lived*; ἑβδόμος (> ἑπτά) – *seventh* supply ἔτει.

56   τελευτάω (> τέλος) – *come to the end* (of), *die*; δεινὸν ποιέομαι – *consider*
     terrible, feel indignant.

57   ὀνείδισμα -ατος τό + dat. – *complaint against*; ἀντιμέμφομαι – *blame in turn*;
     τάδε – 'as follows' (54).

58   πάτρως -ωος ὁ – *uncle*; ἀποκλείω – *shut, close down*.

59   μέμνημαι + gen. – *be mindful of*; ἀλλὰ καί – *instead actually*; φθείρω – *destroy,*
     ruin.

60   βιόω (> βίος) – *live* (55); ἐπὶ πολὺν χρόνον – 'for a long time'; ἐγὼ δ' – 'whereas
     I', contrasting with ὁ μὲν (58); εὐσεβής -ές – *pious, reverent*; ταχέως (adverb of ταχύς)
     – *quickly, soon*.

61   τελευτάω (56).

The oracle's reply to Mycerinus' complaint and the response of Mycerinus. 2.133

ἐκ δὲ τοῦ χρηστηρίου τούτου αὐτῷ δεύτερον ἦλθε λέγον,
'τούτων ἕνεκα καὶ συνταχύνει σοι ὁ βίος· οὐ γὰρ πεποίηκας
ὃ χρεὼν ἦν ποιεῖν. δεῖ γὰρ Αἴγυπτον κακοῦσθαι ἐπ' ἔτη
πεντήκοντά τε καὶ ἑκατόν· καὶ οἱ μὲν δύο βασιλεῖς οἱ πρὸ   65
σοῦ γενόμενοι ἔμαθον τοῦτο, σὺ δὲ οὔ.'

ταῦτα ἀκούσας ὁ Μυκερῖνος, ὡς κατακεκριμένων ἤδη οἱ
τούτων, λύχνα ποιησάμενος πολλά, ἀνάψας αὐτὰ ὅπως
γίγνοιτο νύξ, ἔπινέ τε καὶ ηὐπάθει οὔθ' ἡμέρης οὔτε νυκτὸς
ἀνιείς, εἴς τε τὰ ἕλη καὶ τὰ ἄλση πλανώμενος καὶ ἵνα γῆς   70
πυνθάνοιτο εἶναι ἐνηβητήρια ἐπιτηδειότατα. ταῦτα δὲ
ἐμηχανᾶτο ἐθέλων τὸ μαντεῖον ψευδόμενον ἀποδεῖξαι,
ἵνα οἱ δώδεκα ἔτη ἀντὶ ἓξ ἐτῶν γένοιτο, τῶν νυκτῶν ἡμερῶν
ποιουμένων.

Names and places
Αἴγυπτος ἡ: *Egypt*

Figure 4 *Statue of Mycerinus (the Pharaoh Menkaura)
flanked by the goddesses Hathor (left) and Bat. The
statue was found at Giza in modern Cairo, about 22 km
from Memphis, the capital city of the Old Kingdom.
c. 2500.*
Photo by DeAgostini/Getty Images.

*'My father loved injustice, and lived long;
I loved the gods he scorned, and hated wrong;
Yet surely, O my people, did I deem
Man's justice from the all-just gods was given;
A light that from some upper fount did beam,
Some better archetype, whose seat was heaven.'*
from *'Mycerinus'*, Matthew Arnold 1822–88

Q.   What is the 'moral' of this story?
Q.   What is your impression of gods and oracles from this story?
Q.   What makes this story entertaining? Do you find it unsettling?

GCSE vocabulary: *δεῖ, δύο, γῆ, ἐθέλω, ἤδη, ἡμέρα, μανθάνω, νύξ, πίνω, πυνθάνομαι, τοῦτο (οὗτος), χρή.*

62   χρηστήριον τό – *oracle*; δεύτερον understand μαντεῖον (54) – *'a second (oracle/*
message)'; λέγον – neuter participle

63   ἕνεκα + gen. – *because of*; τούτων ἕνεκα καί . . . – *'it's actually because of this'*,
'that is precisely why'; συνταχύνω (> ταχύς) – *be over soon, be over quickly*; σοι
possesive dative – *'your'*; πεποίηκας perfect tense of ποιέω – *'you have done'*.

64   ὅ (= ὅς ἤ ὅ); χρεών τό (> χρή)– *the necessary thing, what is required*; κακόομαι –
suffer ill-treatment; ἐπί + acc. (expressing extent of time, as in line 60).

65   πεντήκοντα (> πεντε) – *fifty*; ἑκατόν – *a hundred*; πρό + gen. – *before, previous*
to.

66   γενόμενοι (γίγνομαι) – *'who came', 'who were'*

67   ὡς + participle (genitive absolute) – *as, since, on the grounds that*; κατακεκριμένων
perfect passive participle of κατακρίνω with τούτων 68 – *judge, condemn, 'this sentence*
had been passed'; οἱ (= αὐτῷ).

68   λύχνα τά – *lights, lamps*; ποιέομαι – *get made, have made*; ἀνάπτω – *light up*;
ὅπως + optative – *whenever.*

69   ηὐπάθει, imperfect of εὐπαθέω (> πάσχω) – *have a good time*; οὔθ' (= οὔτε, elision);
ἡμέρης (= ἡμέρας) genitive 'time during which'.

70   ἀνιείς present participle of ἀνίημι (49) – *let up*; ἕλος -ους τό – *marsh*; ἄλσος -ους τό
– *grove*; πλανάομαι (< planet) – *wander, roam*; ἵνα γῆς + optative – *anywhere in*
the country.

71   πυνθάνομαι + acc. and infinitive (but usually + participle); ἐνηβητήριον τό – *place of*
amusement; ἐπιτήδειος -α -ον – *suitable, (superlative) 'best'*.

72   μηχανάομαι (< mechanism) – *devise, engineer*; μαντεῖον τό – *oracle* (54); ψεύδομαι
– *lie, be false*; ἀποδεῖξαι aorist infinitive of ἀποδείκνυμι – *demonstrate, show.*

73   οἱ (= αὐτῷ, 67); οἱ . . . γένοιτο – *there might be for him*, i.e. *'he might have'*;
δώδεκα (< dodecahedron) – *twelve*; ἀντί + gen. – *instead of.*

Pygmies

What is known about the river Nile and its source beyond Egypt. 2.31–2

μέχρι μὲν τεττάρων μηνῶν πλοῦ καὶ ὁδοῦ γιγνώσκεται ὁ   75
Νεῖλος, πάρεξ τοῦ ἐν Αἰγύπτῳ ῥεύματος. ῥεῖ δ' ἀφ' ἑσπέρας
τε καὶ ἡλίου δυσμῶν. τὸ δ' ἀπὸ τοῦδε οὐδεὶς ἔχει σαφῶς
φράσαι· ἔρημος γάρ ἐστιν ἡ χώρα αὕτη ὑπὸ καύματος. ἀλλὰ
τάδε μὲν ἤκουσα ἀνδρῶν Κυρηναίων φαμένων ἐλθεῖν τε ἐπὶ
τὸ Ἄμμωνος χρηστήριον καὶ ἀφικέσθαι εἰς λόγους Ἐτεάρχῳ   80
τῷ Ἀμμωνίων βασιλεῖ· καὶ πως ἐκ λόγων ἄλλων ἀφίκοντο εἰς
λέσχην περὶ τοῦ Νείλου, ὡς οὐδεὶς οἶδε τὰς πηγὰς αὐτοῦ.

ὁ δὲ Ἐτέαρχος ἔφη ἐλθεῖν ποτε παρ' ἑαυτὸν Νασαμῶνας
ἄνδρας, οἵ, ἐρωτώμενοι εἴ τι ἔχουσι πλέον λέγειν περὶ τῶν
ἐρήμων τῆς Λιβύης, ἔφασαν παρ' ἑαυτοῖς γενέσθαι ἀνδρῶν   85
δυναστῶν παῖδας ὑβριστάς, οἳ ἄλλα τε μηχανῶντο
ἀνδρωθέντας περιττὰ καὶ δὴ καὶ ἀποκληρώσειαν πέντε
ἑαυτῶν ὀψομένους τὰ ἔρημα τῆς Λιβύης.

Names and places

Νεῖλος ὁ: *the Nile*
The longest river in the world, over 6,400 km in length. Its annual flooding, which Herodotus investigates
in *Histories* 2.19–24, was key to Egypt's prosperity.

Κυρηναῖοι οἱ: *Cyrenaeans, inhabitants of Cyrene*
A city founded by Greek colonists in the seventh century on the north coast of modern Libya, east of the
Gulf of Sirte.

Ἄμμων -ωνος ὁ: *Ammon;* **Ἀμμώνιοι οἱ:** *Ammonians;* **Ἐτέαρχος ὁ:** *Etearchus*
Ammon was the principal Egyptian deity, identified with Zeus by the Greeks. His oracle was in Siwa
about 560 km west of the pyramids in Giza. Ammonium was the ancient name for the Siwa oasis.
Etearchus ruled the Ammonians.

Νασαμῶνες οἱ: *Nasamones*
A tribe from the Gulf of Sirte (Syrtes) on north coast of Libya, east of Tripoli. The coastline was feared
for its treacherous sandbanks.

Λιβύη ἡ: *Libya,* the Greek word for *Africa.*

Q.   Trace the path of Herodotus' sources for information about the upper Nile. Do
they sound reliable?

GCSE vocabulary: ἄλλος, ἀνήρ, αὕτη (οὗτος), γιγνώσκω, ἑαυτόν, ἔφη, ἑσπέρα, ἐρωτάω,
ἔχω, λόγος, ὁδός, οἶδα, οὐδείς, ὄψομαι (ὁράω), παῖς, πέντε, περί + gen., πλέων-ον (*comparative
of* πολύς), τέσσαρες.

75 μέχρι + gen. – *as far as* μέχρι μέν contrasts with τὸ δ' ἀπὸ τοῦδε (77); μήν μηνός ὁ (< moon) – *month*; πλοῦς -οῦ ὁ – *voyage, sailing*; ὁδός ἡ – 'travel'; γιγνώσκεται – *is known*, i.e. 'has been explored'. Herodotus explains that it takes four months' travel by boat, land and on foot (for 40 days) to get beyond Elephantine (Aswan) into Ethiopia (modern Sudan).

76 πάρεξ + gen. – *beyond*; ῥεῦμα -ατος – *stream, river*; ῥέω – *flow*; ἀφ' = ἀπό (elision); ἑσπέρα ἡ – *evening, west*. The Nile flows from south to north, except near modern Lake Nasser where it flows from the southwest.

77 ἥλιος ὁ (< heliocentric) – *sun*; δυσμαί αἱ – *setting*; τὸ δ' ἀπὸ τοῦδε – 'as for the part after this', ἔχω + infinitive – *be able*; σαφῶς – *clearly*.

78 φράσαι, aorist infinitive of φράζω – *say, tell*; ἔρημος -ον – *deserted*, or as noun *desert*; αὕτη (οὗτος); ὑπό + gen. – 'because of'; καῦμα -ατος τό – *heat*.

79 τάδε μέν (points forward; there is no contrasting δε): 'this is what'; ἀκούω – *hear* x (acc.) *from* y (gen.); φαμένων, aorist middle participle of φημί (with understood nominative + infinitive) – 'saying that they'; ἐπί + acc. – *to*.

80 χρηστήριον τό (62); εἰς λόγους ἀφικνέομαι (+ dat.) – *get into conversation with*.

81 πως – *somehow*; ἐκ λόγων ἄλλων – 'following on from other talk'.

82 λέσχη ἡ – *talk, discussion*; ὡς – 'how'; πηγή ἡ – *spring*, pl. 'source'.

83 ἔφη with accusative and infinitive; παρ' (= παρά) + acc. – *to, into the presence of*.

84 οἵ (ὅς ἥ ὅ); εἴ τι – *if . . . anything*; ἔχω + infinitive (77); πλέον – *more*.

85 ἐρήμων – 'desert regions', 'desert' (78); ἔφασαν with accusative and infinitive; παρά + dat. – *with, among*; παρ' ἑαυτοῖς γενέσθαι – 'were among them'.

86 δυνάστης -ου ὁ (< dynasty) – *lord, ruler, aristocrat*; παῖς παιδός ὁ – 'son'; ὑβριστής -οῦ ὁ – *arrogant or unruly (man)*; μηχανάομαι (72) – *devise* x (acc.) *for* y (acc.); ἄλλα τε (περιττά – 87) . . . καὶ δὴ καί (87) – 'a number of strange (rites) . . . including'.

87 ἀνδρωθέντας aorist passive participle of ἀνδρόομαι – *initiate into manhood*; περιττός -ή -όν – *excessive, strange*; καὶ δὴ καί – 'including' (see 86); ἀποκληρόω – *select by lot* optative, in indirect speech like μηχανῷντο (86).

88 ἑαυτῶν – *of themselves*, 'of their number'; ὀψόμενος -η -ον, future participle of ὁράω – expressing purpose – *to see*, 'to explore'.

There are three distinct regions of Africa, as the young Nasamonian aristocrats discover when they set off on their adventures. 2.32

τῆς γὰρ Λιβύης τὰ μὲν κατὰ τὴν βορείαν θάλατταν, ἀπ'
Αἰγύπτου ἀρξάμενοι μέχρι Σολόεντος ἄκρας, ἢ τελευτᾷ τῆς   90
Λιβύης, οἰκοῦσι Λίβυες καὶ Λιβύων ἔθνη πολλά, πλὴν ὅσον
Ἕλληνες καὶ Φοίνικες ἔχουσι· τὰ δὲ καθύπερθε τούτων
θηριώδης ἐστὶν ἡ Λιβύη· τὰ δὲ καθύπερθε τῆς θηριώδους
ψάμμος τέ ἐστι καὶ ἄνυδρος δεινῶς καὶ ἔρημος πάντων.

οἱ οὖν νεανίαι, ὡς ἔφασαν οἱ Νασαμῶνες, ἀποπεμπόμενοι   95
ὑπὸ τῶν ἡλίκων, ὕδατί τε καὶ σιτίοις εὖ ἐξηρτυμένοι, ἦσαν
πρῶτον μὲν διὰ τῆς οἰκουμένης· ταύτην δὲ διεξελθόντες εἰς
τὴν θηριώδη ἀφίκοντο, ἐκ δὲ ταύτης τὴν ἔρημον διεξῆσαν,
τὴν ὁδὸν ποιούμενοι πρὸς ζέφυρον ἄνεμον.

Names and places
Σολόεντος ἄκρα ἡ: *Cape Soloeis*
The precise location is debated, but it is on the Atlantic coast of Africa in or south of Morocco.

Ἕλληνες καὶ Φοίνικες, οἱ: *Greeks and Phoenicians*
The Phoenicians, with their great cities like Tyre and Sidon (in modern Lebanon), were a great trading nation and founded Carthage (in modern Tunisia); the most important Greek colony in north Africa was Cyrene.

African fauna
In another part of his work Herodotus describes the fauna of the parts of Africa infested with wild animals: 'absolutely enormous (ὑπερμεγάθεες) snakes, lions, elephants, bears, asps and asses with antlers, people with dog-heads, and people with no heads at all with eyes in their chests (at least, that's what the Africans say), and savage men and savage women and a mass of creatures you just couldn't make up (ἀκαταψεύστα)' (*Histories* 4.191–2).

Q.   Draw a map of Africa showing what is described in lines 89–99.

Q.   What clue in the text suggests that the initiation rites were not supposed to be too hazardous?

Q.   How appropriate do you think Herodotus' long and varied account of Egypt is in a work about the Persian wars?

Q.   Does the inclusion of details like the list of animals above increase or decrease the credibility of Herodotus' *Histories*?

GCSE vocabulary: ἄνεμος, ἀπό + gen., ἀποπέμπω, ἄρχομαι, διά + gen., εὖ, ἦσαν (εἶμι), θάλασσα, νεανίας, οἰκέω, πολλά (πολύς), πρῶτον, ὕδωρ, ὑπό + gen.

89   τὰ μέν . . . τὰ δέ (92) . . . τὰ δέ (93), Herodotus describes three distinct regions; τὰ μέν is the
     object of οἰκοῦσι (91): perhaps translate as if passive: 'the region . . . is inhabited by . . .'; κατά +
     acc. – along; βόρειος -α -ον (< Aurora Borealis) – northern; θάλαττα – 'coast'.

90   ἀρξάμενοι (ἄρχομαι > ἀρχή) – 'starting'; μέχρι + gen. (75); ἥ refers back to ἄκρα, the
     Cape; τελευτάω + gen. (> τέλος) – 'mark the end of', ἀρχή and τέλος, like our 'beginning'
     and 'end', can mark either 'time' or 'space'; Λιβύες οἱ Herodotus generally uses the word to
     mean Africans, but it can also refer to the Libyan tribe, as here.

91   καί – 'including'; ἔθνος -ους τό (< ethnic) – race, tribe; πλὴν ὅσον – except in as
     far as, except for whatever.

92   ἔχω – hold, 'occupy'; τὰ δέ (see 89); καθύπερθε + gen. – below i.e. south of.

93   θηριώδης-ες – infested with wild beasts; τὰ δέ (89); τῆς θηριώδους – supply γῆς
     (the definite article shows that a feminine noun is implied).

94   ψάμμος ἡ – sand; ἄνυδρος -ον (> ὕδωρ) – without water, dry; δεινῶς – terribly,
     severely; ἔρημος -ον – deserted, (+ gen.) empty of, devoid of.

96   ἥλιξ -ικος ὁ/ἡ – contemporary, peer; ὕδατί (dat. sg. of ὕδωρ τό); σιτία τά (= σῖτος)·
     (32); ἐξαρτύω + dat. – equip with, kit out; ἦσαν imperfect of εἰμί (90).

97   τῆς οἰκουμένης (γῆς) (93) διεξελθόντες (διά + ἐξ + ἦλθον from διεξέρχομαι) – go out
     through, get through.

98   τὴν θηριώδη (= θηριώδε+α) (γῆν); τὴν ἔρημον (γῆν) – i.e the desert; διεξῆσαν (διά
     + ἐξ + εἶμι from διέξειμι, see 97).

99   ὁδὸν ποιέομαι – take a route, travel; πρός + acc. – 'against', 'into'; ζέφυρος ὁ –
     west wind, Zephyr i.e. the wind from the west would be blowing against them.

The Nasamonians report a fabulous story of meeting a tribe of pygmies. Here they also learn of a great river, which some believe to be the Nile. 2.32–3

διεξελθόντες δὲ χῶρον πολὺν ψαμμώδη καὶ ἐν πολλαῖς   100
ἡμέραις, εἶδον δή ποτε δένδρα ἐν πεδίῳ πεφυκότα, καὶ
προσελθόντες ἥπτοντο τοῦ ἐπόντος ἐπὶ τῶν δενδρῶν
καρποῦ· ἁπτομένοις δὲ αὐτοῖς ἐπῆλθον ἄνδρες μικροί,
μετρίων ἐλάττονες ἀνδρῶν, λαβόντες δὲ ἦγον αὐτοὺς δι'
ἑλῶν μεγίστων, καὶ διεξελθόντες ταῦτα ἀφίκοντο εἰς πόλιν   105
ἐν ᾗ πάντες ἦσαν ἴσοι τοῖς ἄγουσι τὸ μέγεθος, χρῶμα δὲ
μέλανες. παρὰ δὲ τὴν πόλιν ἔρρει ποταμὸς μέγας, ἔρρει δ'
ἀφ' ἑσπέρας πρὸς ἥλιον ἀνατέλλοντα, ἐφαίνοντο δὲ ἐν αὐτῷ
κροκόδειλοι.

ὁ μὲν δὴ τοῦ Ἀμμωνίου Ἐτεάρχου λόγος εἰς τοῦτό μοι   110
δεδηλώσθω, πλὴν ὅτι ἀπονοστῆσαί τε ἔφη τοὺς Νασαμῶνας,
ὡς οἱ Κυρηναῖοι ἔλεγον, καὶ τοὺς ἀνθρώπους εἰς οὓς οὗτοι
ἀφίκοντο γόητας εἶναι ἅπαντας. τὸν δὲ δὴ ποταμὸν τοῦτον
Ἐτέαρχος συνεβάλλετο εἶναι τὸν Νεῖλον.

Pygmies and cranes

Around the foot of the Francois Vase (*c.* 570), now in Florence, there is a frieze showing pygmies fighting with cranes, a popular scene in art. The pygmies gallop forwards on goats, armed with slings, clubs and hooks; the cranes target the eyes of their enemy with long beaks. Such stories are the stuff of travellers' tales, like *Gulliver's Travels* by Jonathan Swift (1726) or Lucian's *Vera Historia*. In fact, there are tribes in central Africa where the average height is below 4' 11".

The source of the Nile

The Nile has two major sources: the White Nile flows down from Lake Victoria (in modern Uganda/ Tanzania) and the Blue Nile joins it as a tributary at Khartoum, flowing in from Lake Tana in modern Ethiopia.

Q.   Does the way Herodotus presents his information about Africa and the Nile make you feel that he is a reliable historian?

Q.   How much of Etearchus' story do you find convincing?

GCSE vocabulary: *ἄγω, ἀνήρ, δένδρον, δή, διά* + gen., *εἶδον* (*ὁράω*), *ἐλάσσων* (*comparative of ὀλίγος*), *ἑσπέρα, λαμβάνω, λόγος, μέγας, μέγιστος, μικρός, πόλις, πολύς, ποταμός, φαίνομαι.*

100 διεξελθόντες (97); χῶρος ὁ (= χώρα) – *country, region, area*; ψαμμώδης -ες – *sandy*.

101 καὶ ἐν πολλαῖς ἡμέραις – *'and taken many days'*; ποτέ – *at some point*; πεδίον τό – *plain*; πεφυκώς -υῖα -ός perfect participle of φύω – *'growing'*.

102 ἅπτομαι + gen. – *touch, grasp, grab*; ἐπόντος (= ἐπί + ὤν-οὖσα-ὄν from ἔπειμι) – *be on*; ἐπί + gen. – *on*.

103 καρπός ὁ – *fruit*; ἐπέρχομαι – *come up to, approach*.

104 μετρίος -α -ον – *of normal size*; ἐλάττονες (comparative of ὀλίγοι) – *fewer, lesser, 'smaller'*; ἀνδρῶν (gen. of comparison); δι' (= διά + gen.).

105 ἕλος -ους τό – *marsh* (70);

106 ἥ (ὅς ἥ ὅ); ἴσος -η -ον (< isosceles) – *equal*; τοῖς ἄγουσι (dative plural participle); μέγεθος τό accusative of respect – *'in size'*; χρῶμα -ατος τό (< polychrome) – *skin, colour* (accusative of respect).

107 μέλας -αινα -αν (< melancholy) – *black, dark*; παρά + acc. (< parallel) – *alongside*; ἔρρει imperfect of ῥέω – *flow* (76).

108 ἀφ' (76); ἑσπέρα ἡ – *west* (76); ἥλιος ὁ (77); ἀνατέλλω – *rise*.

109 κροκόδειλος ὁ (27).

110 ὁ μὲν . . . λόγος, μέν is balanced by πλὴν ὅτι (111); εἰς τοῦτο – *thus far*.

111 (μοι) δεδηλώσθω 3rd person perfect passive imperative of δηλόω – *show* lit. *'let it have been shown (by me)'*, i.e. *'that's all I'll say about Etearchus' account'*; εἰς τοῦτο – *up to this point*; πλὴν ὅτι – *except that* (91); ἀπονοστῆσαι aorist infinitive of ἀπονοστέω – *get back home*; τέ – *'both that . . .'*; ἔφη, Etearchus is the subject, followed by acc. (τοὺς Νασαμῶνας) and infinitive (ἀπονοστῆσαι).

112 ὡς – *just as*; οὕς (ὅς ἥ ὅ) i.e. the Pygmies; οὗτοι – i.e. the young aristocrats.

113 γόης -ητος ὁ – *sorcerer, witch-doctor*; εἶναι infinitive of εἰμί, after ἔφη (111); ἅπαντας (= πάντας).

114 συνεβάλλετο, from συμβάλλομαι – *conjecture, guess*. Herodotus concludes his account of what the Cyreneans heard from Etearchus with two final points, the second of which takes us back to the original topic of discussion (λεσχή, line 82), widespread ignorance at the time about the source of the Nile.

What happens next?

After the long digression on Egyptian customs in *Histories* 2, Herodotus returns to his main narrative, the expansion of the Persian empire, at the start of *Histories* 3.

Cambyses led his army, which included Ionian mercenaries, against Amasis, King of Egypt 570–526. He was helped by a deserter, one of Amasis' Greek mercenaries called Phanes, who was originally from Halicarnassus, the city where Herodotus was born. Phanes offered advice to Cambyses on how to enter Egypt via Arabia. The Greek mercenaries loyal to Amasis and his son, Psammenitus, made Phanes pay for this betrayal by killing his sons before the deciding battle and openly drinking their blood (3.4–11). After his conquest Cambyses established the 27th Dynasty in Egypt, but these rulers were *satraps*, provincial governors subject to Persia. Persian rule of Egypt ended briefly in 402, but the land was conquered again by the Persians in 343, then passed to Alexander the Great in 332. His Macedonian *satrap*, Ptolemy Soter, established the final, 32nd Dynasty and Greek became the official administrative language. The last Ptolemy to rule Egypt independently was Cleopatra, the only Ptolemy to learn Egyptian as well as her native Greek. She was defeated by Octavian, the future emperor Augustus, at Actium in 31.

Final questions

- What impressions have you formed of Herodotus from your reading? Do you think he is someone you would have liked to meet?
- Would you agree that Herodotus is a good story-teller?
- Which of these extracts do you find most memorable and why?
- Do you consider what you have been reading to be history? If not, how would you categorize it?

Euripides

Drama is one of the great innovations to have come out of ancient Greece. It continues to have a significant influence on modern theatre and many plays from ancient Greece have been subject to revival over the past 100 years. In the late 1990s Euripides was briefly the most popular West End playwright; in 2016, for example, versions of Aeschylus' *Oresteia* were staged in two major London theatres; Ben Whishaw played Dionysus in Euripides' *Bacchae*; a new play inspired by Euripides' *Hecuba* could be seen at the RSC; and Euripides' *Medea* was streamed live from the National Theatre to cinemas worldwide.

When we talk about Greek drama, we are really speaking of Athenian drama, for it was in Athens that the plays that we have were first written and performed. The rise of drama was closely tied up with the rise of democracy, another great Athenian innovation. The content of the plays may have been based on mythology but the issues explored were often relevant to their time, and continue to be so today. The fact that they were expressed in terms of myth meant that issues could be explored in a safe environment without the passions that discussion in the *Assembly*, the democratic decision-making body of Athens, might bring about.

The presentation of drama was very different from our current practice. Plays are now put on typically for a run for several weeks or even months; they are performed inside with artificial lighting, generally in the evening. Members of the audience come alone, in pairs, or perhaps as a group, with the aim of being entertained or perhaps to learn something. A large theatre today may seat an audience of about 1,000 people.

Greek drama took place in the context of a religious festival. The main one in Athens, the City Dionysia, took place in the spring once sea-travel had restarted after the winter, and lasted for the best part of a week. At the start of the festival there was a procession where taxes from the allies of Athens were paraded through the agora and into the theatre for citizens and visitors to see and admire. Bulls were sacrificed to Dionysus and wine (plenty of it) was drunk to honour him. On this opening day, group choral songs called *dithyrambs* were performed. These involved 1,000 ordinary Athenians, 500 men and 500 boys, arranged into groups of fifty by tribes (a division of the citizen body into smaller units, like the 'house' system some schools have). The next days were filled with theatrical performances: five comedies in one day and three days consisting of four plays by the same author, three tragedies and a less-serious satyr play. At the end, there was a vote by a jury for the best author and the best actor. The Greeks were competitive in many areas.

The plays were written in verse, using a combination of long speeches, line-for-line dialogue (*stichomythia*) and choral odes in a variety of lyric metres sung by the chorus. There were two or three professional actors only, always men, who took on all the speaking roles. In addition to their costumes, they wore full face masks which helped to make their character clear at a distance. Apart from the non-speaking extras, there were fifteen other participants – the chorus. They were financed by a wealthy citizen in a form of taxation known as a *liturgy*. The chorus was recruited from ordinary Athenian citizens (only men were citizens) who spent several months learning the words, music and dance that comprised the performance. The complexity of the choral rhythms meant that this would have been an intense period of hard work. Since many Athenians would have performed choral songs in the *dithyrambs*, the audience would have been knowledgeable and appreciative of this art.

The space for performances was very specific – an open-air space on the south side of the Acropolis which held around 5,000 spectators in a wooden theatre. An area of beaten earth (the *orchestra*) formed the main performance space and spectators sat on the natural slope of the hillside surrounding it with a view of the open countryside beyond. At the back of the *orchestra*, facing the audience, was a wooden stage building (σκηνή < scene) probably on a raised wooden platform with a double door in the middle representing an interior – typically the palace of the king, although it could represent other things such as the peasant cottage of Electra. There were also entrances (*parodoi*) from either side. Since the *orchestra* was about 24 metres in diameter, entrances and exits from the side to the centre would have taken an appreciable amount of time. The theatre was part of a larger complex of the sanctuary of the god, Dionysus, after whom the festival was named (Dionysia).

If you have seen pictures of Greek theatres or have been lucky enough to visit one, it is worth bearing in mind that they may be of a later date. They became grander, with stone seats and a permanent *skene*. The remains of the Theatre of Dionysus in Athens date from the time of the Roman emperor Nero, over 500 years after the plays were originally performed.

Euripides was one of the three most celebrated writers of tragedy in fifth-century Athens. As well as a range of fragments, we have eighteen complete plays out of the ninety or so that he wrote, which is more than the combined total of Aeschylus and Sophocles, the other great playwrights of the period, from whose works seven plays each survive.

Very little hard evidence exists about Euripides' life. There are plenty of stories from ancient authors but they seem to have been invented either from material in his own plays or from the portrayal of him in contemporary comedies by Aristophanes. He was born around 480 and died in 407/406. Since his plays were part of a competition, records were kept of the title, author and position each year. Where there are gaps in the record, changes in an author's written style mean we can date most plays with a reasonable degree of confidence. *Alcestis* is Euripides' earliest surviving play. It was first performed in 438 and won second prize. *Electra* was written around twenty years later. *Bacchae* was written at the end of his life when he was living in Macedonia. It was put on in Athens in 406 by his son and won first prize.

ALCESTIS 280–392 (here 1–113)

2018–2019 Prescription

The story so far . . .

Zeus once forced Apollo to be a slave to a mortal for killing one of the Cyclopes who made his thunderbolts. Apollo served this punishment under Admetus, king of Pherae in Thessaly, and found him to be a good man and very hospitable. As a sign of gratitude for his treatment, he granted a favour to Admetus. Admetus was fated to meet an early death but Apollo persuaded the Fates to agree to a significant delay if he could find someone to die in his place. Admetus asked his parents but they refused; his wife Alcestis agreed to die for him.

Apollo opens the play by explaining the situation: he says he is leaving because he cannot be near **Alcestis** when she dies today. The character, **Death**, enters. Apollo tries to persuade him to let Alcestis reach old age, but Death will not allow this. Apollo warns him that Heracles is coming and will rescue Alcestis from the underworld anyway. A household **Maid** tells the **Chorus** how noble Alcestis has been: she has kept her self-control and only broke down on seeing her marriage bed and imagining some other woman occupying it. Admetus begins to realize that the favour Apollo has granted him is double-edged. Alcestis, **Admetus** and their children come outside the palace for the last time . . .

Alcestis addresses her husband Admetus from her deathbed saying that she is willing to die on his behalf, but criticizing his parents who have refused to die in his place.

Nominative *words or phrases are in* light blue, **verbs** *in* dark blue.

ALCESTIS: Ἄδμηθ', ὁρᾷς γὰρ τἀμὰ πράγμαθ' ὡς ἔχει,
λέξαι θέλω σοι πρὶν θανεῖν ἃ βούλομαι.
ἐγώ σε πρεσβεύουσα κἀντὶ τῆς ἐμῆς
ψυχῆς καταστήσασα φῶς τόδ' εἰσορᾶν
θνήσκω, παρόν μοι μὴ θανεῖν, ὑπὲρ σέθεν,   5
ἀλλ' ἄνδρα τε σχεῖν Θεσσαλῶν ὃν ἤθελον
καὶ δῶμα ναίειν ὄλβιον τυραννίδι.
οὐκ ἠθέλησα ζῆν ἀποσπασθεῖσα σοῦ
σὺν παισὶν ὀρφανοῖσιν, οὐδ' ἐφεισάμην
ἥβης, ἔχουσ' ἐν οἷς ἐτερπόμην ἐγώ.   10
καίτοι σ' ὁ φύσας χἠ τεκοῦσα προύδοσαν,
καλῶς μὲν αὐτοῖς κατθανεῖν ἧκον βίου,
καλῶς δὲ σῶσαι παῖδα κεὐκλεῶς θανεῖν.
μόνος γὰρ αὐτοῖς ἦσθα, κοὔτις ἐλπὶς ἦν
σοῦ κατθανόντος ἄλλα φιτύσειν τέκνα.   15

Names and places

Ἄδμητος ὁ: *Admetus*
King of Pherae in Thessaly and a former Argonaut.

Θεσσαλός ὁ: *Thessalian*
A person from the region of Thessaly in northern Greece.

Farewell speech or challenge?
Alcestis is taking leave of her husband and children. In reminding him of what she is giving up to die in his place, she is challenging him to reflect on the consequences of embarking on this course of action.

Q.   What does Alcestis suggest as an alternative possibility for her own future (lines 6–7)?

Q.   Why does Alcestis suggest that Admetus' parents were better suited to die in her husband's place (lines 11–15)? How valid are her arguments?

Q.   How emotional is the language Alcestis uses in this passage? Identify any words or phrases that seem particularly powerful.

GCSE vocabulary: *ἀλλά, ἄλλος η ο, ἀνήρ, ἀποθνήσκω, βούλομαι, γάρ, ἐγώ, ἐμός, ἔχω, ἐθέλω, ἦσθα* (imperfect of *εἰμί*), *καλῶς, λέγω, μόνος, ὁράω, ὅς, παῖς, ὑπέρ.*

1 Ἄδμηθ' = Ἄδμητε (by elision); τἀμὰ πράγμαθ' = τὰ ἐμὰ πράγματα; πρᾶγμα -ατος τό (> πράσσω) – *affair, situation*; ὡς ἔχει – '*how it is*' (the subject is τὰ ἐμὰ πράγματα (n. pl. subject with a singular verb): '*you see how my situation is*'.

2 θέλω (= ἐθέλω) – *want, be willing*; λέξαι – aorist infinitive of λέγω; πρίν + infinitive – *before*; θανεῖν – aorist infinitive (ἀπο)θνήσκω.

3 πρεσβεύω – *honour, put someone* (acc.) *first*; κἀντί = καὶ ἀντί: ἀντί + gen. – *in place of*.

4 ψυχή ἡ (< psychology) – *soul, life*; καταστήσασα participle from καθίστημι – '*having settled that*', (understand σε) + infinitive; φῶς φωτός τό – *light*; εἰσοράω – *see, look on*, φῶς εἰσορᾶν = '*live*'.

5 θνήσκω = ἀποθνήσκω; παρόν neuter participle from πάρεστι – '*although it is possible*', followed by three infinitives, impersonal verbs use an accusative absolute, not a genitive absolute; θανεῖν (2); σέθεν = σοῦ.

6 σχεῖν – aorist active infinitive of ἔχω.

7 δῶμα -ατος τό – *house*; ναίω – *live in*; ὄλβιος -α -ον – *prosperous, blessed*; τυραννίς -ίδος ἡ (< tyrant) – *royal power*.

8 ζῆν present active infinitive from ζάω – *live*; ἀποσπασθεῖσα aorist passive participle of ἀποσπάω + gen. – *separate from*.

9 σύν + dat. – *with*; ὀρφανός -όν – *orphaned*; οὐδέ – *and not, nor*; φείδομαι + gen. – *spare, begrudge*.

10 ἥβη ἡ – *youth, prime of life*; ἔχουσα – concessive participle '*although I had*'; οἷς supply an antecedent '*things in which*'; τέρπομαι – *have delight*.

11 καίτοι – *and yet*; σ' = σέ; ὁ φύσας aorist participle from φύω – *beget, father*, '*the one who fathered*'; χἠ = καὶ ἡ (by crasis); τίκτω aorist ἔτεκον – *give birth*; προύδοσαν aorist of προδίδωμι – *betray*.

12 καλῶς – *nobly*; καταθνήσκω = ἀποθνήσκω; ἧκον neuter participle (5) of ἥκω – *have come* '*although having reached*' + gen.; βίου – '*a time of life*' ('*for them to die nobly*').

13 κεὐκλεῶς (crasis) = καὶ εὐκλεῶς – *gloriously, famously*; θανεῖν (2).

14 κοὔτις (crasis) = καὶ οὔτις – *and not any*; ἐλπίς -ίδος ἡ (> ἐλπίζω) – *hope*.

15 κατθανόντος (12) is forming a genitive absolute with σοῦ; φιτύω – *bear, produce*; τέκνον τό – *child*.

Alcestis describes the life they could have had together and tells Admetus he must not remarry – a stepmother will treat the children badly.

κἀγώ τ' ἂν ἔζων καὶ σὺ τὸν λοιπὸν χρόνον,
κοὐκ ἂν μονωθεὶς σῆς δάμαρτος ἔστενες
καὶ παῖδας ὠρφάνευες. ἀλλὰ ταῦτα μὲν
θεῶν τις ἐξέπραξεν ὥσθ' οὕτως ἔχειν.
εἶέν· σύ νύν μοι τῶνδ' ἀπόμνησαι χάριν·   20
αἰτήσομαι γάρ σ' ἀξίαν μὲν οὔποτε
(ψυχῆς γὰρ οὐδέν ἐστι τιμιώτερον),
δίκαια δ', ὡς φήσεις σύ· τούσδε γὰρ φιλεῖς
οὐχ ἧσσον ἢ 'γὼ παῖδας, εἴπερ εὖ φρονεῖς.
τούτους ἀνάσχου δεσπότας ἐμῶν δόμων   25
καὶ μὴ 'πιγήμῃς τοῖσδε μητρυιὰν τέκνοις,
ἥτις κακίων οὖσ' ἐμοῦ γυνὴ φθόνῳ
τοῖς σοῖσι κἀμοῖς παισὶ χεῖρα προσβαλεῖ.
μὴ δῆτα δράσῃς ταῦτά γ', αἰτοῦμαί σ' ἐγώ·

Heirs from a previous marriage

It is not uncommon in Greek tragedies for a situation to arise where succession in a royal family is problematical. If the new partner wants their own children to succeed to the throne, pre-existing children could be seen as a potential threat. In *Medea*, a later play by Euripides, Jason tries to argue that by marrying a new wife he will increase the security of the children he and Medea already have, but Medea dismisses this argument as weak.

Q.   Explain Alcestis' reasons for not wanting her husband to remarry (lines 27–8)?

Q.   How would you describe Alcestis' attitude to her imminent death given her statement that some god is behind what has happened (line 19)?

GCSE vocabulary: *αἰτέω, ἄξιος, γε, γυνή, δεσπότης, δίκαιος, εὖ, θεός, ἤ, μέν, νῦν, ὅδε, οὐδείς οὐδεμία οὐδέν, οὐδέποτε, οὗτος, οὕτως, πράσσω, σύ, σός-ή-όν, ταῦτα (οὗτος), τις, χείρ, χρόνος, φημί, φιλέω, ὡς, ὥστε.*

16 **κἀγώ** = καὶ ἐγώ (crasis); **ζάω** – *live* (8): ἄν with indicative shows an impossible condition '*I would be living*'; **λοιπός -ή -όν** – *the rest of* accusative case for time 'how long'.

17 **κοὐκ** = καὶ οὐκ; **μονόω** + gen. (> μόνος) – *be left alone without*; **δάμαρ -αρτος ἡ** – *wife*; **στένω** – *weep, lament* with ἄν (16).

18 **ὀρφάνευω** – *look after orphans.*

19 **ἐκ**πράσσω – *do, bring about*; **ὥσθ'** = ὥστε + accusative + infinitive (the rough breathing of οὕτως has changed the final τ of to ὥστ' to θ); **οὕτως ἔχω** – *be thus, be the case.*

20 **εἶέν** – *very well then, so be it*; **σύ** – not strictly necessary with the imperative; **νυν** – *then*; **ἀπόμνησαι** aorist imperative of ἀπομιμνήσκομαι – *recognize, repay*; **χάρις** + gen. – *favour for something*; **τῶνδε** – *these things*, i.e. my sacrificing my life for you.

21 **αἰτέομαι** = αἰτέω – *ask someone (acc.) for something* (acc.), the middle has the idea of 'ask for my own benefit'; **ἀξίαν** an idiomatic phrase – 'χάριν' is understood – '*the favour I deserve*'. **οὔποτε** = οὐδέποτε.

22 **ψυχή ἡ** – *soul, life* (4); **τίμιος -α -ον** (> τιμή) – *costly, prized.*

23 **δίκαια δ'** is the second object of αἰτήσομαι; **φήσω** future of φημί.

24 **τούσδ'** . . . **παῖδας** – separated to give added emphasis, τούσδε suggests that she is pointing to them –'*these ones here*'; **ἧσσον** – *less*; **'γώ** = ἐγώ; **πέρ** adds emphasis to εἰ; **εὖ φρονέω** – *be sensible.*

25 **ἀνάσχου** strong aorist imperative from ἀνέχομαι – *put up with, allow (to be)*; **δόμος ὁ** – *house* here it is plural for singular.

26 **'πιγήμης** aorist subjunctive from **ἐπιγαμέω** – *marry again*; **μή** + aorist subjunctive is a negative specific command; **μητρυιά ἡ** (> μήτηρ) – *stepmother*; **τέκνον τό** – *child* (15).

27 **ὅστις ἥτις ὅ τι** – *who*; **κακίων** – comparative of κακός; **φθόνος ὁ** – *envy*, in the dative '*because of her envy*'.

28 **κἀμοῖς** = καὶ ἐμοῖς; **προσβάλλω** – *throw towards, hit on*, literally 'she will strike her hand (acc.) on the children (dat.)'.

29 **μή** + aorist subjunctive – *don't!*; **δῆτα** = δή; **δράσῃς** aor. subj. (26) from **δράω** – *do*; **γε** is emphasizing ταῦτα; **αἰτέομαι** = αἰτέω (21).

Alcestis ends her speech by thinking about the future of the children she will never see growing up. She addresses them directly.

ἐχθρὰ γὰρ ἡ 'πιοῦσα μητρυιὰ τέκνοις   30
τοῖς πρόσθ', ἐχίδνης οὐδὲν ἠπιωτέρα.
καὶ παῖς μὲν ἄρσην πατέρ' ἔχει πύργον μέγαν
ὃν καὶ προσεῖπε καὶ προσερρήθη πάλιν·
σὺ δ', ὦ τέκνον μοι, πῶς κορευθήσῃ καλῶς;
ποίας τυχοῦσα συζύγου τῷ σῷ πατρί;   35
μή σοί τιν' αἰσχρὰν προσβαλοῦσα κληδόνα
ἥβης ἐν ἀκμῇ σοὺς διαφθείρῃ γάμους.
οὐ γάρ σε μήτηρ οὔτε νυμφεύσει ποτὲ
οὔτ' ἐν τόκοισι σοῖσι θαρσυνεῖ, τέκνον,
παροῦσ', ἵν' οὐδὲν μητρὸς εὐμενέστερον.   40
δεῖ γὰρ θανεῖν με· καὶ τόδ' οὐκ ἐς αὔριον
οὐδ' ἐς τρίτην μοι μηνὸς ἔρχεται κακόν,
ἀλλ' αὐτίκ' ἐν τοῖς οὐκέτ' οὖσι λέξομαι.
χαίροντες εὐφραίνοισθε· καὶ σοὶ μέν, πόσι,
γυναῖκ' ἀρίστην ἔστι κομπάσαι λαβεῖν,   45
ὑμῖν δέ, παῖδες, μητρὸς ἐκπεφυκέναι.

Childbirth

Bringing up a family of healthy children was a priority in the ancient world, when giving birth was a risky business and infant mortality was high. Writers refer to the religious and practical reasons for a mother to be present when her daughter gives birth and at subsequent thanksgiving ceremonies. We see the strength of this feeling in Euripides' *Electra*: Electra has been thrown out of the palace because her mother Clytemnestra has taken a new husband. She uses the pretext that she has given birth to lure her mother to her house where she will kill her. She knows that Clytemnestra cannot refuse to come.

Q.   Why do you think step-mothers receive such bad press?

Q.   Whom does Alcestis address at greater length – her son or daughter? What reason do you think there might there be for this?

Q.   How does Alcestis emphasize that her death is imminent (lines 41–3)?

Q.   What special qualities does Admetus say Alcestis has (lines 44–5)?

GCSE vocabulary: *αἰσχρός, ἄριστος, δεῖ, διαφθείρω, ἔρχομαι, ἐχθρός, κακός, λαμβάνω, μέγας, μήτηρ, οὔτε . . . οὔτε . . ., πατήρ, ποῖος;, πῶς;, τρίτος, ὑμεῖς.*

30 ἡ 'πιοῦσα from ἐπέρχομαι – *come after*; μητρυιά ἡ – *stepmother* (26).

31 πρόσθε – *previous*; ἔχιδνα ἡ genitive of comparison – *viper*; οὐδέν accusative of respect – *as to nothing, in no way*; ἤπιος -α -ον – *mild, gentle, kind*.

32 ἄρσην -ενος – *masculine, male*; πύργος ὁ – *tower* in apposition to πατέρ'.

33 *This line, very similar to line 195, should be ignored: scholars accept that it makes no sense here ('whom he both spoke to and in turn was spoken to').*

34 κορεύομαι – *grow up to be a woman*; καλῶς – *happily, well*; μοι – a 'possessive' dative 'to me', translate as *'my'*.

35 τυχοῦσα aorist from τυγχάνω + gen. – *meet with, chance upon, 'get'*; συζύγος -ου ἡ – *spouse, partner, yokemate* (i.e. what sort of step-mother).

36 μή – see 37; προσβάλλω – *hurl, launch*; κληδών -όνος ἡ – *name, reputation*.

37 ἥβη ἡ – *youth*; ἀκμή ἡ – *prime*; μή ... διαφθείρῃ – subj. + μή indicates a fear for the future, '*I am afraid that she will ...*'; γάμος ὁ – *marriage*.

38 νυμφεύω (< nymph) – *give in marriage, see married*; οὔτε – two negatives reinforce each other in Greek; ποτέ – *ever*.

39 τόκος ὁ – *childbirth* the dative plural has an extra -ι on the end, which is not at all uncommon in verse; θαρσύνω – *encourage*.

40 παροῦσα participle from πάρειμι – *be present*; ἵνα – *where*; εὐμενής -ές – *sympathetic, helpful*.

41 θανεῖν – (2); τόδ' agrees with κάκον (42); ἐς αὔριον – *tomorrow*.

42 ἐς τρίτην μηνός – '*the day after tomorrow*', '*two days' time*' (literally, '*the third (day) of the month*' – the Greeks counted days inclusively).

43 αὐτίκα – *immediately*; οὐκέτι – *no longer* (οὐκ + ἔτι); τοῖς ... οὖσι – '*those ... who exist*'; λέξομαι (middle for passive) – '*I will be counted*'.

44 χαίρω – *rejoice, farewell*; εὐφραίνομαι optative used to express a wish for the future '*may you be happy*'; πόσις -ιος ὁ – *husband*.

45 ἔστι = ἔξεστι + dative + infinitive; κομπάζω – *boast* introducing an indirect statement with unexpressed nominative (αὐτός or σύ) + infinitive (λαβεῖν).

46 ὑμῖν δέ – contrasts with σοὶ μέν (44): understand '*it is possible for you to boast that ...*' ἐκπεφυκέναι perfect infinitive from ἐκφύω – *be born from*; supply ἀρίστης again to agree with μητρός.

The Chorus says that Admetus will fulfil the last wishes Alcestis has just made.
Admetus says that he will not marry again but will always mourn her.

CHORUS: θάρσει· πρὸ τούτου γὰρ λέγειν οὐχ ἅζομαι·
δράσει τάδ', εἴπερ μὴ φρενῶν ἁμαρτάνει.
ADMETUS: ἔσται τάδ', ἔσται, μὴ τρέσῃς· ἐπεί σ' ἐγὼ
καὶ ζῶσαν εἶχον καὶ θανοῦσ' ἐμὴ γυνή   50
μόνη κεκλήσῃ, κοὔτις ἀντὶ σοῦ ποτε
τόνδ' ἄνδρα νύμφη Θεσσαλὶς προσφθέγξεται.
οὐκ ἔστιν οὕτως οὔτε πατρὸς εὐγενοῦς
οὔτ' εἶδος ἄλλως ἐκπρεπεστάτη γυνή.
ἅλις δὲ παίδων· τῶνδ' ὄνησιν εὔχομαι   55
θεοῖς γενέσθαι· σοῦ γὰρ οὐκ ὠνήμεθα.
οἴσω δὲ πένθος οὐκ ἐτήσιον τὸ σὸν
ἀλλ' ἔστ' ἂν αἰὼν οὑμὸς ἀντέχῃ, γύναι,
στυγῶν μὲν ἥ μ' ἔτικτεν, ἐχθαίρων δ' ἐμὸν
πατέρα· λόγῳ γὰρ ἦσαν οὐκ ἔργῳ φίλοι.   60

Figure 5 *Thanatos (a personification of death) appears*
as a character in this play. He is depicted in Greek art as
a winged male figure. This late fourth-century carving
comes from a column drum from the Temple of Artemis
at Ephesus.
Photo by Universal History Archive/UIG via Getty Images.

Q.   What is Admetus' attitude to his children (line 55) and to his parents (line 60)?
Q.   How do his views differ from those of Alcestis?

GCSE vocabulary: *γίγνομαι, ἐπεί, ἔσται (εἰμί), θεός, λόγος, μόνος, οἴσω (φέρω), φίλος.*

47 θαρσέω – *have courage, cheer up*; τούτου – refers to Admetus; ἅζομαι + infinitive – *shrink from doing something*.

48 δράω future δράσω – *do*; εἴπερ μή – *if not, unless* (περ emphasizes 'if'); φρήν φρενός ἡ – *mind, sense*; ἁμαρτάνω + gen. – *be mistaken in, lose*.

49 ἔσται future of εἰμί; τρέω – *be afraid, run away*; μή + aorist subjunctive (26); σ' = σέ.

50 ζῶσαν present participle of ζάω (8) – *be alive, live*; εἶχον – imperfect of ἔχω; θανοῦσα (2).

51 κεκλήσῃ future perfect passive of καλέω – *'you will be called'*; κοὔτις = καὶ οὔτις – *no-one, no*; ἀντί + gen. – *instead of, in place of*; ποτε – *ever*.

52 νύμφη ἡ (> νυμφεύω 38) – *bride*; τόνδε ἄνδρα – *'this man as husband'*, this word suggests that Admetus is pointing to himself; προσφθέγγομαι – *speak to, address*.

53 εὐγενής -ές (< eugenics) – *noble, well-born*.

54 εἶδος -ους τό accusative of respect – *form, shape, appearance*; ἄλλως – *as well, either* (> ἄλλος); ἐκπρεπής -ές – *distinguished, remarkable*. Translate in the word-order: οὐκ ἔστιν γυνὴ οὕτως ἐκπρεπεστάτη εἶδος, οὔτε (οὕτως) πατρὸς εὐγενοῦς ἄλλως.

55 ἅλις + gen. – *enough (of), sufficient*, i.e. 'I have enough children'; ὄνησις -εως ἡ – *enjoyment (of)*; εὔχομαι – *boast, pray to someone that*.

56 γενέσθαι from γίγνομαι; ὠνέομαι – *have enjoyment of*. Supply a possessive dative μοι with γενέσθαι 'there is be to me', i.e. 'I will have'.

57 οἴσω future of φέρω; πένθος -ους τό – *sorrow* τὸ σὸν πένθος = 'sorrow for you'; ἐτήσιος -ον – *lasting for a year*.

58 ἔστε – *as long as*; αἰών -ῶνος ὁ – *life*; οὑμός = ὁ ἐμός; ἀντέχω – *endure, last*; γύναι irregular voc. sg. of γυνή; ἄν with subjunctive makes the idea indefinite, but does not need to be translated into English in this context.

59 στυγέω – *hate, loathe* supply as an object αὐτήν – 'she who . . .'; ἔτικτεν aor. of τίκτω – *give birth to*; ἐχθαίρω (> ἐχθρός) – *hate*.

60 Note the typically Greek contrast here between word and deed, λόγος and ἔργον.

Admetus will give up all the pleasures of life in the future and will commission a
substitute statue of her for his bed.

σὺ δ' ἀντιδοῦσα τῆς ἐμῆς τὰ φίλτατα
ψυχῆς ἔσωσας. ἆρά μοι στένειν πάρα
τοιᾶσδ' ἁμαρτάνοντι συζύγου σέθεν;
παύσω δὲ κώμους συμποτῶν θ' ὁμιλίας
στεφάνους τε μοῦσάν θ' ἣ κατεῖχ' ἐμοὺς δόμους.   65
οὐ γάρ ποτ' οὔτ' ἂν βαρβίτου θίγοιμ' ἔτι
οὔτ' ἂν φρέν' ἐξάραιμι πρὸς Λίβυν λακεῖν
αὐλόν· σὺ γάρ μου τέρψιν ἐξείλου βίου.
σοφῇ δὲ χειρὶ τεκτόνων δέμας τὸ σὸν
εἰκασθὲν ἐν λέκτροισιν ἐκταθήσεται,   70
ᾧ προσπεσοῦμαι καὶ περιπτύσσων χέρας
ὄνομα καλῶν σὸν τὴν φίλην ἐν ἀγκάλαις
δόξω γυναῖκα καίπερ οὐκ ἔχων ἔχειν·

Drinking parties

In fifth-century Athens *symposia* (drinking parties) were a standard form of entertainment for elite Greek men. The emphasis was on drinking, talking and music and they could easily descend into rowdiness. The *barbiton*, a deeper version of the lyre or small harp, and pipes provided musical accompaniment and guests would wear garlands. Other forms of entertainment were provided by *hetaerae* ('companions'), high-class courtesans who might dance, play music or perform other services.

Statues

Euripides was writing during a golden age in Greek sculpture, with the creation of figures of extraordinary beauty like the statue of Athene for the Parthenon sculpted in gold and ivory by Pheidias. Most sculptures from this period are idealized rather than lifelike portraits. The denouement of this play is not unlike myths in which statues come to life, for example the story of Pygmalion, which perhaps inspired Shakespeare's *The Winter's Tale*.

Q.   What does Admetus say he will give up (lines 64–8)?

Q.   What will he do to remember Alcestis (lines 69–73)?

Q.   What do you imagine Alcestis would think of his promises?

GCSE vocabulary: ἆρα;, εἷλον (αἱρέω), καλέω, ὄνομα, παύω, πεσοῦμαι (πίπτω), τε, χείρ.

61   ἀντιδίδωμι (> ἀντί + δίδωμι) – *give something* (acc.) *instead of* (gen.); **τὰ φίλτατα**
     – *the dearest things, 'what is dearest'*; **τῆς ἐμῆς** with ψυχῆς (62)

62   **ψυχή ἡ** (4); **ἆρα** – *'is it not ... ?'*, **στένω** – *lament, mourn*; **πάρα** = πάρεστι – *it is*
     possible, allowed.

63   **τοιᾶσδε** – *such* (agreeing with συζύγου); **ἁμαρτάνω** dative participle, agreeing with
     μοι + gen. – *lose, be deprived of* (48); **σύζυγος ἡ** – *spouse, partner, wife* (35);
     σέθεν = σοῦ – *'as you'.*

64   **κῶμος ὁ** – *revel, celebration*; **συμπότης ὁ** (< *symposium*) – *fellow-drinker*; **θ'** = τε;
     ὁμιλία ἡ – *gathering.*

65   **στέφανος ὁ** – *garland*; **μοῦσα ἡ** – *muse, music*; **κατέχω** (κατά + ἔχω) – *occupy,*
     fill; **δόμος ὁ** – *house.*

66   **ποτέ** – *ever*; **βάρβιτος ὁ** – *lyre*; **οὔτε ἄν** + potential optative – *'I would not ...'*; **θίγοιμι**
     aorist optative from θιγγάνω – *touch, play*; **ἔτι** – *any more.*

67   **ἐξάραιμι** aorist optative from **ἐξαίρω** – *lift up, stir up*; **φρήν φρενός ἡ** – *heart,*
     mind (48); **πρός** + acc. – *to the accompaniment of*; **Λίβυς -νος** – *Libyan* agreeing
     with αὐλόν; **λάσκω** aorist ἔλακον – *cry out, sing.*

68   **αὐλός ὁ** – *pipe,* an instrument like two oboes in one; **τέρψις -εως ἡ** – *enjoyment*;
     ἐξείλου from ἐξαιρέω + gen. – *take away from someone.*

69   **σοφός -ή -όν** – *wise, skilled*; **τέκτων -ονος ὁ** – *craftsman*; **δέμας -ατος τό** –
     body.

70   **εἰκασθέν** neuter aorist passive participle of εἰκάζω – *fashion, make copy*; **λέκτρον τό**
     – *bed*; **ἐκταθήσεται** future passive of ἐκτείνω – *stretch out, lay on.*

71   **πεσοῦμαι** – future of πίπτω; **περιτύσσω** – *fold around, embrace with*; **χέρας** =
     χεῖρας (acc. pl.)

72   **ἀγκάλη ἡ** – *arm*; τὴν φίλην agrees with γυναῖκα in the following line.

73   **δοκέω** – *think, imagine*, introducing an indirect statement with an infinitive (ἔχειν),
     nominative 'I' is understood (> δοκεῖ *it seems good* is the same verb, used impersonally).

Admetus promises to join up with Alcestis again in the underworld.

ψυχρὰν μέν, οἶμαι, τέρψιν, ἀλλ' ὅμως βάρος
ψυχῆς ἀπαντλοίην ἄν. ἐν δ' ὀνείρασιν   75
φοιτῶσά μ' εὐφραίνοις ἄν· ἡδὺ γὰρ φίλους
κἀν νυκτὶ λεύσσειν, ὅντιν' ἂν παρῇ χρόνον.
εἰ δ' Ὀρφέως μοι γλῶσσα καὶ μέλος παρῆν,
ὥστ' ἢ κόρην Δήμητρος ἢ κείνης πόσιν
ὕμνοισι κηλήσαντά σ' ἐξ Ἅιδου λαβεῖν,   80
κατῆλθον ἄν, καί μ' οὔθ' ὁ Πλούτωνος κύων
οὔθ' οὑπὶ κώπῃ ψυχοπομπὸς ἂν Χάρων
ἔσχ' ἄν, πρὶν ἐς φῶς σὸν καταστῆσαι βίον.
ἀλλ' οὖν ἐκεῖσε προσδόκα μ', ὅταν θάνω,
καὶ δῶμ' ἑτοίμαζ', ὡς συνοικήσουσά μοι.   85
ἐν ταῖσιν αὐταῖς γάρ μ' ἐπισκήψω κέδροις
σοὶ τούσδε θεῖναι πλευρά τ' ἐκτεῖναι πέλας
πλευροῖσι τοῖς σοῖς· μηδὲ γὰρ θανών ποτε
σοῦ χωρὶς εἴην τῆς μόνης πιστῆς ἐμοί.

Names and places

Ὀρφεύς -έως ὁ: *Orpheus, husband of Eurydice.*

Δημήτηρ -τρος ἡ: *Demeter, mother of Hades' wife, Persephone.*

Ἅιδης -ου ὁ: *Hades, also known as* **Πλούτων -ωνος ὁ**: *Pluto.*

Χάρων -ωνος ὁ: *Charon, ferries dead souls across the river Styx.*

Escape from the underworld

The underworld was presided over by Hades ('not-seen' – ἀ+ἰδ-) god of the dead, sometimes known as Pluto ('wealth-giver'), and his consort Persephone. Crossing to the other side of the river Styx via the ferryman Charon ('fierce-eyes') was a one-way trip. In Greek mythology only a very few heroes ventured into the underworld alive: Theseus and Pirithous went down to abduct Persephone; Heracles kidnapped the three-headed dog Cerberus as the last of his Twelve Labours; Orpheus, the most famous and best parallel for Admetus, tried and failed to bring back his wife who had died of a snake-bite. The first two attempts relied on brute force; Orpheus used the power of music.

Q.   To what extent does, Admetus see himself as a successor to the heroes he
      mentions?

GCSE vocabulary: *αὐτός, βίος, γλῶσσα, εἰ, ἐκεῖνος, ἡδύς, νύξ, πιστός.*

74   ψυχρός -ά -ον – *cold*; οἶμαι – *I think*; τέρψις (68); ὅμως – *nevertheless*; βάρος τό – *weight*.

75   ἀπαντλοίην potential optative with ἄν meaning '*would, might*' from ἀπαντλέω – *bail water out of a boat, lighten*; ὄναρ ὀνείρατος τό – *dream*.

76   φοιτάω – *visit frequently*; εὐφραίνω optative, as verb in previous line – *cheer up*; ἡδύ is neuter – supply ἐστί before translating the infinitive.

77   κἄν = καὶ ἐν; λεύσσω – *gaze on, see*; ὅστις (ἄν) + subj. – ὅντινα agrees with χρόνον, acc. time 'how long' – *for whatever (time)*; πάρειμι – *be present, be there*.

78   μέλος τό (< melody) – *music, poetry*; εἰ δ' ... παρῆν ... κατῆλθον ἄν (81) the condition should be translated, '*If I had* ... (lit, *if there were to me*) *I would have* ...'; παρῆν is singular as if after each of the two subjects.

79   ὥστε (με, agreeing with κηλήσαντα (80) is understood) + infinitive λαβεῖν; κόρη ἡ – *maiden*; κεῖνος = ἐκεῖνος; πόσις ὁ – *husband*.

80   κηλέω – *charm*; ὕμνος ου ὁ – *hymn*; ἐξ Ἅιδου – *from (the house) of Hades*.

81   κατέρχομαι see note on 78 – *go down*; οὔθ' = οὔτε; κύων κυνός ὁ – *dog* a reference to Cerberus – see opposite page.

82   κώπη ἡ – *oar*; οὑπί = ὁ ἐπί '*the one at* ...'; ψυχοπομπός ὁ (> πέμπω + ψυχή) – *(one) who escorts souls*.

83   ἔσχον aorist of ἔχω – *hold, restrain*; πρίν (+ infinitive) – *before*; φῶς φωτός τό – *light*; καταστῆσαι aorist infinitive of καθίστημι, the subject 'I' has to be supplied – *establish, bring, restore*.

84   ἀλλ' οὖν expresses resignation – *at least*; ἐκεῖσε – *there*; προσδοκάω – *wait for*; ὅταν + subjunctive – *when, when(ever)*.

85   δῶμα (7); ἑτοίμαζω – *make ready*; συνοικήσουσα (> σύν – with + οἰκέω), ὡς + future participle is used to express purpose.

86   ἐπισκήπτω – *command*; με – object of θεῖναι (87); κέδρος ἡ – *cedar-wood coffin* (plural for singular).

87   τούσδε referring to the children of; θεῖναι infinitive from τίθημι – *put, place*; ἐκτείνω – *lay out*; πέλας + gen. – *near*.

88   πλευρόν τό (< pleurisy) – *rib, side*

89   χωρίς + gen. – *apart from, separated*; εἴην – optative of εἰμί expressing a wish; πιστός (> πιστεύω) – *trustworthy, faithful*.

Alcestis entrusts the children to Admetus.

Chorus	καὶ μὴν ἐγώ σοι πένθος ὡς φίλος φίλῳ	90
	λυπρὸν συνοίσω τῆσδε· καὶ γὰρ ἀξία.	
Alcestis	ὦ παῖδες, αὐτοὶ δὴ τάδ' εἰσηκούσατε	
	πατρὸς λέγοντος μὴ γαμεῖν ἄλλην ποτὲ	
	γυναῖκ' ἐφ' ὑμῖν μηδ' ἀτιμάσειν ἐμέ.	
Admetus	καὶ νῦν γέ φημι καὶ τελευτήσω τάδε.	95
Al.	ἐπὶ τοῖσδε παῖδας χειρὸς ἐξ ἐμῆς δέχου.	
Ad.	δέχομαι, φίλον γε δῶρον ἐκ φίλης χερός.	
Al.	σύ νυν γενοῦ τοῖσδ' ἀντ' ἐμοῦ μήτηρ τέκνοις.	
Ad.	πολλή μ' ἀνάγκη, σοῦ γ' ἀπεστερημένοις.	
Al.	ὦ τέκν', ὅτε ζῆν χρῆν μ', ἀπέρχομαι κάτω.	100
Ad.	οἴμοι, τί δράσω δῆτα σοῦ μονούμενος;	
Al.	χρόνος μαλάξει σ'· οὐδέν ἐσθ' ὁ κατθανών.	
Ad.	ἄγου με σὺν σοί, πρὸς θεῶν, ἄγου κάτω.	
Al.	ἀρκοῦμεν ἡμεῖς οἱ προθνῄσκοντες σέθεν.	

Children on the stage

In Greek tragedies, children were almost always non-speaking parts. However, from the words spoken by the other characters, it is clear that they could appear on stage and their presence could be a significant point of emotional focus.

Q. Where does the text suggest the children appeared on stage? List the Greek words or phrases.

Q. How would the presence of the children on stage add to the feelings of an audience in this situation?

Q. How is Admetus' despair suggested here?

GCSE vocabulary: ἄγω, ἀκούω, ἄξιος, δέχομαι, δῶρον, ἡμεῖς, νῦν, ὅδε ἥδε τόδε, πολύς πολλή πολύ, ὑμεῖς, φημί, φίλος, χρή.

90   μήν – *indeed*; πένθος τό – *sorrow grief*; ὡς – *as*.

91   λυπρός -ή -όν – *wretched, painful*; συνοίσω (> σύν + φέρω) – *bring together, bear
     with*; τῆσδε grief of this woman = grief for this woman, i.e. Alcestis; καὶ γάρ – *for truly*.

92   εἰσακούω + gen. of person.

93   λέγοντος as well as having an object also introduces an indirect statement with infinitive;
     γαμέω future γαμῶ – *marry* (used of a man only; the middle is used for a female).

94   ἐπί + dat. – *over*; ἀτιμάζω – *dishonour* (> ἀ + τιμάω).

95   καί . . . καί – *both* . . . *and*; γέ emphasizes νῦν to contrast with the future tense of τελευτήσω;
     φημί – *say, think, assert*; τελευτάω (> τέλος) – *bring to an end, accomplish*.

96   ἐπὶ τοῖσδε – *on these things, 'on these conditions'*.

98   γενοῦ – aorist imperative of γίγνομαι; ἀντί (51).

99   ἀνάγκη ἡ (> ἀναγκάζω) – *necessity*; μ' = μοι; ἀπεστερημένοις dative participle
     (referring to the children) from ἀποστερέω – *deprive someone* (*acc.*) *of something* (*gen.*).

100 ὅτε – *when*; ζῆν irregular present infinitive of ζάω (8); χρῆν = ἐχρῆν (imperfect tense);
     κάτω (adv. > κατά) – *below*.

101 οἴμοι – *alas, oh no*; δράω (48); δῆτα = δή; μονόω + gen. (> μόνος) – *be left alone,
     deserted* (17).

102 μαλάσσω – *soften*; ἐσθ' = ἐστί; κατθανών (12).

103 ἄγομαι = ἄγω; σύν + dat. – *with*; πρός + gen. – *by* (as an exclamation or swearing an
     oath).

104 ἀρκέω – *be sufficient, enough*; προθνήσκω – *die for* + gen.; σέθεν = σοῦ.

Alcestis says her final farewell to her husband.

Ad.   ὦ δαῖμον, οἵας συζύγου μ' ἀποστερεῖς.   105
Al.   καὶ μὴν σκοτεινὸν ὄμμα μου βαρύνεται.
Ad.   ἀπωλόμην ἄρ', εἴ με δὴ λείψεις, γύναι.
Al.   ὡς οὐκέτ' οὖσαν οὐδὲν ἂν λέγοις ἐμέ.
Ad.   ὄρθου πρόσωπον, μὴ λίπῃς παῖδας σέθεν.
Al.   οὐ δῆθ' ἑκοῦσά γ'· ἀλλὰ χαίρετ', ὦ τέκνα.   110
Ad.   βλέψον πρὸς αὐτούς, βλέψον.
Al.   οὐδέν εἰμ' ἔτι.
Ad.   τί δρᾷς; προλείπεις;
Al.   χαῖρ'.
                                          ἀπωλόμην τάλας.
Ch.   βέβηκεν, οὐκέτ' ἔστιν Ἀδμήτου γυνή.

Building to a climax

In Greek tragedy, characters often give extended speeches, answering each other's points in a stylized, rhetorical way as Alcestis and Admetus have done until line 89. To heighten the emotional content, dramatists used **stichomythia**, where characters speak alternate lines, often picking up on words or flow of the other speaker as in 95–110. It is unusual for characters to interrupt each other midline (*antilabē*) as in lines 111-12. When it occurs, it suggests a climax has been reached.

The position of women in Athens

Well-off women living in Athens led a restricted life. They lived in their own quarters and did not mix with any male guests their husbands invited into their home: instead, they had to keep within the women's quarters which were physically separate. They had to be chaperoned when they went outside, except when attending religious ceremonies. They did have an important role to play in running the household and, as this play shows, their lower public profile did not mean there was necessarily any less feeling within a marriage.

Q.   What do the tenses of the verbs in lines 106–7 suggest?
Q.   What clues to the actions of this final scene do we get from the Greek?
Q.   How does the language on this page contribute to the emotional intensity of this scene in the play?

GCSE vocabulary: *δή, ἔτι, λείπω.*

105 δαίμων -ονος ὁ (> demon) – *god, fate*; οἷος -η -ον – *what sort of, what a*; ἀποστερέω – *deprive* (99).

106 καὶ μήν – *certainly, indeed*; σκοτεινός ή όν – *dark*; ὄμμα -ατος τό – *eye*; βαρύνω (βάρος 74) – *weigh down*.

107 ἀπωλόμην aorist from ἀπόλλυμαι – *perish, die, be destroyed*; ἄρα – *then* (not the question ἆρα with a circumflex).

108 εἰμί – *be, exist, live*; οὐκέτι . . . οὐδέν the two negatives give added emphasis, and do not cancel each other out; ἂν λέγοις is a **potential optative** – *'you could speak'*.

109 ὀρθόω (< orthodontist) singular middle imperative – *set straight, raise up*; πρόσωπον τό – *face*; μή + aorist subjunctive (26); λίπῃς – aorist subjunctive of λείπω.

110 δῆθ' = δῆτα = δή; ἑκών ἑκοῦσα ἑκόν – *willing*; χαίρετε – *farewell*.

111 βλέπω – *look*; ἔτι – *still, any more*.

112 προλείπω – *leave behind, abandon*; τάλας -αινα -αν – *wretched, unhappy*.

113 βέβηκεν (> ἔβην) perfect tense – *'she has gone'*.

What happens next?

Alcestis' **son** sings a song of mourning for his mother. **Admetus** commands the Thessalians to mourn with him for twelve months and takes the body of Alcestis back into the palace. The **Chorus** predict that she will be remembered in song; they remind us how Admetus' elderly parents refused to die for him.

Heracles enters. He explains that he is on his way north to capture the man-eating horses of Diomedes in Thrace as one of his Twelve Labours. As a guest-friend (ξένος) of Admetus he can expect to be well-received. When he sees Admetus dressed in mourning and asks who has died, Admetus says that it was a stranger and insists that Heracles stay, putting him in a separate guest-wing so that the sound of mourning does not put him off his food (Heracles is notorious for his appetite). Admetus acts in accordance with the conventions of hospitality. The Chorus praise this action, remembering his treatment of Apollo.

Admetus brings out the corpse of his wife for burial and meets his father, **Pheres**, who has come to pay his respects. Admetus disowns him, setting out the arguments why Pheres should have agreed to die in his place. In response, Pheres calls him a coward, responsible for Alcestis' death.

A **slave** comes onto the empty stage and tells how Heracles has been eating and drinking. He is followed by Heracles himself who tries to encourage the gloomy-looking slave to eat and drink while he has the chance. On being told the that the dead woman is Alcestis, Heracles immediately vows to wrestle her back from Death. He leaves to find her tomb.

Admetus enters with the Chorus. The realization of his loss hits him and he wishes he had died when the Fates had decreed. He thinks of the empty house which will remind him of Alcestis and imagines the comments and scorn of other people.

Heracles enters, leading a veiled **woman**. He says he has won her as a prize in a local athletics contest. He asks Admetus to look after her until he returns from his labour with the horses of Diomedes. Admetus refuses, citing practical reasons. The two argue and Heracles insists that he look after the woman. Very much against his will, Admetus agrees. Heracles hands her over as he would a guest-gift. While Admetus is reluctantly holding her right hand in his, Heracles flings off her veil so that Admetus can see who she actually is – his wife, Alcestis. Heracles explains that he wrestled Death by the tomb. He tells Admetus to take her into the palace. Admetus orders dance, song and sacrifice to the gods in thanks for the return of his wife from the dead.

Final questions

- Why do you think Alcestis is classified as a tragedy?
- How honourable do you consider the character of Admetus to be?
- Hold a debate about the conduct of Admetus' parents.
- How does Heracles change the tone of the play?
- Who is your favourite character in this play and why?
- Choose any one scene from the play, either from the lines you have read or from the summaries, and consider how to stage it.

ELECTRA 215–331 (here 1–117)

2020–2021 Prescription

See pages 139–40 for an introduction to Euripides.

Electra is the daughter of Agamemnon, King of Mycenae. Her story is part of the Trojan War cycle. As commander-in-chief of the Greek army, Agamemnon takes the decision to sacrifice his first daughter Iphigenia to secure favourable winds for the crossing to Troy. During his absence for the ten-year war at Troy, his wife Clytemnestra broods on Agamemnon's action and takes as a lover his cousin, Aegisthus, who has his own reasons for revenge: Aegisthus' father Thyestes was tricked into eating his own children by Atreus, the father of Agamemnon. On Agamemnon's triumphant return ten years later, the lovers murder the king as he takes a bath. Agamemnon's young son and heir, Orestes, is smuggled out of the country to safety by people still loyal to the memory of Agamemnon. Electra remains in the palace.

The story of Electra is the only one we have remaining told by each of the three great Greek tragedians: Aeschylus (*The Libation Bearers*, the central play in his trilogy, the *Oresteia*), Sophocles (*Electra*) and Euripides. Since there was no fixed version of myths, dramatists felt free to change details for their own purpose and explore the issues that interested them. One question, however, remains central to all three versions: if one murder must be avenged by another, where will the cycle of killing end? The version you are reading is the one by Euripides and was written around forty years after Aeschylus' *Libation Bearers*.

The story so far . . .

Aegisthus and **Clytemnestra** have married off **Electra** to a **Farmer** who lives in the countryside, far from the palace. He is of good birth but poor. He opens the play and explains that he treats her honourably, recognizing her status. When Electra enters, lamenting her lot, he tells her not to work so hard and she replies that she does so willingly, out of gratitude for his friendship. Meanwhile **Orestes** has grown to manhood and, with his friend **Pylades**, has come in disguise to take vengeance on his father's killers. After leaving an offering on Agamemnon's tomb, he overhears a group of local women (the **Chorus** in this play) talking to Electra and realizes that he has found his sister. He does not yet reveal his identity.

Electra expresses her alarm to the Chorus of local women when she sees two male strangers near her house. She pleads with the men for her life and is forced to listen.

Nominative *words or phrases are in* light blue, **verbs** *in* dark blue.

Electra	οἴμοι, γυναῖκες, ἐξέβην θρηνημάτων.	
	ξένοι τινὲς παρ' οἶκον οἵδ' ἐφεστίους	
	εὐνὰς ἔχοντες ἐξανίστανται λόχου·	
	φυγῇ σὺ μὲν κατ' οἶμον, ἐς δόμους δ' ἐγὼ	
	φῶτας κακούργους ἐξαλύξωμεν ποδί.	5
Orestes	μέν', ὦ τάλαινα· μὴ τρέσῃς ἐμὴν χέρα.	
El.	ὦ Φοῖβ' Ἄπολλον, προσπίτνω σε μὴ θανεῖν.	
Or.	ἄλλους κτάνοιμι μᾶλλον ἐχθίους σέθεν.	
El.	ἄπελθε, μὴ ψαῦ' ὧν σε μὴ ψαύειν χρεών.	
Or.	οὐκ ἔσθ' ὅτου θίγοιμ' ἂν ἐνδικώτερον.	10
El.	καὶ πῶς ξιφήρης πρὸς δόμοις λοχᾷς ἐμοῖς;	
Or.	μείνασ' ἄκουσον, καὶ τάχ' οὐκ ἄλλως ἐρεῖς.	
El.	ἕστηκα· πάντως δ' εἰμὶ σή· κρείσσων γὰρ εἶ.	

Names and places
Φοῖβος Ἀπόλλων ὁ: *Phoebus Apollo*
Phoebus ('the shining one') recalls Apollo's association with the sun.

Stichomythia
Line-for-line dialogue, as in lines 6–75, is typical of Greek tragedy and creates a fast, tense pace. Characters often pick up on the direction of the previous line, which can be reflected in the grammar.

The setting of the play
The play is set outside the house where Electra is now forced to live. Regardless of rank, it was the expectation of Greek society that females should not meet men from outside the family. Electra tries to protect herself – and the chorus – both physically and from criticism. The men lurk near an altar (3) in the orchestra, which is used both for public sacrifice and as a stage prop. Electra appeals for protection to a statue of Apollo in front of her house (7).

Dramatic irony
Electra is not aware of who the strangers are. We, the audience, know more and see that some words (e.g. line 10) have greater significance than Electra realizes.

Q.   How is Electra's anxiety on seeing the strangers conveyed?

Q.   How does Orestes persuade Electra to listen in lines 11–13?

GCSE vocabulary: ἀκούω, βαίνω, γυνή, μέν, μένω, ξένος, πῶς;, σύ, χείρ, χρή.

1 οἴμοι – *alas!* (a frequent word in tragedy); ἐξέβην aorist of ἐκβαίνω + gen. – *leave off, break off*; θρήνημα -ατος τό – *lament* (Electra is still in mourning for her dead father).

2 παρά + acc. (< parallel) – *near, alongside*; οἶκος ὁ = οἰκία; ἐφεστίος -ον – *at the altar*; οἵδ′ = οἵδε (elision, from ὅδε) – *these ones here*.

3 εὐνή ἡ – *bed*; εὐνὰς ἔχοντες – *'lying low', 'lurking'*; ἐξανίστανται present of ἐξανίστημι (ἐκ + ἀνα) – *get up from*; λόχος ὁ – *hiding place, ambush*.

4 φυγή ἡ (> φεύγω) – *flight*; σὺ μέν – Electra addresses the Chorus leader; κατά + acc. – *towards*; οἷμος ὁ – *road, path*; δόμος ὁ – *house* (often plural).

5 φώς φωτός ὁ – *man*; κακοῦργος -ον (> κακός + ἔργον) – *harmful, bad, evil*; ἐξαλύξωμεν (aorist subjunctive of ἐξαλύσκω – *escape*) – *'let us flee'* (jussive subjunctive) reinforced by φυγῇ (4); ποδί (> πούς) – *'on foot'*.

6 μέν′ = μένε; τάλας -αινα -αν – *wretched, unhappy*; μή + aorist subjunctive – *don't!*; τρέω – *flee from in terror, tremble at* + acc.; χέρα = χεῖρα.

7 προσπίτνω (= πρός + πίπτω) – *supplicate, beg*; θανεῖν = ἀποθανεῖν, used as the passive of ἀποκτείνω – *be killed*; μή + infinitive.

8 κτάνοιμι = ἀποκτάνοιμι aorist optative of ἀποκτείνω, expressing a wish; μᾶλλον – *more, rather*; ἐχθίους comparative of ἐχθρός – *more hostile, more the enemy*; σέθεν = σοῦ genitive of comparison.

9 ψαύω + gen. – *touch*; ὧν (ὅς ἥ ὅ) – *which, things which* (Greek often leaves out the antecedent); χρεών (ἐστι) = χρή.

10 ἔσθ′ = ἐστί: τ′ becomes θ′ because the next letter is aspirated; ὅτου gen. sg. of ὅστις – *who, which*; θίγοιμι – *'potential'* optative, aorist, with ἄν from θιγγάνω, + gen. *touch, 'I might touch'*; ἐνδικώτερον (> ἐν + δίκαιος comparative adverb) – *more justly, with more right*.

11 πῶς – *how, how is it?*; ξιφήρης -ες – *armed with a* ξίφος; λοχάω – *lurk, hide*; πρός + dat. – *near, at*. The combination καὶ πῶς asks an indignant question: Electra is frightened and outraged by the stranger's behaviour.

12 τάχα (> ταχύς) (adv.) – *soon*; ἄλλως (> ἄλλος) – *otherwise*; ἄλλως λέγω – future ἐρῶ – *disagree* (with his claim in 10).

13 ἔστηκα (perfect of ἵστημι < Latin sto) – *stand, 'I am standing (here)'*; πάντως (> πᾶς) – *entirely*; κρείσσων -ον – *stronger, more powerful*.

Orestes, without revealing who he is, reports that her brother is alive.
Electra questions the stranger about her brother.

Or.	ἥκω φέρων σοι σοῦ κασιγνήτου λόγους.
El.	ὦ φίλτατ', ἆρα ζῶντος ἢ τεθνηκότος; 15
Or.	ζῇ· πρῶτα γάρ σοι τἀγάθ' ἀγγέλλειν θέλω.
El.	εὐδαιμονοίης, μισθὸν ἡδίστων λόγων.
Or.	κοινῇ δίδωμι τοῦτο νῷν ἀμφοῖν ἔχειν.
El.	ποῦ γῆς ὁ τλήμων τλήμονας φυγὰς ἔχων;
Or.	οὐχ ἕνα νομίζων φθείρεται πόλεως νόμον. 20
El.	οὔ που σπανίζων τοῦ καθ' ἡμέραν βίου;
Or.	ἔχει μέν, ἀσθενὴς δὲ δὴ φεύγων ἀνήρ.
El.	λόγον δὲ δὴ τίν' ἦλθες ἐκ κείνου φέρων;
Or.	εἰ ζῇς, ὅπως τε ζῶσα συμφορᾶς ἔχεις.
El.	οὐκοῦν ὁρᾷς μου πρῶτον ὡς ξηρὸν δέμας. 25
Or.	λύπαις γε συντετηκός, ὥστε με στένειν.
El.	καὶ κρᾶτα πλόκαμόν τ' ἐσκυθισμένον ξυρῷ.

Figure 6 *Detail from an Attic red-figure vase by the Cleophrades Painter showing a mourner tearing her hair.*
Photo © Marie-Lan Nguyen/Wikimedia Commons.

Electra's appearance

Electra's shorn hair is a sign of her continued mourning, even though enough years have now passed for Orestes to grow to manhood. Traditional signs of mourning in ancient Greece included wailing, beating the head and breasts, tearing the cheeks, cutting hair short, becoming squalid and wearing dark clothing. Women played a key role within the family in mourning the dead.

Q. How do Electra's feelings towards the stranger change and why?

Q. What picture of Orestes' life is presented in these lines?

Q. How may the sounds of Electra's words in 27 reinforce their meaning?

GCSE vocabulary: ἀγαθός, ἀγγέλλω, ἆρα, ἀσθενής, βίος, γῆ, ἐθέλω, εἷς μία ἕν, ἐρέω (λέγω), ἔχω, ἦλθον (ἔρχομαι), ἡμέρα, λόγος, νόμος, ὁράω, πόλις, πρῶτος, συμφορά, φέρω, ὥστε.

14   ἥκω – *have come*; κασιγνήτος -ου ὁ – *brother.*

15   φίλτατε superlative of φίλος – *dear*; ζάω – *live*; τεθνηκότος perfect participle of (ἀπο)θνήσκω. The two participles agree with κασιγνήτου (14).

16   ζῇ – present 3rd sg. of ζάω (15); πρῶτα (adv.) = πρῶτον; τἀγάθ' = τὰ ἀγαθά by crasis – '*the good news*'; θέλω = ἐθέλω

17   εὐδαιμονέω optative used to express a wish – *be happy, prosperous*; μισθός ὁ – *reward*; ἥδιστος -η -ον – superlative of ἡδύς.

18   κοινῇ – *in common*; νῷν – *for us*; ἀμφοῖν – *both* -οῖν and -ῷν are gen/dat. dual endings used to refer to a pair; τοῦτο – *this* i.e. '*being happy*' (17).

19   ποῦ γῆς – *where on earth?*; τλήμων -ονος – *poor man, wretched*; φυγή ἡ – *flight, exile*; ἔχων – the verb ζῇ is understood (*live*) *having . . .* (i.e. '*in exile*'); τλήμων is used twice, once as a noun (*poor man*) and once as an adjective (*wretched*). The repetition and juxtaposition of the same word emphasizes Electra's sympathy.

20   οὐχ ἕνα (εἰς μία ἕν) – *not one, no single* in sense, translate with πόλεως; νομίζω – *think, respect, adopt*; φθείρομαι (> διαφθείρω) – *tire oneself out, wander wretchedly.*

21   πού – *surely, I suppose*; σπανίζω + gen. – *need, be in want of*; καθ' ἡμέραν – *daily, day by day*; βίος ὁ – *life*, '*what is needed for life*'.

22   δή emphasizes ἀσθενής; φεύγω – *flee, be in exile* (19). The μέν . . . δέ . . . shows that there are two sides to Orestes' answer. In **stichomythia**, it may help to add in translation 'yes' or 'no', for example, '*Yes, he has that, but . . .*'

23   τίν' = τίνα the accent show it is the question word, agreeing with λόγον – *word*, '*message*' κείνος = ἐκεῖνος (i.e. Orestes).

24   ὅπως + gen. (συμφορᾶς) '*in what kind of circumstances*' (συμφορά does not always have negative connotations); ζῶσα present participle of ζάω (15), ἔχεις – '*you live your life*'.

25   οὐκοῦν (= οὖν) – *then, so*; ὡς – *how* the verb ἐστί is understood; ξηρός -ά -όν – *wasted, gaunt*; δέμας τό – *body.*

26   λύπη ἡ – *grief*; γε, reinforces the idea of grief – '*Yes* (22); συντετηκός perfect participle of συντήκω, agreeing with δέμας – *wasted away*; ὥστε introduces a result clause with the accusative subject (με) and infinitive –'*so much so that . . .*'; στένω – *lament, pity, grieve.*

27   κρᾶτα (acc.) – *head*; πλόκαμος ὁ – *lock* (*of hair*), *hair*; ἐσκυθισμένον (< scythe) perfect passive participle of σκυθίζω – *shave*; ξυρόν οὗ τό – *razor*; repetition of ὁρᾷς is implied by the two accusatives.

The stranger guesses that Electra is worn down by the loss of her father and her brother's absence. He asks about her marriage, so that he can inform her brother.

Or.　δάκνει σ' ἀδελφὸς ὅ τε θανὼν ἴσως πατήρ.

El.　οἴμοι· τί γάρ μοι τῶνδέ γ' ἐστὶ φίλτερον;

Or.　φεῦ φεῦ· τί δ' αὖ σοῦ σῷ κασιγνήτῳ, δοκεῖς;　　30

El.　ἀπὼν ἐκεῖνος, οὐ παρὼν ἡμῖν φίλος.

Or.　ἐκ τοῦ δὲ ναίεις ἐνθάδ' ἄστεως ἑκάς;

El.　ἐγημάμεσθ', ὦ ξεῖνε, θανάσιμον γάμον.

Or.　ᾤμωξ' ἀδελφὸν σόν. Μυκηναίων τίνι;

El.　οὐχ ᾧ πατήρ μ' ἤλπιζεν ἐκδώσειν ποτέ.　　35

Or.　εἴφ', ὡς ἀκούσας σῷ κασιγνήτῳ λέγω.

El.　ἐν τοῖσδ' ἐκείνου τηλουρὸς ναίω δόμοις.

Or.　σκαφεύς τις ἢ βουφορβὸς ἄξιος δόμων.

El.　πένης ἀνὴρ γενναῖος ἔς τ' ἔμ' εὐσεβής.

Or.　ἡ δ' εὐσέβεια τίς πρόσεστι σῷ πόσει;　　40

El.　οὐπώποτ' εὐνῆς τῆς ἐμῆς ἔτλη θιγεῖν.

Names and places

Μυκηναῖος -α -ον: *Mycenaean, person from Mycenae*
Mycenae was the royal city of Agamemnon's family.

Electra's isolation

Electra emphasizes how, without the protection of a male φίλος, she is left on the fringes of society, both physically and in social terms. In practice, the Farmer to whom she is married is very decent, as is made clear at the start of the play, where the Farmer is the first character we meet: after setting the scene, he says he has not slept with his wife out of respect – she is the daughter of a king – and he doesn't care if others think him foolish.

Q.　Orestes asks Electra to describe her life, pretending that he will report her news to her brother (36). What sort of picture does Electra paint in her words?

Q.　How is Orestes made to seem sympathetic to Electra's situation?

GCSE vocabulary: ἀνήρ, ἄξιος, δοκεῖ, ἐκ + gen., ἐκεῖνος, ἐλπίζω, ἐμός, ἐν + dat., ἐνθάδε, ἡμεῖς, λέγω, ὅδε, πατήρ, φίλος.

28 　δάκνω – *bite, gnaw away at, trouble*; ἀδελφός ὁ – *brother*; ἴσως – *perhaps*;
　　ὅ τε θανών aorist participle of (ἀπο)θνήσκω – *and the one who has died, 'the death
　　of . . .'.*

29 　οἴμοι (1); φίλτερον comparative of φίλος -η -ον – *dear, beloved*; τῶνδε (from ὅδε ἥδε
　　τόδε) – i.e. her brother and father, given emphasis by γε.

30 　φεῦ – *alas!* an alternative to οἴμοι; αὖ – *in turn*; κασιγνήτος ὁ – *brother*; δοκέω –
　　think. The sense follows on from (29): τί δ' αὖ δοκεῖς (εἶναι) φίλτερον σῷ κασιγνήτῳ σοῦ (gen. of
　　comparison).

31 　ἄπειμι – *be absent*; πάρειμι – *be present*; φίλος ὁ – *'as a friend'*. There is no main
　　verb; the participles have a concessive sense: *'. . . although he is absent'*. Electra wonders,
　　perhaps, after Orestes' long absence how dear to him she really is.

32 　ἐκ τοῦ; – *why?*; ναίω – *live, dwell*; ἄστυ -εως τό – *city, city-centre*; ἑκάς + gen.
　　– *far from.*

33 　γαμέομαι aorist (< polygamy) – *get married, wed* poetic plural; ξεῖνος = ξένος;
　　θανάσιμος -η -ον (> θάνατος) – *deathly*; γάμος ὁ – *marriage.* Greek, often pairs a verb
　　and related accusative, *marry in marriage*, rather than deliberate variation as in English, *wed
　　in marriage.*

34 　ᾤμωξα aorist of οἰμώζω (> οἴμοι 1) – *lament, grieve for*; ἀδελφός ὁ – *brother* (28).

35 　ᾧ (from ὅς ἥ ὅ) picks up the dat. sg. τίνι (34) – *to whom, 'not one to whom . . .'*;
　　ἐκδώσειν (future infinitive of ἐκδίδωμι) – *give in marriage*; ποτέ – *ever.*

36 　εἴφ' = εἰπέ (imperative); ὡς (= ἵνα) + subjunctive to express purpose.

37 　τηλορός -όν (< telephone) + gen. – *far away, distant*; ἐκείνου – i.e. the Farmer. The
　　position in the line of τηλορός describing Electra, adds to her picture of loneliness; ναίω (32).

38 　σκαφεύς -έως ὁ – *labourer*; βουφορβός ὁ – *herdsman* supply ἐστί; ἄξιος -α -ον
　　Orestes' implication is that the house is very simple and rustic.

39 　πένης -ητος – *poor*; γενναῖος -α -ον – *noble, well-born, noble–minded*; ἐς = εἰς;
　　εὐσεβής -ές – *respectful*; the verb ἐστί is understood. Electra defends her husband: although
　　poor, he is noble, a quality defined not by birth and wealth, but by how one behaves.

41 　εὐσέβεια ἡ – *respect, reverence*; πρόσειμι (> πρός + εἰμί) – *belong to*; πόσις ὁ a
　　possessive dative – *husband.*

41 　οὐπώποτε – *never yet*; εὐνή ἡ – *bed*; τλάω – *dare, bring oneself*; θιγγάνω (10).

Orestes continues his questioning. He learns more about Electra's husband, how Electra has been treated by their mother and Aegisthus, and how she feels about them.

Or.	ἅγνευμ' ἔχων τι θεῖον ἤ σ' ἀπαξιῶν;	
El.	γονέας ὑβρίζειν τοὺς ἐμοὺς οὐκ ἠξίου.	
Or.	καὶ πῶς γάμον τοιοῦτον οὐχ ἥσθη λαβών;	
El.	οὐ κύριον τὸν δόντα μ' ἡγεῖται, ξένε.	45
Or.	ξυνῆκ'· Ὀρέστῃ μή ποτ' ἐκτείσῃ δίκην.	
El.	τοῦτ' αὐτὸ ταρβῶν· πρὸς δὲ καὶ σώφρων ἔφυ.	
Or.	φεῦ· γενναῖον ἄνδρ' ἔλεξας, εὖ τε δραστέον.	
El.	εἰ δή ποθ' ἥξει γ' ἐς δόμους ὁ νῦν ἀπών.	
Or.	μήτηρ δέ σ' ἡ τεκοῦσα ταῦτ' ἠνέσχετο;	50
El.	γυναῖκες ἀνδρῶν, ὦ ξέν', οὐ παίδων φίλαι.	
Or.	τίνος δέ σ' οὕνεχ' ὕβρισ' Αἴγισθος τάδε;	
El.	τεκεῖν μ' ἐβούλετ' ἀσθενῆ, τοιῷδε δούς.	
Or.	ὡς δῆθε παῖδας μὴ τέκοις ποινάτορας;	
El.	τοιαῦτ' ἐβούλευσ'· ὧν ἐμοὶ δοίη δίκην.	55

Names and places
Ὀρέστης ὁ: *Orestes*

Αἴγισθος ὁ: *Aegisthus*

Nobility
Electra described her husband as γενναῖος (*noble*, 39). Orestes has come to accept the Farmer's nobility by line 48, not because of his birth or descent, but because of his behaviour. He asks for more intimate details of their marriage than one would normally expect from a stranger, but Electra is clearly willing to let others know of her situation and of the outrages that have been done to her by her mother and step-father.

Q.   How does our view of the Farmer develop in these lines?

Q.   The dictionary associates φεῦ with the following emotions: grief, anger, astonishment, admiration. Which do you think is appropriate in Orestes' response at line 48, and why?

Q.   What picture of Clytemnestra and Aegisthus emerges from lines 50–4?

Q.   What do we learn of Electra's attitude towards them?

GCSE vocabulary: *βούλομαι, εὖ, λαμβάνω, μήτηρ, νῦν, παῖς, τοῦτο (οὗτος).*

42   ἄγνευμα -ματος τό – *chastity, purity*; θεῖος -α -ον (> θεός) – *divine, religious*;
     ἀπαξιόω (> ἄξιος) – *think unworthy*. Orestes offers two possible reasons for the Farmer's
     scruples (ἤ . . . ἤ . . .). The participles pick up on the verb from the previous line (ἔτλη) ('*having . . . ,
     because he has . . . ?*').

43   γονεύς -έως ὁ – *father, forefather, parent*; ὑβρίζω – *insult, outrage*; ἠξίου 3rd sg.
     imperfect of o-contracted verb ἀξιόω (> ἄξιος) – *think it right*.

44   καὶ πῶς (11); γάμος ὁ – *marriage*; ἥσθην aorist of ἥδομαι – *enjoy, take pleasure*.

45   κύριος -α -ον – *having authority, entitled*; τὸν δόντα aorist participle of δίδωμι – '*the
     one who gave*' + acc: με; ἡγέομαι – *consider, regard as*.

46   ξυνῆκα aorist of συνίημι – *understand*; μή ποτε + subjunctive – *lest ever, in case
     some day*; δίκη ἡ – *justice, penalty*; δίκην ἐκτίνω aor. ἐξέτεισα + dat. – *be
     punished by*.

47   ταρβέω = φοβέομαι; τοῦτ' αὐτὸ ταρβῶν – '*this is exactly what he fears*'; πρός
     (adv.) – *in addition*; σώφρων -ονος – *self–controlled*; ἔφυ aor. of φύω (< physics) –
     '*he is by nature*'.

48   φεῦ (30); δραστέος (gerundive) – *must be treated, dealt with*.

49   ποθ' = ποτέ – *ever*; ἥκω – *come, have come*; ὁ νῦν ἀπών (< ἄπειμι) – '*the one now
     absent*'.

50   ἡ τεκοῦσα aorist participle of τίκτω – *give birth*; ἀνέχομαι (> ἀνά + ἔχω) – *put up
     with, endure*.

51   ἀνδρῶν – '*husbands*': Electra expresses her bitter thought in a balanced phrase: γυναῖκες
     [εἰσιν] φίλαι ἀνδρῶν, [καὶ] οὐ [φίλαι εἰσιν] παίδων.

52   τίνος οὔνεκα – *for what reason, why*; τάδε – '*in this*', '*over this*' (acc. of respect).

53   τεκεῖν – aorist infin. of τίκτω (50); ἀσθενῆ – n. pl. of ἀσθενής – supply '*children*'; τοιόσδε
     – (*a man*) *such as this*; δούς aorist participle of δίδωμι.

54   ὡς (+ opt.) = ἵνα; δῆθε = δή; ποινάτωρ -ορος ὁ/ἡ – *avenger* (in apposition to παῖδας).

55   βουλεύω (> βουλή) – *plan*; δίκην δίδωμι – *pay the penalty for something* (gen.) *to
     someone* (dat.), δοίη is an aorist optative used to express a wish '*may he pay . . .*'; ὧν (from
     ὅς ἥ ὅ).

Orestes asks further questions, the first of which is important to the plot. He tests the loyalty and sympathies of the Chorus and of Electra herself.

Or.	οἶδεν δέ σ' οὖσαν παρθένον μητρὸς πόσις;
El.	οὐκ οἶδε· σιγῇ τοῦθ' ὑφαιρούμεσθά νιν.
Or.	αἵδ' οὖν φίλαι σοι τούσδ' ἀκούουσιν λόγους;
El.	ὥστε στέγειν γε τἀμὰ καὶ σ' ἔπη καλῶς.
Or.	τί δῆτ' Ὀρέστης πρὸς τόδ', Ἄργος ἢν μόλῃ; 60
El.	ἤρου τόδ'; αἰσχρόν γ' εἶπας · οὐ γὰρ νῦν ἀκμή;
Or.	ἐλθὼν δὲ δὴ πῶς φονέας ἂν κτάνοι πατρός;
El.	τολμῶν ὑπ' ἐχθρῶν οἷ' ἐτολμήθη πατήρ.
Or.	ἦ καὶ μετ' αὐτοῦ μητέρ' ἂν τλαίης κτανεῖν;
El.	ταὐτῷ γε πελέκει τῷ πατὴρ ἀπώλετο. 65
Or.	λέγω τάδ' αὐτῷ, καὶ βέβαια τἀπὸ σοῦ;
El.	θάνοιμι μητρὸς αἷμ' ἐπισφάξασ' ἐμῆς.
Or.	φεῦ· εἴθ' ἦν Ὀρέστης πλησίον κλύων τάδε.
El.	ἀλλ', ὦ ξέν', οὐ γνοίην ἂν εἰσιδοῦσά νιν.
Or.	νέα γάρ, οὐδὲν θαῦμ', ἀπεζεύχθης νέου. 70
El.	εἷς ἂν μόνος νιν τῶν ἐμῶν γνοίη φίλων.

Names and places
Ἄργος -ους τό: *Argos*
Argos is the area around Mycenae and a city 11 km from Mycenae itself.

Recognition
Orestes comes closer and closer to revealing his identity. Although Electra has no means of recognizing her brother, she reminds him in line 71 that there is someone who would be able to recognize him. In this play, as in Homer's *Odyssey*, the true identity of the stranger is eventually revealed by a scar.

Revenge
Orestes's present situation is not unlike that of Shakespeare's Hamlet: both are intelligent and sensitive young men faced with the prospect of having to commit murder to avenge their father's untimely death. When we first meet Orestes in the play, it is clear he has come to kill Aegisthus, but his question to Electra about their own mother at line 64 is more tentative. In any culture, matricide seems a particularly shocking and unnatural crime.

Q.   Who seems to be more resolute about taking revenge, Electra or Orestes?
      How does the language they use reveal their attitudes?
Q.   Find an example of dramatic irony and explain its effect in this passage.

GCSE vocabulary: *αἰσχρός, ὁ αὐτός, γάρ, γιγνώσκω, ἐχθρός, καλῶς, οἶδα, σιγή, τίς τί.*

56 οἶδα indirect statement with acc. + participle; **παρθένος ἡ** – *virgin*; **πόσις ὁ** – *husband*.

57 **σιγῇ** – *by (our) silence*; **τοῦθ'** = τοῦτο; **ὑφαιρέομαι** (> ὑπό + αἱρέω) – *keep something* (acc.) *from someone* (acc.); **νιν** = αὐτόν. This detail becomes significant later in the play, when Electra pretends to be pregnant.

58 **αἵδε** (from ὅδε) – the **-δε** suffix indicates that Orestes gestures to the Chorus; **φίλαι σοί** (in apposition to αἵδε) – '*as your friends*'.

59 **ὥστε** + infinitive (26); **στέγω** – *cover, conceal, keep hidden*; **τἀμά** = τὰ ἐμά; **σ'** = σά (σός σή σόν); **ἔπος -ους τό** (< epic) – *word*; **καλῶς** – *well, nobly*.

60 **δῆτα** = emphatic form of δή; **πρὸς τόδ'** – *in response to this*; **ἤν** = ἐάν + subjunctive; **ἔμολον** – '*come to*'; supply verb 'do' or 'say' for the subject – 'Orestes'.

61 **ἠρόμην** aorist of ἐρωτάω; **εἶπας** = εἶπες; **ἀκμή ἡ** (< acme) – *perfect moment*.

62 **ἐλθών** participle substituting for an εἰ clause – '*if he came*'; **φονεύς -έως ὁ** – *murderer*; **κτάνοι** aorist from (ἀπο)κτείνω, ἄν + **potential** optative: '*would he kill*'.

63 **τολμάω** – *dare*; **οἷος -α -ον** – *such things as*. There may be a textual error, but the sense is clear: '*daring*' (τολμῶν) *such things as were dared by his enemies* (*against my father*).

64 **ἦ καί** – *would you also?*; **τλάω** (41) – for the optative see 62.

65 **ταὐτῷ** crasis for τῷ αὐτῷ – *the same*; **γε** – *yes*; **πέλεκυς -εως ὁ** – *axe*; **τῷ** = ᾧ (ὅς ἥ ὅ); **ἀπώλετο** (aorist of ἀπόλλυμαι) – '*perished*', '*was killed*'.

66 **λέγω** – deliberative subjunctive *am I to ...?, should I?*; **αὐτῷ** – i.e. Orestes; **βέβαιος -α -ον** – *firm, fixed, resolute*; **τἀπὸ σοῦ** = τὰ ἀπὸ σοῦ – *the things from you, your intention*.

67 **θάνοιμι** aorist optative for a wish for the future – '*may I die*', '*if only I could die*'; **αἷμα -ατος τό** (< haematology) – *blood*; **ἐπισφάζω** – *slaughter, shed* (usually of animal sacrifices).

68 **φεῦ** (48); **εἴθε** (of wishes for the past) – *if only*; **πλησίον** – *nearby*; **κλύω** = ἀκούω.

69 **γνοίην** potential aorist optative of γιγνώσκω; **εἰσιδοῦσα** from εἰσοράω; **νιν** = αὐτόν

70 **γάρ** – '*yes, for*'; **θαῦμα -ατος τό** – *wonder, surprise*; **ἀπεζεύχθης** aorist of ἀποζεύγνυμαι – *be unyoked, be separated from* + gen.

71 **γνοίη** (69) **potential** optative from γιγνώσκω; **τῶν ἐμῶν φίλων** – *my friends, those friendly to me*.

Orestes realizes that Electra is referring to the elderly tutor who rescued him.
He now asks Electra to describe her unhappy life, so that he can tell Orestes. The
Chorus of women also encourage Electra to speak about her suffering.

Or. ἆρ' ὃν λέγουσιν αὐτὸν ἐκκλέψαι φόνου;

El. πατρός γε παιδαγωγὸς ἀρχαῖος γέρων.

Or. ὁ κατθανών δὲ σὸς πατὴρ τύμβου κυρεῖ;

El. ἔκυρσεν ὡς ἔκυρσεν, ἐκβληθεὶς δόμων.   75

Or. οἴμοι, τόδ' οἷον εἶπας· αἴσθησις γὰρ οὖν
      καὶ τῶν θυραίων πημάτων δάκνει βροτούς.
      λέξον δ', ἵν' εἰδὼς σῷ κασιγνήτῳ φέρω
      λόγους ἀτερπεῖς, ἀλλ' ἀναγκαίους κλύειν.
      ἔνεστι δ' οἶκτος ἀμαθίᾳ μὲν οὐδαμοῦ,   80
      σοφοῖσι δ' ἀνδρῶν· καὶ γὰρ οὐδ' ἀζήμιον
      γνώμην ἐνεῖναι τοῖς σοφοῖς λίαν σοφήν.

Ch. κἀγὼ τὸν αὐτὸν τῷδ' ἔρον ψυχῆς ἔχω.
      πρόσω γὰρ ἄστεως οὖσα τὰν πόλει κακὰ
      οὐκ οἶδα, νῦν δὲ βούλομαι κἀγὼ μαθεῖν.   85

Orestes

Immediately after the death of Agamemnon, the palace was a dangerous place for Agamemnon's heir, Orestes, with a particular threat from Aegisthus, the new king. The **Tutor** (he appears as a character later in the play), was one of those loyal to the old king who helped Orestes get away to safety.

Knowing too much

The repetition of σοφός in lines 81–2 is striking. This word had a resonance for a late fifth-century Athenian, a little like our word 'clever' when it contains an element of suspicion; one view of sophists was that they manipulated people's views rather than gained a better understanding of the truth. Orestes, on the other hand, seems apprehensive of the truth he is about to hear from Electra.

Q.   Explain in your own words what you think Orestes is trying to say in lines 76–82.

Q.   Do you feel more sympathy for Orestes or Electra at this point in the play? Explain why.

Q.   Why do you think Orestes still does not reveal who he is to his sister?

GCSE vocabulary: αἰσθάνομαι, αὐτός, γέρων, ἐβλήθην (βάλλω), ἐγώ, εἶπον (λέγω), ἵνα + subj./opt., κακός, κλέπτω, μανθάνω, ὅς, οὖν, σοφός.

72   ἆρ' ὅν ... *is it the man whom* ...? ἐκκλέπτω (> κλέπτω) + gen. – *steal from*; φόνος ὁ (> φονεύω) – *murder.* Orestes quickly identifies the Tutor, who rescued him at the time of Agamemnon's murder, and who proves to be a key character later in the play.

73   γε – '*yes*'; παιδαγωγός ὁ (> παῖς + ἄγω) – *tutor*; ἀρχαῖος -α -ον (> archaic) – *ancient, old.* If Agamemnon was in his forties on his return from Troy, his tutor could easily be over seventy.

74   καταθνήσκω = ἀποθνήσκω; τύμβος ὁ – *tomb, monument*; κυρέω + gen. – *obtain, get, meet with.*

75   ἔκυρσεν (74); ὡς – *as, what*; ἐκβληθείς aorist passive of ἐκβάλλω – *throw out, cast out.*

76   οἴμοι (1); οἷον – *of what sort, 'what a thing'*; εἶπας (61); αἴσθησις -εως ἡ (> αἰσθάνομαι) – *perception*; γὰρ οὖν = γάρ.

77   θυραῖος -α -ον (> θύρα) – '*from outdoors', 'of other people'*; πῆμα -ατα τό – *trouble, misery*; δάκνω – *eat away at* (28); βροτός ὁ (< ambrosia) – *mortal.*

78   λέξον aorist imperative of λέγω; ἵν' = ἵνα + subjunctive; εἰδώς -υῖα -ός participle of οἶδα; κασίγνητος ὁ – *brother* (14). The imperative invites Electra to tell him more about her situation and will eventually be answered in a long speech (lines 86–117).

79   ἀτερπής -ές – *unhappy, joyless*; ἀναγκαῖος -α -ον (> ἀναγκάζω) – *necessary* + infinitive; κλύω (68).

80   ἔνεστι + dat. – *is present, is in*; οἶκτος ὁ – *pity*; ἀμαθία ἡ (> μανθάνω) – *ignorance*; οὐδαμοῦ – *nowhere, not ... anywhere.* The μέν ... δέ ... clause shows Orestes contrasting σοφοῖσι ἀνδρῶν (81), with those in a state of ignorance (ἀμαθία): people don't feel pity for what they are unaware of or don't understand.

81   σοφοῖσι ἀνδρῶν – '*men who are wise', 'the educated'*; καὶ γάρ – *and yet*; ἀζήμιος -ον – *without penalty, without cost*; οὐδ' ἀζήμιον (ἐστί) – *it is not ...* followed by accusative and infinitive in 82.

82   γνώμη ἡ – *opinion, mind*; ἐνεῖναι (80); λίαν – *excessively, too much.* A person needs to know the facts in order to be σοφός and feel pity, but too much of anything can prove damaging. The Delphic proverb 'μηδὲν ἄγαν' ('*nothing in excess*') encapsulates this caution.

83   κἀγώ = καὶ ἐγώ (crasis – also in 85); ἔρος ὁ (< erotic) – *desire*; ψυχή ἡ (< psychiatrist) – *soul, mind, 'in my mind'*; τὸν αὐτὸν τῷδ' – *the same ... as this man here* (i.e. Orestes).

84   πρόσω + gen. – *far away from*; ἄστυ -εως τό – *city* (32); τἀν = τὰ (κακά) ἐν + dat. The Chorus are also keen to hear the full story, implying that they themselves know very little.

Electra speaks about her pitiable living conditions and sense of exclusion.

El.   λέγοιμ' ἄν, εἰ χρή (χρὴ δὲ πρὸς φίλον λέγειν)
      τύχας βαρείας τὰς ἐμὰς κἀμοῦ πατρός.
      ἐπεὶ δὲ κινεῖς μῦθον, ἱκετεύω, ξένε,
      ἄγγελλ' Ὀρέστῃ τἀμὰ κἀκείνου κακά,
      πρῶτον μὲν οἵοις ἐν πέπλοις αὐλίζομαι,   90
      πίνῳ θ' ὅσῳ βέβριθ', ὑπὸ στέγαισί τε
      οἵαισι ναίω βασιλικῶν ἐκ δωμάτων,
      αὐτὴ μὲν ἐκμοχθοῦσα κερκίσιν πέπλους
      ἢ γυμνὸν ἔξω σῶμα καὶ στερήσομαι
      αὐτὴ δὲ πηγὰς ποταμίους φορουμένη,   95
      ἀνέορτος ἱερῶν καὶ χορῶν τητωμένη.
      ἀναίνομαι γυναῖκας οὖσα παρθένος,
      αἰσχύνομαι δὲ Κάστορ', ὃς πρὶν ἐς θεοὺς
      ἐλθεῖν ἔμ' ἐμνήστευεν, οὖσαν ἐγγενῆ.

Names and places

Κάστωρ -ορος ὁ: *Castor, one of the Heavenly Twins*
Castor appears as a god at the end of the play. He died in a fight but shared immortality with his divine
brother, Pollux or Polydeuces. Clytemnestra and Helen were their sisters, all four born from two eggs after
their mother Leda was impregnated by Zeus in disguise as a swan.

Q.   How effectively does Electra convey the oppressiveness of her day-to-day life
     and sense of isolation in lines 86–99? What values does she reveal?

Q.   Does she exaggerate or show too much self-pity in this part of her speech or is
     this simply a fair representation of her situation?

GCSE vocabulary: γυνή, ἐπεί, μῦθος, ξένος, πρῶτον, σῶμα, χρή.

86 λέγοιμ' ἄν potential optative – *I might speak of* (+ acc.) Electra makes a tentative start; χρή + infinitive – *must, should* (both meanings are used in this line). Electra has now accepted the ξένος as a φίλος since hearing of his connection to her brother (14).

87 βαρύς -εῖα -ύ – *heavy, oppressive*; κἀμοῦ = καὶ ἐμοῦ.

88 κινέω – *set in motion, prompt*; ἱκετεύω – *beg, beseech*.

89 κἀκείνου = καὶ ἐκείνου (i.e. Agamemnon).

90 πρῶτον μέν – instead of an answering ἔπειτα δέ, there follows a long list, opening with three indirect questions: οἴοις ... ὅσῳ ... οἴαισι; οἷος -α -ον (> ποῖος) – *what kind of*; πέπλος ὁ – *dress, robe*; αὐλίζομαι – *be stalled, be kept (like an animal)*.

91 πίνος ὁ – *squalor, filth*; ὅσος -η -ον (> πόσος) – *how much*; βέβριθα (perfect of βρίθω) – *be weighed down, be burdened*; ὑπό + dat. – *under*; στέγη ἡ – *roof*.

92 ναίω – *live, dwell*; ἐκ – 'instead of'; βασιλικός -ή -όν (> βασιλεύς) – *royal*; δώματα τά – *palace, house*.

93 αὐτὴ μέν ... αὐτὴ δέ ... (95) – adds to the sense of drudgery; ἐκμοχθέω – *work hard at*; κερκίς -ίδος ἡ – *shuttle* (used for weaving).

94 γυμνός -ή -όν (< gymnastics) – *naked*; ἕξω future of ἔχω; στερέομαι – *go without*. Women of royal rank and even goddesses might choose to weave alongside their maids, like Circe or Penelope in Homer's *Odyssey*.

95 πηγή ἡ – *water*; ποταμίος -η -ον (> ποταμός) – *from the river*; φορέομαι (> φέρω) – *fetch for oneself, collect*.

96 ἀνέορτος -ον + gen. – *not celebrating*; ἱερά -ῶν τά (> ἱερός) – *sacred rites*; χορός ὁ – *dance*; τητάομαι + gen. – *be deprived of*.

97 ἀναίνομαι – *reject, renounce, avoid*; γυνή ἡ – *married woman*; παρθένος ἡ – *virgin, unmarried woman*.

98 αἰσχύνομαι (> αἰσχρός) + acc. – *feel shame at, embarrassment at*; πρίν + infinitive – *before*.

99 μνηστεύω – *woo, be a suitor*; ἐγγενής -ές – *related, kin*; οὖσαν – 'since I was': being uncle and niece is presented as an advantage to marriage here.

Electra speaks of the luxury of the royal palace and laments the wrongs to her father.

μήτηρ δ' ἐμὴ Φρυγίοισιν ἐν σκυλεύμασιν	100
θρόνῳ κάθηται, πρὸς δ' ἕδραισιν Ἀσίδες	
δμωαὶ στατίζουσ', ἃς ἕπερσ' ἐμὸς πατήρ,	
Ἰδαῖα φάρη χρυσέαις ἐζευγμέναι	
πόρπαισιν. αἷμα δ' ἔτι πατρὸς κατὰ στέγας	
μέλαν σέσηπεν, ὃς δ' ἐκεῖνον ἔκτανεν	105
ἐς ταὐτὰ βαίνων ἅρματ' ἐκφοιτᾷ πατρί,	
καὶ σκῆπτρ' ἐν οἷς Ἕλλησιν ἐστρατηλάτει	
μιαιφόνοισι χερσὶ γαυροῦται λαβών.	
Ἀγαμέμνονος δὲ τύμβος ἠτιμασμένος	
οὔπω χοάς ποτ' οὐδὲ κλῶνα μυρσίνης	110
ἔλαβε, πυρᾷ δὲ χέρσος ἀγλαϊσμάτων.	
μέθῃ δὲ βρεχθεὶς τῆς ἐμῆς μητρὸς πόσις	
ὁ κλεινός, ὡς λέγουσιν, ἐνθρῴσκει τάφῳ	
πέτροις τε λεύει μνῆμα λάϊνον πατρός,	
καὶ τοῦτο τολμᾷ τοὔπος εἰς ἡμᾶς λέγειν·	115
'ποῦ παῖς Ὀρέστης; ἆρά σοι τύμβῳ καλῶς	
παρὼν ἀμύνει;' ταῦτ' ἀπὼν ὑβρίζεται.	

Names and places

Φρύγιος -α -ον: *Phrygian*; **Ἀσίς -ίδος**: *Asian*; **Ἰδαῖος -α -ον**: *from Mt Ida*
Three ways of referring to Troy: Phrygia is the region in which Troy lies, Asia refers to Asia Minor (modern Turkey); Mt Ida was the mountain near Troy.

Ἀγαμέμνων -ονος ὁ: *Agamemnon*

Aegisthus
Electra does not refer to Aegisthus by name but uses Orestes' phrase, μητρὸς πόσις ('*mother's husband*' 56, 112). Aegisthus is blamed for Agamemnon's murder by Zeus in Homer's *Odyssey* (*Odyssey* 1), whereas Agamemnon blames his wife (*Odyssey* 11); Clytemnestra is in control in Aeschylus' *Agamemnon*. The respective roles of Orestes and Electra also vary from version to version.

Q.   What themes does Electra focus on in describing life in the palace?
        How does she make the picture she paints particularly vivid and shocking.
Q.   Who comes out of this description worse, Clytemnestra or Aegisthus?
Q.   How would you expect Orestes to react as he listens to this speech?

GCSE vocabulary: ἔτι, τὰ αὐτά (ὁ αὐτός), ταῦτα (οὗτος), ὡς.

100 ἐν + dat. pl. – *among*; σκύλευμα -ατος τό – *spoils (of war)*.

101 θρόνος ὁ – *throne*; κάθημαι – *sit*; πρός – *by*; ἕδραι αἱ – *seat*.

102 δμωή ἡ – *(house) slave*; στατίζω – *stand*; πέρθω, aor. ἔπερσα – *plunder*.

103 φᾶρος -ους τό – *cloak*; χρύσεος -α -ον – *golden*; ἐζευγμέναι, perf. pass. participle of ζεύγνυμι – yoke – '*(their cloaks) fastened*' (φάρη – acc. of respect).

104 πόρπη ἡ – *clasp*; αἷμα -ατος τό – *blood*; κατά + acc. – *throughout*; στέγαι αἱ (< stegosaurus) – *house* (91).

105 μέλας -αινα -αν – *dark*; σήπω perfect σέσηπεν – '*has congealed*'; ὃς δ' ἐκεῖνον – ὃς refers to Aegisthus; ἐκεῖνον is Agamemnon; κτείνω aorist ἔκτανον – kill.

106 ταὐτά = τὰ αὐτά (pl. for sg.); ἅρμα -ατος τό – *chariot*; ἐκφοιτάω – *drive around*; πατρί – '*as my father*'.

107 σκῆπτρον τό – *sceptre*; ἐν οἷς – '*with which*' (referring back to σκῆπτρα); στρατηλατέω (> στρατιά) + dat. – *command, give commands to*.

108 μιαιφόνος -ον (agreeing with χερσί) – *blood-stained*; γαυρόομαι – *exult, rejoice*.

109 τύμβος ὁ – *tomb* (74); ἠτιμασμένος (perf. pass. partic. ἀτιμάζω) – *dishonoured*.

110 οὔπω – *not yet* (reinforced by ποτέ – *ever*); χοή ἡ – *drink–offering*; οὐδέ – *and not, not even, nor*; κλών -νός ὁ – *twig, spray*; μυρσίνη ἡ – *myrtle*.

111 λαμβάνω – '*receive*'; πυρά ἡ – *altar*; χέρσος -ον – *dry*; ἀγλάϊσμα -ατος τό – *offering* supply ἐστί. The **diaeresis** (¨) shows the vowels are pronounced separately.

112 μέθη ἡ – *strong drink*; βρέχω – *get wet, 'soaked'*; πόσις ὁ – *husband* (56).

113 κλεινός -ή -όν – *famous*; ἐνθρῴσκω + dat. – *leap onto*; τάφος ὁ – *tomb, grave*.

114 πέτρος ὁ – *stone, rock*; λεύω – *pelt*; μνῆμα -ατος τό – *memorial*; λάϊνος -η -ον – *made of stone, stone*.

115 τολμάω – *dare*; ἔπος -ους τό – *word, phrase, speech*.

116 σοι ('polite' dative) – '*I ask you*'; καλῶς – *nobly, well*.

117 πάρειμι/ἄπειμι – *I am present/absent* (31); ἀμύνω + dat. – *defend*; ταῦτα ὑβρίζεται – '*these are the insults he receives*', '*this is outrage he suffers*'; ἀπών refers to Orestes.

What happens next . . .

The **Farmer** returns and invites Orestes into his house. Electra scolds her husband for inviting in noble guests without the means to entertain them properly; she sends for her father's old **Tutor** (mentioned at line 73) to bring food. On arrival he reports his surprise in finding that an offering has recently been made at Agamemnon's tomb. His suspicions aroused, he looks carefully at Orestes and recognizes him from a scar by his eyebrow. Brother and sister are overjoyed.

The Tutor advises Orestes that Aegisthus has left town with a small group of slaves to make a sacrifice, an ideal opportunity to kill him without the danger of going into the city. Electra takes the lead in the death of her mother: she will pretend she has given birth and her mother will come to see her to undertake the birth ceremonies.

Orestes returns with the body of Aegisthus. A **Messenger** reports the details of how he was killed and Electra recalls the wrongs she suffered at her step-father's hands. Just as Orestes takes the body into the house, **Clytemnestra** arrives. Electra and Clytemnestra each argue their case until Clytemnestra steps inside to make a sacrifice for the new baby. Electra follows and screams are heard. The bodies of Clytemnestra and Aegisthus inside the house are revealed, brought out to view on a rolling platform (*eccyclema*).

The god **Castor** (mentioned at line 98) appears from above the stage (*ex machina*) to resolve the situation: Electra is to marry Pylades, but Orestes must go to Athens to face trial on the Areopagus (the Hill of Ares, close to the theatre in Athens where the audience first watched the play). Orestes argues in his defence that he had to obey the commands of Apollo's oracle at Delphi, a point Castor accepts, indicating that Orestes will be acquitted and go on to found a city in Arcadia. After a tearful leave-taking between brother and sister, Orestes leaves for Athens, pursued by the Furies.

Final questions

- Do you think that Orestes was right to murder Aegisthus? Give reasons for your answer.
- Do you consider the murder of Clytemnestra equally justifiable?
- Who do you think is more convincingly characterized by Euripides, Orestes or Electra? Which character do you find more sympathetic and why?
- Euripides introduces some new characters into his plot (e.g. the Farmer, the Tutor and Castor). Consider how they affect the story.
- Do you find the extract you have read dramatic? What do you understand by the term dramatic?

BACCHAE 434–508, 800–38 (here 1–114)

2022–2023 Prescription

See pages 139–40 for an introduction to Euripides.

The story so far . . .

Dionysus opens the play by revealing to the audience who he is and that he has come to the city of Thebes to introduce his worship to Greece, after establishing it in Asia. Thebes has a special significance because it was the home city of his mother, Semele. Zeus loved Semele but destroyed her when, at Hera's prompting, Semele asked Zeus to appear before her not in his usual mortal disguise, but as a god. Semele was pregnant at the moment of her death and Zeus sewed the embryo of Dionysus into his thigh to gestate, so Dionysus was 'twice-born'. Semele was the daughter of Cadmus, king of Thebes. Her family did not believe that her lover was Zeus, assuming she had made up the story to avoid disgrace. Dionysus and his followers, the **Chorus** of *bacchants* (see Fig. 7), have therefore come to make an example of Thebes to demonstrate his power. He has driven the women mad and they have gone out onto Mount Cithaeron, just outside Thebes, neglecting their homes. Among them are Cadmus' other daughters, including Agave, the mother of Pentheus who now rules Thebes in his grandfather's place.

The former king, **Cadmus** and the blind seer **Tiresias** agree that they should pay the god due honour and have dressed for the part in symbols associated with bacchic ritual, fawnskins and the *thyrsus* (a fennel stalk wrapped in ivy – see Fig. 7); they discuss how they will get to Cithaeron, even though they are old and, in Tiresias' case, blind. **Pentheus** returns to his city to find these two looking ridiculous. He has heard that an effeminate stranger has arrived and led some of the women of Thebes to the mountain. Pentheus is suspicious of these rites, which he assumes involve drinking wine and sexual activity. Tiresias, who knows the ways of the gods because he is a seer, lectures Pentheus on why he should honour Dionysus. Pentheus rejects his advice and orders his slaves to find and arrest the stranger . . .

Figure 7 *A follower of Dionysus, also known as a bacchant or maenad, carrying a thyrsus. The play takes its name from these Bacchae. This vase was painted c. 480.*
Photo © Marie-Lan Nguyen/Wikimedia Commons.

A servant brings in the stranger, who has allowed himself to be arrested easily. They have had less success in rounding up Dionysus's female followers, the bacchants.

Nominative words or phrases are in light blue, **verbs** in dark blue.

SERVANT:	Πενθεῦ, πάρεσμεν τήνδ' ἄγραν ἠγρευκότες
	ἐφ' ἣν ἔπεμψας, οὐδ' ἄκρανθ' ὡρμήσαμεν.
	ὁ θὴρ δ' ὅδ' ἡμῖν πρᾶος οὐδ' ὑπέσπασεν
	φυγῇ πόδ', ἀλλ' ἔδωκεν οὐκ ἄκων χέρας
	οὐδ' ὠχρός, οὐδ' ἤλλαξεν οἰνωπὸν γένυν, 5
	γελῶν δὲ καὶ δεῖν κἀπάγειν ἐφίετο
	ἔμενέ τε, τοὐμὸν εὐτρεπὲς ποιούμενος.
	κἀγὼ δι' αἰδοῦς εἶπον· 'ὦ ξέν', οὐχ ἑκὼν
	ἄγω σε, Πενθέως δ' ὅς μ' ἔπεμψ' ἐπιστολαῖς.'
	ἃς δ' αὖ σὺ βάκχας εἷρξας, ἃς συνήρπασας 10
	κἄδησας ἐν δεσμοῖσι πανδήμου στέγης,
	φροῦδαί γ' ἐκεῖναι λελυμέναι πρὸς ὀργάδας
	σκιρτῶσι Βρόμιον ἀνακαλούμεναι θεόν·

Names and places

Πενθεύς -έως ὁ: *Pentheus*
Grandson of Cadmus, the founder of Thebes. The meaning of his name is explained at line 75.

Βρόμιος ὁ: *Bromios* – a cult name of Dionysus.

Dionysus

He became one of the Twelve Olympians, after Hestia, goddess of the hearth, gave up her place to him. Also known as Bacchus and Bromios, he is the god of wine, madness, illusion and theatre. The subversive powers and contradictory nature of this elusive and enigmatic god are explored in this play, which was first performed in Athens at the dramatic festival dedicated to the god, known as the Great Dionysia.

Q.   What picture of the stranger and his followers is painted in these lines?

Q.   How would you expect Pentheus, the King of Thebes who has ordered the stranger's arrest, to react on hearing this speech?

GCSE vocabulary ἄγω, ἀλλά, γε, γελάω, ἐγώ, ἔδωκα (δίδωμι), ἐκεῖνος, εἶπον (λέγω), ἐπιστολή, ἡμεῖς, θεός, μένω, ξένος, ὅδε, οἶνος, ὅς, πέμπω, χείρ.

1   πάρειμι – *be present*; ἄγρα ἡ – *prey*; ἠγρευκότες perfect participle from ἀγρεύω
    '*having caught*'.

2   ἐφ' = ἐπί elision of the final iota; ἄκραντος -ον – *unfulfilled, unfinished*; ὁρμάω –
    start. Translate '*and I have not started something that is unfinished*'.

3   θήρ -ός ὁ – *wild animal* supply ἦν as the verb; ὅδ' = ὅδε (elision) – *this one here*;
    πρᾶος -α -ον – *gentle, tame*; οὐδέ – *and not*; ὑποσπάω – *withdraw secretly*.

4   πόδ' = πόδα by elision from πούς; φυγή ἡ – *flight*; lit: 'did not withdraw his foot secretly in
    flight', '*take off in flight*'; ἔδωκεν aorist of δίδωμι; ἄ(ε)κων -ουσα -ον – *unwilling*;
    χέρας = χεῖρας (an alternative spelling).

5   ὠχρός -ά -όν – *pale* (< ochre); ἀλλάσσω – *change*; οἰνωπός -ή -όν – *wine-faced*,
    '*red-faced*'; γένυς -υος ἡ – *cheek*.

6   δέω – *tie up, bind*; ἐπάγω – *lead in*; κἀπάγειν = καί + ἀπάγειν by crasis, where two
    words merge; ἀπάγειν = ἀπό + ἄγειν; ἐφίημι – *incite someone* (acc.) *to*.

7   τοὐμόν = τὸ ἐμόν by crasis – *my thing*, '*my task*'; εὐτρεπής -ές – *easy*.

8   κἀγώ = καὶ ἐγώ by crasis; αἰδώς -οῦς ἡ – *shame*; ἑκών -οῦσα -όν – *willing*.

9   ἔπεμψ' = ἔπεμψε by elision; ἐπιστολή ἡ – *letter, instruction, command*; the genitive
    Πενθέως belongs with ἐπιστολαῖς.

10 ἄς...ἄς... (ὅς ἥ ὅ), both refer to βάκχας – '*bacchants whom . . .*'; βάκχη ἡ – *bacchant*,
    maenad, female follower of Bacchus; αὖ – *again, moreover* (> αὖθις); εἷρξας
    aorist of εἴργω – *shut up, imprison*; συναρπάζω – *seize*.

11 κἄδησας = καὶ ἔδησας, (crasis) from δέω (6); δεσμός ὁ – *chain*; πάνδημος -α -ον –
    public; στέγη ἡ – *building*; πανδήμος στέγη = '*public prison*'.

12 φροῦδος -η -ον – *gone*; λελυμέναι perfect passive participle from λύω – '*having been
    released*'; ὀργάς -άδος, ἡ – *meadow*.

13 σκιρτάω – *leap*; ἀνακαλέω (> καλέω)– *invoke, call on*.

Pentheus confidently orders the prisoner's hands to be untied and remarks on his effeminate appearance.

αὐτόματα δ' αὐταῖς δεσμὰ διελύθη ποδῶν
κλῇδές τ' ἀνῆκαν θύρετρ' ἄνευ θνητῆς χερός.   15
πολλῶν δ' ὅδ' ἀνὴρ θαυμάτων ἥκει πλέως
ἐς τάσδε Θήβας. σοὶ δὲ τἄλλα χρὴ μέλειν.

PENTHEUS: μέθεσθε χειρῶν τοῦδ'· ἐν ἄρκυσιν γὰρ ὢν
οὐκ ἔστιν οὕτως ὠκὺς ὥστε μ' ἐκφυγεῖν.
ἀτὰρ τὸ μὲν σῶμ' οὐκ ἄμορφος εἶ, ξένε,   20
ὡς ἐς γυναῖκας, ἐφ' ὅπερ ἐς Θήβας πάρει·
πλόκαμός τε γάρ σου ταναὸς οὐ πάλης ὕπο,
γένυν παρ' αὐτὴν κεχυμένος, πόθου πλέως·
λευκὴν δὲ χροιὰν ἐκ παρασκευῆς ἔχεις,
οὐχ ἡλίου βολαῖσιν, ἀλλ' ὑπὸ σκιᾶς,   25
τὴν Ἀφροδίτην καλλονῇ θηρώμενος.
πρῶτον μὲν οὖν μοι λέξον ὅστις εἶ γένος.

Names and places
Θῆβαι -ῶν αἱ: *Thebes*
A city in Boeotia about 120 km northwest of Athens. It was founded by Cadmus after he was exiled from Phoenicia, and is the setting for many Greek tragedies.

Wonders
At various points in the play things occur against the natural order of things. Here, the chains have fallen off the women so they can escape. The servant, unlike Pentheus, is clearly impressed by these signs of the god's power.

The effeminate appearance of Dionysus
Dionysus' feminine qualities are emphasized throughout the play yet he has a hold over the women who come flocking to him – indeed Pentheus suspects Dionysus has sexual designs on them. These ambiguities and contradictions prove fatally attractive to Pentheus and eventually bring about his undoing.

Q.   How does the servant emphasize the wonders of what he has seen?

Q.   What details does Pentheus notice about Dionysus' appearance? How does he account for these?

Q.   Who seems the more powerful presence on stage, Pentheus or Dionysus?

GCSE vocabulary: *ἄλλος, ἀνήρ, αὐτός, γυνή, εἶ (εἰμί), ἐκφεύγω, θαυμάζω, λύω, ὅδε, οὖν, οὕτως, πολύς, πρῶτον, σύ, σῶμα, φεύγω, χρή, ὤν (εἰμί).*

14   αὐτόματος -η -ον (> automatic) – *by themselves*; αὐταῖς – *to them* ('possessive' dat.), *'their'*; δεσμά τά – *chains, bonds*; διαλύω – *loosen* (> λύω); ποδῶν – genitive is used to show separation from.

15   κλής -ηδός ἡ – *bar, bolt*; ἀνῆκαν aorist of ἀνίημι – *undo, open*; θύρετρα τά = θύρα; θνητός -ή -όν – *mortal*; χερός = χειρός (4).

16   ἀνήρ = ὁ ἀνήρ; θαῦμα -ατος τό (> θαυμάζω) – *marvel, amazing thing*; πλέως -έων + gen. – *full of*.

17   τἄλλα = τὰ ἄλλα; μέλω – *be a concern to*.

18   μέθεσθε – aorist imperative plural of μεθίημι + gen. – *let go of*; τοῦδε – *this man* (i.e. the stranger); ἄρκυς -υος ἡ – *(hunter's) net*.

19   ὠκύς -εῖα -ύ – *swift, quick*; οὕτως ... ὥστε – '*so quick that . . .*' or '*swift enough to . . .*' with infinitive showing the likelihood of the result; ἐκφεύγω – *escape*.

20   ἀτάρ = *yet*; ἄμορφος -ον – *unattractive*; σῶμα – acc. sg. '*as to your body*' (accusative of respect).

21   ὡς ἐς γυναῖκας – '*as regards women*', '*as far as women are concerned*'; ἐφ' ὅπερ – '*for which reason*'; ἐς (= εἰς) – '*in*'; πάρειμι – *be present* (1).

22   πλόκαμος ὁ – *(lock of) hair, curl*; ταναός -ή -όν – *long*; πάλη ἡ – *wrestling*.

23   γένυς -υος ἡ – *cheek* (5); παρά + acc. – *next to, by*; κεχυμένος perfect middle participle from χέω – *flow*; πόθος ὁ – *desire*; πλέως (16).

24   λευκός -ή -όν (< leukaemia) – *white, pale*; χροιά ἡ – *skin*; παρασκευή ἡ – *preparation, care, attention*.

25   ἥλιος ὁ (< heliocentric) – *sun*; βολή ἡ – *ray* (> βάλλω); σκιά ἡ – *shade*.

26   Ἀφροδίτη ἡ – either the goddess *Aphrodite* or what she represents *(sexual) love*; καλλονή ἡ – *beauty* (> καλός); θηράω – *hunt, chase* (> θήρ 3).

27   πρῶτον (adv.) – *first* (> πρῶτος); λέξον aorist imperative singular of λέγω; ὅστις ἥτις ὅ τι – *who* (interrogative): γένος τό (< genetic) – *race*, accusative of respect, lit. '*who you are as to race*', i.e. '*what race you are*'.

Pentheus questions the stranger about the nature of his cult.

Dionysus	οὐ κόμπος οὐδείς, ῥᾴδιον δ' εἰπεῖν τόδε.	
	τὸν ἀνθεμώδη Τμῶλον οἶσθά που κλύων.	
Pentheus	οἶδ', ὃς τὸ Σάρδεων ἄστυ περιβάλλει κύκλῳ.	30
Di.	ἐντεῦθέν εἰμι, Λυδία δέ μοι πατρίς.	
Pe.	πόθεν δὲ τελετὰς τάσδ' ἄγεις ἐς Ἑλλάδα;	
Di.	Διόνυσος αὐτός μ' εἰσέβησ', ὁ τοῦ Διός.	
Pe.	Ζεὺς δ' ἔστ' ἐκεῖ τις ὃς νέους τίκτει θεούς;	
Di.	οὔκ, ἀλλ' ὁ Σεμέλην ἐνθάδε ζεύξας γάμοις.	35
Pe.	πότερα δὲ νύκτωρ σ' ἢ κατ' ὄμμ' ἠνάγκασεν;	
Di.	ὁρῶν ὁρῶντα, καὶ δίδωσιν ὄργια.	
Pe.	τὰ δ' ὄργι' ἐστὶ τίν' ἰδέαν ἔχοντά σοι;	
Di.	ἄρρητ' ἀβακχεύτοισιν εἰδέναι βροτῶν.	
Pe.	ἔχει δ' ὄνησιν τοῖσι θύουσιν τίνα;	40
Di.	οὐ θέμις ἀκοῦσαί σ', ἔστι δ' ἄξι' εἰδέναι.	

Names and places

Τμῶλος ὁ: *Tmolus*; **Σάρδεις -εων αἱ:** *Sardis*; **Λυδία -ας ἡ:** *Lydia*
Lydia was a kingdom in Asia Minor whose capital, Sardis, was near Mt Tmolus.

Διόνυσος ὁ: *Dionysus, Bacchus*; **Σεμέλη ἡ:** *Semele*
By using this form of his name in the same breath as **Διός** (Ζεύς, < deus (Latin), deity), Dionysus emphasizes his paternity. Semele was Dionysus' mother.

Dramatic tension

The characters move from longer speeches to line by line in quick-fire responses known as **stichomythia**. This faster pace generally heightens the tension.

Eastern cults

A number of 'mystery' cults like those of Attis, Cybele, Mithras and Christianity, came from the east to Greece and Rome and were viewed with suspicion at first. They demanded personal commitment from their followers and required initiation into secret rites, often with the promise of a joyful after-life.

Q. What tone does Dionysus adopt in his answers to the king?

Q. Is Pentheus suspicious of all gods, or just of Dionysus? What other suspicions does he reveal?

GCSE vocabulary: *ἀκούω, ἀναγκάζω, ἄξιος, βαίνω, βάλλω, εἰδέναι (οἶδα), ἐκεῖ, Ἑλλάς, ἐνθάδε, ἔχω, θύω, νέος, νύξ, ὁράω, οὐδείς, πόθεν, ῥᾴδιος.*

28 κόμπος ὁ – *boast*; οὐ . . . οὐδείς – do not cancel each other out, but emphasize the
negative; ῥᾴδιον – neuter, supply ἐστί – *'it is easy to . . .'*.

29 ἀνθεμώδης -ες – *full of flowers*; οἶσθα present tense of οἶδα; που – *I suppose, no
doubt*; κλύω = ἀκούω.

30 ὅς – *'the one which'*; ἄστυ -εως τό – *city* (centre rather than the surrounding territory);
περιβάλλω – *surround* (>περί + βάλλω); κύκλος ὁ (< cycle) – *circle*; οἶδα – *'Yes, I
know'* in line for line dialogue (**stichomythia**), Greek doesn't usually use words for 'yes' or 'no';
these may need to be supplied in an English translation.

31 ἐντεῦθεν – *from there*; πατρίς -ίδος ἡ – *native land*, supply the verb ἐστί.

32 πόθεν – *from where?*; τελετή ἡ – *ceremony, rite*.

33 εἰσέβησε – aorist from εἰσβαίνω; ὁ τοῦ Διός – supply υἱός.

34 ἐκεῖ – *there* (i.e. in Lydia); τίκτω – *I give birth to*.

35 οὔκ – *'no'* (30); ἐνθάδε – *here*; ζεύξας – aorist participle from ζεύγνυμι – *yoke, join,
couple with*; γάμος ὁ – *marriage*, (dat.) *'in marriage'*.

36 πότερα . . . ἤ – *'(whether) . . . or'*; νύκτωρ – *at night* (> νύξ); σ' = σέ (acc.); ὄμμα
-ατος τό – *eye*; κατ' ὄμμα – *'to your face'*, *'when you could see him'*. πότερα –
introduces a question with two possible responses. In English, it is usually better to leave 'whether'
out.

37 ὁρῶν ὁρῶντα – literally *'(I) seeing (him) seeing (me)'*: Greek can often be very compressed in
verse and you need to take very careful notice of the cases; δίδωσιν present of δίδωμι – *give,
establish*; ὄργια -ίων τά (< orgy) – *rites, mysteries*.

38 ἰδέα ἡ – *kind, sort*; σοί – *'in your opinion'*.

39 ἄρρητος -ον (< rhetoric) – *not to be spoken, must not be spoken*, supply ἐστί – *'these
things are'*; ἀβάκχευτος -ον – *non-Bacchant*; εἰδέναι = infinitive of οἶδα; βροτός ὁ
– *mortal*.

40 ὄνησις -εως ἡ – *advantage, profit*; τοῖσι θύουσιν – dat. pl. participle of θύω.

41 θέμις – *lawful, right* (supply ἐστί + accusative + infinitive); ἄξιος -α, -ον + infin. – *worth
doing*; εἰδέναι (39).

Dionysus' answers to Pentheus' questions are evasive and clever.

Pe. εὖ τοῦτ' ἐκιβδήλευσας, ἵν' ἀκοῦσαι θέλω.

Di. ἀσέβειαν ἀσκοῦντ' ὄργι' ἐχθαίρει θεοῦ.

Pe. ὁ θεός, ὁρᾶν γὰρ φὴς σαφῶς, ποῖός τις ἦν;

Di. ὁποῖος ἤθελ'· οὐκ ἐγὼ 'τασσον τόδε.   45

Pe. τοῦτ' αὖ παρωχέτευσας εὖ γ' οὐδὲν λέγων.

Di. δόξει τις ἀμαθεῖ σοφὰ λέγων οὐκ εὖ φρονεῖν.

Pe. ἦλθες δὲ πρῶτα δεῦρ' ἄγων τὸν δαίμονα;

Di. πᾶς ἀναχορεύει βαρβάρων τάδ' ὄργια.

Pe. φρονοῦσι γὰρ κάκιον Ἑλλήνων πολύ.   50

Di. τάδ' εὖ γε μᾶλλον· οἱ νόμοι δὲ διάφοροι.

Pe. τὰ δ' ἱερὰ νύκτωρ ἢ μεθ' ἡμέραν τελεῖς;

Di. νύκτωρ τὰ πολλά· σεμνότητ' ἔχει σκότος.

Pe. τοῦτ' ἐς γυναῖκας δόλιόν ἐστι καὶ σαθρόν.

Di. κἀν ἡμέρᾳ τό γ' αἰσχρὸν ἐξεύροι τις ἄν.   55

Talking in riddles

Dionysus is starting to entrap Pentheus with his own curiosity, even though Pentheus remains suspicious (42). There is an emphasis on knowledge and ignorance, appropriate to a secret cult. What σοφὰ λέγων (*speaking cleverly*) in 47 implies was an issue in Athens in the late fifth century. People had become suspicious of the way an argument could be manipulated so that truth became obscured rather than clarified. Such 'cleverness' is satirized in Aristophanes' comedy *Clouds*, where he targets freelance teachers of rhetoric known as *sophists*.

Q. How does Dionysus increase Pentheus' curiosity in his ceremonies?

Q. How specific is the information Dionysus gives?

Q. Does this dialogue alter your impressions of Pentheus?

GCSE vocabulary: ἄγω, αἰσχρός, δοκεῖ, ἐθέλω, Ἕλλην, εὖ, ἡμέρα, ἦλθον (ἔρχομαι), ἵνα, κακός, μᾶλλον, νόμος, οὐδείς, οὗτος, πᾶς, ποῖος, σοφός, φημί.

42   **κιβδηλεύω** – *play a trick on* – the literal meaning is to give someone a fake coin (κίβδος – alloy); **ἵν'** = ἵνα + subj./opt. – purpose clause; **θέλω** = ἐθέλω.

43   **ἀσέβεια ἡ** – *disrespect, impiety*; **ἀσκοῦντα** – '*the person who practises . . .*'; **ἐχθαίρω** – *hate, abhor* (> ἐχθρός), the subject is ὄργια – '*the god's rites hate . . .*'.

44   **γάρ** – '*since*'; **φής** – from φημί (which introduces an indirect statement); **σαφῶς** – *clearly*; (ὁ)ποῖος – *what sort of, 'what was he like?'*

45   **ἤθελ'** = ἤθελε; **'τασσον** from τάσσω – *arrange, manage.*

46   **αὖ** = αὖθις (10); **παροχετεύω** – *divert, side-track.*

47   **δοκέω** – *seem to someone* (dat.) *to be* (infin.); **ἀμαθής -ές** – *ignorant, stupid* (> ἀ + (ἔ)μαθον); **εὖ φρονεῖν** – *be sensible.*

48   **πρῶτα** (adv.) – *for the first time*; **δεῦρο** – *(to) here*; **δαίμων -ονος ὁ** (> demon) – *god, power.*

49   **ἀναχορεύω** (> chorus) – *dance*; πᾶς βαρβάρων is stronger than πάντες βάρβαροι because it focuses on each individual.

50   **γάρ** – '*yes, because*'; **κακὰ φρονέω** – *be foolish,* the opposite of εὖ φρονεῖν (47); **κάκιον** is comparative; **Ἑλλήνων** – gen. of comparison; **πολύ** – *much, by much.*

51   **τάδε** – accusative of respect *as to these things, in this respect*; **μᾶλλον** – *rather*; **διάφορος -ον** (> φέρω) – *different.*

52   **τὰ δ' ἱερά** – *the holy things, ceremonies,* a synonym for τὰ ὄργια but more respectful; **νύκτωρ** – *at night* (36); **μετὰ ἡμέραν** – *by day*; **τελέω** – *perform.*

53   **τὰ πολλά** (accusative of respect) – '*as for most things, mostly*'; **σεμνότης -ητος ἡ** – *solemnity, dignity*; **σκότος ὁ** – *darkness.*

54   **ἐς** – '*for*'; **δόλιος -α -ον** – *treacherous*; **σαθρός -ά -όν** – *unsound, unhealthy.*

55   **κἂν** (καὶ ἐν) **ἡμέρᾳ** – '*even during the day*'; **τό γ' αἰσχρόν** – τό + adjective makes a noun – '*something shameful*'; **ἐξευρίσκω** + ἄν is a **potential optative** – *might find out, discover.*

Pentheus becomes aggressive towards his prisoner, who taunts him in return.

Pe.   δίκην σε δοῦναι δεῖ σοφισμάτων κακῶν.

Di.   σὲ δ᾽ ἀμαθίας γε κἀσεβοῦντ᾽ ἐς τὸν θεόν.

Pe.   ὡς θρασὺς ὁ βάκχος κοὐκ ἀγύμναστος λόγων.

Di.   εἴφ᾽ ὅτι παθεῖν δεῖ· τί με τὸ δεινὸν ἐργάσῃ;

Pe.   πρῶτον μὲν ἁβρὸν βόστρυχον τεμῶ σέθεν.   60

Di.   ἱερὸς ὁ πλόκαμος· τῷ θεῷ δ᾽ αὐτὸν τρέφω.

Pe.   ἔπειτα θύρσον τόνδε παράδος ἐκ χεροῖν.

Di.   αὐτός μ᾽ ἀφαιροῦ· τόνδε Διονύσῳ φορῶ.

Pe.   εἱρκταῖσί τ᾽ ἔνδον σῶμα σὸν φυλάξομεν.

Di.   λύσει μ᾽ ὁ δαίμων αὐτός, ὅταν ἐγὼ θέλω.   65

Pe.   ὅταν γε καλέσῃς αὐτὸν ἐν βάκχαις σταθείς.

Di.   καὶ νῦν ἃ πάσχω πλησίον παρὼν ὁρᾷ.

Pe.   καὶ ποῦ 'στιν; οὐ γὰρ φανερὸς ὄμμασίν γ᾽ ἐμοῖς.

Di.   παρ᾽ ἐμοί· σὺ δ᾽ ἀσεβὴς αὐτὸς ὢν οὐκ εἰσορᾷς.

Dramatic irony

Pentheus believes that the man whom his servant has captured is one of Dionysus' followers – it obviously would not occur to him that he is a god. The audience know otherwise because they have heard the Prologue to the play in which Dionysus reveals himself as a god. The audience understand far more than Pentheus does in this scene.

Q.   What is the tone of line 56? How could the sounds of the words in this line help an actor characterize Pentheus?

Q.   How does Dionysus react to Pentheus' provocation?

Q.   Do you feel any pity for Pentheus in this scene? What other responses might he arouse in an audience.

Q.   What examples of dramatic irony can you find on this page?

GCSE vocabulary: αὐτός, γάρ, δεῖ, δεινός, ἐμός, ἐν + dat., ἔπειτα, καλέω, λόγος, λύω, νῦν, ὅτι, πάσχω, ποῦ, σῶμα.

56   δίκην δίδωμι + gen. – *pay the penalty, be punished for*; **σόφισμα -ατος τό**
     (> σοφός) – *word-play, cleverness* (often in a bad sense)

57   **ἀμαθία ἡ** – *ignorance* (47); **ἀσεβέω** – *dishonour, disrespect* (43). The syntax follows
     on from the previous line and so repeat '*You must pay the penalty*': ἀμαθίας genitive specifying
     the penalty ('*for your ignorance*') and participle κἀσεβοῦντ' agreeing with σέ (lit. '*you being
     disrespectful*') giving a reason ('*because . . .*').

58   **θρασύς -εῖα -ύ–** *bold, confident*; **βάκχος ὁ** – *Bacchant*; **ἀγύμναστος -ον**
     (< gymnast) – *untrained, unpractised in.*

59   **εἶφ'** = εἰπέ; **παθεῖν** – aorist of πάσχω; **τί . . . τὸ δεινόν** – *what terrible thing?*;
     ἐργάζομαι (> ἔργον) – *do something* (acc.) *to someone* (acc.).

60   **ἁβρός -ά -όν** – *pretty, delicate*; **βόστρυχος ὁ** – *curl* (*of hair*); **τέμνω** fut. τεμῶ –
     cut; **σέθεν** = σοῦ.

61   **πλόκαμος ὁ** – *lock* (*of hair*) (22); **τρέφω** – *nourish, grow.*

62   **θύρσος ὁ** – *thyrsus*; **παράδος** aorist imperative from παραδίδωμι – *hand over*; **χεροῖν**
     gen. **dual** of χείρ – (*pair of*) *hands.*

63   **ἀφαιρέομαι** (> ἀπό + αἱρέω) singular imperative; **φορέω** (> φέρω) – *bear, carry.*

64   **εἱρκτή ἡ** (> εἴργω 10) – *prison*; **ἔνδον** (adv.) – *inside.*

65   **δαίμων ὁ** (48); **ὅταν** + subjunctive – *whenever*; **θέλω** (42).

66   **γε** – *yes*; **ἐν βάκχαις** – '*among the Bacchants*'; **σταθείς** nominative singular masculine
     participle (< στ Latin 'sto', English 'stand') – *standing.*

67   **καὶ νῦν** – *even now*; **πλησίον** (adv.) – *close, nearby*; **πάρειμι** – *be present.*

68   **'στιν** = ἐστίν; **φανερός -ά -όν** (> φαίνομαι) – *visible, evident, clear*; **ὄμμα -ατος τό**
     – *eye*; γ' (γέ) emphasizes the previous word '*at least to my eyes*'.

69   **παρά** + dat. – *with, by, next to, in the presence of* – here it seems deliberately vague and
     misleading.; **ἀσεβής ἐς** – *disrespectful* (43); **ὤν** – participle, perhaps giving a reason
     '*because . . .*'; **εἰσοράω** = ὁράω.

Pentheus resorts to force.

Pe.   λάζυσθε· καταφρονεῖ με καὶ Θήβας ὅδε.   70
Di.   αὐδῶ με μὴ δεῖν σωφρονῶν οὐ σώφροσιν.
Pe.   ἐγὼ δὲ δεῖν γε, κυριώτερος σέθεν.
Di.   οὐκ οἶσθ' ὅ τι ζῆς, οὐδ' ὃ δρᾷς, οὐδ' ὅστις εἶ.
Pe.   Πενθεύς, Ἀγαύης παῖς, πατρὸς δ' Ἐχίονος.
Di.   ἐνδυστυχῆσαι τοὔνομ' ἐπιτήδειος εἶ.   75

Names and places

Ἀγαύη ἡ: *Agave* (*'illustrious'*)
Mother of Pentheus. She is leading the women of Thebes on Mt. Cithaeron.

Ἐχίων -ονος ὁ: *Echion* (*'snake-man'*)
Pentheus's father Echion was one of the men who sprung from the serpent's teeth sown by Cadmus to create a population for his new city of Thebes. As a reward for his help, Cadmus gave Echion his daughter, Agave, in marriage.

Q.   Compare Pentheus' orders in lines 18 and 70. Give a brief account of what has changed between the two commands.

Q.   What is the effect of Dionysus' three short statements in line 73?

Q.   Why does Pentheus give a description of his parentage in line 74?

Q.   What is the impact of learning the etymology (> ἔτυμος – *true, real, actual*) of Pentheus's name at this point in the drama?

GCSE vocabulary: *μή, ὄνομα, πατήρ*.

70   λάζυμαι (= λάζομαι, poetic for λαμβάνω) – *seize*; **καταφρονέω** – *despise*.

71   αὐδάω – *say, tell*; with μή + infin. – *tell not to, forbid*; **δέω** – *bind* (6); **σωφρονέω** – *be sensible* (two present participles; Dionysus compares himself (nom.) with the people he is talking to (dat.).

72   **δεῖν** – understand αὐδῶ again; γε emphasizes the preceding word; **κύριος** – *having power, authority*; **σέθεν** = σοῦ gen. of comparison. The first half of this line is ambiguous: it could either be a statement '*I say [that I] am binding you*' or a command '*I tell [them] to bind you*'.

73   **οἶσθα** > οἶδα (29); **ὅ** – *what*; **ζάω** – *live*; **δράω** – *do*; **ὅστις** – *who* (> ὅς + τίς). It is not clear that the words ὅτι ζῆς are correct. Perhaps they mean '*what kind of life you lead*'. Pentheus takes a very literal interpretation in his answer.

75   **ἐνδυστυχέω** – *be unlucky* (> δυστυχής); **τοὔνομ'** = τὸ ὄνομα, here **accusative of respect**; **ἐπιτήδειος -α -ον** + infinitive – *suitable*. Dionysus is deriving the name Pentheus from the word πένθος – *grief, sorrow, mourning*.

509–799: After this initial encounter, Pentheus orders his slaves to imprison the stranger in the stables. Almost immediately, the **Chorus** of Bacchants, Dionysus' true followers, report earth tremors and flames around the tomb of Semele. The stranger emerges, unconcerned, from the rubble that was his prison and his admiring audience of Bacchants enjoy his account of how he deluded Pentheus, disguising himself as a bull, and making the king·look ridiculous.

A **herdsman** comes from Cithaeron. The women he saw there were calm and at first he saw various miracles of nature and nothing wrong. However, when he and his friends decided to try to capture them, they turned violent, tearing apart cows with their bare hands and using their thyrsi as javelins. He repeats Tiresias' advice, that Pentheus should receive the god into Thebes. The Chorus reinforce this view. Pentheus threatens violence, this time by leading an armed force against the women in the mountains.

The lines just before the next section of Greek read:

Dionysus: I'd make a sacrifice to Dionysus rather than kick out against the god in anger – a mortal against a god.
Pentheus: I will make a sacrifice – the slaughter of women, which is what they deserve. I will create havoc in the glens of Cithaeron.
Dionysus: You will be routed, every one of you! This will be your shame – to turn with your bronze shields and flee from the thyrsi of the bacchants.

Pentheus is frustrated at his inability to control the stranger. Dionysus takes charge and offers his help.

Pe. ἀπόρῳ γε τῷδε συμπεπλέγμεθα ξένῳ,
     ὃς οὔτε πάσχων οὔτε δρῶν σιγήσεται.

Di. ὦ τᾶν, ἔτ' ἔστιν εὖ καταστῆσαι τάδε.

Pe. τί δρῶντα; δουλεύοντα δουλείαις ἐμαῖς;

Di. ἐγὼ γυναῖκας δεῦρ' ὅπλων ἄξω δίχα.   80

Pe. οἴμοι· τόδ' ἤδη δόλιον ἐς ἐμὲ μηχανᾷ.

Di. ποῖόν τι, σῶσαί σ' εἰ θέλω τέχναις ἐμαῖς;

Pe. ξυνέθεσθε κοινῇ τάδ', ἵνα βακχεύητ' ἀεί.

Di. καὶ μὴν ξυνεθέμην τοῦτό γ', ἴσθι, τῷ θεῷ.

Pe. ἐκφέρετέ μοι δεῦρ' ὅπλα, σὺ δὲ παῦσαι λέγων.   85

Di. ἄ·
     βούλῃ σφ' ἐν ὄρεσι συγκαθημένας ἰδεῖν;

Pe. μάλιστα, μυρίον γε δοὺς χρυσοῦ σταθμόν.

Di. τί δ' εἰς ἔρωτα τοῦδε πέπτωκας μέγαν;

Q. Many of these lines can be brought to life by thinking how they might be spoken. Try directing this scene, experimenting with different approaches to delivering the Greek lines. What does ἄ· (86) signify?

Q. Consider how and when Dionysus uses questions in this passage.

Q. How does Dionysus make the foolish plan of going to the mountains seem logical to Pentheus?

GCSE vocabulary: ἀεί, βούλομαι, δοῦλος, ἔτι, μάλιστα, ὅπλα, οὔτε ... οὔτε ..., παύω, πίπτω, ποῖος;, σῴζω, χρυσός.

76   ἄπορος -ον – *unmanageable, impossible*; συμπεπλέγμεθα perfect passive of
συμπλέκω – *entangle, lock together* (a metaphor from wrestling).

77   δράω – (73); σιγάω (> σιγή) – *be silent.*

78   τᾶν – *sir*; ἔστιν = ἔξεστι supply σέ; καταστῆσαι aorist infinitive of καθίστημι – *settle.*

79   δρῶντα – participle from δράω (73) agreeing with (the implied) σέ in 78; δουλεύω – *be a
slave*; δουλεία ἡ = δοῦλος.

80   δεῦρο – (*to*) *here*; ἄξω from ἄγω; δίχα + gen. – *without.*

81   οἴμοι – *alas! oh no!*; ἤδη – '*now*'; δόλιος – *deceitful*, take with τόδ'; ἐς – '*against*';
μηχανάομαι – *devise, plan* (μηχανᾷ is 2nd person sing.).

82   ποῖον (44) understand δόλιον from the previous line; τέχνη ἡ (< technique) – *skill.*

83   ξυνέθεσθε aorist from συντίθεμαι – *make an agreement*; κοινῇ – *in common,
'together'*; τάδ' – *with respect to these things, about this*; βακχεύω – *celebrate
the bacchic rites.*

84   καὶ μήν – *indeed, certainly*; ἴσθι – imperative from οἶδα.

85   δεῦρο (80); παῦσαι middle imperative; σύ does not need to be translated into English but
adds emphasis to the command.

86   ἅ – *ah!* exclamation expressing pity, envy, or contempt. This word occurs outside the regular
metre and so achieves greater force in delivery.

87   σφε = αὐτάς; συγκάθημαι participle, feminine plural – *be seated*; ἰδεῖν from εἶδον.

88   μυρίος -α -ον – *countless, immense*; δούς – aorist participle from δίδωμι – '*I would
give*'; σταθμός ὁ – *weight*

89   τί = διὰ τί; ἔρως -ωτος ὁ (> erotic) – *love, desire*; τοῦδε – *of this, for this* (i.e. seeing the
bacchants); πέπτωκας perfect 2nd singular of πίπτω.

Dionysus persuades Pentheus to go to Mt Cithaeron to see the women.

Pe.	λυπρῶς νιν εἰσίδοιμ' ἂν ἐξῳνωμένας.	90
Di.	ὅμως δ' ἴδοις ἂν ἡδέως ἅ σοι πικρά;	
Pe.	σάφ' ἴσθι, σιγῇ γ' ὑπ' ἐλάταις καθήμενος.	
Di.	ἀλλ' ἐξιχνεύσουσίν σε, κἂν ἔλθῃς λάθρα.	
Pe.	ἀλλ' ἐμφανῶς· καλῶς γὰρ ἐξεῖπας τάδε.	
Di.	ἄγωμεν οὖν σε κἀπιχειρήσεις ὁδῷ;	95
Pe.	ἄγ' ὡς τάχιστα· τοῦ χρόνου δέ σοι φθονῶ.	
Di.	στεῖλαί νυν ἀμφὶ χρωτὶ βυσσίνους πέπλους.	
Pe.	τί δὴ τόδ'; ἐς γυναῖκας ἐξ ἀνδρὸς τελῶ;	
Di.	μή σε κτάνωσιν, ἢν ἀνὴρ ὀφθῇς ἐκεῖ.	
Pe.	εὖ γ' εἶπας αὖ τόδ'· ὥς τις εἶ πάλαι σοφός.	100
Di.	Διόνυσος ἡμᾶς ἐξεμούσωσεν τάδε.	

Seeing the forbidden

Dionysus understands Pentheus better than Pentheus knows himself. As a ruler Pentheus has been outraged and reacted with violence to his imagined picture of debauched women roaming Cithaeron and having sex there; as a young man, however, he is really rather curious about such things, though he tries to hide it from himself as well as from others. Dionysus uses his superior powers and understanding to spring his pitiless trap and wreak his revenge.

Q.   Does Dionysus give Pentheus any good advice here?

Q.   Do any of Pentheus' responses surprise you, and if so why?

Q.   Do you think that Pentheus is still thinking rationally?

GCSE vocabulary: *ἄν, αὖθις, ἐάν, ἐκ/ἐξ* + gen., *ἡδύς, ἡμεῖς, καλῶς, λάθρα, ὁδός, πάλαι, χρόνος, ὡς τάχιστα, ὤφθην (ὁράω).*

90 **λυπρῶς** – *painfully, distressingly*; **εἰσίδοιμι ἄν** – potential optative from εἰσοράω – '*I would be distressed to see . . .*'; **νιν** = αὐτάς; **ἐξοινόομαι** (> ἐξ + οἶνος) feminine participle – *be very drunk*.

91 **ὅμως** – *nevertheless*; **ἴδοις ἄν** (90); **ἡδέως** (> ἡδύς) – *sweetly, gladly*; **πικρός -ά -όν** – *bitter, hateful*.

92 **σάφα** – *clearly*; **ἴσθι** (84); **σιγῇ** (> σιγή) – *silently*; **γε** – emphasizes σιγῇ; **ὑπό** + dat. – *under*; **ἐλάτη ἡ** – *pine tree*; **καθήμενος** present participle of κάθημαι – *sit*.

93 **ἐξιχνεύω** – *track down*; **κἄν** = καὶ ἐάν followed by subjunctive – *even if*.

94 **ἐμφανῶς** (> φαίνομαι, ἐφάνην) – *openly*; **ἀλλά** – marks an objection '*no, in that case*'.

95 **ἄγωμεν** is a jussive subjunctive – '*let us take, lead*'; **ἐπιχειρέω** (> ἐπί + χείρ – put one's hand to) – *make a start on*.

96 **ἄγε** (> ἄγω) – *come on*; **φθονέω** – *grudge, resent, someone* (dat.) *something* (gen.); **χρόνος ὁ** – *time spent, 'delay'*.

97 **στεῖλαι** (from στέλλω) – '*put on!*'; **νυν** – *then*; **ἀμφί** + dat. *around, next to*; **χρώς χρωτός ὁ** – *skin*; **βύσσινος -α -ον** – *made of linen*; **πέπλος ὁ** – *dress, peplos* (*robe worn only by females*).

98 **τί δὴ τόδε** – *why this indeed, why on earth?*; **τελέω** – *be classified, enrolled as*. τελῶ is here a subjunctive denoting a **deliberative question** '*Am I to be classified . . .*'.

99 **μή** + subjunctive, understand ἵνα – '*so that . . . not*'; **κτάνωσιν** aorist subjunctive from (ἀπο)κτείνω; **ἤν** = ἐάν; **ἀνήρ** in apposition to the subject, you '*as a man*'; **ὀφθῇς** aorist passive subjunctive of ὁράω.

100 **εἶπας** = εἶπες; **αὖ** = αὖθις; **πάλαι** – *long ago, 'for a long time'*.

101 **ἐκμουσόω** (< Muse) – *teach fully, inspire* (+ two accusatives).

Dionysus overcomes the last traces of resistance of Pentheus who is worried about putting on women's clothes.

Pe.	πῶς οὖν γένοιτ' ἂν ἃ σύ με νουθετεῖς καλῶς;
Di.	ἐγὼ στελῶ σε δωμάτων ἔσω μολών.
Pe.	τίνα στολήν; ἢ θῆλυν; ἀλλ' αἰδώς μ' ἔχει.
Di.	οὐκέτι θεατὴς μαινάδων πρόθυμος εἶ; 105
Pe.	στολὴν δὲ τίνα φῂς ἀμφὶ χρῶτ' ἐμὸν βαλεῖν;
Di.	κόμην μὲν ἐπὶ σῷ κρατὶ ταναὸν ἐκτενῶ.
Pe.	τὸ δεύτερον δὲ σχῆμα τοῦ κόσμου τί μοι;
Di.	πέπλοι ποδήρεις· ἐπὶ κάρᾳ δ' ἔσται μίτρα.
Pe.	ἦ καί τι πρὸς τοῖσδ' ἄλλο προσθήσεις ἐμοί; 110
Di.	θύρσον γε χειρὶ καὶ νεβροῦ στικτὸν δέρος.
Pe.	οὐκ ἂν δυναίμην θῆλυν ἐνδῦναι στολήν.
Di.	ἀλλ' αἷμα θήσεις συμβαλὼν βάκχαις μάχην.
Pe.	ὀρθῶς· μολεῖν χρὴ πρῶτον ἐς κατασκοπήν.

Comedy or tragedy

We tend to assume that Greek drama falls clearly into the two distinct genres, but there is some cross-over, with humorous scenes in some of Euripides' tragedies and sublime choral lyrics in some of Aristophanes' comedies. At the end of Plato's *Symposium*, Socrates argues that there is no significant difference between the art of a tragedian and a comedian. Laughter is often a nervous response and a way of dealing with troubling issues. The comic elements in this play could, if anything, contribute to the horror to which events are leading.

Q.   Paying close attention to the Greek, consider how to bring out the humour in this dressing-up scene.

Q.   What sort of incidental music might work if this scene were being staged for performance today?

GCSE vocabulary: γίγνομαι, δεύτερος, μάχη, πῶς, σύ, τίς;.

102 γένοιτο ἄν – aorist **potential optative** from γίγνομαι – '*how could this happen*'; νουθετέω – *advise someone* (acc.) *of something* (acc.).

103 στελῶ future of **στέλλω** – *dress, clothe*; ἔσω + gen. = εἰς; **μολών** aorist participle from ἔμολον – *go* (present = βλώσκω).

104 στολή ή (> στέλλω) – *clothes*; ἦ – '*is it really?*'; θῆλυς -εια -υ – *female*; αἰδώς -οῦς ή – *shame, shame has me* – '*I am ashamed*'.

105 θεατής ὁ – *spectator* (< theatre); μαινάς -άδος, ή – *Maenad*; πρόθυμος -η -ον – *eager*.

106 ἀμφί (97).

107 κόμη -ης ή – *hair, wig*; κράς κρατός τό – *head*; ταναός -ή -όν – *long-flowing*; ἐκτείνω – *spread*.

108 σχῆμα -ατος τό (< scheme) – *feature*; κόσμος, ὁ – *arrangement, decoration, get-up, disguise*.

109 πέπλος ὁ (97); ποδήρης -ες – *full-length, reaching to the feet* (> πούς, ποδός); κάρα τό – *head*; μιτρά ή – *headband, snood*.

110 ἦ καί – *surely* (expects the answer 'yes'); πρός (+ dat.) – *in addition to*; προσθήσεις future tense of προστίθημι – *add*.

111 νεβρός ὁ – *fawn*; στικτός -ή -όν – *dappled, spotted*; δέρος το – *skin*.

112 ἄν δυναίμην – **potential** optative of δύναμαι – *be able*; θῆλυς (104); ἐνέδυν aorist of ἐνδύω – *put on*.

113 αἷμα -ατος τό – *blood, bloodshed*; θήσεις future of τίθημι – *put, place cause*; (μάχην) συμβάλλω – *join in, clash in,* the participle acts as the first part of a conditional clause: '*if you clash . . .*'.

114 ὀρθῶς – *straightly, 'quite right'*; μολεῖν (103); κατασκοπή ή – *spying, reconnaissance*, ἐς κατασκοπήν '*to spy*'.

What happens next . . .

Pentheus, dressed in women's clothes, is led off to Mt Cithaeron through the streets of the city. After an ominous interlude from the Chorus, a **messenger** returns to describe how Pentheus was raised to the top of a tree to get a better view, but was spotted. The women failed to reach him with their missiles and so tore the tree from the ground with their bare hands, his mother Agave taking the lead. Pentheus fell and appealed to his mother to recognize him and spare him but, possessed by Dionysus, she tore his shoulder from his torso; his body parts are scattered over the mountain, his head is impaled on a thyrsus.

The Chorus rejoice in Dionysus' triumph.

Agave enters. In a state of delusion, she believes she is carrying the head of a young lion that she has killed, not that of her son. Cadmus arrives bearing a stretcher on which some scattered body parts of Pentheus have been collected. He gradually brings Agave back to a rational state and to a crushing realization of what she has done.

Dionysus finally manifests himself in his true form as a god; Agave is to be sent into exile and Cadmus will be turned into a snake. Dionysus asserts that his harsh punishment is right because Thebes insulted him, a god.

Harming enemies

We should try to see Dionysus' revenge on the unbelieving Pentheus not only from a modern perspective but also through ancient Greek eyes, where the idea of harming enemies was morally acceptable: Solon, hailed as laying foundations in the sixth century for the Athenian democratic constitution, prays:

> εἶναι δὲ γλυκὺν ὧδε φίλοις, ἐχθροῖσι δὲ πικρόν,
> τοῖσι μὲν αἰδοῖον, τοῖσι δὲ δεινὸν ἰδεῖν. *CURFRAG.tlg-0263.13*
> to be sweet to my friends but bitter to my enemies in this way;
> to the former, a man deserving of respect; to the latter, a man fearful to look on.

Final questions

- Do you think, by ancient or modern standards, the punishment of Pentheus was deserved? Was he warned? Is that relevant?

- Write an obituary for Pentheus.

- In lines 860–1 of the play Dionysus describes himself as 'θεὸς δεινότατος, ἀνθρώποισι δ' ἠπιώτατος' – '*a god most terrible, but most gentle to mankind*'. What picture of the god emerges in this play? Do you find the character of Dionysus attractive? Are the things he stands for important?

- *Bacchae* was Euripides' last play, produced after his death by his son. There are many theatrical elements in the story – men dressing up as women, viewing and being viewed, an actor carrying around a head that looks like a mask. How far could this play be said to be about the power of theatre?

PLATO, PHAEDO

59c–60a, 115b–d, 116b–d, 117c–118a

The Martyrdom of Socrates

2022–2023 Prescription

Plato's *Phaedo* is, among other things, an account of the death of Socrates. The work is written in the form of a dialogue: a friend, who knows that Phaedo was a close companion of Socrates, asks him to describe what happened during those final hours in prison.

As Socrates left nothing in writing, we rely on the works of Plato for an understanding of the philosopher's life and ideas. Socrates was an Athenian who was condemned to death in 399 at the age of seventy by hundreds of his fellow citizens. Plato, who was about thirty at the time, clearly admired him. In the *Apology* he dramatizes Socrates as he unsuccessfully defends himself in court.

Socrates argued that he had been confused with the 'Socrates' who appeared in Aristophanes' comedy, *Clouds*, a satire on the so-called 'sophists' who claimed to teach wisdom. Aristophanes represented this Socrates as teaching people to argue that wrong is right, undermining moral and religious values. In practice, Socrates denied that he had any knowledge at all to impart. He liked to engage in discussions on serious topics, like 'Can you teach someone to be good?', 'What is justice?' or 'What happens to the soul after death?' He usually demonstrated that anyone who thought they knew anything was wrong – and this irritated people.

The formal charges against Socrates were two-fold: that he corrupted the young and introduced new gods. As there was no state prosecution, his case was brought to court by private individuals. The Athenians were litigious and could use the courts to get at their enemies or win popularity. Socrates is sometimes presented as a scapegoat for Athens' defeat by the Spartans five years earlier. In 404 the Spartans put in place a puppet government of nobles that was overthrown within a year; some of these oligarchs included followers of Socrates such as Critias. Alcibiades was another 'corrupted' youth who betrayed Athens more than once on her road to defeat and troubled the Athenians, but had his many conversations with Socrates made him a better or worse citizen?

Socrates was found guilty. It was the custom of the court that the prosecution and defence each suggested the penalty: a fine or death, perhaps satisfied by exile. In Socrates' case, the prosecution proposed the death penalty, but Socrates, on the grounds that his irritating questions were good for Athens, suggested free meals for life, the reward of an Olympic victor. Given no serious alternative, the jury voted for the death penalty.

In the section you are about to read, Socrates is in prison awaiting death by hemlock. For religious reasons his execution may not take place until the return of a ship which set out for Delos the day before his trial. Yesterday evening, news arrived that the ship would be in Athens on the next day . . . .

Phaedo 59c–60a

Phaedo tells Echecrates how they used to visit the prison every day to see Socrates.
59c–d

Nominative *words or phrases are in* light blue, **verbs** *in* dark blue.

PHAEDO: ἐγώ σοι ἐξ ἀρχῆς πάντα πειράσομαι
διηγήσασθαι. ἀεὶ γὰρ δὴ καὶ τὰς πρόσθεν ἡμέρας
εἰώθεμεν φοιτᾶν καὶ ἐγὼ καὶ οἱ ἄλλοι παρὰ τὸν
Σωκράτη, συλλεγόμενοι ἕωθεν εἰς τὸ δικαστήριον ἐν
ᾧ καὶ ἡ δίκη ἐγένετο· πλησίον γὰρ ἦν τοῦ δεσμωτηρίου.   5

περιεμένομεν οὖν ἑκάστοτε ἕως ἀνοιχθείη τὸ
δεσμωτήριον, διατρίβοντες μετ' ἀλλήλων, ἀνεῴγετο
γὰρ οὐ πρῴ· ἐπειδὴ δὲ ἀνοιχθείη, εἰσῇμεν παρὰ τὸν
Σωκράτη καὶ τὰ πολλὰ διημερεύομεν μετ' αὐτοῦ. καὶ
δὴ καὶ τότε πρωαίτερον συνελέγημεν· τῇ γὰρ προτεραίᾳ   10
ἡμέρᾳ ἐπειδὴ ἐξήλθομεν ἐκ τοῦ δεσμωτηρίου ἑσπέρας,
ἐπυθόμεθα ὅτι τὸ πλοῖον ἐκ Δήλου ἀφιγμένον εἴη.

Names and places
Σωκράτης -ους (accusative **Σωκράτη**) ὁ – *Socrates*

Δῆλος ὁ – *Delos*
A sacred island in the Aegean believed to be the birthplace of Apollo and Artemis. The ship sent there in thanksgiving was believed to be Theseus' ship.

Timing of the execution
The day after the return of Theseus' ship from the island of Delos was the day appointed by the court for Socrates' death.

Plato and Phaedo
Plato's dialogue begins in the Peloponnese, shortly after Socrates' death, when Phaedo meets Echecrates in his home city of Elis. Phaedo lists the people who were with him in Athens with Socrates when he died, ending with '*I think Plato was ill*' 59b10.

Q. Why did Socrates' friends continue to go to the law court after the trial?
Q. How does their timing on this day compare with previous days (10)?
Q. What had his friends learnt on the previous evening (12)?
Q. What first impression of Socrates do you get from the words and actions of his friends?

GCSE vocabulary: ἀεί, ἀρχή, γίγνομαι, ἑσπέρα, ἡμέρα, ὅτι, πᾶς, σύ, συλλέγω, τότε.

1   πειράομαι – *try*; σοί is Echecrates, a friend.

2   διηγέομαι – *set out in detail*; πρόσθεν – *previous*, καὶ τὰς πρόσθεν ἡμέρας – '*even on the previous days*'.

3   εἴωθα – *be accustomed*; φοιτάω παρά + acc. – *visit someone*; καί . . . καί = τέ . . . καί.

4   ἕωθεν – *at dawn*; εἰς – '*at*'; δικαστήριον τό – *law-court*.

5   ᾧ from ὅς ἥ ὅ – *who, which*; καί – '*itself*', '*as well*'; δίκη ἡ (> δίκαιος) – *trial*; πλησίον + gen. – *near*; δεσμωτήριον τό – *prison*.

6   περιμένω = μένω; ἑκάστοτε (> ἕκαστος) – *each time*; ἀνοιχθείη aorist passive optative from ἀνοίγνυμι – *open* where ἕως has the idea of purpose: '*until it was opened*', '*for it to be opened*'.

7   διατρίβω – *spend time*; μετ' = μετά (elision of the alpha); ἀλλήλους -ας -α – *each other*; ἀνεῴγετο – imperfect passive of ἀνοίγνυμι – '*it was opened*'.

8   πρῴ – *early*; ἐπειδή = ἐπεί; εἰσῆμεν – imperfect of εἰσέρχομαι; παρά + acc. – *to*.

9   τὰ πολλά accusative used as an adverb – *for the most part, mostly*; διημερεύω (> διά + ἡμέρα) – *spend the day*.

10 καὶ δὴ καί τότε – '*on this particular occasion*'; πρῳαίτερον – *earlier*; συνελέγημεν aorist passive of συλλέγω; προτεραία ἡ – *previous*, dative for time '*when*'.

11 δεσμωτήριον τό (5); ἑσπέρας – genitive for time '*during which*'.

12 πλοῖον τό (> πλέω) – *boat*; ἀφιγμένον εἴη perfect optative from ἀφικνέομαι – '*had arrived*'.

Socrates asks Crito to take Xanthippe home. 59e–60a

παρηγγείλαμεν οὖν ἀλλήλοις ἥκειν ὡς πρῳαίτατα εἰς
τὸ εἰωθός. καὶ ἥκομεν καὶ ἡμῖν ἐξελθὼν ὁ θυρωρός,
ὅσπερ εἰώθει ὑπακούειν, εἶπεν περιμένειν καὶ μὴ   15
πρότερον παριέναι ἕως ἂν αὐτὸς κελεύσῃ· 'λύουσι γάρ,'
ἔφη, 'οἱ ἕνδεκα Σωκράτη καὶ παραγγέλλουσιν ὅπως
ἂν τῇδε τῇ ἡμέρᾳ τελευτᾷ.' οὐ πολὺν δ' οὖν χρόνον
ἐπισχὼν ἧκεν καὶ ἐκέλευεν ἡμᾶς εἰσιέναι. εἰσιόντες
οὖν κατελαμβάνομεν τὸν μὲν Σωκράτη ἄρτι λελυμένον,   20
τὴν δὲ Ξανθίππην — γιγνώσκεις γάρ — ἔχουσάν τε τὸ
παιδίον αὐτοῦ καὶ παρακαθημένην. ὡς οὖν εἶδεν ἡμᾶς
ἡ Ξανθίππη, ἀνηυφήμησέ τε καὶ τοιαῦτ' ἄττα εἶπεν, οἷα
δὴ εἰώθασιν αἱ γυναῖκες, ὅτι 'ὦ Σώκρατες, ὕστατον
δή σε προσεροῦσι νῦν οἱ ἐπιτήδειοι καὶ σὺ τούτους.'   25
καὶ ὁ Σωκράτης βλέψας εἰς τὸν Κρίτωνα, 'ὦ Κρίτων,'
ἔφη, 'ἀπαγέτω τις αὐτὴν οἴκαδε.'

Names and places

Ξανθίππη ἡ: *Xanthippe*
Socrates' wife, presented in later literature as very difficult and ill-tempered.

Κρίτων -ωνος ὁ: *Crito*
A wealthy and loyal friend of Socrates, keen to help Socrates to escape.

A woman's place

The removal of Xanthippe and one of Socrates' young sons underlines how the world of Socrates as presented by Plato is a very masculine one: Socrates dismisses his wife, depicted as too emotional, in order to spend his final hours in tranquillity with his (male) friends.

Q.   Why do Socrates' friends have to wait for entry on this day?

Q.   What impression do we get of Xanthippe here?

Q.   How does Socrates show what he thinks of his wife's behaviour?

GCSE vocabulary: γιγνώσκω, γυνή, ἔρχομαι, εἶναι, ἡμεῖς, ἰέναι, ἕως, μένω, νῦν, ὁράω, οὖν, τοιοῦτος.

After this, Xanthippe is led home. Socrates is relieved that his leg-irons have been taken off: the pain has been replaced by pleasure. He discusses the arguments for the immortality of the soul. If a person has led a good life, then the soul has a good future and so there is nothing to fear from death.

13 παραγγέλλω (> ἀγγέλλω) – *give orders to, tell*; ἀλλήλους -ας -α – *each other* (7); ἥκω – *(have) come*; ὡς πρῳαίτατα – *as early as possible* (10).

14 εἰωθός τό – *accustomed place*; θυρωρός ὁ (< θύρα) – *door-keeper*.

15 ὅσπερ = ὅς; ἔθω perfect εἴωθα (> ethos) – *be accustomed, usually do*; ὑπακούω (> ἀκούω) – *answer the door*; λέγω – *tell* someone to do something; περιμένω = μένω; πρότερον – *before* but best omitted in translation when used together with ἕως.

16 παριέναι from πάρειμι – *enter* (do not confuse ἰέναι – *to go* with εἶναι – *to be*); ἄν is used with the subjunctive to show indefiniteness, but does not need to be translated here; λύω here means release from chains, not release from prison.

17 οἱ ἕνδεκα – *The Eleven*, a group of officials who carried out the decisions of the court; ὅπως (= ἵνα) + subjunctive – *so that*.

18 τελευτάω – *die*; ἡμέρα – dative used for 'time when'.

19 ἐπέχω (> ἔχω) – *wait*; εἰσιέναι and εἰσιόντες – infinitive and participle of εἰσέρχομαι 'enter'.

20 καταλαμβάνω (> λαμβάνω) – *find*; ἄρτι – *recently, just now*; λελυμένον perfect passive participle of λύω, the first of three forming an indirect statement.

22 παιδίον τό (diminutive of παῖς) – *little boy* Socrates had two young sons, both probably under seven, and one older one; αὐτοῦ – *of him*, i.e. of Socrates; παρακάθημαι – *sit next to*; εἶδον aorist of ὁράω.

23 ἀνευφημέω (> φημί) – *shout out, give a cry*; ἄττα – *something*; οἷος -α – *like*.

24 εἴωθα – *be accustomed* (15); ὅτι – does not need to be translated because direct speech follows; ὕστατον (> ὕστερον) – *the last time*.

25 δή emphasizes the previous word – '*for the very last time*'; προσεροῦσι future of προσλέγω; ἐπιτήδεος ὁ – *close friend*; σὺ τούτους supply 'speak to' from the previous clause – this is a typically balanced Greek clause.

26 βλέπω – *look (at)*.

27 ἀπαγέτω (> ἀπό + ἄγω) third person singular imperative – '*let someone take away*'; οἴκαδε (> οἰκία) – the suffix –δε signifies movement towards.

Phaedo 115b–d

There has been a great deal of philosophical discussion between Socrates and his friends in which he has made it clear why he is calm in the face of death. It is getting towards the end of the final day and he knows that the time for his execution is imminent. He decides that he ought to have a bath so that the women do not have to wash his body after he is dead.

Socrates tells his friends how they should act. 115b

ταῦτα δὴ εἰπόντος αὐτοῦ ὁ Κρίτων, 'εἶεν,' ἔφη,
'ὦ Σώκρατες· τί δὲ τούτοις ἢ ἐμοὶ ἐπιστέλλεις ἢ περὶ
τῶν παίδων ἢ περὶ ἄλλου του, ὅτι ἄν σοι ποιοῦντες　　30
ἡμεῖς ἐν χάριτι μάλιστα ποιοῖμεν;'

'ἅπερ ἀεὶ λέγω,' ἔφη, 'ὦ Κρίτων, οὐδὲν καινότερον·
ὅτι ὑμῶν αὐτῶν ἐπιμελούμενοι ὑμεῖς καὶ ἐμοὶ καὶ τοῖς
ἐμοῖς καὶ ὑμῖν αὐτοῖς ἐν χάριτι ποιήσετε ἅττ' ἄν ποιῆτε,
κἂν μὴ νῦν ὁμολογήσητε· ἐὰν δὲ ὑμῶν μὲν αὐτῶν　　35
ἀμελῆτε καὶ μὴ 'θέλητε ὥσπερ κατ' ἴχνη κατὰ τὰ νῦν
τε εἰρημένα καὶ τὰ ἐν τῷ ἔμπροσθεν χρόνῳ ζῆν, οὐδὲ
ἐὰν πολλὰ ὁμολογήσητε ἐν τῷ παρόντι καὶ σφόδρα,
οὐδὲν πλέον ποιήσετε.'

'ταῦτα μὲν τοίνυν προθυμησόμεθα,' ἔφη, 'οὕτω　　40
ποιεῖν. θάπτωμεν δέ σε τίνα τρόπον;'

How can we help you?

Socrates' friends are keen to help him as much as possible in the final hours. The way he expresses his response in 32–9 is compressed. He is telling them that there is no new course of action they can try (οὐδὲν καινότερον). If they look after themselves (ὑμῶν αὐτῶν ἐπιμελούμενοι), i.e. their souls, even if this is counter-intuitive at the moment (κἂν μὴ νῦν ὁμολογήσητε), then they will bring pleasure to him as well as to themselves.

However, if they don't care for themselves and their souls (ἐὰν δὲ ὑμῶν μὲν αὐτῶν ἀμελῆτε), and are not willing to live a good life (ζῆν), as they have been discussing just now (τὰ νῦν τε εἰρημένα) and as they have discussed in the past (τὰ ἐν τῷ ἔμπροσθεν χρόνῳ), even if they pretend to agree in order to humour him, this will not be of any use.

In other words, what he wants them to do is to continue to live the philosophical life that he has been discussing with them.

GCSE vocabulary: *ἐγώ, οὗτος, μάλιστα, περί, πλείων, ποιέω, φημί.*

28 ἐιπόντος αὐτοῦ – a genitive absolute, referring to Socrates; εἶεν – *very well.*

29 ἐπιστέλλω – *give an instruction* a slightly formal word.

30 ἄλλου του (= τινός) – *anything else*; ὅτι from ὅστις – *which*; ἄν belongs with ποιοῖμεν in the next line; ποιοῦντες – present participle, perhaps translate as if substituting for a protasis '*if we were to do . . .*'.

31 χάρις -ιτος ἡ (< charity) – *favour*; ἐν χάριτι – '*as a favour*' ποιοῖμεν a potential optative with ἄν '*we might . . .*'.

32 ἅπερ (> ὅς + περ) – *the things which*, '*what*'; καινός (= νέος) – *new, strange, surprising.*

33 ἐπιμελέομαι + gen. – *take care of*; τοῖς ἐμοῖς – *my affairs, my situation.*

34 ἄττα – '*whatever*'; subjunctive + ἄν makes the verb indefinite.

35 κἄν = καὶ ἐάν; ὁμολογήσητε subjunctive of ὁμολογέω after ἐάν in a future condition – *agree, promise.*

36 ἀμελέω + gen. – *do not care for*; ἐθέλητε = ἐθέλητε; ὡσπερ – *as if, as it were*; κατά + acc. – *along*; ἴχνος τό – *track, path* κατιἴχνη – '*in my footsteps*'; κατά + acc. – *according to.*

37 τὰ νῦν εἰρημένα perfect participle of λέγω – '*the things we have talked about now*'; ἔμπροσθεν – *previously, in the past*: τὰ ἐν τῷ ἔμπροσθεν χρόνῳ supply εἰρημένα again – '*the things we have been talking about in the past*'; ζῆν infinitive of ζάω used with ἐθέλητε from the previous line – *live*; οὐδέ here is a double negative giving additional emphasis to οὐδέν in line 39, translate '*even*'.

38 πολλά – '*many things*'; ἐν τῷ παρόντι – '*at the present time*'; σφόδρα – *strongly, firmly.*

39 πλέον ποιέω – *be of use, do any good.*

40 τοίνυν – *so, accordingly*; προθυμέομαι – *be eager, very keen*; ἔφη – the subject is Crito.

41 τρόπος ὁ acc. of respect – *way*, '*as to what way*', '*how*'; θάπτω subjunctive for a deliberative question '*should we bury*', '*are we to bury*'.

Socrates explains what he expects after death.

'ὅπως ἄν,' ἔφη, 'βούλησθε, ἐάνπερ γε λάβητέ με καὶ
μὴ ἐκφύγω ὑμᾶς.' γελάσας δὲ ἅμα ἡσυχῇ καὶ πρὸς
ἡμᾶς ἀποβλέψας εἶπεν· 'οὐ πείθω, ὦ ἄνδρες, Κρίτωνα,
ὡς ἐγώ εἰμι οὗτος Σωκράτης, ὁ νυνὶ διαλεγόμενος καὶ   45
διατάττων ἕκαστον τῶν λεγομένων, ἀλλ' οἴεταί με
ἐκεῖνον εἶναι ὃν ὄψεται ὀλίγον ὕστερον νεκρόν, καὶ
ἐρωτᾷ δὴ πῶς με θάπτῃ. ὅτι δὲ ἐγώ πάλαι πολὺν
λόγον πεποίημαι, ὡς, ἐπειδὰν πίω τὸ φάρμακον, οὐκέτι
ὑμῖν παραμενῶ, ἀλλ' οἰχήσομαι ἀπιὼν εἰς μακάρων δή   50
τινας εὐδαιμονίας, ταῦτά μοι δοκῶ αὐτῷ ἄλλως λέγειν,
παραμυθούμενος ἅμα μὲν ὑμᾶς, ἅμα δ' ἐμαυτόν'.

Making fun of Crito

In this dialogue, Crito is characterized as being the practical one. When he raises the concerns about what
to do with the body after death (a key decision in any society) Socrates makes gentle fun, pretending that
Crito has not understand his teaching on the person being the soul, not the body. His body, which will be
buried, is different from the 'real' Socrates, the soul.

Q.   Explain why Socrates is amused in 42–3.

Q.   What does this gentle humour tell us about Socrates?

Q.   Why do you think the word νεκρόν is delayed in 47?

Q.   How clear an idea does Socrates give here about his ideas after death? Why do
      you think he expresses it in the way he does?

GCSE vocabulary: *βούλομαι, γελάω, ἕκαστος, ἐμαυτόν, ἐρωτάω, θάπτω, μένω, νεκρός,
πῶς;.*

42 ὅπως ἄν + subjunctive making idea indefinite – *in whatever way, however*; ἐάνπερ =
    ἐάν; γε – emphasizes the previous word (ἐάνπερ) but Socrates is being ironic; λαμβάνω –
    seize, catch; ἐκφεύγω – *escape*.

43 ἅμα – *at the same time*; ἡσυχῇ – *quietly, gently*.

44 ἀποβλέπω – *look away from* (26); πείθω – be careful always to distinguish πείθω + acc.
    (persuade) from πείθομαι + dat. (obey).

45 ὡς = ὅτι; νυνί is a stronger form of νῦν – *at this moment*; διαλέγομαι (< dialogue) –
    discuss, argue.

46 διατάττω – *set out in order, arrange*; τῶν λεγομένων – *the things being said*,
    '*the arguments*'; οἴομαι (+ acc. + infinitive) – *think, suppose*.

47 ἐκεῖνον agrees with the delayed noun νεκρόν; ὄψεται future of ὁράω; ὀλίγον ὕστερον –
    '*a little later*'.

48 θάπτῃ – deliberative subjunctive in an indirect question '*how he should bury*', '*how is
    he to bury*'; ὅτι = ὅ τι (30).

49 λόγος – '*argument*'; πεποίημαι – perfect of ποιέω, in conjunction with πάλαι '*I have
    been making for a long time*'; ὡς – *that*; ἐπειδάν = ἐπεί with subjunctive referring to
    indefinite time in the future; πίω – aor. subj. πίνω; φάρμακον τό – (< pharmaceutical)
    poison; οὐκέτι (> ἔτι) – *no longer*. Socrates is quoting back Crito's words to him ironically:
    he implies that Crito, a great supporter of his, has not really understood what he has been teaching.

50 παραμενῶ = contracted future tense of μένω; οἴχομαι ἀπιών – '*I will be gone*' (both
    words mean 'go away'); μάκαρ -αρος – *blest*.

51 εὐδαιμονία ἡ – *good fortune*, '*happy places*'; μοι δοκέω – '*I seem to me to*', '*I
    think that I*'; ἄλλως λέγω – *speak in vain*.

52 παραμυθέομαι (> μῦθος) – *reassure, comfort*; ἅμα – *at the same time* (43).

Phaedo 116b–d

There is a small gap after Passage 2. Socrates takes his bath sees his wife and children for the last time. He is calm, and prepares to say his farewells to his close friends.

An attendant of the officials arrives and politely tells Socrates that the time has come. 116b

καὶ ἦν ἤδη ἐγγὺς ἡλίου δυσμῶν· χρόνον γὰρ πολὺν
διέτριψεν ἔνδον. ἐλθὼν δ' ἐκαθέζετο λελουμένος καὶ
οὐ πολλὰ ἄττα μετὰ ταῦτα διελέχθη, καὶ ἧκεν ὁ τῶν   55
ἕνδεκα ὑπηρέτης καὶ στὰς παρ' αὐτόν, 'ὦ Σώκρατες,'
ἔφη, 'οὐ καταγνώσομαί γε σοῦ ὅπερ ἄλλων καταγιγνώσκω,
ὅτι μοι χαλεπαίνουσι καὶ καταρῶνται ἐπειδὰν
αὐτοῖς παραγγείλω πίνειν τὸ φάρμακον ἀναγκαζόντων
τῶν ἀρχόντων. σὲ δὲ ἐγὼ καὶ ἄλλως ἔγνωκα ἐν τούτῳ   60
τῷ χρόνῳ γενναιότατον καὶ πρᾳότατον καὶ ἄριστον
ἄνδρα ὄντα τῶν πώποτε δεῦρο ἀφικομένων, καὶ δὴ καὶ
νῦν εὖ οἶδ' ὅτι οὐκ ἐμοὶ χαλεπαίνεις, γιγνώσκεις γὰρ
τοὺς αἰτίους, ἀλλὰ ἐκείνοις. νῦν οὖν, οἶσθα γὰρ ἃ ἦλθον
ἀγγέλλων, χαῖρέ τε καὶ πειρῶ ὡς ῥᾷστα φέρειν τὰ   65
ἀναγκαῖα.' καὶ ἅμα δακρύσας μεταστρεφόμενος ἀπήει.

Bringing the message

Although The Eleven (see 17) were responsible for carrying out the decision of the court, they had delegated the actual task to an attendant, perhaps a slave rather than freed-man.

Q.   What is significant about the mention of sun-set here?

Q.   Why do you think Socrates had spent a long time bathing?

Q.   Why do you think not much was said after Socrates returned from his bath?

Q.   What had been the attendant's experience of previous executions?

Q.   How does Socrates appear to the attendant?

GCSE vocabulary: ἀναγκάζω, ἄρχων, γνώσομαι (γιγνώσκω), δακρύω, ἤδη, ἦλθον (ἔρχομαι), καθίζω, οἶδα, πειράομαι, πίνω, χρόνος.

53 ἐγγύς + gen. – *near*; ἥλιος ὁ – *sun*; δυσμαί αἱ (usually plural) – *setting*.

54 διατρίβω – *spend*; ἔνδον – *inside*; λελουμένος perfect participle of λούω wash – *'having washed'*, *'after washing'*. Socrates had gone into another room to bathe, giving his friends the opportunity to talk about him and has now returned.

55 ἄττα = τινά; οὐ πολλὰ ἄττα – *'not many things'*, *'a few things'*; διελέχθη from διαλέγομαι (45); ἥκω – *came*.

56 ὑπηρέτης ὁ – *attendant, slave*; στάς (< Latin *sto*)– *'standing'*; παρά + acc. – *next to*.

57 καταγιγνώσκω + gen. – *condemn, blame, hold against someone*; ὅπερ – *thing which*; ἄλλων – *'other men'*.

58 ὅτι – *because*; χαλεπαίνω + dat. (> χαλεπός) – *be annoyed at, be angry*; καταράομαι – *curse*; ἐπειδάν (49).

59 παραγγείλω aorist subjunctive of παραγγέλλω + dat. – *order, command*; φάρμακον τό (< pharmaceutical) – *poison*, (49); ἀναγκαζόντων τῶν ἀρχόντων – genitive absolute, referring to the Eleven.

60 καὶ ἄλλως – *besides*; ἔγνωκα perfect of γιγνώσκω, introducing an indirect statement with accusative and participle *'I have known that …'*; ἐν τούτῳ τῷ χρόνῳ, i.e. the time Socrates has been in prison.

61 γενναῖος -α -ον – *noble*; πρᾶος -ον – *gentle, moderate, affable*; ἄριστος -η -ον (> ἀγαθός) – *excellent, best*.

62 πώποτε – *ever*; δεῦρο – *(to) here*; τῶν … ἀφικομένων – *'best of those'* partitive genitive; καὶ δὴ καί – *moreover*.

63 οἶδ' = οἶδα; χαλεπαίνω (58).

64 ἐκείνοις – *'them'*, i.e. the officials who have given the order contrasing with ἐμοί; νῦν οὖν < *so then*; ἅ from ὅς ἥ ὅ – *'the things which'*.

65 χαῖρε – *farewell*; πειρῶ an imperative from πειράομαι, forming a pair with χαῖρε; ὡς ῥᾷστον (> ῥᾴδιος) – *as easily as possible*.

66 τὰ ἀναγκαῖα (> ἀναγκάζω) – *'the necessary things'*, *'what is necessary'*; ἅμα (43); δακρύσας – *having cried*, *'he burst into tears'*; μεταστρέφομαι – *turn oneself away*; ἀπήει – imperfect of ἄπειμι.

Socrates appreciates the courtesy with which he has been treated. 116d

καὶ ὁ Σωκράτης ἀναβλέψας πρὸς αὐτόν, 'καὶ σύ,'
ἔφη, 'χαῖρε, καὶ ἡμεῖς ταῦτα ποιήσομεν.' καὶ ἅμα πρὸς
ἡμᾶς, 'ὡς ἀστεῖος,' ἔφη, 'ὁ ἄνθρωπος· καὶ παρὰ πάντα
μοι τὸν χρόνον προσῄει καὶ διελέγετο ἐνίοτε καὶ ἦν   70
ἀνδρῶν λῷστος, καὶ νῦν ὡς γενναίως με ἀποδακρύει.
ἀλλ' ἄγε δή, ὦ Κρίτων, πειθώμεθα αὐτῷ, καὶ ἐνεγκάτω
τις τὸ φάρμακον, εἰ τέτριπται· εἰ δὲ μή, τριψάτω
ὁ ἄνθρωπος.'

Q.   What does Socrates think about the attendant?

Q.   Are the actions of the attendant what we might expect?

Q.   What does this tell us about Socrates?

Q.   Discuss this eighteenth-century representation of the moment when Socrates is
      handed the cup of hemlock.

Figure 8 *Engraving after David*, The Death of Socrates, *in the Bibliotheque
Nationale, Paris.*
Photo by Photo12/UIG/Getty Images.

---

*After this discussion about the poison, Crito suggests that Socrates should delay a
little: other condemned prisoners have taken a last meal with their family and friends
at this stage. Socrates disagrees: he does not want to prolong his life, because he is
ready to take the poison. His friends summon the attendant who explains that after
he drinks it, Socrates should walk around until his legs become heavy, and then lie
down and wait for the poison to take its course.*

67 ἀναβλέπω – *look up* (26).

68 χαῖρε (65); ποιήσομεν – plural used with a singular meaning 'Ι'.

69 ὡς – *how, what a*; ἀστεῖος -α -ον – *polite, charming, witty*; παρά + acc. –'*throughout*'.

70 μοί – '*my (time)* . . .'; προσῄει imperfect of πρόσειμι – *come to visit*; διαλέγομαι (45); ἐνίοτε – *sometimes*.

71 λῷστος -η -ον – *most agreeable, excellent*; ὡς – *how!* (69) γενναῖος -α -ον (61); ἀποδακρύω – *cry for.*

72 ἀλλ' ἄγε δή – *come on then*; πειθώμεθα jussive subjunctive – '*let us . . .*'; ἐνεγκάτω (> ἐν + φέρω) aorist 3rd person imperative – '*let someone bring in*'.

73 τρίβω – *grind, prepare* (literally, 'pounded': hemlock leaves were crushed to make the poison); τέτριπται perfect passive – '*it has been prepared*'; τριψάτω aorist 3rd person imperative – '*let him prepare it*'.

74 ἄνθρωπος – referring to the attendant.

Phaedo 117c–118a

Socrates drinks the poison. His friends cannot stop themselves from crying for him.
117c–d

καὶ ἅμ' εἰπὼν ταῦτα ἐπισχόμενος καὶ μάλα εὐχερῶς   75
καὶ εὐκόλως ἐξέπιεν. καὶ ἡμῶν οἱ πολλοὶ τέως μὲν
ἐπιεικῶς οἷοί τε ἦσαν κατέχειν τὸ μὴ δακρύειν, ὡς δὲ
εἴδομεν πίνοντά τε καὶ πεπωκότα, οὐκέτι, ἀλλ' ἐμοῦ γε
βίᾳ καὶ αὐτοῦ ἀστακτὶ ἐχώρει τὰ δάκρυα, ὥστε ἐγκα-
λυψάμενος ἀπέκλαον ἐμαυτόν – οὐ γὰρ δὴ ἐκεῖνόν γε,   80
ἀλλὰ τὴν ἐμαυτοῦ τύχην, οἵου ἀνδρὸς ἑταίρου ἐστερημένος εἴην. ὁ δὲ Κρίτων ἔτι πρότερος ἐμοῦ, ἐπειδὴ
οὐχ οἷός τ' ἦν κατέχειν τὰ δάκρυα, ἐξανέστη. Ἀπολλό-
δωρος δὲ καὶ ἐν τῷ ἔμπροσθεν χρόνῳ οὐδὲν ἐπαύετο
δακρύων, καὶ δὴ καὶ τότε ἀναβρυχησάμενος κλάων καὶ   85
ἀγανακτῶν οὐδένα ὅντινα οὐ κατέκλασε τῶν παρόντων
πλήν γε αὐτοῦ Σωκράτους.

Names and places
Ἀπολλόδωρος ὁ: *Apollodorus*
He is mentioned right at the start of this dialogue as one of the close friends of Socrates. Phaedo comments on him there, using much the same words as he does in the current passage, as follows:

> 'All of us there were in much the same state – sometimes laughing, sometimes crying and one of us in particular, Apollodorus. Of course, you know the man and his character.'

Q. Judging from his actions, what is Socrates' state of mind when he drinks the poison?

Q. When did the outburst of tears actually start?

Q. What did Phaedo do when he started crying? Why do you think he acted in this way?

Q. How would you characterize Apollodorus' reaction.

Q. Who is the one person not mentioned? Why do you think this is?

GCSE vocabulary: δακρύω, εἶπον, ἡμεῖς, οἷός τ' εἰμί, παύομαι, χρόνος.

75 ἅμα (43); ἐπέχω (aor. ἐπέσχον) – *hold up the (cup)*; μάλα – *very*; εὐχερῶς – *fearlessly.*

76 εὐκόλως – *calmly*; ἐκπίνω (> πίνω) – *drink up, drain*; τέως – *for a while.*

77 ἐπιεικῶς – *pretty well*; κατέχω + gen. – *hold back from, keep from*; τὸ μὴ δακρύειν – '*crying*' (the neuter article with an infinitive makes a noun; μή reinforces rather than cancels out the idea of restraint); ὡς – *when.*

78 εἴδομεν introduces an indirect statement with acc. + participle; πεπωκότα perfect acc. participle of πίνω – '*had drunk*'; οὐκέτι – *no longer*, i.e. they no longer held back from crying after seeing him actually take the poison.

79 βίᾳ + gen. – *in spite of* ἐμοῦ γε βίᾳ καὶ αὐτοῦ – '*very much* (γε) *in spite of myself*'; ἀστακτί (adverb) – *in floods*; χωρέω – *go*, '*flow*'; δάκρυον τό – *tear* this nom. pl. takes a singular verb.

80 ἐγκαλύπτομαι – *cover one's head*; ἀποκλάω – *weep for*; ἐμαυτόν (> ἐμός + αὐτός) – *myself*; γε – emphasizes ἐκεῖνον, i.e. Socrates.

81 τύχη ἡ – *misfortune*; οἷος -α -ον – *such*; ἑταῖρος ὁ – *companion* in apposition; ἐστερημένος εἴην perfect optative passive of στερέω + gen. – '*I had been deprived of*' the optative suggests he is reporting his thoughts so add '*thinking*'.

82 ἔτι – *even*; πρότερος -α -ον + gen. – *earlier, before.*

83 κατέχω – *restrain, hold back*; ἐξανέστη (ἐξ + ἀνά + < st) – '*he stood up and went out*'.

84 ἔμπροσθεν – *former*, καὶ ἐν τῷ ἔμπροσθεν χρόνῳ – '*even in the time up to now*'; οὐδέν accusative of respect – *as to nothing, not.*

85 καὶ δὴ καί – *especially*; ἀναβρυχάομαι – *bellow, roar*; κλάω (= δακρύω) '*cried his eyes out*'.

86 ἀγανακτέω – *be upset, distressed* (forms a pair of present participles with κλάων); κατακλάω – *make someone break down, make dissolve into tears*; οὐδένα . . . οὐ the double negative (litotes) gives added emphasis – '*there was no-one at all whom he did not make to break down*'; τῶν παρόντων from πάρειμι be present – '*of those present*'.

87 πλήν + gen. – *except*; γε emphasizes the one exception.

Socrates shames his friends into silence. Phaedo describes how the effects of the poison travel up the body of Socrates. 117d–118a

ἐκεῖνος δέ, 'οἷα,' ἔφη, 'ποιεῖτε, ὦ θαυμάσιοι. ἐγὼ
μέντοι οὐχ ἥκιστα τούτου ἕνεκα τὰς γυναῖκας ἀπέπεμψα,
ἵνα μὴ τοιαῦτα πλημμελοῖεν· καὶ γὰρ ἀκήκοα ὅτι ἐν 90
εὐφημίᾳ χρὴ τελευτᾶν. ἀλλ' ἡσυχίαν τε ἄγετε καὶ
καρτερεῖτε.'

καὶ ἡμεῖς ἀκούσαντες ᾐσχύνθημέν τε καὶ ἐπέσχομεν
τοῦ δακρύειν. ὁ δὲ περιελθών, ἐπειδή οἱ βαρύνεσθαι
ἔφη τὰ σκέλη, κατεκλίνη ὕπτιος —οὕτω γὰρ ἐκέλευεν 95
ὁ ἄνθρωπος— καὶ ἅμα ἐφαπτόμενος αὐτοῦ οὗτος ὁ δοὺς
τὸ φάρμακον, διαλιπὼν χρόνον ἐπεσκόπει τοὺς πόδας
καὶ τὰ σκέλη, κἄπειτα σφόδρα πιέσας αὐτοῦ τὸν πόδα
ἤρετο εἰ αἰσθάνοιτο, ὁ δ' οὐκ ἔφη. καὶ μετὰ τοῦτο
αὖθις τὰς κνήμας· καὶ ἐπανιὼν οὕτως ἡμῖν ἐπεδείκνυτο 100
ὅτι ψύχοιτό τε καὶ πήγνυτο. καὶ αὐτὸς ἥπτετο καὶ
εἶπεν ὅτι, ἐπειδὰν πρὸς τῇ καρδίᾳ γένηται αὐτῷ, τότε
οἰχήσεται.

Silence

In order to avoid offending the gods, sacrifices and other religious ceremonies were often performed in silence. Socrates' call for silence suggests that he is regarding his death as a ceremony of this type: his argument earlier in the dialogue, where there is a long philosophical discussion of the nature of the soul, has been that at death the soul enters the presence of the gods.

Q.   What approaches does Socrates use to stop his companions crying?

Q.   What stages does Phaedo record as the effects of the hemlock take hold?

Q.   How effective is the additional description of what the attendant does and says?

GCSE vocabulary: *αἰσθάνομαι, γίγνομαι, ἵνα, μέντοι, πούς, χρή.*

88 ἐκεῖνος – refers to Socrates; οἷα – *what sort of things, what's all this!* showing astonishment; θαυμάσιος -α -ον (> θαυμάζω) – *strange, odd* perhaps translate the vocative more idiomatically here as '*you. . . .*'.

89 ἥκιστα – *least*; ἕνεκα + gen. – *because of* the preposition ἕνεκα is unusual in that it is a 'post-positive' preposition that comes after its noun.

90 τοιαῦτα – '*in such a way*'; πλημμελέω (3rd person pl. optative) – *make a mistake, behave badly*; καὶ γάρ – *for truly*; ἀκήκοα – perfect tense of ἀκούω '*I have heard*'.

91 εὐφημία ἡ – *silence*; τελευτάω (> τέλος) – *die*; ἀλλά – *come then* (usual meaning with an imperative); ἡσυχίαν ἄγω – *be still, keep quiet*.

92 καρτερέω – *be strong, endure*.

93 αἰσχύνομαι – *be ashamed*; ἐπέχω + gen. – *keep from doing, stop doing something*; τὸ δακρύειν article plus infinitive (77) – *crying*.

94 περιέρχομαι – *walk around*; οἱ – *to him*, '*his*'; βαρύνομαι – *become heavy*.

95 σκέλος τό (< isosceles) – *leg*; κατακλίνω (< recline) – *lie down* κατεκλίνη is aorist passive – Socrates is helped; ὕπτιος -α -ον – *on the back*.

96 ἄνθρωπος refers to the attendant; ἐφάπτομαι + gen. – *hold onto* perhaps to stop shaking or convulsions; ὁ δούς (> δίδωμι) article plus aorist participle – '*the one who had given*'.

97 φάρμακον τό (49); διαλείπω (> λείπω) – *leave* used especially of a gap of time; ἐπισκοπέω (< microscope) – *inspect*.

98 κἄπειτα = καὶ ἔπειτα by crasis; σφόδρα – *hard*; πιέζω – *squeeze, pinch*.

99 ἤρετο – strong aorist of ἐρωτάω; οὐ φημί – *say . . . not*.

100 κνήμη ἡ ἡ – *lower leg* supply 'squeezed' again; ἐπάνειμι – *go up*, i.e. he squeezes further up the leg to show how the poison is travelling; ἐπιδείκνυμι – *demonstrate*.

101 ψύχομαι – *be cold*; πήγνυμι – *become stiff*; ἅπτομαι – *touch, grasp*; αὐτός refers to the attendant and suggests others had had to hold on to Socrates as well.

102 πρός + dat. – *at*; καρδία ἡ (< cardiac) – *heart*; γένηται aorist subjunctive of γίγνομαι; αὐτῷ – possessive dative '*his*'.

103 οἴχομαι – *depart, be gone* a euphemistic way of saying '*die*'.

Socrates make his last request and dies. 118a

ἤδη οὖν σχεδόν τι αὐτοῦ ἦν τὰ περὶ τὸ ἦτρον
ψυχόμενα, καὶ ἐκκαλυψάμενος – ἐνεκεκάλυπτο γάρ –   105
εἶπεν – ὃ δὴ τελευταῖον ἐφθέγξατο – 'ὦ Κρίτων,' ἔφη,
'τῷ Ἀσκληπιῷ ὀφείλομεν ἀλεκτρυόνα· ἀλλὰ ἀπόδοτε καὶ
μὴ ἀμελήσητε.'

'ἀλλὰ ταῦτα,' ἔφη, 'ἔσται,' ὁ Κρίτων· 'ἀλλ' ὅρα εἴ τι
ἄλλο λέγεις.'   110

ταῦτα ἐρομένου αὐτοῦ οὐδὲν ἔτι ἀπεκρίνατο,
ἀλλ' ὀλίγον χρόνον διαλιπὼν ἐκινήθη τε καὶ ὁ ἄνθρωπος
ἐξεκάλυψεν αὐτόν, καὶ ὃς τὰ ὄμματα ἔστησεν· ἰδὼν δὲ
ὁ Κρίτων συνέλαβε τὸ στόμα καὶ τοὺς ὀφθαλμούς.

ἤδε ἡ τελευτή, ὦ Ἐχέκρατες, τοῦ ἑταίρου ἡμῖν   115
ἐγένετο, ἀνδρός, ὡς ἡμεῖς φαῖμεν ἄν, τῶν τότε ὧν
ἐπειράθημεν ἀρίστου καὶ ἄλλως φρονιμωτάτου καὶ
δικαιοτάτου.

The effects of hemlock

Hemlock is a poison which affects the central nervous system. If not treated, it results in respiratory failure and death because the heart and brain do not get oxygen. Before this point, there may be other symptoms: in the early stages nausea, vomiting, abdominal pain, rapid heartbeat, tremors, seizures, and in the later stages very slow heartbeat, ascending paralysis, coma and respiratory failure leading to death.

An offering to Asclepius

Asclepius was the god of healing. When someone recovered from an illness, they would often make an offering to Asclepius in gratitude for his help. At first sight this seems inappropriate in the current case, but for Socrates his imminent death is a recovery from the 'illness' of life on earth as he contemplates moving on to the better life that he has been discussing with his friends.

Q.   What potential symptoms are not described? Why do you think this is?

Q.   What is the impression we have of Socrates in his dying moments?

Q.   How consistent have Socrates' actions been in what you have read?

Final questions

- This is the very end of the dialogue. What impressions of Socrates have you formed from what you have read?

- Do you find Plato's account moving or inspiring? Why do you think he chose to narrate it from Phaedo's point of view? How well-written and reliable do you think it is?

104 σχεδόν τι – *almost*; αὐτοῦ – *of him, his*; ἦτρον τό – *(lower) abdomen*; ψύχομαι
– *be cold, 'getting cold'*, the subject is the phrase τὰ περὶ τὸ ἦτρον 'the part around the
abdomen'. The paralysis is gradually moving up the body, from foot, to lower leg and now lower
abdomen. When it reaches the heart, Socrates will die.

105 ἐκκαλυψάμενος aorist middle passive of ἐκκαλύπτομαι (ἐκ-) – *'having uncovered his
face'*; ἐνεκεκάλυπτο pluperfect passive from ἐγκαλύπτομαι (ἐν-) – *'he had hidden
his face'*.

106 ὅ δή – (> ὅς ἥ ὅ) *'which was indeed'*; τελευταῖον τό (> τέλος) – *last thing*;
φθέγγομαι – *utter, speak*.

107 ὀφείλω – *owe*; ἀλεκτρυών -όνος ὁ – *cock, chicken*; ἀλλά – *come then* (91);
ἀπόδοτε a plural aorist imperative of ἀποδίδωμι – *give back, pay a debt*.

108 ἀμελήσητε aorist subjunctive of ἀμελέω – *be negligent, fail to do something*, μή +
aorist subjunctive is used for a specific prohibition.

109 ἔσται – 3rd sg. future of εἰμί.

111 ἐρομένου – aorist participle from ἐρωτάω; αὐτοῦ refers to Crito; ἔτι – *any more*.

112 διαλείπω (> λείπω) – *leave* especially used of a gap of time; κινέομαι (< cinema) – *move*,
passive has active meaning here.

113 ἐκκαλύπτομαι (105); ὅς marking a change of subject change of subject – *'Socrates'*;
ἔστησεν – *he set, 'he fixed'*; ὄμμα -ατος τό – *eye*. His eyes stop responding and become
lifeless, so we know that he has died.

114 συλλαμβάνω – *take together, 'close'*; στόμα -ατος τό – *mouth*; ὀφθαλμός ὁ –
eye

115 τελευτή ἡ (> τέλος) – *end*; ἑταῖρος ὁ – *companion*; ἡμῖν dative of possession –
'our'.

116 φαῖμεν ἄν potential optative from φημί – *'we might say'*.

117 πειράομαι + gen. – *have experience of*; ἀρίστός -η -ον – *best*; ἄλλως – *otherwise*;
φρόνιμος -α -ον – *wise*. Sorting out the genitives: singulars are describing 'the end of Socrates'
(ἀνδρός); plurals describe 'best etc. of those who' (τῶν . . . ὤν)

Plutarch and Lucian

2018–2019 Prescription

The two authors Plutarch and Lucian were both writing long after the glory days of Greece. Indeed, Greece had been absorbed into the Roman empire for well over 200 years and Latin was the official language. Despite this, the legacy of Greece continued to command great interest, not only because of the immense cultural debt the Romans had to the Greeks but also because Greek remained the most commonly spoken language in the eastern part of the empire. There had been some changes from Attic Greek, the dialect spoken in Athens 600 years previously, both in vocabulary and grammar. Plutarch and Lucian each made a conscious effort to return to a pure Attic style.

Both authors began life far from the centre of power in Rome. **Plutarch** (50–*c.* 120 CE) came from Chaeronea in central Greece, not far from Delphi, where he served as a priest for thirty years and helped to revive the fame of the sanctuary. He had a high profile in Greece as an intellectual, lecturer and prolific writer. His best known work is the *Parallel Lives*, biographies of famous Greeks and Romans paired together, drawing comparisons between their characters: Alexander the Great, for example, is paired with Julius Caesar.

Lucian was born *c.* 120 CE in Samosata, a city on the banks of the river Euphrates deep in the south of modern Turkey not far from the northern border with Syria. His native language was probably Aramaic, but he seems to have had the standard training in Greek rhetoric leading to a career in law before, aged about forty, he reinvented himself as a lecturer on literary and philosophical topics and travelled around the Roman empire.

Plutarch: A Spartan Childhood

(Taylor, *Greek Beyond GCSE*, Reading 9, pp. 129–33)

Education of the Spartans is taken from Plutarch's *Life of Lycurgus*. Lycurgus was credited with founding the Spartan system of *eunomia* or 'good laws/customs' in the earliest days of Sparta. Plutarch paired him with Numa Pompilius, a legendary king of Rome, who established many of its basic religious structures.

The Spartan system was designed to support a small number of full citizens (*Spartiates*) who were focused on being the best at fighting, both physically and psychologically. The system instilled a fearless attitude in the young, taking boys aged seven away from their parents and subjecting them to tough physical training, known and to an extent admired far and wide.

This highly stratified society was supported by a free class, the *perioikoi*, who also fought but were not so highly trained, and a serf population, the *helots*. The steady decline in number of *Spartiates* led to the demise of Sparta as a significant power, particluarly after defeat by the Thebans at Leuctra in 371, but her reputation lived on and some rituals survived: for example, the cheese-stealing ritual at the sanctuary of Artemis Orthia, where Spartan boys tried to steal cheeses placed on the altar guarded by men with whips. Originally this would have been intended to train the boys in evading the enemy and in enduring pain. Cicero was a typical Roman tourist who toured around Greece in the mid first century BCE; he visited Sparta and witnesed this 500-year-old ritual: *'they receive so many blows at the altar that a lot of blood flows from their bodies, and sometimes, as I heard when I was there, death. Yet none of them shouts out, there isn't even a whimper'*. Two hundred years after Cicero's visit, the spectacle had become so popular that stone seating for the crowds was constructed. The remains of this seating form one of the few structures from ancient Sparta that remain visible today.

Lucian: Anacharsis and Athletics

(Taylor, *Greek Beyond GCSE*, Reading 10, pp. 134–40)

Lucian's work takes the form of a dialogue between two wise men: **Solon**, one of the seven sages of ancient Greece, has invited **Anacharsis**, a legendary wise 'barbarian' (non-Greek) from Scythia, a territory north of the Black Sea, to visit a gymnasium on the outskirts of Athens to watch the young men at their exercise. Anacharsis asks the innocent questions of an outsider. Solon is forced to defend and explain Greek practices.

Solon was regarded as the first founder of Athenian democracy, rather as Lycurgus was credited with creating the Sparta system, but, unlike Lycurgus, Solon is a documented historical figure: he held the important post of *archon* in 594/593, presumably when he introduced his reforms. His reputation for wisdom is based in part on the way he left Athens and travelled for ten years to give his radical reforms, which included cancellation of debts, time to bed down.

The word *gymnasium* derives from the Greek word γυμνός – *nude*, since Greek athletes exercised naked. As an institution, it was part not only of Athenian life, but of Greek culture in general. The Greeks were competitive in all areas, but particularly in sport and exercise. Physical fitness was regarded as an important part of life and, indeed, as a duty for young men, who would be expected to fight for their city and its allies.

This competitive spirit was seen in the four major pan-Hellenic games (held at Olympia, Delphi, Corinth and Nemea) that brought together all Greek cities, even in times of war. The most famous of these were the Olympic Games, which featured wresting and pancration, two sports mentioned in this dialogue. These games were said to have been founded in 776 and were still going strong when Lucian wrote his dialogue. A contemporary of Lucian, the Greek travel writer Pausanias, has left a detailed description of the site of Olympia, which remains a good guide on a visit. The philosopher Epictetus (*c.* 55–135 CE) gives us an insight into the timeless appeal of the Olympic Games: *'Some unpleasant and harsh things happen in life. They don't happen in Olympia? Don't you get sunburnt? Aren't you squashed together? Isn't it difficult to have a wash? Aren't you treated to crowds and noise and other hardships? But I think you weigh up all these things against the wow-factor of the spectacle and put up with the discomfort.'*

PLUTARCH, LIFE OF LYCURGUS 16–18

A Spartan Childhood

New-born babies were inspected soon after birth to decide whether they should be brought up or killed.

Nominative *words or phrases are in* light blue, **verbs** *in* dark blue.

τὸ δὲ γεννηθὲν οὐκ ἦν κύριος ὁ γεννήσας τρέφειν, ἀλλ'
ἔφερε λαβὼν εἰς τόπον τινὰ λέσχην καλούμενον, ἐν ᾧ
καθήμενοι τῶν φυλετῶν οἱ πρεσβύτατοι καταμάθοντες τὸ
παιδάριον, εἰ μὲν εὐπαγὲς εἴη καὶ ῥωμαλέον, τρέφειν
ἐκέλευον, κλῆρον αὐτῷ τῶν ἐνακισχιλίων προσνείμαντες·   5
εἰ δ᾽ ἀγεννὲς καὶ ἄμορφον, ἀπέπεμπον εἰς τὰς λεγομένας
Ἀποθέτας, παρὰ Ταΰγετον βαραθρώδη τόπον, ὡς οὔτε
αὐτῷ ζῆν ἄμεινον ὂν οὔτε τῇ πόλει τὸ μὴ καλῶς εὐθὺς ἐξ
ἀρχῆς πρὸς εὐεξίαν καὶ ῥώμην πεφυκός. ὅθεν οὐδὲ ὕδατι
τὰ βρέφη, ἀλλ᾽ οἴνῳ περιέλουον αἱ γυναῖκες, βάσανόν τινα   10
ποιούμεναι τῆς κράσεως αὐτῶν. λέγεται γὰρ ἐξίστασθαι τὰ
ἐπιληπτικὰ καὶ νοσώδη πρὸς τὸν ἄκρατον ἀποσφακελίζοντα,
τὰ δ᾽ ὑγιεινὰ μᾶλλον στομοῦσθαι καὶ κρατύνεσθαι τὴν ἕξιν.

Names and places

Ἀπόθεται -ων αἱ: *Apothetae*
The place where Spartan babies were taken to be killed, literally *'set aside'*.

Ταΰγετος ὁ: *Mt Taygetus*
The highest mountain in a range that dominates Sparta, separating Laconia from Messenia.

Spartans

The treatment described applies to male full citizens or *Spartiates*. A different regime existed for girls, equally focused on developing the qualities needed for a successful military state. Two other classes of Spartan society were included in the more general term Λακεδαιμόνιοι: the *perioikoi* (> περί + οἰκέω), a class of free people who 'lived around' them providing support services, and the *helots* (> εἵλον) a captive serf population who worked the land that fed the *Spartiates*.

Q.   What happened when a baby was healthy?

Q.   What two reasons are given for taking unhealthy infants to the Apothetae?

Q.   Explain how women could determine whether their baby was healthy.

GCSE vocabulary: αὐτός, γυνή, εἰ, εἰς + acc, καλέω, κελεύω, λαμβάνω, λέγω, μᾶλλον, οἶνος, οὔτε . . . οὔτε, πέμπω, ποιέω, ὅς, τόπος, ὕδωρ, φέρω.

1   γεννάω aor. ἐγέννησα – *beget, father*: the two participles are used with an article to make a noun *'what has been fathered'*, i.e. *'a baby'*, and *'the person who fathered'*: note that the nominative is delayed; κύριος -α -ον – *authorized, entitled*; τρέφω – *nourish, bring up*; ἀλλ' = ἀλλά (elision) – *but*.

2   ἔφερε – the imperfect tense is used here for a habitual action; λαβών from λαμβάνω, note that the normal Greek word order (participle followed by the main verb) has been reversed; λέσχη ἡ – *assembly hall*.

3   κάθημαι – sit; φυλέτης ὁ – *tribesman*, the partitive genitive here precedes the superlative; πρεσβύτατος -η -ον – *oldest*, note that this nominative is delayed (1); καταμανθάνω (> μανθάνω) – *examine*.

4   παιδάριον τό (> παῖς) – *infant, baby*; εὐπαγής -ές – *sturdy*; εἴη – optative of εἰμί; ῥωμαλέος -α -ον (< Rome) – *strong*; τρέφω – *bring up, rear* (1).

5   ἐκέλευον imperfect (2), supply αὐτόν, i.e. 'the father', as the object; κλῆρος ὁ – *plot of land*; ἐνακισχίλιοι -αι -α – *9,000*; προσνέμω aor. προσένειμα – *assign, allocate*; since only 9,000 plots of land were available, they were assigned only to those babies likely to become good warriors.

6   ἀγεννής -ές – *of poor birth, not of healthy birth*; ἄμορφος -ον – *deformed*, supply εἴη again from 4; λεγομένας from λέγω – *'being called'*, *'so-called'*.

7   παρά + acc. – *by, on the side of*; βαραθρώδης -ες – *full of chasms*; ὡς + participle – *on the grounds that*; οὔτε ... οὔτε – these two words are important signposts for the structure of the sentence.

8   ζῆν infin. of ζάω – *live*; ἀμείνων -ον (comparative of ἀγαθός) – *better*; τὸ μὴ ...... πεφυκός (9) the subject is delayed (1) – *'the baby that does not grow ... '*, translate before the first half of 8.

9   εὐεξία ἡ – *good health*; ῥώμη ἡ – *strength* (4); πεφυκώς -υῖα -ός perf. participle from φύω – *grow, be by nature*; ὅθεν – *from which, 'this is why'*.

10   βρέφος -ους τό – *baby, infant*; περιλούω – *wash, bathe*; the English word order is almost the exact reverse of the Greek; βάσανος ἡ – *trial, test*.

11   κρᾶσις -εως ἡ – *constitution, make-up*; αὐτῶν refers to βρέφη; λέγεται – the subject is τὰ ἐπιληπτικά; ἐξίσταμαι – *stand outside, lose one's senses*.

12   ἐπιληπτικός -ή -όν– *epileptic*; νοσώδης -ες (> νόσος) – *sickly, ill*; προς + acc. – *'at'*; ἄκρατος -ον – *unmixed wine*; ἀποσφακελίζω translate the participle before ἐξίστασθαι, (2) – *fall into convulsions at*.

13   ὑγιεινός -ή -όν (< hygiene) – *healthy*; στομόω (repeat λέγεται) – *harden, make tough*; κρατύνω – *strengthen*; ἕξις -εως ἡ – *condition*, acc. of respect, *'in condition'*.

The skill of nurses made infants healthy and unafraid; other Greeks hired Spartan nurses for this reason.

ἦν δὲ περὶ τὰς τροφοὺς ἐπιμέλειά τις μετὰ τέχνης, ὥστ'
ἄνευ σπαργάνων ἐκτρεφούσας τὰ βρέφη τοῖς μέλεσι καὶ   15
τοῖς εἴδεσιν ἐλευθέρια ποιεῖν, ἔτι δὲ εὔκολα ταῖς διαίταις
καὶ ἄσικχα καὶ ἀθαμβῆ σκότου καὶ πρὸς ἐρημίαν ἄφοβα
καὶ ἄπειρα δυσκολίας ἀγεννοῦς καὶ κλαυθμυρισμῶν. διὸ καὶ
τῶν ἔξωθεν ἔνιοι τοῖς τέκνοις Λακωνικὰς ἐωνοῦντο τίτθας.

Once the boys were old enough to be educated, Lycurgus made sure they were brought up communally by the state

τοὺς δὲ Σπαρτιατῶν παῖδας οὐκ ἐπὶ ὠνητοῖς οὐδὲ μισθίοις   20
ἐποιήσατο παιδαγωγοῖς ὁ Λυκοῦργος, οὐδ' ἐξῆν ἑκάστῳ
τρέφειν οὐδὲ παιδεύειν ὡς ἐβούλετο τὸν υἱόν, ἀλλὰ πάντας
εὐθὺς ἑπταετεῖς γενομένους παραλαμβάνων αὐτὸς εἰς
ἀγέλας κατελόχιζε, καὶ συννόμους ποιῶν καὶ συντρόφους
μετ' ἀλλήλων εἴθιζε συμπαίζειν καὶ συσχολάζειν. ἄρχοντα   25
δ' αὐτοῖς παρίστατο τῆς ἀγέλης τὸν τῷ φρονεῖν διαφέροντα
καὶ θυμοειδέστατον ἐν τῷ μάχεσθαι·

Names and places

Λακωνικός -ή -όν: *Laconian, Spartan;* **Σπαρτιάτης ὁ:** a *Spartiate, Spartan*
Lacedaemonia was the usual name for Sparta; the adjective Laconian means Spartan. *Spartiate*s, the male warrior class, were the only full citizens.

Λυκοῦργος ὁ: *Lycurgus*
The legendary founder of the Spartan constitution, credited with creating a system of sound laws (εὐνομία) which raised citizens who were not only skilled and brave in battle, but also fully supportive of the aims of the state.

Q. What benefits came from not swaddling the babies?
Q. How were older boys educated elsewhere in Greece?
Q. What qualities did Lycurgus look for in a platoon leader?

GCSE vocabulary: *ἄνευ, ἄρχων, βούλομαι, γίγνομαι, ἐλεύθερος, ἔξεστι, εὐθύς, μάχομαι, παῖς, πᾶς, υἱός, φόβος, ὥστε.*

14 περί + acc. – *'among'*; τρόφος ἡ – *nurse*; ἐπιμέλεια ἡ – *care, concern*; τέχνη ἡ (> technique) – *skill, craft, art*; μετὰ τέχνης – *'for their art'*; ὥστε is followed by an acc. subject (ἐκτρεφούσας 15) and an infinitive (ποιεῖν 16).

15 σπάργανα -ων τά – *swaddling clothes*; ἐκτρέφω – *bring up*, rear (supply τάς to the participle); βρέφος (10); μέλος τό – *limb*. Swaddling a baby means wrapping it tightly, keeping the arms and legs still to encourage sleep.

16 εἶδος τό – *appearance, body*; ἐλευθέριος = ἐλεύθερος, here used predicatively *'made them* (i.e. τὰ βρέφη) *free in'* + dat.; ἔτι δε – *and besides*; εὔκολος -ον + dat. – *easy, contented with*; δίαιτα ἡ (< diet) – *way of living, life*.

17 ἄσικχος -ον – *not fussy about food*; ἀθαμβής -ές – *fearless*; σκότος ὁ – *darkness*; ἐρημία ἡ – *solitude, being left alone*; ἄφοβος -ον (> φοβέομαι) – *not scared, fearless*.

18 ἄπειρος -ον – *inexperienced in, not used to* (> ἀ + πειράομαι); δυσκολία ἡ – *bad-temper, grumpiness*; ἀγεννής -ές – *discreditable* (6); κλαυθμυρισμός ὁ – *whining*; διό – *for that reason*.

19 ἔξωθεν – *from outside*, οἱ ἔξωθεν *'outsiders'*; ἔνιοι -αι -α – *some* + gen. (for this word order, see 3); τέκνον τό – *child*; ἐωνοῦντο imperfect of ὠνέομαι – *buy*; τίτθη ἡ – *nurse*.

20 ἐπί + dat. – *in the power of*; ὠνητός -ή -όν – *bought*; μίσθιος -α -ον – *hired*.

21 παιδαγωγός ὁ (> παῖς + ἄγω) – *tutor*; Λυκοῦργος Plutarch often delays the nominative (1); ἑκάστῳ – *'each man'*, i.e. each father.

22 τρέφω – (1); παιδεύω (> παῖς) – *bring up, educate*.

23 εὐθύς – *immediately*, *'as soon as'*; ἑπταετής -ές (> ἑπτα + ἔτος) – *seven years old*; γενομένους aor. participle γίγνομαι; παραλαμβάνω – *hand over*.

24 ἀγέλη ἡ – *unit, platoon*; καταλοχίζω – *enrol, put a name down*; σύννομος -ον – *eating together*; σύντροφος -ον (> τρέφω) – *reared together*.

25 μετ' = μετά (elision); ἀλλήλους – *each other*; εἴθιζε, imperf. of ἐθίζω + inf. – *get x used to*; συμπαίζω – *play together*; συσχολάζω (< scholar) – *learn together*; ἄρχων in apposition – *'as leader'*.

26 αὐτοῖς = ἑαυτοῖς; παρίστατο (παρίσταμαι) – *put someone* (acc.) *in charge of something* (gen.); ἀγέλη (24); διαφέρω – *be different, stand out*, τὸν διαφέροντα *'the one standing out . . .'*; φρονέω – *be sensible*, τὸ φρονεῖν *'having good sense'*.

27 θυμοειδής -ές – *brave, courageous*; τῷ μάχεσθαι article plus infinitive – *'in fighting'*.

The boys' education, supervized by elders, focused on the skills that they would need.

καὶ πρὸς τοῦτον ἀφεώρων καὶ προστάττοντος ἠκροῶντο
καὶ κολάζοντος ἐκαρτέρουν, ὥστε τὴν παιδείαν εἶναι
μελέτην εὐπειθείας. ἐπεσκόπουν δὲ οἱ πρεσβύτεροι   30
παίζοντας αὐτούς, καὶ τὰ πολλὰ μάχας τινὰς ἐμβάλλοντες
ἀεὶ καὶ φιλονεικίας, οὐ παρέργως κατεμάνθανον ὁποῖός
ἐστι τὴν φύσιν ἕκαστος αὐτῶν πρὸς τὸ τολμᾶν καὶ μὴ
φυγομαχεῖν ἐν ταῖς ἁμίλλαις.

γράμματα μὲν οὖν ἕνεκα τῆς χρείας ἐμάνθανον· ἡ δ ἄλλη   35
πᾶσα παιδεία πρὸς τὸ ἄρχεσθαι καλῶς ἐγίνετο καὶ
καρτερεῖν πονοῦντα καὶ νικᾶν μαχόμενον. διὸ καὶ τῆς
ἡλικίας προερχομένης ἐπέτεινον αὐτῶν τὴν ἄσκησιν, ἐν
χρῷ τε κείροντες καὶ βαδίζειν ἀνυποδήτους παίζειν τε
γυμνοὺς ὡς τὰ πολλὰ συνεθίζοντες.   40

Q.   What skills did the boys learn from this training?

Q.   What qualities did the elders look out for in the boys?

Q.   How would you describe the balance of the boys' education?

Q.   What three things changed in their education when they get older?

Q.   What are the advantages and disadvantages of the training described here?

GCSE vocabulary: *ἀεί, ἄρχω, ἄρχομαι, καλῶς, κολάζω, μάχη, μάχομαι, νικάω, ὁράω, πολύς, ὥστε.*

28   τοῦτον – i.e. the boy chosen as leader; ἀφεώρων 3rd pl. imperf. of ἀφοράω (> ὁράω) – keep
      one's eyes on; προστάττω – give orders, instruct προστάττοντος – 'the one giving
      orders'; ἠκροῶντο imperf. of ἀκροάομαι + gen. – pay close attention to, obey.

29   καρτερέω + gen. – put up with, endure; ὥστε – (14); παιδεία ἡ – education;
      εἶναι inf. of εἰμί.

30   μελέτη ἡ – practice, rehearsal; εὐπειθεία ἡ (> εὖ + πείθω) – ready obedience,
      doing what you are told; ἐπισκοπέω (< microscope) – watch over, oversee;
      πρεσβύτεροι comparative – older men.

31   παίζω – play; τὰ πολλά – for the most part, 'often'; ἐμβάλλω – throw in,
      introduce the subject is in line 30.

32   φιλονεικία ἡ – rivalry; παρέργως – as a by-product, co-incidentally;
      καταμανθάνω (3); ὁποῖος = ποῖος.

33   τὴν φύσιν (< physics) acc. of respect – 'as to their nature', 'what nature each had';
      πρός + acc. – with regard to; τολμάω – dare, τὸ τολμᾶν 'daring' (for τό + infinitive as
      a noun, see 27).

34   φυγομαχεῖν – run from a fight; ἅμιλλα ἡ – contest, fight.

35   γράμμα -ατος τό – letter, writing; ἕνεκα + gen. – 'for the sake of ', 'in accordance
      with'; χρεία ἡ – need, use.

36   παιδεία ἡ (29); πρός + acc. – for, 'aimed at' is followed by an infinitive and two participles;
      τὸ ἄρχεσθαι καλῶς – being ruled nobly, 'taking orders well'; ἐγίνετο = ἐγίγνετο
      – 'was'.

37   καρτερέω – put up with, endure; πονέω – toil, endure hardship, πονοῦντα,
      understand τόν with this participle; νικᾶν – infinitive of νικάω; διό – wherefore, for this
      reason (18).

38   ἡλικία ἡ – age; προέρχομαι– advance, increase (genitive absolute); ἐπιτείνω –
      stretch out, increase the subject is an unspecified 'they', 'the boys' teachers' or 'the Spartans';
      ἄσκησις -εως ἡ – exercise, training.

39   χρώς ὁ – skin, ἐν χρῷ 'down to the skin'; κείρω – cut hair, shear; βαδίζω = βαίνω
      infinitive after συνεθίζοντες (40), which is parallel to κείροντες; ἀνυπόδητος -η -ον –
      without shoes.

40   γυμνός -ή -όν – naked; ὡς τὰ πολλά (31); συνεθίζω + inf. – accustom x to.

At twelve years old the education became tougher both physically and psychologically.

γενόμενοι δωδεκαετεῖς ἄνευ χιτῶνος ἤδη διετέλουν, ἓν
ἱμάτιον εἰς τὸν ἐνιαυτὸν λαμβάνοντες, αὐχμηροὶ τὰ σώματα
καὶ λουτρῶν καὶ ἀλειμμάτων ἄπειροι· πλὴν ὀλίγας
ἡμέρας τινὰς τοῦ ἐνιαυτοῦ τῆς τοιαύτης φιλανθρωπίας
μετεῖχον. ἐκάθευδον δὲ ὁμοῦ κατ᾽ ἴλην καὶ ἀγέλην ἐπὶ   45
στιβάδων, ἃς αὐτοῖς συνεφόρουν, τοῦ παρὰ τὸν Εὐρώταν
πεφυκότος καλάμου τὰ ἄκρα ταῖς χερσὶν ἄνευ σιδήρου
κατακλάσαντες.

ἤδη δὲ τοῖς τηλικούτοις ἐρασταὶ τῶν εὐδοκίμων νέων
συνανεστρέφοντο· καὶ προσεῖχον οἱ πρεσβύτεροι, καὶ   50
μᾶλλον ἐπιφοιτῶντες εἰς τὰ γυμνάσια, καὶ μαχομένοις
καὶ σκώπτουσιν ἀλλήλους παρατυγχάνοντες, οὐ παρέργως,
ἀλλὰ τρόπον τινὰ πάντες οἰόμενοι πάντων καὶ πατέρες εἶναι
καὶ παιδαγωγοὶ καὶ ἄρχοντες, ὥστε μήτε καιρὸν ἀπολείπεσθαι
μήτε χωρίον ἔρημον τοῦ νουθετοῦντος τὸν ἁμαρτάνοντα καὶ   55
κολάζοντος.

Names and places

Εὐρώτας ὁ: *Eurotas*
The river that flows through the plain of Sparta.

Clothing

The toughening process gathered pace from the age of twelve, as boys were denied a *chiton* and allowed
only one *himation*. The *chiton* was the basic garment worn next to the skin, like a long, baggy T-shirt or
Roman tunic. The function of the *himation* ('cloak') was to provide a warmer outer layer; it was made of
coarser material and draped over the body, more like a Roman toga. The boys trained naked and their one
himation was for when they were not exercising.

Q.   What do we learn about the Spartans' personal hygiene? What might the word
     φιλανθρωπίας (44) suggest about Plutarch's views on this subject?

Q.   How does Plutarch emphasize the toughness of the sleeping arrangements?

Q.   What relationships do they develop at this age. Does this surprise you?

Q.   What role did the older men play (50–2)? What made them conscientious in
     carrying out their duties (53–4)?

Q.   Overall, how closely were the boys supervized?

Greek vocabulary: *ἄνευ, γίγνομαι, ἕν, εἰς, λαμβάνω, μᾶλλον, νέος, πατήρ, πειράομαι,
σῶμα, τοιοῦτος, χείρ.*

41   γενόμενοι – aorist participle of γίγνομαι; δωδεκαετής -ές – *twelve years old;* χιτών
     -ῶνος ὁ – *tunic;* ἤδη – *now;* διατελέω – *continue, carry on.*

42   ἱμάτιον τό – *cloak;* εἰς – '*for*'; ἐνιαυτός ὁ – *year;* αὐχμηρός -ά -όν – *dry, rough,*
     unkempt (most Greeks used olive oil to keep their skin soft and clean); σώματα – acc. of
     respect '*as to their bodies*', '*their bodies were*'.

43   λουτρόν τό – *bath;* ἄλειμμα -ατος τό – *ointment;* ἄπειρος -ον + gen. (> πειράομαι)
     – *unused to* understand ἦσαν; πλήν adv. – *except that.*

44   ἐνιαυτός ὁ – (42); φιλανθρωπία ἡ – *kindness, courtesy, indulgence.*

45   μετέχω + gen. – *share in, partake of;* ὁμοῦ adv. – *together;* κατά + acc. – *according*
     to, by; ἴλη ἡ – *troop;* ἀγέλη (24); ἐπί + gen. – *on.*

46   στιβάς -άδος ἡ – *bed of rushes;* ἅς (ὅς ἥ ὅ); αὐτοῖς (25); συνφορέω (> φέρω) –
     gather; τοῦ – start from 48 and work back; παρά + acc. – *beside.*

47   πεφυκότος – perfect participle of φύω (9) agreeing with τοῦ – '*of the . . . which grow*';
     κάλαμος ὁ – *reeds;* ἄκρον τό – (< acropolis) *top, tip;* σίδηρος ὁ – *iron, knife.*

48   κατακλάω – *break off.*

49   τηλικοῦτος -η -ον – *of this age* (i.e. boys of this age); ἐραστής ὁ – *lover;* εὐδόκιμος
     -α -ον – *well-thought of, reputable;* νέων – *new,* i.e. '*young men*'.

50   συναναστρέφομαι + dat. – *mix with;* προσέχω – *pay attention to;* πρεσβύτεροι
     (30).

51   ἐπιφοιτάω – *go regularly to, haunt;* γυμνάσιον τό – *exercise ground;* καί . . .
     καί = . . . τέ . . . καί (also 53–4); μαχομένοις is a dative plural participle, referring to the
     boys.

52   σκώπτουσιν, dat. pl. participle, like μαχομένοις, of σκώπτω – *make fun of, joke with;*
     ἀλλήλους – *each other* (refers to the boys); παρατυγχάνω + dat. – *happen to be*
     near; παρέργως – *incidentally, by accident* (32).

53   τρόπον τινά – '*in some way*'; πάντες refers to the men, πάντων to the boys; οἴομαι
     – *think,* introduces an indirect statement with nom. + infin.

54   παιδαγωγός ὁ – *tutor* (21); ἄρχοντες – *ruler,* '*in charge of*'; ὥστε + infin.; μήτε . . .
     μήτε – *neither . . . nor;* καιρός ὁ – *(right) time, opportunity.*

55   ἀπολείπω (> λείπω) – *leave;* χωρίον τό – *place;* ἐρῆμος -η -ον + gen. *deserted,*
     '*without*'; νουθετέω – *advise* νουθετοῦντος (article + participle making a noun) –
     '*advising*'.

56   ἁμαρτάνω – *err, make a mistake* τὸν ἁμαρτάνοντα – '*the one making a mistake*';
     κολάζοντος is parallel to τοῦ νουθετοῦντος (55).

Official supervision was entrusted to a 20-year-old called an 'eiren' whom the boys
themselves chose. The boys were expected to supplement their own food.

οὐ μὴν ἀλλὰ καὶ παιδονόμος ἐκ τῶν καλῶν καὶ ἀγαθῶν
ἀνδρῶν ἐτάττετο, καὶ κατ' ἀγέλας αὐτοὶ προΐσταντο τῶν
λεγομένων εἰρένων ἀεὶ τὸν σωφρονέστατον καὶ μαχιμώτατον
(εἴρενας δὲ καλοῦσι τοὺς ἔτος ἤδη δεύτερον ἐκ παίδων   60
γεγονότας).

οὗτος οὖν ὁ εἴρην, εἴκοσι ἔτη γεγονώς, ἄρχει τε τῶν
ὑποτεταγμένων ἐν ταῖς μάχαις, καὶ κατ' οἶκον ὑπηρέταις
χρῆται πρὸς τὸ δεῖπνον. ἐπιτάσσει δὲ τοῖς μὲν ἁδροῖς ξύλα
φέρειν, τοῖς δὲ μικροτέροις λάχανα. καὶ φέρουσι   65
κλέπτοντες, οἱ μὲν ἐπὶ τοὺς κήπους βαδίζοντες, οἱ δὲ εἰς τὰ
τῶν ἀνδρῶν συσσίτια παρεισρέοντες εὖ μάλα πανούργως
καὶ πεφυλαγμένως· ἂν δ᾽ ἁλῷ, πολλὰς λαμβάνει πληγὰς τῇ
μάστιγι, ῥαθύμως δοκῶν κλέπτειν καὶ ἀτέχνως. κλέπτουσι
δὲ καὶ τῶν σιτίων ὅ τι ἂν δύνωνται, μανθάνοντες εὐφυῶς   70
ἐπιτίθεσθαι τοῖς καθεύδουσιν ἢ ῥαθύμως φυλάττουσιν.

Names and places
εἴρην -ενος ὁ: *eiren*.
A Spartan youth of around 20 years old, two years out of his training who acted as platoon leader and
role-model for the younger boys.

Q.   What qualities were sought in an *eiren*?

Q.   What chores did the *eiren* impose on the boys?

Q.   Where did the boys go to get food?

Q.   Why do you think boys were made to find their own food rather than have it
provided by slaves?

Greek vocabulary: *ἀγαθός, ἀεί, δεῖπνον, δεύτερος, ἐάν, ἔτος, ἤ, ἤδη, καλός, κλέπτω, οὖν,
φέρω.*

57 οὐ μὴν ἀλλά – *and furthermore, in addition*; παιδονόμος ὁ – *inspector of boys*; καλὸς καὶ ἀγαθός – a common phrase meaning '*aristocrat*'.

58 τάττω – *draw up, appoint*; κατ' ἀγέλας – *by platoon* (24, 45); αὐτοί refers to the boys; προίσταντο + gen. – '*chose as leader*', '*put someone in command*'.

59 λεγομένων – '*so-called*' (6); εἴρην -ενος ὁ – *eiren*; σώφρων -ον – *self-controlled, sensible*; μάχιμος -α -ον (> μάχη) – *good at fighting*.

60 τοὺς ... γεγονότας (61) (> γίγνομαι) perfect participle – '*those who have been*'; ἔτος ... δεύτερον – '*for the second year now*' i.e. two years have elapsed; ἐκ παίδων – '*out of the class of boys*', '*since they were boys*'.

62 εἴκοσι ἔτη – *twenty years* (acc: time 'how long'); γεγονώς – perfect participle of γίγνομαι i.e. '*20 years old*'; ἄρχω + gen. – *command*.

63 ὑποτεταγμένων perfect passive participle of ὑποτάσσω – *put under authority*, '*those under his authority*'; μάχη ἡ – (here) '*military exercise*'; κατ' οἶκον – *at home, indoors*; ὑπηρέτης ὁ – *attendant, waiter*.

64 χρῆται, 3rd sg. present of χράομαι + dat. – '*use as*'; πρός – '*at*'; ἐπιτάσσω + dat. – *order, command*; τοῖς μέν ... τοῖς δέ – *those who are ...*; ἁδρός -ά -όν – *thick, strong, large*; ξύλον τό (< xylophone) – *wood*.

65 λάχανον τό – *vegetables*.

66 κῆπος ὁ – *orchard*; βαδίζω (39).

67 συσσίτιον τό (> σῖτος) – *mess, communal dining-room*; παρεισρέω – *creep*; μάλα (> μάλιστα) – *very*; πανούργως – *cunningly, daringly*.

68 πεφυλαγμένως (> φυλάσσω) – *carefully, cautiously*; ἄν = ἐάν; ἁλῷ aorist subjunctive of ἁλίσκομαι – '*he is caught*'; λαμβάνω – '*receive*'; πληγή ἡ – *blow*.

69 μάστιξ -ιγος ἡ – *whip, lash*; ῥαθύμως – *lazily, carelessly*; δοκέω participle giving a reason – *seem, appear*; ἀτέχνως (> ἀ + τέχνη) – *unskilfully*.

70 καί (postponed) – *also, as well*; σιτίον = σῖτος here, a partitive genitive; ὅ τι – *what*; ἄν + subjunctive makes phrase indefinite – *ever*; ὅ τι ἄν = '*whatever*'; δύναμαι (< dynamic) – *be able*; εὐφυῶς – *cleverly, instinctively*.

71 ἐπιτίθεμαι + dat. – *attack, make an attempt*; τοῖς καθεύδουσιν, φυλάττουσιν are both dative participles.

The reason for allowing meagre rations and stealing was to encourage bravery.

τῷ δὲ ἁλόντι ζημία πληγαὶ καὶ τὸ πεινῆν. γλίσχρον γὰρ
αὐτοῖς ἐστι δεῖπνον, ὅπως δι᾽ αὐτῶν ἀμυνόμενοι τὴν
ἔνδειαν ἀναγκάζωνται τολμᾶν καὶ πανουργεῖν. οὕτω δὲ
κλέπτουσι πεφροντισμένως οἱ παῖδες, ὥστε λέγεταί τις ἤδη   75
σκύμνον ἀλώπεκος κεκλοφὼς καὶ τῷ τριβωνίῳ
περιστέλλων, σπαρασσόμενος ὑπὸ τοῦ θηρίου τὴν γαστέρα
τοῖς ὄνυξι καὶ τοῖς ὀδοῦσι, ὑπὲρ τοῦ λαθεῖν ἐγκαρτερῶν
ἀποθανεῖν.

Effect of diet

Plutarch explains elsewhere that a secondary reason for restricting the diet is to make Spartan boys grow tall, arguing that the weight of too much food can impede growth, whereas a restricted diet leads to beauty, since light people can move their limbs gracefully. A number of works on medicine by Greek writers survive and, although they make mistakes which seem basic to us with our greater scientific knowledge, their reasoning is usually based on careful observation.

Q.   What could a boy expect if he was caught stealing food?

Q.   What did the fox-cub do to the boy?

Q.   Why did the boy continue to hide the fox-cub?

Q.   What does the story demonstrate about the training Spartan boys experienced?

GCSE vocabulary: *ἀποθνήσκω, ἀναγκάζω, οὕτω, ἵνα, ὑπέρ* + gen.

Final questions on Plutarch, Life of Lycurgus

- How attractive does the childhood of a Spartan boy seem to you compared with a typical childhood of today?

- What advantages and disadvantages might this sort of training bring to society today?

- Do you think Plutarch admires or is he critical of the Spartan system?

- What impression do you get of Lycurgus?

- Explain the significance of '*With it, or on it.*'

72   τῷ δὲ ἁλόντι aorist passive participle – *'for the one who has been caught'* (68); ζημία ἡ – *penalty*; πληγή (68); πεινῆν infinitive of πεινάω – *be hungry*, for τό + infinitive, see 27 and 33; the verb ἐστί needs to be supplied; γλίσχρος -α -ον – *scanty, meagre*.

73   ὅπως = ἵνα; δι' αὐτῶν – *through themselves*, *'by their own resources'*; ἀμύνομαι – *keep away, repel*.

74   ἔνδεια ἡ – *lack (of food)*, *'hunger'*; τολμάω – *endure, be daring*; πανουργέω – *do wrong*.

75   πεφροντισμένως – *carefully, with skill*.

76   σκύμνος ὁ – *cub*; ἀλώπηξ -εκος ὁ – *fox*; κεκλοφώς perfect participle of κλέπτω – *'having stolen'*; τριβώνιον τό – *cloak*.

77   περιστέλλω – *wrap up*; σπαράσσω – *tear, rip to sheds*; θηρίον τό – *wild animal*; γαστήρ -ρός ἡ (< gastric) accusative of respect – *stomach, belly*.

78   ὄνυξ -υχος ὁ – *claw*; ὀδούς -όντος ὁ – *tooth*; ὑπὲρ τοῦ λαθεῖν – literally *for the purpose of escaping the attention*, i.e. *'to avoid detection'*; ἐγκαρτερέω – *hold out, remain firm*.

79   ἀποθανεῖν infinitive because of λέγεται (75) – *'he is said to have . . .'*.

Plutarch, like Cicero, witnessed and commented on Spartan rituals that had survived into his time: '*I can actually believe this story from the adolescents of today that I have seen, many of whom I have seen dying of a beating at the altar of Artemis Orthia.*'

Spartan life was not all suffering: after dinner, the *eiren* would order a boy to sing a song, and another might be questioned on a moral issue, such as 'who is the bravest man?', which would require a short, well-considered answer. The Spartans were famous for their economy with words (the word 'laconic' can be used of someone who seldom says much). One famous laconic remark was supposed to have been said by a mother to her son as he departed for battle, '*With it, or on it.*', referring to his shield. The Greek is: ἢ τὰν ἢ ἐπὶ τᾶς (τὰν and τᾶς are the definite article using the long alpha of the Spartan dialect rather than the eta of Attic Greek).

LUCIAN, ANACHARSIS AND ATHLETICS

The Scythian visitor Anacharses asks his guide Solon why the young men they are watching are strangling each other one minute and behaving like friends the next.

ANACHARSIS: ταῦτα δὲ ὑμῖν, ὦ Σόλων, τίνος ἕνεκα οἱ νέοι ποιοῦσιν;
οἱ μὲν αὐτῶν περιπλεκόμενοι ἀλλήλους ὑποσκελίζουσιν, οἱ δὲ
ἄγχουσι καὶ λυγίζουσι καὶ ἐν τῷ πηλῷ συναναφύρονται
κυλινδούμενοι ὥσπερ σύες. καίτοι κατ' ἀρχὰς εὐθὺς ἀποδυσάμενοι
(ἑώρων γάρ) λίπα τε ἠλείψαντο καὶ κατέψησε μάλα εἰρηνικῶς   5
ἅτερος τὸν ἕτερον ἐν τῷ μέρει. μετὰ δὲ οὐκ οἶδ' ὅ τι παθόντες
ὠθοῦσί τε ἀλλήλους συννενευκότες καὶ τὰ μέτωπα συναράττουσιν
ὥσπερ οἱ κριοί. καὶ ἢν ἰδοὺ ἀράμενος ἐκεινοσὶ τὸν ἕτερον ἐκ τοῖν
σκελοῖν ἀφῆκεν εἰς τὸ ἔδαφος, εἶτ' ἐπικαταπεσὼν ἀνακύπτειν οὐκ
ἐᾷ, συνωθῶν κάτω εἰς τὸν πηλόν· τέλος δὲ ἤδη περιπλέξας αὐτῷ τὰ   10
σκέλη κατὰ τὴν γαστέρα τὸν πῆχυν ὑποβαλὼν τῷ λαιμῷ ἄγχει
ἄθλιον, ὁ δὲ παρακροτεῖ εἰς τὸν ὦμον, ἱκετεύων οἶμαι, ὡς μὴ τέλεον
ἀποπνιγείη. καὶ οὐδὲ τοῦ ἐλαίου ἕνεκα φείδονται μὴ μολύνεσθαι,
ἀλλ' ἀφανίσαντες τὸ χρῖσμα καὶ τοῦ βορβόρου ἀναπλησθέντες ἐν
ἱδρῶτι ἅμα πολλῷ γέλωτα ἐμοὶ γοῦν παρέχουσιν ὥσπερ αἱ   15
ἐγχέλυες ἐκ τῶν χειρῶν διολισθαίνοντες.

Names and places
Ἀνάχαρσις ὁ: *Anacharsis*; Σόλων ὁ: *Solon*

Figure 9 *The pankration shown on an Attic red figure kylix from Vulci, c. 480, now in the British Museum. Solon's attempt to explain wrestling to a non-Greek, is not entirely unlike trying to explain cricket to a US citizen.*
Photo © Marie-Lan Nguyen/Wikimedia Commons/ CC-BY 2.5.

Q.   Describe in your own words what Anacharsis observes.
Q.   How does Lucian make Anacharsis seem both engaged and confused at the same time?

GCSE vocabulary: εὐθύς, εἰρήνη, νέος, οἶδα, ὁράω, οὗτος, πάσχω, ποιέω, πολύς.

1 ἕνεκα + gen. – *on account of* (comes after its genitive, τίνος); οἱ νέοι – '*the young men*'; ὕμιν – possessive dative '*why do your young men . . .?*'

2 οἱ μὲν αὐτῶν, answered by οἱ δέ; περιπλέκομαι – *wind oneself around*; ἀλλήλους -ας -α (> ἄλλος) – *each other*; ὑποσκελίζω – *trip up*.

3 ἄγχω – *choke*; λυγίζω – *twist, bend, force back*; πηλός ὁ – *mud*; συναναφύρομαι – *roll around together*.

4 κυλινδέομαι (< cylinder) – *roll, wallow*; ὥσπερ – *like*; σῦς συός ὁ/ἡ – *pig*; καίτοι – *yet*; κατ' ἀρχάς – *at the beginning, start*; ἀποδύομαι – *undress*.

5 ἑώρων imperfect of ὁράω; λίπα – *lavishly*; ἀλείφομαι – *pour oil on, anoint*; καταψάω – *rub*; μάλα – *very much*; εἰρηνικῶς (> εἰρήνη) – *peacefully*.

6 ἅτερος = ὁ ἕτερος by crasis; ἕτερος -α -ον (< heterosexual) – *other*; μέρος τό – *part, turn*; μετά adv. – *afterwards*; οὐκ οἶδ' ὅ τι – '*I know not what*'.

7 ὠθέω – *push*; ἀλλήλους – (2); συννενευκότες, perfect participle of συννεύω – '*lowering their heads*'; μέτωπον τό – *forehead*; συναράττω – *butt*.

8 ὥσπερ (4); κριός ὁ – *ram*; ἢν ἰδού – both words mean 'look': '*look, over there!*'; αἴρομαι aorist ἠράμην – *lift up, carry off*; ἐκεινοσί – *that man there*.

9 σκέλος τό – *leg*; ἐκ τοῖν σκελοῖν (the ending -οῖν is dual) – '*by both legs*'; ἀφίημι aorist ἀφῆκα – *throw*; ἔδαφος τό – *ground*; εἶτ' = εἶτα – *then*; ἐπικαταπίπτω (> ἐπί + κατά) – *fall down on top of*; ἀνακύπτω – *get up*.

10 ἐάω – *allow, let*; συνωθέω = ὠθέω (7); κάτω adv. – *down*; πηλός ὁ (3); περιπλέκω – *wind something* + acc. (σκέλη 11) + dat. *around*.

11 κατά + acc. – '*by*'; γαστήρ -τρός ἡ – *stomach*; ὑποβάλλω – *throw X (acc.) under (dat.)*; πῆχυς -εως ὁ – *forearm*; λαιμός ὁ – *throat*; ἄγχω – *throttle*.

12 ἄθλιος -α -ον – *poor, wretched*, '*the poor man*'; ὁ δέ – marks a change of subject; παρακροτέω – *slap*; ὦμος ὁ – *shoulder*; ἱκετεύω – *beg, beseech*; οἶμαι – *think*; ὡς = ἵνα; τέλεον (> τέλος) adv. – *completely*.

13 ἀπεπνιγείη aorist pass. opt. of ἀποπνίγω – *strangle*; ἔλαιον τό – *olive oil*; ἕνεκα (1); φείδομαι + μή – *spare, avoid doing*; μολύνομαι – *get dirty*.

14 ἀφανίζω – *remove, rub off*; χρῖσμα -ατος τό – *oil that has been put on*; βόρβορος ὁ – *mud*; ἀναπίμπλημι aor. pass. participle – *plaster, cover*.

15 ἱδρώς -ῶτος ὁ – *sweat*; ἅμα – *together*; γέλως -ωτος ὁ (> γελάω) – *laughter*; γοῦν (= γε).

16 ἔγχελυς -υος ἡ – *eel*; διολισθαίνω – *slip*.

Anacharsis watches similar activities going on in other places and wonders why the umpires don't step in to stop the young men hurting each other.

ἕτεροι δὲ ἐν τῷ αἰθρίῳ τῆς αὐλῆς τὸ αὐτὸ τοῦτο δρῶσιν, οὐκ
ἐν πηλῷ οὗτοί γε, ἀλλὰ ψάμμον ταύτην βαθεῖαν ὑποβαλόμενοι
ἐν τῷ ὀρύγματι πάττουσίν τε ἀλλήλους καὶ αὐτοὶ ἑκόντες
ἐπαμῶνται τὴν κόνιν ἀλεκτρυόνων δίκην, ὡς ἀφυκτότεροι εἶεν   20
ἐν ταῖς συμπλοκαῖς, οἶμαι, τῆς ψάμμου τὸν ὄλισθον ἀφαιρούσης
καὶ βεβαιοτέραν ἐν ξηρῷ παρεχούσης τὴν ἀντίληψιν.

οἱ δὲ ὀρθοστάδην κεκονιμένοι καὶ αὐτοὶ παίουσιν ἀλλήλους
προσπεσόντες καὶ λακτίζουσιν. οὑτοσὶ γοῦν καὶ τοὺς ὀδόντας
ἔοικεν ἀποπτύσειν ὁ κακοδαίμων, οὕτως αἵματος αὐτῷ καὶ   25
ψάμμου ἀναπέπλησται τὸ στόμα, πύξ, ὡς ὁρᾷς, παταχθέντος εἰς
τὴν γνάθον. ἀλλ᾽ οὐδὲ ὁ ἄρχων οὑτοσὶ διίστησιν αὐτοὺς καὶ λύει
τὴν μάχην (τεκμαίρομαι γὰρ τῇ πορφυρίδι τῶν ἀρχόντων τινὰ
τοῦτον εἶναι) ὁ δὲ καὶ ἐποτρύνει καὶ τὸν πατάξαντα ἐπαινεῖ.

Three wrestling styles

Solon distinguishes three styles of fighting. The first of these involves wrestling (πάλη) in mud (πηλός); throwing, tripping and strangling were allowed and the contest lasted until one party submitted (2–16). A second style of wrestling (also called πάλη) took place in a pit of sand (ψάμμος); the competitors fought standing up and the winner was the one who threw their competitor to the ground three times (17–22). The third is the pancration (παγκράτιον), the toughest of the three, where, as the name ('all force') suggests, anything – except biting or gouging – was allowed, including hitting (παίω), kicking (λακτίζω), jumping on an opponent or dislocating limbs (23–29). Greek athletes competed naked (γυμνός < gymnasium); in all these sports they anointed themselves with oil then coated themselves in sand or dust to improve their grip.

Q.   What elements of humour are there in Anacharsis' description of wrestling in mud and on sand?

Q.   How does Anacharsis make it clear that the third discipline (23–9) is more violent?

Q.   What surprises Anacharsis about the umpires?

Q.   Why do you think Anacharsis uses so many animal similes? Which one do you find most effective?

GCSE vocabulary: ἀλλά, ἄρχων, αὐτός, εἰς, μάχη, ὁράω, παρέχω, ὡς.

17 ἕτερος -α -ον (6); αἴθριον τό – *open-air area*; αὐλή ἡ – *courtyard*; δράω – *do*.

18 πηλός ὁ (3); γε – *at least*; ψάμμος ἡ – *sand*; βαθύς -εῖα -ύ – *deep*; ὑποβάλλομαι – *throw underneath oneself* (11).

19 ὄρυγμα -ατος τό – *pit*; πάττω – *sprinkle*; ἀλλήλους (2); ἑκών -οῦσα -όν – *willingly*.

20 ἐπαμάομαι – *heap up*; κόνις -εως ἡ – *dust*; ἀλεκτρυών -όνος ὁ – *cock, chicken*; δικήν + gen. which comes before it – *like, in the manner of*; ὡς + optative – *in order that*; ἄφυκτος -ον (> ἀ + φεύγω) – *unable to escape*; εἶεν optative of εἰμί – *be*.

21 συμπλοκή ἡ – *encounter*; ψάμμου (18) – this has two participles agreeing with it, ἀφαιρούσης and παρεχούσης in a long genitive absolute giving a reason; ὄλισθος ὁ – *slipperiness*; ἀφαιρέω (> ἀπό + αἱρέω) – *take away*.

22 βέβαιος -ον – *firm* (agrees with ἀντίληψις); ξηρός -ά -όν – *dry*, here used a noun '*the dry*'; ἀντίληψις -εως ἡ – *grip*.

23 ὀρθοστάδην adv. – *standing upright*; κεκόνιμαι perfect passive of κονίω (> κόνις, 20) – '*have been covered in dust*'; παίω – *hit*.

24 προσπεσόντες aorist participle from προσπίπτω: translate before the main verb παίουσιν (reversed word order is common in Lucian); λακτίζω – *kick*; οὑτοσί = οὗτος; γοῦν = γε + οὖν, a more emphatic '*at any rate*' (15); ὀδούς -όντος ὁ (< orthodontist) – *tooth*.

25 ἔοικα – *seem, look like*; ἀποπτύω – *spit out*; κακοδαίμων -ον – *unlucky*; αὐτῷ is a possessive dative '*his*'.

26 ἀναπέπλησται + gen. perfect passive of ἀναπίμπλημι – '*has become full of*'; στόμα -ατος τό – *mouth*; πύξ adv. – '*by a fist*'; παταχθείς, aorist pass. participle of πατάσσω – *strike, hit* (understand αὐτοῦ, referring in sense to κακοδαίμων, but now in a genitive absolute); εἰς – '*on*'.

27 γνάθος ἡ – *jaw*; ἄρχων -οντος ὁ – *official, umpire*; διίστησιν from διίστημι – '*(he) separates*'; λύω – *release, end*.

28 τεκμαίρομαι – *judge, conclude, infer* introduces an indirect statement with acc. + infinitive; πορφυρίς -ίδος ἡ – *purple cloak*.

29 ὁ δέ – i.e. the umpire; ἐποτρύνω – *urge on*; πατάξαντα aor. participle from πατάσσω (26) – *hit, strike*; ἐπαινέω – *praise, applaud*.

Anacharsis also watches some warming-up routines that look very strange to him. Solon explains that Anacharsis is unfamiliar with Greek ways, and that's why they seem odd.

ἄλλοι δὲ ἀλλαχόθι πάντες ἐγκονοῦσιν καὶ ἀναπηδῶσιν ὥσπερ   30
θέοντες ἐπὶ τοῦ αὐτοῦ μένοντες καὶ εἰς τὸ ἄνω συναλλόμενοι
λακτίζουσιν τὸν ἀέρα. ταῦτα οὖν ἐθέλω εἰδέναι τίνος ἀγαθοῦ ἂν
εἴη ποιεῖν· ὡς ἔμοιγε μανίᾳ μᾶλλον ἐοικέναι δοκεῖ τὸ πρᾶγμα,
καὶ οὐκ ἔστιν ὅστις ἂν ῥᾳδίως μεταπείσειέ με ὡς οὐ
παραπαίουσιν οἱ ταῦτα δρῶντες.   35

SOLON: καὶ εἰκότως, ὦ Ἀνάχαρσι, τοιαῦτά σοι τὰ γιγνόμενα
φαίνεται, ξένα γε ὄντα καὶ πάμπολυ τῶν Σκυθικῶν ἐθῶν
ἀπάδοντα, καθάπερ καὶ ὑμῖν πολλὰ εἰκὸς εἶναι μαθήματα καὶ
ἐπιτηδεύματα τοῖς Ἕλλησιν ἡμῖν ἀλλόκοτα εἶναι δόξαντα ἄν,
εἴ τις ἡμῶν ὥσπερ σὺ νῦν ἐπισταίη αὐτοῖς. πλὴν ἀλλὰ θάρρει,   40
ὦγαθέ· οὐ γὰρ μανία τὰ γιγνόμενά ἐστιν οὐδ' ἐφ' ὕβρει οὗτοι
παίουσιν ἀλλήλους καὶ κυλίουσιν ἐν τῷ πηλῷ ἢ ἐπιπάττουσιν
τὴν κόνιν, ἀλλ' ἔχει τινὰ χρείαν οὐκ ἀτερπῆ τὸ πρᾶγμα καὶ
ἀκμὴν οὐ μικρὰν ἐπάγει τοῖς σώμασιν·

Names and places
Σκυθικός -ή -όν *Scythian*
A remote region beyond the Black Sea, associated by the Greeks with barbaric customs like drinking the blood of the first man you kill and 'no head, no plunder'.

The importance of training
Greek city-states in the fifth century were in a constant state of readiness for war, often against each other. Since most citizens were expected to fight, physical fitness was the duty of each citizen. As warfare became increasingly professionalized, mercenaries took on the major role, but the games culture and the cult of the body continued until Lucian's time and beyond, both as an end in itself and as part a balanced education: **mens sana in corpore sano** – *'a healthy mind in a healthy body'* (*Satire* 10), as the Roman poet Juvenal (d.130 CE) put it.

Q.   Describe a modern warm-up routine that would look odd to an outsider.

Q.   What are the benefits of training according to Solon? Do similar arguments apply today?

Q.   What examples of your 'normal' behaviour might surprise an outsider?

GCSE vocabulary: *ἀγαθός, ἐγώ, ἐθέλω, ἡμεῖς, νῦν, οὖν, πᾶς, ῥᾴδιος, σύ, σῶμα, τοιοῦτος, φαίνομαι.*

30 ἀλλαχόθι (> ἄλλος) – *in another place, 'over there'*; ἐγκονέω – *exert oneself, be active*; ἀναπηδάω – *jump up*; ὥσπερ – *as if*.

31 θέω – *run*; ἐπὶ τοῦ αὐτοῦ – *on the same (place), 'on the spot'*; ἄνω (> ἀνά) adv. – *upwards*; συνάλλομαι – *leap together*.

32 λακτίζω (24); ἀήρ ἀέρος ὁ – *air*; εἰδέναι – infinitive of οἶδα; τίνος ἀγαθοῦ ἂν εἴη – *'of what good would it be . . .?'*.

33 εἴη – optative of εἰμί; ἔμοιγε, -γε adds emphasis – *'in my opinion'*; μανία ἡ (> mania) – *madness*; ἐοικέναι infinitive of ἔοικα – *resemble, look like*; δοκεῖ – *seems*; πρᾶγμα -ατος τό (> πράσσω) – *action, activity*.

34 ὅστις (> ὅς + τις) – *anyone who*; ἄν + optative (32); μεταπείθω (> πείθω) – *change someone's mind*; ὡς = ὅτι.

35 παραπαίω – *be mad*; οἱ ταῦτα δρῶντες – *do* (17), the nominative is delayed until after the verb.

36 εἰκότως – *reasonably, 'it is reasonable that . . .'*; τὰ γιγνόμενα – *'things that are happening'*.

37 ὄντα participle giving a reason; πάμπολυ – *very much*; ἔθος τό – *custom, character*.

38 ἀπᾴδω + gen. – *sing out of tune with, be different from*; καθάπερ – *just as*; εἰκός – (ἐστί is understood) – *'it is likely that . . .'* + acc. (πολλά) + infinitive (εἶναι); ὑμῖν – possessive dative *'you* (i.e. Scythians), *too* (καί), *have many . . .'*; μάθημα -ατος τό – *theory*.

39 ἐπιτήδευμα -ατος τό – *practice*; τοῖς . . . ἡμῖν – *us* (Greeks), starts the contrast with ὑμῖν (38); ἀλλόκοτος -ον – *strange*; δόξαντα ἄν – *'which would seem'*.

40 ἐπισταίη – aor. optative of ἐφίστημι + dat. – *pay attention to*; πλήν (adv.) – *instead, rather*; ἀλλά – *'come on'* (as encouragement); θαρρέω – *cheer up*.

41 ὦγαθέ = ὦ ἀγαθέ by crasis – *my dear chap, my good man*; μανία (33) is the complement; τὰ γιγνόμενα is the subject; ὕβρις -εως ἡ – *wanton violence, brutality*.

42 παίω (23); ἀλλήλους -ας -α (2) – *each other*; κυλίω (< cylinder) – *roll around, wallow* (4); πηλός ὁ (3); ἐπιπάττω – *sprinkle on*.

43 κόνις -εως ἡ (20); χρεία ἡ – *usefulness, purpose*; ἀτερπής -ές – *unpleasant*; πρᾶγμα (33).

44 ἀκμή ἡ – *strength*; ἐπάγω (ἐπί + ἄγω) – *bring on, provide*.

A lesson in some of the technical terms connected with what Anacharsis has just seen.

ἢν γοῦν ἐνδιατρίψῃς, ὥσπερ οἶμαί σε ποιήσειν, τῇ Ἑλλάδι, οὐκ εἰς   45
μακρὰν εἷς καὶ αὐτὸς ἔσῃ τῶν πεπηλωμένων ἢ κεκονιμένων·
οὕτω σοι τὸ πρᾶγμα ἡδύ τε ἅμα καὶ λυσιτελὲς εἶναι δόξει.

ANA.: ἄπαγε, ὦ Σόλων, ὑμῖν ταῦτα γένοιτο τὰ ὠφέλιμα
καὶ τερπνά, ἐμὲ δὲ εἴ τις ὑμῶν τοιοῦτό τι διαθείη, εἴσεται ὡς οὐ
μάτην παρεζώσμεθα τὸν ἀκινάκην. ἀτὰρ εἰπέ μοι, τί ὄνομα   50
ἔθεσθε τοῖς γιγνομένοις, ἢ τί φῶμεν ποιεῖν αὐτούς;

SOL.: ὁ μὲν χῶρος αὐτός, ὦ Ἀνάχαρσι, γυμνάσιον ὑφ' ἡμῶν
ὀνομάζεται καὶ ἔστιν ἱερὸν Ἀπόλλωνος τοῦ Λυκείου. καὶ τὸ
ἄγαλμα δὲ αὐτοῦ ὁρᾷς, τὸν ἐπὶ τῇ στήλῃ κεκλιμένον, τῇ
ἀριστερᾷ μὲν τὸ τόξον ἔχοντα, ἡ δεξιὰ δὲ ὑπὲρ τῆς κεφαλῆς   55
ἀνακεκλασμένη ὥσπερ ἐκ καμάτου μακροῦ ἀναπαυόμενον
δείκνυσι τὸν θεόν. τῶν γυμνασμάτων δὲ τούτων τὸ μὲν ἐν τῷ
πηλῷ ἐκεῖνο πάλη καλεῖται, οἱ δ' ἐν τῇ κόνει παλαίουσι καὶ αὐτοί,
τὸ δὲ παίειν ἀλλήλους ὀρθοστάδην παγκρατιάζειν λέγομεν.

Names and places
Ἀπόλλων -ωνος ὁ: *Apollo;* **Λύκειος -α -ον:** *Lycean*
Lycean is a cult title of Apollo, derived by the Greeks either from λύκος (wolf) or from λύκη (light, < *lux,
lucis* in Latin), which would reflect Apollo's association with the sun. One gymnasium in Athens took its
name from the adjacent temple of Lycean Apollo.

Intellectual exercise
There was another Lyceum founded by Aristotle, a place where philosophers could exercise their minds
through discussion and debate. Like the gymnasia, this provided a meeting place where wealthier citizens
with lesiure time could socialize with others.

Q.   How does Solon make fun of Anacharsis' ignorance in 45–7? How does
Anacharsis react to Solon's remark?

Q.   In what ways is the Lyceum mentioned in the passage different from a modern
sports centre?

GCSE vocabulary: *εἷς, γίγνομαι, εἰ, εἶναι, εἴσομαι, ἐκεῖνος, Ἑλλάς, ἱερός, καλέω, κεφαλή,
ποιέω, ὑμεῖς, φημί.*

45 ἤν = ἐάν + subj.; γοῦν (24); ἐνδιατρίβω + dat. – *spend time somewhere* (subjunctive because it is an open condition for the future); οἴμαι – *think.*

46 οὐκ εἰς μακράν – *not for a long time, 'before long';* ἔσῃ – 2nd sg. fut of εἰμί; πεπήλωμενος perfect participle of πηλόομαι – *'wallows in mud';* κεκονιμένος perfect participle of κονίω (23) – *'covered in dust'.*

47 ἄμα – *'both';* λυσιτελής -ές – *giving a payback, profitable;* δοκέω – *seem.*

48 ἄπαγε – *'away with you!', 'come off it!';* γένοιτο optative from γίγνομαι, expressing a wish – *'I hope these things are . . .';* ὠφέλιμος -ον – *useful.*

49 τερπνός -ή -όν – *enjoyable;* διαθείη active aorist optative (remote condition) of διατίθημι – *deal with, 'treat';* τοιοῦτό τι – *'in a way like this'* (accusative of respect); εἴσομαι – future of οἶδα; ὡς = ὅτι.

50 μάτην – *for no reason;* παραζώννυμι (here, aorist) – *fasten to one's belt, put on;* ἀκινάκης ὁ – *sword,* the *akinanakes* was the short sword about 40 cm long, favoured by Persians and Scythians; ἀτάρ = ἀλλά.

51 ἔθεσθε aorist middle of τίθημι – *'you put', 'you assign';* γιγνομένοις (36); φῶμεν jussive subjunctive (φημί) – *'are we to say?'* introducing an indirect statement.

52 χῶρος ὁ (> χώρα) – *place;* γυμνάσιον τό – *gymnasium.*

53 ὀνομάζω (> ὄνομα) – *name, call.*

54 ἄγαλμα -ατος τό *statue;* στήλη ἡ – *pillar, stele;* κεκλιμένος perfect passive participle of κλίνω (< recline) – *lean, rest.*

55 ἀριστερά ἡ – *left hand;* τόξον τό – *bow;* δεξιά ἡ – *right hand;* ὑπέρ + gen. (= Latin *super*) – *above.* The subject shifts to ἡ δεξία part way through the sentence, indicated by δέ.

56 ἀνακεκλασμένη perfect participle from ἀνακλάω – *'bent back';* κάματος ὁ – *exertion, exercise;* μακρός -ά -όν (< macron) – *long;* ἀναπαύομαι (> παύω) – *rest, take a break.*

57 δείκνυσι 3rd sg. present of δείκνυμι – *show, represent;* γύμνασμα -ατος τό – *athletic exercise;* τὸ μέν answered by τὸ δέ – *'the one . . . the other'.*

58 πάλη ἡ – *wrestling;* παλαίω (> πάλη) – *wrestle.*

59 παίω – *hit,* τό παίειν is a noun *'hitting';* ὀρθοστάδην adv. – *'standing up';* παγκρατιάζω – *take part in pancration, all-in wrestling.*

What happens next . . .

Anacharsis next asks Solon about the prizes to which all this pain and struggle might lead. When he is told that, although they vary according to where the games are held, they amount to little more than a wreath of olive or pine or parsley, Anacharsis replies sarcastically that these sound marvellous prizes, well worth all the pain, blood and bruises. He also expresses astonishment that athletes should allow people to watch their pain and humiliation when training and is confused as to why busy people should take time off to travel and see people beating each other up at these major events. It is clear that Anacharsis is having second thoughts about the wisdom of his long journey from Scythia to ask Solon about constitutional reform.

Solon, however, rises to the occasion: he uses a 'no pain, no gain' theory, that without toil (πόνος), one cannot gain glory (δόξα). The garland is an outward symbol of victory that others can view, just as they can view beforehand the painful process that led to victory. All this leads to an analogy with political life in general: '*For there is another contest open to all good citizens; its prize garlands are not made of olive or pine or parsley, but are picked and made up of human happiness – I'm talking about freedom, both for every individual and for the collective state, and wealth, and reputation, and appreciation of our traditional festivals, and domestic security; in short, the fairest gifts that one could pray for from the gods. All these things, I say, are woven into that garland and they come as a result of that contest to which all that training and all that toil lead.*' At these words, Anacharsis begins to perceive Solon's wisdom.

Final questions on Lucian, Anacharsis and Athletics

- Compare the impressions of physical training you have formed from your reading about Spartan upbringing in Plutarch with the picture painted by Solon and Anacharsis in Lucian's work. Which is more appealing?

- What percentage of the school curriculum today should be given over to physical training?

- Do you think Solon, Anacharsis or even Lycurgus would appreciate the way the Olympic Games are run in modern times?

- What are the advantages of the dialogue form adopted by Lucian? Compare this with the biographical approach of Plutarch.

- Which of the characters you have met in these readings have you found most engaging – Lycurgus, Anacharsis or Solon? Explain your choice.

LUCIAN, THE ISLE OF THE BLEST

2020–2021 Prescription

See pages 216–7 for an introduction to Lucian.

*This selection corresponds as follows to the edition of **Lucian** by K Sidwell (ed.):*
Pages 240 to 247: Section 10 **Shangri La** (VH 2.11–14)
Pages 248 to 251: Section 11 **The Homeric Question** (VH 2.20)
Pages 252 to 257: Section 12 **The Face that Launched**
                a Thousand Ships (VH 2.25–7)

Life and times of Lucian

Lucian's works were designed as light entertainment. He wrote in a variety of genres using humour, wit and allusion in an imaginative way that appeals, in particular, to the educated reader. By calling his work *A True History/Story* (*Vera Historia*), Lucian is being provocative: he claims to have been inspired to write this work after reading works by other authors which contain very little truth. The implication is that this book will be different, but later he claims that readers will find his work entertaining '*because I have set out intricate, persuasive and plausible lies*'. Like Epimenides of Crete who formulated the so-called 'Cretan liar' paradox 'all Cretans are liars', Lucian challenges us not to break the illusion that he himself breaks. Lucian's *Vera Historia* is in two books. The extracts you will read come from the second book.

The story so far

The narrator, Lucian, sails out into the Atlantic with some companions. After finding traces of Heracles and Dionysus, their ship gets caught up in a whirlwind which takes them high up into the sky as far as the moon. There, they are drawn into a battle between the forces of the moon and the sun. Everything is described as if it were a typical Greek battle, except for the troops of imaginary animals, like horse-vultures (Ἱππόγυποι) and flea-archers (Ψυλλοτοξόται). This episode has earned Lucian the title 'Father of Science Fiction'.

Lucian and his men survive the battle and manage to get back to the sea, only to be swallowed by a large whale, where they find an entire community living inside. The first people they meet are an old man, Scintharos, and his son, Cinthyras, who join Lucian in his adventures. They find life in the whale not too bad, but the book ends with Lucian and his men once more involved in a battle between the local residents.

After twenty months in the whale, Lucian and his men manage to escape by setting fire to the forest inside it and making their way out through its mouth. After enduring icebergs and sailing past an island of cheese in a sea of milk and one of cork, where men can walk on water, they come to a sweet-smelling place, the Isle of the Blest. Here, king Rhadamanthys presides as judge over various cases, for example, who should have superior status, Hannibal or Alexander.

The isle of the blest

Lucian describes the materials which make up the city of the Isle of the Blest.

Nominative *words or phrases are in* light blue, **verbs** *in* dark blue.

αὐτὴ μὲν οὖν ἡ πόλις πᾶσα χρυσῆ, τὸ δὲ τεῖχος
περίκειται σμαράγδινον· πύλαι δέ εἰσιν ἑπτά, πᾶσαι
μονόξυλοι κινναμώμινοι· τὸ μέντοι ἔδαφος τῆς πόλεως καὶ
ἡ ἐντὸς τοῦ τείχους γῆ ἐλεφαντίνη· ναοὶ δὲ πάντων θεῶν
βηρύλλου λίθου ᾠκοδομημένοι, καὶ βωμοὶ ἐν αὐτοῖς   5
μέγιστοι μονόλιθοι ἀμεθύστινοι, ἐφ' ὧν ποιοῦσι τὰς
ἑκατόμβας. περὶ δὲ τὴν πόλιν ῥεῖ ποταμὸς μύρου τοῦ
καλλίστου, τὸ πλάτος πήχεων ἑκατὸν βασιλικῶν, βάθος δὲ
πέντε ὥστε νεῖν εὐμαρῶς. λουτρὰ δέ ἐστιν αὐτοῖς οἶκοι
μεγάλοι ὑάλινοι, τῷ κινναμώμῳ ἐγκαιόμενοι· ἀντὶ μέντοι   10
τοῦ ὕδατος ἐν ταῖς πυέλοις δρόσος θερμὴ ἔστιν.

Conceptions of the underworld

Tales of eternal punishment for the wicked, like Sisyphus, Tantalus or Prometheus, are well known in Greek mythology, but the idea of each soul being judged after death was not established until later. When Odysseus encounters great heroes like Achilles in the underworld in *Odyssey* 11, their existence in the Elysian Fields with its meadows of asphodel seems empty. A more attractive picture is presented to Menelaus in *Odyssey 4.563ff.* by Proteus, the old man of the sea. He describes a land where there is no rain, snow or strong winds, just a refreshing western breeze. Lucian does not distinguish between the Elysian Fields (τὸ Ἠλύσιον πεδίον) and Isle or Isles of the Blest (ἡ Μακάρων νῆσος), which, in his time were sometimes identified with the Canary Islands, appropriate since Lucian's voyages were beyond the Pillars of Hercules into the Atlantic.

Q.   Write down in Greek all the expensive materials mentioned. Which have an English derivation?

Q.   Pick out three details which show how rich life is in the Isles of the Blest.

GCSE vocabulary: *αὐτός (all three uses), γῆ, ἑπτά, θεός, λίθος, μέγας, μέγιστος, μέντοι, ποιέω, πόλις, πᾶς, πέντε, περί + acc., ποταμός, πύλη, τεῖχος, ὕδωρ, ὥστε.*

1   αὐτή ... ἡ πόλις – note the word order of αὐτή and supply a verb, ἐστί; χρυσοῦς -ῆ -οῦν (> χρυσός) – *made of gold.*

2   περίκειμαι – *lie around, surround;* σμαράγδινος -η -ον – *made of emeralds.*

3   μονόξυλος -η -ον (> μόνος) – *made from one trunk;* κινναμώμινος -η -ον – *of cinnamon;* cinnamon was an exotic spice, imported from India, and consequently very expensive. It could be burnt as an offering as well as eaten. ἔδαφος τό – *ground, land.*

4   ἐντός + gen. – *inside;* ἐλεφάντινος -η -ον – *made of ivory;* the verb ἐστί needs to be supplied again: the clue is all the nominatives (subject and complement) and no accusatives; ναός ὁ (= ἱερόν) – *temple, shrine.*

5   βήρυλλος ἡ – *beryl* a precious crystalline mineral; ᾠκοδομημένος perfect passive participle of οἰκοδομέω – '*built of*'; βωμός ὁ – *altar.*

6   μονόλιθος -η -ον (> monolithic) – (*made from a*) *single stone;* ἀμεθύστινος -η -ον – *of amethyst;* ἐφ' = ἐπί by elision and the π has been aspirated; ὧν – relative pronoun ὅς ἥ ὅ.

7   ἑκατόμβη ἡ – *sacrifice* (strictly speaking, of a hundred animals); ῥέω (< diarrhoea) – *flow, run;* μύρον τό – *perfume.*

8   πλάτος τό – *breadth;* πῆχυς -εως ὁ – *cubit;* ἑκατόν – *hundred* (see previous line); βασιλικός -ή -όν (> βασιλεύς) – *royal* (notice how the Greek says 'one hundred of royal cubits'); βάθος τό – *depth.* A cubit was the length of the forearm, from the tip of the middle finger to the elbow. The royal cubit was a little longer.

9   νέω – *swim* supply 'it is possible'; εὐμαρῶς – *easily, comfortably;* λουτρόν τό – *bath;* αὐτοῖς – *to them,* '*their*' a possessive dative; οἶκος ὁ – *room.*

10   ὑάλινος -η -ον – *crystal;* κιννάμωμον τό – *cinnamon wood;* ἐγκαίομαι (> καίω) – *be heated;* ἀντί + gen. – *instead of.*

11   πυέλος ἡ – *trough, bath;* δρόσος ἡ – *dew;* θερμός -ή -όν (< thermal) – *warm, hot.* Note the detail of using dew instead of water – not just expensive like previous details but actually impossible to collect.

The inhabitants of the Isle of the Blest look real, but have no actual substance.

ἐσθῆτι δὲ χρῶνται ἀραχνίοις λεπτοῖς, πορφυροῖς. αὐτοὶ δὲ
σώματα μὲν οὐκ ἔχουσιν, ἀλλ' ἀναφεῖς καὶ ἄσαρκοί εἰσιν,
μορφὴν καὶ ἰδέαν μόνην ἐμφαίνουσιν, καὶ ἀσώματοι ὄντες
ὅμως συνεστᾶσιν καὶ κινοῦνται καὶ φρονοῦσι καὶ φωνὴν   15
ἀφιᾶσιν, καὶ ὅλως ἔοικε γυμνή τις ἡ ψυχὴ αὐτῶν περιπολεῖν
τὴν τοῦ σώματος ὁμοιότητα περικειμένη· εἰ γοῦν μὴ ἅψαιτό
τις, οὐκ ἂν ἐξελέγξειε μὴ εἶναι σῶμα τὸ ὁρώμενον· εἰσὶ γὰρ
ὥσπερ σκιαὶ ὀρθαί, οὐ μέλαιναι. γηράσκει δὲ οὐδείς, ἀλλ'
ἐφ' ἧς ἂν ἡλικίας ἔλθη παραμένει.   20

The spirits of the dead

In Book 11 of the *Odyssey*, Odysseus and his men do not go down to the underworld, but sail to the
Ocean at the edge of the world and dig a trench to summon up the spirits of the dead. Odysseus was told
to question the prophet Tiresias about how to get home. While there, Odysseus speaks to his mother and
tries to embrace her, but finds her, like the spirits on the isle, insubstantial.

*I was troubled in my heart and wanted to capture the soul (ψυχή) of my dead mother. Three times I
rushed at her, as my spirit urged me to hold her. Three times she fluttered from my hands like a
shadow (σκιά) or a dream.*

Odyssey 11 204–8

> Q.   Explain what the dead appear like to an observer. What is their true nature?

GCSE vocabulary: *εἰ, ἔχω, ἦλθον (ἔρχομαι), μόνος, οὐδείς, σῶμα, φωνή, χράομαι, ὤν
οὖσα ὄν (εἰμί).*

12   ἐσθής -ῆτος ἡ – *clothes* in apposition; χρῶνται contracted present of χράομαι – *use*, *'wear'*; ἀράχνιον τό (< arachnaphobia) – *spider's web*; λεπτός -ή -όν – *fine, delicate*; πορφυροῦς -ᾶ -οῦν – *purple:* purple dye, made from shellfish, was very expensive to produce and so was used as a status symbol in the ancient world; αὐτοί Lucian now changes focus to describe the inhabitants of the Isle of the Blest.

13   ἀναφής -ές – *insubstantial, can't be touched*; ἄσαρκος -ον (< sarcophagus) – *without flesh.*

14   μορφή ἡ (< metamorphosis) – *shape*; ἰδέα ἡ – *appearance, form*; μόνην – *only* applies in sense to both nouns, and is best translated as an adverb; ἐμφαίνω – *display*, i.e. they only look like solid bodies; ἀσώματος (= ἄσαρκος) – *without real body*; ὄντες – participle used concessively as if with καίπερ *'although they are'.*

15   ὅμως – *nevertheless*; συνεστᾶσιν perfect of συνίσταμαι (< συν + st from Latin sto) – *stand together, gather together*; κινέομαι (< cinema) – *move*; φρονέω – *think.*

16   φωνὴν ἀφίημι – *send out a voice, speak*; ὅλως (< holistic) – *in general*; ἔοικα + infinitive – *seem, appear*; γυμνός -ή -όν (< gymnast) – *naked* γυμνή τις (in apposition) 'as someone naked'; ψυχή ἡ (< psychiatrist) is the subject – *soul*; περιπολέω (> περί) – *wander about, around.*

17   ὁμοιότης -ητος ἡ – *likeness, appearance*; περικειμένος -η -ον – *having around oneself*; γοῦν – *at any rate*; εἰ μή – *unless*; ἅπτομαι using optative for future remote condition – *touch, get hold of.*

18   ἐξελέγχω – *refute, prove something is not* introducing an indirect statement; σῶμα – **complement** of εἶναι – *'real body'*; τὸ ὁρώμενον passive participle from ὁράω, subject of εἶναι – *'the thing that was seen'.*

19   ὥσπερ – *just like*; σκιά ἡ – *shadow*; ὀρθός -ή -όν (< orthodontist) – *straight, upright*; μέλας -αινα -αν – *dark, black*; γηράσκω – *grow old.*

20   ἐφ' = ἐπί + gen. – *'at'*; ἡλικία ἡ – *age*; ἄν + subjunctive (ἔρχομαι) indefinite construction ('at whatever age he reaches . . .'); παραμένω (> μένω) – *stay, remain.*

There is no night and only one season; the land produces crops more abundantly than on earth and in ready-made form.

οὐ μὴν οὐδὲ νὺξ παρ' αὐτοῖς γίνεται, οὐδὲ ἡμέρα πάνυ
λαμπρά· καθάπερ δὲ τὸ λυκαυγὲς ἤδη πρὸς ἔω, μηδέπω
ἀνατείλαντος ἡλίου, τοιοῦτο φῶς ἐπέχει τὴν γῆν. καὶ μέντοι
καὶ ὥραν μίαν ἴσασιν τοῦ ἔτους· αἰεὶ γὰρ παρ' αὐτοῖς ἔαρ
ἐστὶ καὶ εἷς ἄνεμος πνεῖ παρ' αὐτοῖς ὁ Ζέφυρος. ἡ δὲ χώρα   25
πᾶσι μὲν ἄνθεσιν, πᾶσι δὲ φυτοῖς ἡμέροις τε καὶ σκιεροῖς
τέθηλεν· αἱ μὲν γὰρ ἄμπελοι δωδεκάφοροί εἰσιν καὶ κατὰ
μῆνα ἕκαστον καρποφοροῦσιν· τὰς δὲ ῥοιὰς καὶ τὰς μηλέας
καὶ τὴν ἄλλην ὀπώραν ἔλεγον εἶναι τρισκαιδεκάφορον· ἑνὸς
γὰρ μηνὸς τοῦ παρ' αὐτοῖς Μινῴου δὶς καρποφορεῖν· ἀντὶ δὲ   30
πυροῦ οἱ στάχυες ἄρτον ἕτοιμον ἐπ' ἄκρων φύουσιν ὥσπερ
μύκητας. πηγαὶ δὲ περὶ τὴν πόλιν ὕδατος μὲν πέντε καὶ
ἑξήκοντα καὶ τριακόσιαι, μέλιτος δὲ ἄλλαι τοσαῦτα, μύρου δὲ
πεντακόσιαι, μικρότεραι μέντοι αὗται, καὶ ποταμοὶ γάλακτος
ἑπτὰ καὶ οἴνου ὀκτώ.   35

Names and places
Ζέφυρος ὁ: *Zephyr*
Zephyrus was a gentle wind who blew from the West and was said to produce flowers and fruits by the sweetness of his breath. Homer is the first to list all four winds: Boreas (N) Notus (S) Eurus (E) Zephyrus (W) in *Odyssey 5*.

Μινῷον τό: *Minoan*
A month, named after Minos, the king of Crete, brother of Rhadamanthys and one of the judges of the underworld. There was no standardized Greek calendar so individual states (or isles) might name their months as they chose.

Parody
Lucian's story of a voyage full of unbelievable places and events is a bit like Homer's *Odyssey* with its tales of one-eyed Cyclopes and Circe, who changes men into pigs. Lucian is constantly referencing works by authors like Homer and Herodotus for his more educated readers to pick out. We are used to this kind of humour, as in, for example, the films of the Coen brothers or the James Bond spoof at the opening of the 2012 Olympics.

Q.   Explain what the light is like on the island.

Q.   What makes the climate so attractive? Compare this with what a
     Mediterranean reader might be used to.

Q.   What is it about the wheat that makes it look like mushrooms?

GCSE vocabulary: *ἄνεμος, εἷς, ἕκαστος, ἕτοιμος, ἔτος, ἡμέρα, οἶνος, πῦρ.*

21 οὐ μήν – *furthermore*; παρά + dat. – *among*; γίνεται = γίγνεται – '*is*'; πάνυ – *very*.

22 λαμπρός -ά -όν (< lamp) – *bright*; καθάπερ – *like*; λυκαυγές -ους τό – *twilight*; πρός + acc. – '*just before*'; ἕως ἡ acc. ἔω – *dawn*; μηδέπω – *not yet*.

23 ἀνατέλλω aor. ἀνέτειλα – *rise*; ἥλιος ὁ – *sun* (here part of a genitive absolute); φῶς φωτός τό (< photograph) – *light*; ἐπέχω – *hold*, '*stretch over*'; καὶ μέντοι – '*what is more*'.

24 ὥρα ἡ – *season*; ἴσασιν from οἶδα; αἰεί = ἀεί; παρ' αὐτοῖς (21); ἔαρ ἦρος τό – *spring*, considered the fairest season.

25 πνέω (< pneumatic) – *blow*.

26 ἄνθος τό – *flower*; φυτόν τό – *plant*; ἥμερος -α -ον – *cultivated*; σκιερός -ά -όν (> σκιά, 19) – *shady*, '*in the shade*'.

27 τέθηλεν – perfect of θάλλω – *bloom, flourish*, '*abounds in*', subject is ἡ χώρα (25); ἄμπελος ἡ – *vine*; δωδεκαφόρος -ον (> φέρω) – *producing twelve times a year*; κατά + acc. – *during, in the course of*.

28 μήν μηνός ὁ – *month*; καρποφορέω (> φέρω) – *bear fruit*; ῥοιά ἡ – *pomegranate tree*; μηλέα ἡ – *apple tree*.

29 ὀπώρα ἡ – *fruit*; τρισκαιδεκάφορος -ον – compare with 27.

30 μήν, μηνός ὁ (28), the genitive expresses 'time during which'; τοῦ παρ' αὐτοῖς – '*the one among them that is . . .*'; δίς – *twice*; καρποφορεῖν (28) the infinitive suggests we need to repeat ἔλεγον from the previous line; ἀντί + gen. (10).

31 πυρός ὁ – *wheat*; στάχυς -υος ὁ – *ear of corn*; ἄρτος ὁ – *loaf of bread*; ἄκρον τό (< acropolis) – *peak, tip*; φύω – *grow, produce*; ὥσπερ – *just like*.

32 μύκης -ητος ὁ – *mushroom*; πηγή ἡ – *running water, streams*.

33 ἑξήκοντα – *sixty*; τριακόσιοι -αι -α – *three hundred*; μέλι -ιτος τό – *honey*, τοσαῦτα – *so many*, '*as many*'; μύρον τό (7).

34 πεντακόσιοι -αι -α – *five hundred*; γάλα -ακτος τό (< galaxy) – *milk*.

Lucian describes the idyllic setting for a party that never ends, where the wine glasses never need to be filled.

τὸ δὲ συμπόσιον ἔξω τῆς πόλεως πεποίηνται ἐν τῷ Ἠλυσίῳ
καλουμένῳ πεδίῳ· λειμὼν δέ ἐστιν κάλλιστος καὶ περὶ
αὐτὸν ὕλη παντοία πυκνή, ἐπισκιάζουσα τοὺς
κατακειμένους. καὶ στρωμνὴν μὲν ἐκ τῶν ἀνθῶν
ὑποβέβληνται, διακονοῦνται δὲ καὶ παραφέρουσιν ἕκαστα   40
οἱ ἄνεμοι πλήν γε τοῦ οἰνοχοεῖν· τούτου γὰρ οὐδὲν δέονται,
ἀλλ' ἔστι δένδρα περὶ τὸ συμπόσιον ὑάλινα μεγάλα τῆς
διαυγεστάτης ὑάλου, καὶ καρπός ἐστι τῶν δένδρων τούτων
ποτήρια παντοῖα καὶ τὰς κατασκευὰς καὶ τὰ μεγέθη.

ἐπειδὰν οὖν παρίῃ τις ἐς τὸ συμπόσιον, τρυγήσας ἐν ἢ καὶ   45
δύο τῶν ἐκπωμάτων παρατίθεται, τὰ δὲ αὐτίκα οἴνου
πλήρη γίνεται. οὕτω μὲν πίνουσιν, ἀντὶ δὲ τῶν στεφάνων
αἱ ἀηδόνες καὶ τὰ ἄλλα τὰ μουσικὰ ὄρνεα ἐκ τῶν πλησίον
λειμώνων τοῖς στόμασιν ἀνθολογοῦντα κατανίφει αὐτοὺς
μετ' ᾠδῆς ὑπερπετόμενα. καὶ μὴν καὶ μυρίζονται ὧδε.   50

νεφέλαι πυκναὶ ἀνασπάσασαι μύρον ἐκ τῶν πηγῶν καὶ τοῦ
ποταμοῦ καὶ ἐπιστᾶσαι ὑπὲρ τὸ συμπόσιον ἠρέμα τῶν
ἀνέμων ὑποθλιβόντων ὕουσι λεπτὸν ὥσπερ δρόσον.

Names and places
Ἠλύσιον πεδίον τό: *Plain of Elysium, Elysian Fields*

Symposium
This magical symposium is a variation on the usual style of Greek drinking party so well illustrated on ancient vases with its variety of cups, mixing bowls and pouring vessels used on such occasions. It was an activity for men, mainly the elite. Participants would wear garlands and recline on couches, waited on by attendants, male or female, who might provide other entertainment. The absence of any servants makes this symposium an even more exclusive affair.

Q.   What atmosphere does Lucian create in this scene?

Q.   What is surprising about the wine cups?

Q.   In what ways have the winds been significant in creating the idyllic feel on this
      island?

GCSE vocabulary: *γάρ, γίγνομαι, δένδρον, δύο, εἷς, ἐκ* + gen., *καλέω, μετά* + gen., *οὐδέν, πίνω, πλήν, ποιέω, ὕλη.*

36 συμπόσιον τό – *symposium*; ἔξω + gen. – *outside*; πεποίηνται perfect middle of ποιέω – *they have made for themselves, they hold*.

37 καλουμένῳ passive participle of καλέω – '*so-called*'; λειμών -ῶνος ὁ – *meadow*.

38 παντοῖος -α -ον – *of all sorts*, i.e. '*with trees of all types*'; πυκνός -ή -όν – *thick, dense*; ἐπισκιάζω + acc. (> σκια 19) – *provide shade for*.

39 κατάκειμαι – *recline*; στρωμνή ἡ – *bedding*; ἄνθος -εος τό – *flower* (26).

40 ὑποβέβληνται perfect of ὑποβάλλομαι – '*they have spread under themselves*'; διακονέομαι + dat. – *serve*; παραφέρω (> φέρω) – *bring, provide*; ἕκαστα n. pl. – *each thing*, i.e. '*everything*'.

41 πλήν + gen. – *except for*; οἰνοχοέω – *pour wine* τό + infinitive = noun '*pouring wine*'; οὐδέν – *not at all*; δέομαι + gen. – *lack, need*.

42 ἔστι δένδρα – *there are trees* (n. pl. subject); ὑάλινος -η -ον (10) – *of glass*.

43 διαυγής -ές – *translucent, transparent*; ὕαλος ἡ – *glass*; καρπός ὁ – *fruit*.

44 ποτήριον τό – *cup, wine-cup*; παντοῖος -α -ον (38); κατασκευή ἡ – *design, construction*; μέγεθος τό – *size*; accusative of respect, '*in their. . .*'.

45 ἐπειδάν + subj. – *whenever*; παρίῃ subj. of παρέρχομαι εἰς – *arrive at*; τρυγάω – *pick*.

46 ἔκπωμα -ατα τό – *cup*; παρατίθεμαι – *put beside oneself*; τά, i.e. the cups; αὐτίκα *immediately, straightaway*.

47 πλήρης -ες – *full (of)*; γίνεται (21) subject is τὰ δέ; στέφανος ὁ – *garland*.

48 ἀηδών -όνος ἡ – *nightingale*; μουσικός -ή -όν – *musical*; ὄρνεον τό – *bird*; πλησίον (adv.) – *nearby*.

49 λειμών (37); στόμα -τος τό – *mouth*; ἀνθολογέω (< anthology) – *pick flowers*; κατανίφω – *sprinkle like snow* (the subject is τὰ ὄρνεα, the object αὐτούς).

50 μετ' = μετά; ᾠδή ἡ (< ode) – *song, singing*; ὑπερπέτομαι – *fly overhead*; καὶ μήν – *moreover*; μυρίζομαι (> μύρον) the subject has changed back to the guests – *perfume onself*; ὧδε – *like this, as follows*.

51 νεφέλη ἡ – *cloud*; πυκνός -ή -όν (38); ἀνασπάω – *draw up*; πηγή ἡ (32) – *stream*.

52 ἐπιστάς -ᾶσα -άν aor. participle of ἐφίσταμαι – *stand over*; ἠρέμα (adv.) – *gently*.

53 ὑποθλίβω – *press softly*; ὕω – *rain*; λεπτόν (12) – *gentle, fine*; ὥσπερ (19); δρόσος ἡ – *dew* (11).

The party is followed by poetry and song. Lucian spots Homer and Odysseus nearby, as well as Socrates and other great men; the only philosophers missing are the Sceptics, who cannot agree whether the island exists, and Plato who inhabits his own ideal state. We rejoin the story when, after a couple of days, Lucian builds up courage to ask Homer questions about his birth and spurious lines.

οὔπω δὲ δύο ἢ τρεῖς ἡμέραι διεληλύθεσαν, καὶ προσελθὼν
ἐγὼ Ὁμήρῳ τῷ ποιητῇ, σχολῆς οὔσης ἀμφοῖν, τά τε ἄλλα   55
ἐπυνθανόμην καὶ ὅθεν εἴη, λέγων τοῦτο μάλιστα παρ' ἡμῖν
εἰσέτι νῦν ζητεῖσθαι. ὁ δὲ οὐδ' αὐτὸς μὲν ἀγνοεῖν ἔφασκεν
ὡς οἱ μὲν Χῖον, οἱ δὲ Σμυρναῖον, πολλοὶ δὲ Κολοφώνιον
αὐτὸν νομίζουσιν· εἶναι μέντοι γε ἔλεγεν Βαβυλώνιος, καὶ
παρά γε τοῖς πολίταις οὐχ Ὅμηρος, ἀλλὰ Τιγράνης   60
καλεῖσθαι· ὕστερον δὲ ὁμηρεύσας παρὰ τοῖς Ἕλλησιν
ἀλλάξαι τὴν προσηγορίαν. ἔτι δὲ καὶ περὶ τῶν ἀθετουμένων
στίχων ἐπηρώτων, εἰ ὑπ' ἐκείνου εἰσὶ γεγραμμένοι. καὶ
ὃς ἔφασκε πάντας αὑτοῦ εἶναι. κατεγίνωσκον οὖν τῶν ἀμφὶ
τὸν Ζηνόδοτον καὶ Ἀρίσταρχον γραμματικῶν πολλὴν τὴν   65
ψυχρολογίαν.

Names and places

Ὅμηρος ὁ: *Homer*
The man credited with creating the *Odyssey* and *Iliad*, the backbone of literary education for hundreds of years: school texts of Homer from 1st to 6th centuries CE have been found amongst papyri excavated at Oxyrhynchus in Egypt and professional *rhapsodes*, who could recite the two poems by heart, could still be heard in Lucian's day. Although Homer's works were well known, the identity of the author remained a mystery.

Χῖος: *from Chios;* **Σμυρναῖος:** *from Smyrna;* **Κολοφώνιος:** *from Colophon*
Three Greek city states about 30 km apart on or near the Aegean coast of Turkey.

Βαβυλώνιος -α -ον – *from Babylon, Babylonian*
Babylon is an ancient city in Iraq, about 2,400 km from the Greek cities above.

Τιγράνης ὁ – *Tigranes* a common name for the kings of Armenia.

Ζηνόδοτος ὁ: *Zenodotus* (b. 325); **Ἀρίσταρχος ὁ:** *Aristarchus* (b. 216)
Two head librarians of the great library at Alexandria. Zenodotus divided the *Odyssey and Iliad* into the twenty-four 'books' we have today, each representing the amount that can be conveniently written on a scroll. He and Aristarchus both identified various lines they thought spurious (not written by Homer).

GCSE vocabulary: *ἀλλά, εἶναι (εἰμί), ἐκεῖνος, ἐρωτάω, ἡμέρα, ἡμεῖς, καλέω, νομίζω, πολύς, πυνθάνομαι, οὗτος, τρεῖς, ὑπό* + gen.

54   οὔπω – *not yet*; διεληλύθεσαν pluperfect from διέρχομαι '*(they) had passed by*';
     προσελθών + (dat.) aorist participle from προσέρχομαι.

55   ποιητής ὁ – *poet*; σχολή ἡ part of a genitive absolute – *spare time, leisure*; ἀμφοῖν
     possessive dative – '*to both of us*', '*we both had*'; τά τε ἄλλα . . . καί (56) – lit. '*both
     other (questions) . . . and*' – '*amongst other questions*'.

56   ἐπυνθανόμην – imperfect, perhaps '*began to . . .*' it has both a direct object and a reported
     (indirect) question; ὅθεν – *where from*; εἴη optative of εἰμί; τοῦτο – i.e. '*this answer*';
     παρά + dat. – *among, by*.

57   εἰσέτι – *still, even*; ζητεῖσθαι – passive infinitive from ζητέω, because of λέγων in the
     previous line; ὁ δέ changes the subject clearly, so to have the same effect in English '*but
     Homer*'; ἀγνοέω – *be ignorant, unaware*, but οὐδέ with ἔφασκεν makes a double negative
     (litotes) '*not unaware*'; φάσκω – *claim, assert* + nom. + infinitive.

58   ὡς = ὅτι, an indirect statement introduced by ἀγνοέω; οἱ μέν . . . οἱ δέ – *some . . . others*.

59   γε – *at least* (suggesting some doubt in Lucian's mind).

60   παρά + dat. (56)

61   ὁμηρεύω – *be a hostage* is a pun on Homer's name, suggesting that it came about because
     he had been taken by the Greeks as a hostage.

62   ἀλλάσσω – *alter, change* here as an aorist infinitive because it is continued indirect speech;
     προσηγορία ἡ – *form of address, name*; ἔτι – *again*; ἀθετέω – *lay aside, regard
     as spurious*.

63   στίχος ὁ – *verse, line of poetry*; ἐπηρώτων contracted imperfect of ἐπερωτάω = ἐρωτάω;
     γεγραμμένοι perfect passive participle of γράφω – '*they had been written*'.

64   ὅς ἥ ὅ – *who, 'he*'; φάσκω (57); αὑτοῦ note the breathing = ἑαυτοῦ – '*his own*';
     καταγιγνώσκω – *accuse someone* (gen.) *of something* (acc.).

65   γραμματικῶν (the words between τῶν and γραμματικῶν are all part of the phrase) –
     grammarian, literary critic; ἀμφί (< amphitheatre) + acc. – *around*.

66   ψυχρολογία ἡ – (lit. cold words) *pedantry, frigid words*.

Lucian takes the opportunity to ask Homer more about his work.

ἐπεὶ δὲ ταῦτα ἱκανῶς ἀπεκέκριτο, πάλιν αὐτὸν ἠρώτων
τί δή ποτε ἀπὸ τῆς μήνιδος τὴν ἀρχὴν ἐποιήσατο·
καὶ ὅς εἶπεν οὕτως ἐπελθεῖν αὐτῷ μηδὲν ἐπιτηδεύσαντι.
καὶ μὴν κἀκεῖνο ἐπεθύμουν εἰδέναι, εἰ προτέραν   70
ἔγραψεν τὴν Ὀδύσσειαν τῆς Ἰλιάδος, ὡς οἱ πολλοί φασιν·
ὁ δὲ ἠρνεῖτο. ὅτι μὲν γὰρ οὐδὲ τυφλὸς ἦν, ὃ καὶ αὐτὸ
περὶ αὐτοῦ λέγουσιν, αὐτίκα ἠπιστάμην· ἑώρα γάρ,
ὥστε οὐδὲ πυνθάνεσθαι ἐδεόμην. πολλάκις δὲ
καὶ ἄλλοτε τοῦτο ἐποίουν, εἴ ποτε αὐτὸν σχολὴν   75
ἄγοντα ἑώρων· προσιὼν γὰρ ἄν τι ἐπυνθανόμην αὐτοῦ,
καὶ ὃς προθύμως πάντα ἀπεκρίνετο, καὶ μάλιστα
μετὰ τὴν δίκην, ἐπειδὴ ἐκράτησεν· ἦν γάρ τις γραφὴ κατ'
αὐτοῦ ἀπενηνεγμένη ὕβρεως ὑπὸ Θερσίτου ἐφ' οἷς αὐτὸν
ἐν τῇ ποιήσει ἔσκωψεν, καὶ ἐνίκησεν ὁ Ὅμηρος Ὀδυσσέως   80
συναγορεύοντος.

Names and places
Ὀδύσσεια ἡ: *the Odyssey*; **Ἰλιάς -άδος ἡ**: *the Iliad*
The first line of the *Iliad* is:

> μῆνιν ἄειδε θεὰ Πηληϊάδεω Ἀχιλῆος,
> *Sing of the wrath, goddess, of the son of Peleus, Achilles.*

Θερσίτης ὁ – *Thersites*; Ὀδυσσεύς -έως ὁ – *Odysseus*
Thersites is an outspoken common soldier who appears in *Iliad* 2 when he insults his commander, Agamemnon. Homer describes his physical ugliness in considerable detail, '*the most shameful/ugly* (αἰσχρός) *man who came to Troy, bow-legged, lame in one foot, shoulders hunched onto his chest, pointy-headed and balding*' (*Iliad* 2.216–9). Odysseus wins credit amongst the troops by beating him up.

Biography of Homer
There were various stories about Homer, including the tradition that he was blind, probably based on the blind bard Demodocus who figures in the *Odyssey*. Various cities were keen to claim Homer as their own. Whether he wrote both the *Odyssey* and the *Iliad*, and if so in what order, are some of the many questions that are still argued over today.

Q.   What questions does Lucian choose to ask Homer? How different are they, do you think, from those a modern scholar would ask?

Q.   What do you think of Homer's answers? What picture of the great man emerges from Lucian's account?

Q.   What is amusing about Thersites' court case and the subsequent outcome?

Q.   Why is it so appropriate for Lucian to satirize the debate on the authenticity of Homer in *Vera Historia*?

GCSE Vocabulary: *ἐπεί, μάλιστα, νικάω, ὁράω, πολλάκις, πυνθάνομαι, ὥστε.*

67 ἱκανῶς – *sufficiently;* ἀπεκέκριτο pluperfect passive of ἀποκρίνομαι – *'had been answered';* πάλιν – *again.*

68 τί = διὰ τί; ποτε – *once, at some time;* μῆνις -ιδος ἡ – *wrath,* the first word of the *Iliad,* see note opposite.

69 ὅς (64); ἐπελθεῖν (> ἐπέρχομαι + dat.) – *come into (the mind of)* infinitive because it is part of an indirect statement, supply accusative 'it' (i.e. 'the word μῆνις'); αὐτῷ (note the breathing) = ἑαυτῷ; ἐπιτηδεύσαντι aorist dative participle of ἐπιτηδεύω – *do something on purpose, do something deliberately;* μηδέν (adv.) – *in no way.*

70 καὶ μήν (50); κἀκεῖνο crasis for καὶ ἐκεῖνο – *'that thing as well';* ἐπιθυμέω – *be keen;* εἰδέναι infinitive from οἶδα; προτέρος -α -ον + gen. (> πρότερον) – *before, prior to, earlier than.*

71 φασίν from φημί.

72 ἀρνέομαι – *deny, say no;* τυφλός -ή -όν – *blind;* ὃ καὶ αὐτό – *'which is itself something'.*

73 αὐτίκα (46); ἐπίσταμαι – *know, understand;* ἑώρα imperfect of ὁράω – *see, have sight.*

74 δέομαι – *need to, have to.*

75 ἄλλοτε (> ἄλλος) – *at other times;* ποτε – *ever;* σχολή ἡ – *leisure, spare time* (55).

76 ἄγοντα participle, indirect statement with a verb of perception – *'have', 'enjoy';* ἑώρων (73); προσιών from προσέρχομαι (54) with conditional sense *'if I approached . . .';* ἄν used with imperfect indicative *'I would ask something* (τι) *from him . . .'*

77 προθύμως – *willingly, readily, eagerly.*

78 δίκη ἡ – *trial, court case;* ἐπειδή = ἐπεί; κρατέω – *be strong, win;* γραφή ἡ – *charge, accusation;* κατά + gen. – *against.*

79 ἀπενηνεγμένη perfect passive participle from ἀποφέρω – *bring a charge of something* (gen.) *against* (κατά) *someone;* ὕβρις -εως ἡ – *insult, insolence, violence;* ἐφ' = ἐπί by elision – *'on the grounds that'.*

80 ποιήσις -εως ἡ (> ποιέω) – *poem, poetry;* σκώπτω – *make fun of, mock.*

81 συναγορεύω here part of a genitive absolute – *join in speaking, back up someone.*

The wicked break out of their place of punishment and try to gate-crash Elysium.
The heroes win a great battle and Homer writes a new epic poem beginning, 'Sing
of the battle, Muse, of the corpses of heroes'; he presents Lucian with a copy (what
a coup!) but unfortunately Lucian will lose it later on his journey home.

When Lucian and his men are preparing to leave after six very pleasant months,
a problem arises ... Cinyras has met Helen of Troy and fallen in love with her.

ἤδη δὲ μηνῶν ἓξ διεληλυθότων περὶ μεσοῦντα τὸν ἕβδομον
νεώτερα συνίστατο πράγματα· Κινύρας ὁ τοῦ Σκινθάρου
παῖς, μέγας ὢν καὶ καλός, ἤρα πολὺν ἤδη χρόνον τῆς
Ἑλένης, καὶ αὐτὴ δὲ οὐκ ἀφανὴς ἦν ἐπιμανῶς ἀγαπῶσα   85
τὸν νεανίσκον· πολλάκις γοῦν καὶ διένευον ἀλλήλοις ἐν τῷ
συμποσίῳ καὶ προὔπινον καὶ μόνοι ἐξανιστάμενοι
ἐπλανῶντο περὶ τὴν ὕλην. καὶ δή ποτε ὑπ' ἔρωτος καὶ
ἀμηχανίας ἐβουλεύσατο ὁ Κινύρας ἁρπάσας τὴν Ἑλένην —
ἐδόκει δὲ κἀκείνῃ ταῦτα — οἴχεσθαι ἀπιόντας ἔς τινα   90
τῶν ἐπικειμένων νήσων, ἤτοι ἐς τὴν Φελλὼ ἢ ἐς τὴν
Τυρόεσσαν. συνωμότας δὲ πάλαι προσειλήφεσαν τρεῖς τῶν
ἑταίρων τῶν ἐμῶν τοὺς θρασυτάτους. τῷ μέντοι πατρὶ οὐκ
ἐμήνυσε ταῦτα· ἠπίστατο γὰρ ὑπ' αὐτοῦ κωλυθησόμενος.

Names and places

Κινύρας ὁ τοῦ Σκινθάρου: *Cinyras, the (son) of Scintharos*
The son and father whom Lucian met in the whale and who escaped with him.

Ἑλένη ἡ – *Helen*
Wife of Menelaus, abducted by Paris and so the cause of the Trojan war, she is often referred to as '*the*
face that launched a thousand ships', after a line by Shakespeare's contemporary, Christopher Marlowe,
in *Doctor Faustus, c.* 1600 CE:

   Was this the face that launch'd a thousand ships
   And burnt the topless towers of Ilium?
   Sweet Helen, make me immortal with a kiss.

Φελλὼ ἡ – *Corkland;* **Τυρόεσσα ἡ –** *Cheeseland*
Two places visited by Lucian and his companions before the Isle of the Blest. Helen and Paris, too,
escaped first to an island not far from Sparta (*Iliad* 3.445).

Q.   Why does Lucian use two different words for love in 84 and 85?

Q.   What do the imperfect tenses (86–7) suggest about the relationship between
     Cinyras and Helen?

Q.   Does Lucian make it clear how far Helen is responsible for what happens?

GCSE vocabulary: *δή, δοκεῖ, εἰς* + acc, *ἕξ, ἐμός, ἤδη, καλός, κωλύω, παῖς.*

82 μήν μηνός ὁ (28); διεληλυθότων (compare with 54) genitive perfect participle from διέρχομαι 'after . . . had passed'; περί – around, approximately; μεσόω – be in the middle; ἕβδομος -η -ον (> ἑπτά) – seventh.

83 συνίστατο – 'arose'; πρᾶγμα -ατα τό (> πράσσω) – matter, thing, situation. plural for singular.

84 ἐράω (< erotic) + gen. – love, be in love with; ἤδη for idiomatic English, we need to change the tense from imperfect 'had already been . . .'.

85 ἀφανής ές – unseen, unobserved, notice the double negative to create a positive: in effect it means 'clearly', 'obviously'; ἐπιμανῶς (< manic) – madly, tremendously; ἀγαπάω – be fond of, love, the word for love in this line tends to be used for affection, whereas the verb in the previous line is used of sexual love.

86 νεανίσκος ὁ = νεανίας but less formal 'lad'; γοῦν – at any rate; διανεύω – nod; ἀλλήλους (> ἄλλος) each other.

87 προπίνω – drink a health, toast; μόνοι – alone, 'were the only ones', i.e. in the sense that no-one else joined them; ἐξανιστάμενοι aorist participle formed of ἐξ+ ἀνά + στ < stand – stand up and leave.

88 πλανάομαι – roam, wander; ποτε (68); ἔρως -ωτος ὁ – (sexual) love.

89 ἀμηχανία ἡ – helplessness, desperation; βουλεύομαι (acc. + infin.) – plan, decide; ἁρπάζω (> harpies) – seize, grab.

90 κἀκείνη = καὶ ἐκείνη crasis; ταῦτα is the subject of ἐδόκει; ἀπιόντας participle ἄπειμι – go away; ἐς = εἰς.

91 ἐπίκειμαι – be made to lie on, be situated off the coast; ἤτοι . . . ἤ – either . . . or.

92 συνωμότης ὁ – 'as fellow-conspirators', 'as partners-in-crime' in apposition rather than direct object; πάλαι – a long time ago, previously; προσειλήφεσαν pluperfect of προσλαμβάνω – get as a helper.

93 ἑταῖρος ὁ – companion; θρασύς -εῖα -ύ – bold, courageous, reckless; τῷ πατρί – i.e. Scintharus.

94 μηνύω – mention, inform; ἐπίσταμαι – know, understood; κωλυθησόμενος – indirect statement with nominative and participle referring to Cinyras, the subject of ἠπίστατο.

The couple try to sail away undetected but are chased and caught.

ὡς δὲ ἐδόκει αὐτοῖς, ἐτέλουν τὴν ἐπιβουλήν. καὶ ἐπειδὴ νὺξ   95
ἐγένετο — ἐγὼ μὲν οὐ παρήμην· ἐτύγχανον γὰρ ἐν τῷ
συμποσίῳ κοιμώμενος — οἱ δὲ λαθόντες τοὺς ἄλλους
ἀναλαβόντες τὴν Ἑλένην ὑπὸ σπουδῆς ἀνήχθησαν.

περὶ δὲ τὸ μεσονύκτιον ἀνεγρόμενος ὁ Μενέλαος ἐπεὶ
ἔμαθεν τὴν εὐνὴν κενὴν τῆς γυναικός, βοήν τε ἠφίει καὶ   100
τὸν ἀδελφὸν παραλαβὼν ἦλθε πρὸς τὸν βασιλέα τὸν
Ῥαδάμανθυν. ἡμέρας δὲ ὑποφαινούσης ἔλεγον οἱ σκοποὶ
καθορᾶν τὴν ναῦν πολὺ ἀπέχουσαν· οὕτω δὴ ἐμβιβάσας ὁ
Ῥαδάμανθυς πεντήκοντα τῶν ἡρώων εἰς ναῦν μονόξυλον
ἀσφοδελίνην παρήγγειλε διώκειν· οἱ δὲ ὑπὸ προθυμίας   105
ἐλαύνοντες περὶ μεσημβρίαν καταλαμβάνουσιν αὐτοὺς
ἄρτι ἐς τὸν γαλακτώδη τοῦ ὠκεανοῦ τόπον ἐμβαίνοντας
πλησίον τῆς Τυροέσσης· παρὰ τοσοῦτον ἦλθον διαδρᾶναι·

Names and places
Μενέλαος ὁ: *Menelaus*
Husband of Helen.

Ῥαδάμανθυς ὁ: *Rhadamanthys*
King of the Elysian Fields.

Menelaus and his troublesome wife
When Helen eloped with Paris to Troy, Menelaus wanted to get her back but did not have the authority or ability to command the Greek army. Consequently he had to seek the help of his older brother, Agamemnon. Something similar happens again here, though with a twist.

Q.   How does Lucian seek to avoid any blame for the escape of the couple?

Q.   What impression do we get of Menelaus when he finds his bed empty?

Q.   What details remind us that we are still in the Elysian Fields?

GCSE vocabulary: *ἄλλος, βοή, γυνή, διώκω, ἐγώ, λαμβάνω, μανθάνω, ναῦς, οὕτω, ὡς.*

95 τελέω – *complete, put into practice*; ἐπιβουλή ἡ – *plot, plan*.

96 παρήμην pluperfect of πάρημαι – '*I was sitting nearby*'; τυγχάνω + participle – *happen to* (do something).

97 κοιμάομαι – *be asleep*; οἱ δέ refers to Cinyras and his conspirators; λανθάνω ἔλαθον + participle – *escape the notice of someone* (acc.) *doing something* (participle), *do something* (participle) *unseen by others* (acc.), because it sounds better to make the Greek participle into the main verb in English.

98 ἀναλαμβάνω – *pick up*; ὑπὸ σπουδῆς – '*with speed*'; ἀνήχθησαν aorist passive of ἀνάγομαι – *put to sea, set sail*.

99 μεσονύκτιον τό (> μεσόω + νύξ) – *midnight*; ἀνεγείρομαι – *wake up*.

100 ἔμαθεν introduces an indirect statement, understand εἶναι; εὐνή ἡ – *bed*; κενός -ή -όν (< cenotaph) – *empty (of)*; ἠφίει – '*he let out*'.

101 ἀδελφός ὁ (< Philadelphia) – *brother*, i.e. Agamemnon; παραλαμβάνω – *take along*.

102 ὑποφαίνω here a genitive participle – *begin to appear, break*; σκοπός ὁ – *lookout*.

103 καθοράω = κατά + ὁράω – *see*; πολύ (adv.); ἀπέχω – *be far away* indirect statement introduced by ἔλεγον (+ infinitive); ἐμβιβάζω – *put on board*.

104 πεντήκοντα – *fifty*; ἥρως -ωος ὁ (< hero); μονόξυλος (3).

105 ἀσφοδελίνος -η -ον – *made of asphodel*, a tall, spiky flower. In Homer's underworld the heroes stride through fields of asphodel (*Odyssey* 11); παραγγέλλω – *order*; προθυμία ἡ (ὑπό as in 98) – *eagerness*.

106 ἐλαύνω – *row*; μεσημβρία ἡ – *mid-day*; καταλαμβάνω – *overtake*. The sudden change into the present tense is for excitement, a **historic present**; feel free to translate as an aorist, in line with the other verbs around it.

107 ἄρτι – *recently, just after*; γαλακτώδης -ες – *milky*; ὠκεανός ὁ – *sea, ocean*; τόπος ὁ – *place, part, area*; ἐμβαίνω (= ἐν + βαίνω) – *enter*.

108 πλησίον + gen. – *near*; Τυροέσση (92); παρὰ τοσοῦτον ἔρχομαι – *come very close to doing*; διαδρᾶναι aorist infinitive of διαδιδράσκω – *run away, escape*.

King Rhadamanthys decrees the punishment for the couple; Lucian and his men are told to leave.

καὶ ἀναδησάμενοι τὴν ναῦν ἁλύσει ῥοδίνη κατέπλεον. ἡ
μὲν οὖν Ἑλένη ἐδάκρυέν τε καὶ ᾐσχύνετο καὶ   110
ἐνεκαλύπτετο, τοὺς δὲ ἀμφὶ τὸν Κινύραν ἀνακρίνας
πρότερον ὁ Ῥαδάμανθυς, εἴ τινες καὶ ἄλλοι αὐτοῖς
συνίσασιν, ὡς οὐδένα εἶπον, ἐκ τῶν αἰδοίων δήσας
ἀπέπεμψεν ἐς τὸν τῶν ἀσεβῶν χῶρον μαλάχη πρότερον
μαστιγωθέντας. ἐψηφίσαντο δὲ καὶ ἡμᾶς ἐμπροθέσμους   115
ἐκπέμπειν ἐκ τῆς νήσου, τὴν ἐπιοῦσαν ἡμέραν μόνην
ἐπιμείναντας.

> Q.   How fairly do you think those involved were punished?
>
> Q.   What details of the punishment seem particularly appropriate to this paradise?

Figure 10 *A red-figure vase c. 450–440 (now in the Louvre) showing the moment, during the sack of Troy, when Menelaus sees Helen again. He drops the sword with which he intended to punish her and falls in love all over again (indicated by the little winged figure of Eros). Helen remains one of the most enigmatic figures in Greek mythology.*
Photo by Wikimedia Commons.

GCSE vocabulary: δακρύω, εἶπον (λέγω), ἡμέρα, μένω, μόνος, νῆσος, οὐδείς, πέμπω, πρότερον, τις.

109 ἀναδέομαι – *tie up*; ἅλυσις -εως ἡ – *chain*; ῥόδινος -η -ον – *made of roses*; καταπλέω – *sail back*.

110 αἰσχύνομαι – *be ashamed*.

111 ἐγκαλύπτομαι – *cover one's face*; ἀμφί + acc. – *round, with*; ἀνακρίνω – *examine, interrogate*.

112 πρότερον – *first of all*; εἰ – supply '*to find out if . . .*'; αὐτοῖς refers to the three who had accompanied Cinyras (92–3).

113 σύνοιδα + dat. – *share in knowing, be implicated*; ὡς – *when*; οὐδένα – acc. masculine not neuter – '*that there was no-one (else)*'; αἰδοῖα τά – *shameful bits, private parts, genitals*; δέω – *tie up*.

114 ἀσεβής -ές – *impious, wicked*; χῶρος ὁ = χώρα; μαλάχη ἡ – *mallow*, a very soft plant, better known for its soothing medicinal uses.

115 μαστιγόω – *whip, beat*; ψηφίζω + infinitive – *vote* (the unexpressed subject is the islanders); ἡμᾶς i.e. Lucian and his men; ἐμπρόθεσμος -η -ον – *before the proper time*.

116 ἐπιοῦσαν – participle from ἐπέρχομαι – *follow*.

117 ἐπιμείνω accusative plural participle, agreeing with ἡμᾶς – *stay, remain*.

What happens next . . .

Lucian leaves the Isle of the Blest in tears, until his men remind him that he'll be back there again soon enough (meaning when he dies). Rhadamanthys prophesies that Lucian will reach his homeland at the end of his wanderings; Homer sends him off with a little poem; Odysseus asks him to pass a letter on to Calypso, without Penelope knowing. They pass the Isles of Punishments and see Cinyras, still tied up by his private parts, being smoked over a fire, and also a couple of historians – including Herodotus – being punished for telling lies. Lucian remarks on how that sight filled him with hope, since his own works contain nothing but the truth. They reach the Isle of Dreams, and after that Calypso's island, where Lucian drops off Odysseus' letter (after having a look inside to see what it says). After many more adventures, Lucian ends with the promise of a third book – which, of course, turns out to be another lie.

In his introduction to Book 1, Lucian writes,

> I think I can escape the accusation of others by agreeing that I have not said anything true. I write about things I have neither seen nor experienced nor heard from others, things which do not and could not exist at all. So, dear reader, you must not believe them at all.

(VH 1.4)

Final questions

- How well do you think the Isle of the Blest is governed?
- What impressions does Lucian present of himself and his crew? Which figure from Homer's works do you think he is most like?
- How many elements of parody can you identify in Lucian's story?
- What makes Lucian's writing so entertaining to read?
- Do you think 'Vera Historia' ('true story') is an appropriate title for Lucian's work?

OCR GREEK GCSE DEFINED VOCABULARY LIST

A

ἀγαθός, ἀγαθή, ἀγαθόν	good
ἀγγέλλω, ἀγγελῶ, ἤγγειλα, ἠγγέλθην	I announce
ἄγγελος, ἀγγέλου, ὁ	messenger
ἀγορά, ἀγορᾶς, ἡ	market-place
ἀγρός, ἀγροῦ, ὁ	field, countryside
ἄγω, ἄξω, ἤγαγον, ἤχθην	I lead, bring
ἀγών, ἀγῶνος, ὁ	contest, trial
ἀδικέω	I do wrong, injure
ἄδικος, ἄδικος, ἄδικον	unjust, wrong
ἀεί	always
Ἀθῆναι, Ἀθηνῶν, αἱ	Athens
Ἀθηναῖοι, Ἀθηναίων, οἱ	the Athenians
Ἀθηναῖος, Ἀθηναία, Ἀθηναῖον	Athenian
ἄθλον, ἄθλου, τό	prize, reward
αἱρέω, αἱρήσω, εἷλον, ᾑρέθην	I take
αἰσθάνομαι, αἰσθήσομαι, ᾐσθόμην	I notice, perceive
αἰσχρός, αἰσχρά, αἰσχρόν	shameful, ugly, disgraceful
αἰτέω	I ask, ask for
αἴτιος, αἰτία, αἴτιον + gen	responsible for, guilty of
αἰχμάλωτος, αἰχμαλώτου, ὁ	prisoner (of war)
ἀκούω, ἀκούσομαι, ἤκουσα, ἠκούσθην	I hear, listen
ἀληθής, ἀληθής, ἀληθές	true
ἀλλά	but
ἄλλος, ἄλλη, ἄλλο	other, another
ἄν	[*in conditional sentence, makes aorist verb mean* 'would have . . .']
ἀνά + acc	up
ἀναγκάζω, ἀναγκάσω, ἠνάγκασα, ἠναγκάσθην	I force, compel
ἀναχωρέω	I retreat, withdraw
ἀνδρεῖος, ἀνδρεία, ἀνδρεῖον	brave, manly

ἄνεμος, ἀνέμου, ὁ	wind
ἄνευ + gen	without
ἀνήρ, ἀνδρός, ὁ	man, husband
ἄνθρωπος, ἀνθρώπου, ὁ	man, person
ἄξιος, ἀξία, ἄξιον + gen	worthy of, deserving
ἀπό + gen	from, away from
ἀποθνήσκω, ἀποθανοῦμαι, ἀπέθανον	I die, am killed
ἀποκρίνομαι, ἀποκρινοῦμαι, ἀπεκριν άμην	I reply, answer
ἀποκτείνω, ἀποκτενῶ, ἀπέκτεινα	I kill
ἆρα;	[*introduces a question*]
ἀρχή, ἀρχῆς, ἡ	beginning, rule, power, empire
ἄρχω + gen	I rule
ἄρχομαι + gen	I begin
ἄρχων, ἄρχοντος, ὁ	ruler, magistrate
ἀσθενής, ἀσθενής, ἀσθενές	weak
ἀσπίς, ἀσπίδος, ἡ	shield
ἀσφαλής, ἀσφαλής, ἀσφαλές	safe
αὖθις	again, in turn
αὐτός, αὐτή, αὐτό	self, himself, herself, itself (*emphatic*)
ὁ αὐτός, ἡ αὐτή, τὸ αὐτό	the same
αὐτόν, αὐτήν, αὐτό (acc/gen/dat only – also plural)	him, her, it, them
ἀφικνέομαι, ἀφίξομαι, ἀφικόμην	I arrive

B

βαίνω, βήσομαι, ἔβην	I go
βάλλω, βαλῶ, ἔβαλον, ἐβλήθην	I throw, fire at, hit (with missile)
βάρβαροι, βαρβάρων, οἱ	foreigners, barbarians, non-Greek
βασιλεύς, βασιλέως, ὁ	king
βία, βίας, ἡ	force, strength
βίβλος, βίβλου, ἡ	book
βίος, βίου, ὁ	life
βλάπτω	I harm, damage
βοάω	I shout
βοή, βοῆς, ἡ	shout
βοηθέω + dat	I help, come to help
βουλή, βουλῆς, ἡ	plan, a council
βούλομαι, βουλήσομαι, ἐβουλήθην	I wish
βραδύς, βραδεῖα, βραδύ	slow

Γ

γάρ	for
γε	at any rate, even, at least
γελάω, γελάσομαι, ἐγέλασα	I laugh
γέρων, γέροντος, ὁ	old man
γῆ, γῆς, ἡ	land, earth
γίγνομαι, γενήσομαι, ἐγενόμην	I become, happen, occur
γιγνώσκω, γνώσομαι. ἔγνων, ἐγνώσθην	I know, realise, understand
γλῶσσα, γλώσσης, ἡ	tongue, language
γράφω	I write, draw
γυνή, γυναικός, ἡ	woman, wife

Δ

δακρύω	I cry, weep
δέ	but, and
δεῖ, δεήσει, ἐδέησε (with acc + infin)	it is necessary
δεινός, δεινή, δεινόν	terrible, strange, clever
δεῖπνον, δείπνου, τό	dinner, meal
δέκα	ten
δένδρον, δένδρου, τό	tree
δεσπότης, δεσπότου, ὁ	master
δεύτερος, δευτέρα, δεύτερον	second
δέχομαι, δέξομαι, ἐδεξάμην	I receive, welcome
δή	indeed
δῆμος, δήμου, ὁ	people, community
διά + acc	because of, on account of
διὰ τί;	why?
διά + gen	through
δι' ὀλίγου	soon
διαφθείρω, διαφθερῶ, διέφθειρα, διεφθάρην	I destroy, corrupt
(δίδωμι), δώσω, ἔδωκα	I give (*future and aorist indicative active and infinitives only*)
δίκαιος, δικαία, δίκαιον	just, fair, upright
διδάσκω, διδάξω, ἐδίδαξα, ἐδιδάχθην	I teach, tell
διότι	because
διώκω	I chase, pursue, prosecute
δοκεῖ (μοι), δόξει, ἔδοξε	(I) decide (= it seems good (to me))
δοῦλος, δούλου, ὁ	slave
δοῦναι (cf. δίδωμι)	to give, to have given (*aor infin*)

δύο, δύο, δύο — two
δυστυχής, δυστυχής, δυστυχές — unlucky
δῶρον, δώρου, τό — present, gift

E
ἐάν — if
ἑαυτόν, ἑαυτήν, ἑαυτό — himself, herself, itself, *plural* themselves
   (*reflexive*)

ἐγώ, ἐμοῦ — I, (*acc etc*) me
  ἐμός, ἐμή, ἐμόν — my
ἐθέλω, ἐθελήσω, ἠθέλησα — I wish, am willing
εἰ — if
εἰδέναι (cf. οἶδα) — to know
εἰδώς, εἰδυῖα, εἰδός (cf. οἶδα) — knowing
εἰμί, ἔσομαι, ἦν (imperfect) — I am
εἶμι (cf. ἔρχομαι) — I shall go
εἰρήνη, εἰρήνης, ἡ — peace
εἰς + acc — to, into
  εἰς τοσοῦτον — to such an extent
εἷς, μία, ἕν — one
εἰσβάλλω — I throw into, invade
ἐκ or ἐξ + gen — out of, from
ἕκαστος, ἑκάστη, ἕκαστον — each
ἐκεῖ — there
ἐκεῖνος, ἐκείνη, ἐκεῖνο — that, *plural* those
ἐκκλησία, ἐκκλησίας, ἡ — assembly, meeting
ἐκφεύγω — I escape
ἐλεύθερος, ἐλευθέρα, ἐλεύθερον — free
Ἑλλάς, Ἑλλάδος, ἡ — Greece
Ἕλλην, Ἕλληνος, ὁ — a Greek, Greek man
ἐλπίζω, ἐλπιῶ, ἤλπισα — I hope, expect
ἐν + dat — in, among
ἐνθάδε — here, there
ἐννέα — nine
ἔνοικος, ἐνοίκου, ὁ — inhabitant
ἕξ — six
ἔξεστι(ν) (μοι) — I am allowed, I can (= it is permitted to me/
  possible for me)
ἐπεί — when, since
ἔπειτα — then, afterwards
ἐπί + acc — against, onto, on, at

ἐπιστολή, ἐπιστολῆς, ἡ	letter
ἕπομαι, ἕψομαι, ἑσπόμην + dat	I follow
ἑπτά	seven
ἔργον, ἔργου, τό	work, task, deed, action
ἔρχομαι, εἶμι, ἦλθον	I go, come
ἐρωτάω, ἐρωτήσω, ἠρόμην (or ἠρώτησα)	I ask (a question)
ἐσθίω, (ἔδομαι), ἔφαγον	I eat
ἑσπέρα, ἑσπέρας, ἡ	evening
ἔτι	still, yet
ἕτοιμος, ἑτοίμη, ἕτοιμον	ready
ἔτος, ἔτους, τό	year
εὖ	well
εὐθύς	immediately, at once
εὑρίσκω, εὑρήσω, ηὗρον, ηὑρέθην	I find
εὐρύς, εὐρεῖα, εὐρύ	wide, broad
εὐτυχής, εὐτυχής, εὐτυχές	lucky, fortunate
ἔφη (cf. φήμι)	he/she said (*with direct speech*)
ἐχθρός, ἐχθρά, ἐχθρόν	hostile
ἐχθρός, ἐχθροῦ, ὁ	(personal) enemy
ἔχω (imperfect εἶχον), ἕξω, ἔσχον	I have
ἕως	while, until

Z

Ζεύς, Διός, ὁ	Zeus
ζητέω	I seek

H

ἤ	or, than
ἤ ... ἤ	either ... or ...
ἡγεμών, ἡγεμόνος, ὁ	guide, leader
ἤδη	already, by now
ἡδύς, ἡδεῖα, ἡδύ	pleasant, sweet
ἡμεῖς, ἡμῶν	we, (*acc etc*) us
ἡμέτερος, ἡμετέρα, ἡμέτερον	our
ἡμερα, ἡμέρας, ἡ	day

Θ

θάλασσα, θαλάσσης, ἡ	sea
θάνατος, θανάτου, ὁ	death
θάπτω, θάψω, ἔθαψα	I bury

θαυμάζω	I am amazed at, admire
θεά, θεᾶς, ἡ	goddess
θεός, θεοῦ, ὁ	god
θυγάτηρ, θυγατρός, ἡ	daughter
θύρα, θύρας, ἡ	door
θύω	I sacrifice

I

ἰατρός, ἰατροῦ, ὁ	doctor
ἰέναι (cf. εἶμι)	to go
ἱερόν, ἱεροῦ, τό	temple
ἱερός, ἱερά, ἱερόν	sacred, holy
ἵνα + subj or opt	in order that, in order to
ἱππεύς, ἱππέως, ὁ	cavalryman, *in plural* (the) cavalry
ἵππος, ἵππου, ὁ	horse
ἰσχυρός, ἰσχυρά, ἰσχυρόν	strong
ἰών, ἰοῦσα, ἰόν (cf. εἶμι)	going

K

καθεύδω	I sleep
καθίζω, καθιῶ, ἐκάθισα	I (make to) sit down
καί	and, also, even, too
καίπερ + participle	although
καίω, καύσω, ἔκαυσα, ἐκαύθην	I burn, set on fire
κακός, κακή, κακόν	bad, wicked, cowardly
καλέω, καλῶ, ἐκάλεσα, ἐκλήθην	I call, summon
καλός, καλή, καλόν	beautiful, handsome, fine
κατά + acc	according to, by, down, along
κατὰ γῆν	by land
καλὰ θάλασσαν	by sea
κατά + gen	down, down from
κελεύω	I order
κεφαλή, κεφαλῆς, ἡ	head
κίνδυνος, κινδύνου, ὁ	danger
κλέπτω, κλέψω, ἔκλεψα, ἐκλάπην	I steal
κολάζω	I punish
κόπτω, κόψω, ἔκοψα	I cut (down)
κρύπτω	I hide (something)
κρύπτομαι	I hide (myself)

κτάομαι, κτήσομαι, ἐκτησάμην	I obtain, get
κωλύω + infin	I hinder, prevent (someone from doing)

Λ

λάθρᾳ	in secret, secretly
Λακεδαιμόνιοι, Λακεδαιμονίων, οἱ	the Spartans
λαμβάνω, λήψομαι, ἔλαβον, ἐλήφθην	I take, capture
λέγω, ἐρῶ, εἶπον, ἐρρήθην	I say, speak, tell
λείπω, λείψω, ἔλιπον, ἐλείφθην	I leave (behind)
λίθος, λίθου, ὁ	stone
λιμήν, λιμένος, ὁ	harbour
λόγος, λόγου, ὁ	word, speech, argument, story, account, reason
λύω	I loose, untie, set free

Μ

μάλιστα	most, very much, especially
μᾶλλον	more
μανθάνω, μαθήσομαι, ἔμαθον	I learn, understand
μάχη, μάχης, ἡ	battle, fight
μάχομαι, μαχοῦμαι, ἐμαχεσάμην	I fight
μέγας, μεγάλη, μέγα	big, great
μέλλω, μελλήσω, ἐμέλλησα + fut infin	I intend, am going to, hesitate
... μέν ... δέ	[*marks a contrast*]
μέντοι	however
μένω, μενῶ, ἔμεινα	I wait, remain
μετά + acc	after
μετά + gen	with
μή	not
μηδείς, μηδεμία, μηδέν	no-one, nothing, no
μηδέποτε	never
μήτε ... μήτε ...	neither ... nor ...
μήτηρ, μητρός, ἡ	mother
μικρός, μικρά, μικρόν	little, small
μισέω	I hate
μόνος, μόνη, μόνον	alone, only
μόνον	only
μῦθος, μύθου, ὁ	story
μῶρος, μώρα, μῶρον	foolish, stupid

N

ναῦς, νεώς, ἡ	ship, **warship**
ναύτης, ναύτου, ὁ	sailor
ναυτικόν, ναυτικοῦ, τό	fleet
νεανίας, νεανίου, ὁ	young man
νεκρός, νεκροῦ, ὁ	corpse
νέος, νέα, νέον	new, young, recent
νῆσος, νήσου, ἡ	island
νικάω	I win, conquer
νίκη, νίκης, ἡ	victory
νομίζω, νομιῶ, ἐνόμισα	I think, consider, believe
νόμος, νόμου, ὁ	law, custom
νόσος, νόσου, ἡ	disease, illness
νῦν	now
νύξ, νυκτός, ἡ	night

Ξ

ξένος, ξένου, ὁ	stranger, foreigner, host, guest, friend
ξίφος, ξίφους, τό	sword

O

ὁ, ἡ, τό	the
ὅδε, ἥδε, τόδε	this
ὁδός, ὁδοῦ, ἡ	road, path, way, journey
οἶδα	I know (*present, participle and infinitive only*)
οἰκέω	I live (in), inhabit, dwell
οἰκία, οἰκίας, ἡ	house, home
οἶνος, οἴνου, ὁ	wine
οἷος τ' εἰμί	I am able, can
ὀκτώ	eight
ὀλίγος, ὀλίγη, ὀλίγον	little
ὀλίγοι, ὀλίγαι ὀλίγα	few
ὄνομα, ὀνόματος, τό	name
ὅπλα, ὅπλων, τά	weapons, arms, armour
ὁράω, ὄψομαι, εἶδον, ὤφθην	I see
ὀργίζομαι, ὀργιοῦμαι, ὠργίσθην + dat	I grow angry (with)
ὄρος, ὄρους, τό	mountain, hill

ὅς, ἥ, ὅ	who, which
ὅτι	that
οὐ, οὐκ, οὐχ	not
οὐδείς, οὐδεμία, οὐδέν	no-one, nothing, no
οὐδέποτε	never
οὔτε . . . οὔτε	neither . . . nor . . .
οὖν	therefore, and so
οὐρανός, οὐρανοῦ, ὁ	sky, heaven
οὗτος, αὕτη, τοῦτο	this
οὕτω(ς)	so, in this way

Π

παῖς, παιδός, ὁ and ἡ	child, son, daughter, boy, girl
πάλαι	long ago, in the past, formerly
παρά + acc	contrary to, along, to
παρά + gen	from (a person)
παρασκευάζω	I prepare
παρέχω	I provide, cause, produce
πᾶς, πᾶσα, πᾶν	all, every
πάσχω, πείσομαι, ἔπαθον	I suffer, experience
πατήρ, πατρός, ὁ	father
παύω	I stop
παύομαι (middle)	I stop, cease from (doing something)
πείθω	I persuade
πείθομαι, πείσομαι, ἐπιθόμην + dat	I obey
πειράομαι, πειράσομαι	I try
πέμπτος, πέμπτη, πέμπτον	fifth
πέμπω	I send, escort
πέντε	five
περί + acc	round
περί + gen	about, concerning
πίνω, πιοῦμαι, ἔπιον	I drink
πίπτω, πεσοῦμαι, ἔπεσον	I fall
πιστεύω + dat	I trust, believe
πιστός, πιστή, πιστόν	faithful, reliable
πλέω, πλεύσομαι, ἔπλευσα	I sail
πλήν	except
πλοῖον, πλοίου, τό	boat, cargo ship
πλούσιος, πλουσία, πλούσιον	rich

ποιέω	I do, make
ποῖος, ποία, ποῖον;	what sort of?
πόλεμος, πολέμου, ὁ	war
πολέμιοι, πολεμίων, οἱ	the enemy
πόλις, πόλεως, ἡ	city, state
πολίτης, πολίτου, ὁ	citizen
πολλάκις	often
πολύς, πολλή, πολύ	much
πολλοί, πολλαί, πολλά	many
πορεύομαι, πορεύσομαι, ἐπορεύθην	I travel, march
πόσος, πόση, πόσον;	how big? how much?
πόσοι, πόσαι, πόσα;	how many?
ποταμός, ποταμοῦ, ὁ	river
πότε;	when?
ποῦ;	where?
ποῖ;	to where?
πόθεν;	from where?
πούς, ποδός, ὁ	foot
πράσσω, πράξω, ἔπραξα, ἐπράχθην	I do, fare, manage
πρό + gen	before, in front of
πρός + acc	to, towards, against
προσβάλλω + dat	I attack
πρότερον	before, formerly
πρῶτος, πρώτη, πρῶτον	first
πρῶτον	at first, first
πύλη, πύλης, ἡ	gate
πυνθάνομαι, πεύσομαι, ἐπυθόμην	I learn, ascertain, ask
πῦρ, πυρός, τό	fire
πῶς;	how?

Ρ

ῥᾴδιος, ῥᾳδία, ῥᾴδιον	easy

Σ

σιγή, σιγῆς, ἡ	silence
σῖτος, σίτου, ὁ	food, corn, bread
σοφός, σοφή, σοφόν	wise, clever
στρατηγός, στρατηγοῦ, ὁ	general, commander
στρατιά, στρατιᾶς, ἡ	army

στρατιώτης, στρατιώτου, ὁ	soldier
σύ	you
σός, σή, σόν	your
συλλέγω, συλλέξω, συνέλεξα	I collect, assemble
σύμμαχοι, συμμάχων, οἱ	allies
συμφορά, συμφορᾶς, ἡ	misfortune, disaster, event
σῴζω, σώσω, ἔσωσα, ἐσώθην	I save, keep, get away safely (passive)
σῶμα, σώματος, τό	body

T

ταχύς, ταχεῖα, ταχύ	fast, quick
. . . τε . . . καί	both . . . and
τεῖχος, τείχους, τό	wall
τέλος	end (adv. in the end), at last, finally,
τέσσαρες, τέσσαρες, τεσσαρα	four
τέταρτος, τετάρτη, τέταρτον	fourth
τιμάω	I honour, respect
τίμη, τιμῆς, ἡ	honour
τις, τι	(a) certain, someone, something
τίς; τί;	who? what? which?
τοιοῦτος, τοιαύτη, τοιοῦτο	such
τόπος, τόπου, ὁ	place
τοσοῦτος, τοσαύτη, τοσοῦτο	so great
τοσοῦτοι, τοσαῦται, τοσαῦτα	so many
τότε	then, at that time
τρεῖς, τρεῖς, τρία	three
τρέχω, δραμοῦμαι, ἔδραμον	I run
τρίτος, τρίτη, τρίτον	third
τύχη, τύχης, ἡ	chance, luck, fortune (good or bad)

Υ

ὕδωρ, ὕδατος, τό	water
υἱός, υἱοῦ, ὁ	son
ὕλη, ὕλης, ἡ	wood, forest
ὑμεῖς, ὑμῶν	you (plural)
ὑμέτερος, ὑμετέρα, ὑμέτερον	your
ὑπέρ + gen	on behalf of
ὑπισχνέομαι, ὑποσχήσομαι, ὑπεσχόμην	I promise
ὕπνος, ὕπνου, ὁ	sleep

ὑπό + gen	by (*with the agent of passive verbs*)
ὕστερον	later
ὑψηλός, ὑψηλή, ὑψηλόν	high

Φ

φαίνομαι, φανοῦμαι, ἐφάνην	I seem, appear
φέρω, οἴσω, ἤνεγκα, ἠνέχθην	I carry, bear, endure
φεύγω, φεύξομαι, ἔφυγον	I run away, flee, am accused, am banished
φημί, φήσω, ἔφην	I say
φιλέω	I love, like, am accustomed
φίλη, φίλης, ἡ	(female) friend
φίλος, φίλου, ὁ	(male) friend
φοβέομαι, φοβήσομαι, ἐφοβήθην	I am afraid, fear
φόβος, φόβου, ὁ	fear
φονεύω	I murder, kill
φύλαξ, φύλακος, ὁ	guard
φυλάσσω	I guard
φωνή, φωνῆς, ἡ	voice

Χ

χαλεπός, χαλεπή, χαλεπόν	difficult, dangerous, harsh
χειμών, χειμῶνος, ὁ	storm, winter
χείρ, χειρός, ἡ	hand
χράομαι, χρήσομαι, ἐχρησάμην + dat	I use, treat
χρή (with acc + infin)	it is necessary
χρήματα, χρημάτων, τά	money, goods, property
χρήσιμος, χρησίμη, χρήσιμον	useful
χρόνος, χρόνου, ὁ	time
χρυσός, χρυσοῦ, ὁ	gold
χώρα, χώρας, ἡ	country, land

Ω

ὦ	o . . . (addressing someone)
ὡς	when, as, because
ὡς τάχιστα	as quickly (etc) as possible
ὥστε	that, so that, with the result that